CALIFORNIA

D0965289

ALSO BY ANDREW ROLLE

Riviera Path, 1946
An American in California: The Biography of William Heath Davis, 1956
The Road to Virginia City: The Diary of James Knox Polk Miller, 1960
Lincoln: A Contemporary Portrait (with Allan Nevins, Irving Stone, and others),
 1961
Occidental: The First Seventy-Five Years, 1962
Editor of Helen Hunt Jackson, A Century of Dishonor: The Early Crusade for
 Indian Reform, 1965
The Golden State: A History of California, 4th Ed. (with John Gaines), 2000
The Lost Cause: Confederate Exiles in Mexico, 2nd Ed., 1990
Los Angeles, A Student's Guide to Localized History, 1965
The Immigrant Upraised: Italian Adventurers and Colonists in an Expanding
 America, 1968
Editor of Alfred Robinson, Life in California, 1971
The American Italians, 1973
Essays and Assays: California History Reconsidered (with George Knoles and
 others), 1973
Studies in Italian American Social History (with Francesco Cordasco and others),
 1975
Los Angeles: The Biography of a City (with John Caughey and others), 1976
Crisis in America (with Allan Weinstein and others), 1977
Perspectives in Italian Immigration and Ethnicity (with Silvano Tomasi and oth-
 ers), 1977
The Italian Americans: Troubled Roots, 1981
Los Angeles: From Pueblo to City of the Future, 2nd Ed., 1995
Occidental College: A Centennial History, 1987
Henry Mayo Newhall and His Times, 1991
John Charles Frémont: Character as Destiny, 1992
Westward the Immigrants, 2000
Gli Emigrati Vittoriosi (The Victorious Immigrants), 2005

ALSO BY ARTHUR VERGE

Paradise Transformed: Los Angeles During the Second World War, 1993
Los Angeles County Lifeguards, 2005

CALIFORNIA

A HISTORY

SEVENTH EDITION

Andrew Rolle
Cleland Professor of History Emeritus
Occidental College
Research Scholar
Huntington Library

with Arthur Verge
Professor of History
El Camino College

Harlan Davidson, Inc.
Wheeling, Illinois 60090-6000

Visit us on the World Wide Web at www.harlandavidson.com.

Library of Congress Cataloging-in-Publication Data

Rolle, Andrew F.
  California : a history / Andrew Rolle ; with Arthur Verge. – Rev. and expanded 7th ed.
    p. cm.
  Includes bibliographical references and indexes.
  ISBN 978-0-88295-256-7 (alk. paper)
  1. California–History I. Verge, Arthur C. II. Title.

F861.R78 2008
979.4–dc22

                                            2007033101

Cover photograph: Monterey coastline along northern California first explored by Cabrillo. © Photographer: Cathy Figuli/Agency: Dreamstime. com.
Cover design: Linda Gaio

Manufactured in the United States of America
10 09 08 1 2 3 4 VP

CONTENTS

PREFACE

Like its predecessors, this seventh edition of *California: A History* is designed to serve the general reader and students alike. Since its original publication, the work has been enjoyed by almost 100,000 persons. The book's aim is to recount the state's history from its origins to the present in an engaging manner, while seeking a balance between conflicting viewpoints.

Any history of California must do justice to its indigenous Indian peoples, the first inhabitants of the land, and then to Spanish and Mexican colonists. Both shaped the past and still influence the present. The historian also must chronicle those dramatic, sometimes violent, changes that began after the American conquest of the province. Today especially, Californians face severe implications of the state's overwhelming diversity and continuing population explosion.

Enormous social and material changes have recently overcome the state. This seventh edition incorporates new developments in a historical context, pondering implications for the future. Likewise, those sections of the book devoted to women, the environment, immigration (legal and illegal), crime, sports, energy, and transportation have all been expanded.

An avalanche of writing about contemporary California often verges on sociology rather than history. Much of this emphasis concerns ethnic groups that are fast outgrowing the minority label. This new scholarship is reflected in the updated chapter bibliographies. And, as always, this edition features a separate "Index of Authors." Finally, new maps, charts, and photographs are provided.

Professor Arthur Verge joins me as the coauthor of this new edition. Among those persons who have been helpful in its preparation are Larry Kocher, Galal Kernahan, Charles Johnson, Professors Robert T. Smith and William Doyle, as well as Selena Spurgeon, Louise Gabriel, Milton Slade, Elayne Alexander, and Gilbert Estrada.

A. R.

LIST OF PHOTOGRAPHS, MAPS, AND TABLES

CHAPTER ONE

CALIFORNIA'S DISTINCTIVENESS

The name California brings to mind extremes in both geography and climate. The state's variety is overwhelming. Its mountains are the highest in the continental United States outside Alaska. Redwood forests are the oldest, containing the tallest trees alive. Its sandy beaches are in sharp contrast to its bleak deserts. Death Valley is an unforgiving wasteland. Yet, rains, floods, and fires can be catastrophic. Droughts too are severe and earthquakes highly destructive.

In 1906, over 3,000 people were killed in a San Francisco earthquake. That catastrophe left a quarter of a million persons homeless. Major quakes later occurred in 1940, 1992, and 2003. There are many underground faults, known and unknown.

California offers virtually every climatic, geologic, and botanical combination. Its weather ranges from the wettest to the driest. The soil in its deserts is sandy, while rich and loamy in the Central Valley. Mount Whitney (14,496 feet) is the second-highest peak in the United States, while Bad Water in Death Valley (282 feet below sea level) is the lowest point in North America. In the summer time, the Central Valley's temperature rises to well over a sweltering 100 degrees. Yet, in half an hour one can travel into the San Francisco Bay area, fogbound at less than 50 degrees. In midwinter, the orange groves of southern California lie in valleys framed by distant snowy peaks.

California's literature expresses all of its distinctive regionality, which underlies the "local color" of the short stories of Bret Harte, the wit of Mark Twain's tall tales, the humanity of John Steinbeck's novels, as well as the celebration of nature in the stark poetry of Robinson Jeffers. Its archi-

Anza-Borrego Desert State Park, east of San Diego. In the foreground are chollo cactus. Courtesy of Lynne Blanton.

tecture, a fusion of the New England and Spanish heritages has produced the Monterey-style house, with its balconies, adobe walls, red-tiled roofs, and white-washed woodwork. A Hispanic fantasy heritage became overblown by Yankee developers and dreamy amateur historians.

Variety remains at the heart of California's past and present. No other American state would, standing alone, resemble a nation. California ranks third in size, but first in population. By 2007, it approached 38 million inhabitants. The fourteen counties that make up southern California are nearly as large as all six of the New England states combined, and are larger than Illinois, Iowa, or Alabama. More people live in southern California's Orange County than in all of Montana. There is, however, a great disparity of population within the state's 58 counties. The Los Angeles area, with some 10 million residents, stands in contrast to tiny Alpine County, with only 1,200 inhabitants.

Under Spain and Mexico, the province's natural wealth lay unexploited. Gold, shining on the bottoms of mountain streams, awaited the picks and shovels of Yankee miners. The melting snows of the Sierra rushed down unharnessed rivers into the sea. Magnificent timber stands stood untouched. Underground reservoirs of petroleum lay untapped. But, all too quickly the missions and *ranchos* gave way to vineyards and orange groves. Next came oil derricks, aircraft factories, steel mills, residential subdivisions, and Hollywood filmmaking.

California's shoreline spans the Pacific seaboard for 1,200 miles. Its length is 824 miles, while the state's width encompasses 252 miles. The chief surface features are two mountain chains that traverse almost the entire length of California. Its Central Valley lies between the mountains of the Coast Ranges and the Sierra Nevada. The combined San Joaquin and Sacramento Valleys, 400 miles long and 50 miles wide, constitute one of the great granaries of the world. Because farmers can raise crops during three growing seasons—instead of the usual one—California remains the nation's top agricultural state.

It is more accurate to speak of California's "climates" than to refer to a single weather pattern. Scores of specialized microclimates frequently recur. What is usually thought of as the "California climate" prevails mostly south of San Francisco to the Mexican border, and between the Coast Ranges and the Pacific Ocean. In these regions the seasons drift by mildly, almost unperceived. The heat of the day is fanned by prevailing westerly winds. Summer climatic comfort is usually maintained by low-lying fog and clouds.

What Californians call "winter" evokes laughter in other parts of the country. The state's coastline is cooled by a meteorologic process known as "upwelling," wherein warm winds swirl inward from a northwesterly direction even as prevailing currents bring cold ocean water from the depths up to the surface. When the warm air meets the cold surface water, condensation forms. Then fog and low clouds sit over the ocean, creeping inland at night and retreating seaward toward dawn. During the course of the day, heat radiating off the California landmass helps to dissipate this fog.

Although more than half the state's residents live in southern California, most of its raw materials and 90 percent of its fresh water lie in northern California. Annual rainfall in the northwest corner of the state, above Eureka, reaches 110 inches, making the area a virtual rain forest. Precipitation in the Central Valley is heavier at Sacramento and Stockton than at other cities farther south, including Fresno and Bakersfield. At San Francisco, the average annual rainfall is nearly 23 inches; at San Luis Obispo it falls to 19 inches, and at Los Angeles to less than 15 inches. In San Diego, near the Mexican border, rainfall generally amounts to only 10 inches per year. Precipitation, the heaviest from November to April, averages only 6 inches at Bakersfield and as little as 1 or 2 inches in the desert areas.

The Coast Ranges partly control California's weather. In the winter, North Pacific storms crash down on those mountains. Rain clouds push through canyon gaps into the Central Valley. Most fast-moving storms, however, break up along the Sierra crest. Below the eastern Sierra, the scorching temperature sometimes rises to 130 degrees in Death Valley, where there is hardly any vegetation. In the bleak volcanic area of northeastern California, a rocky topography also limits agriculture and ranching.

In northern California, annual floods can be especially severe. Since the Gold Rush era, Sacramento, Stockton, Oroville, and Marysville have repeatedly endured winter inundations. Paradoxically, one of the most serious flood threats exists in semiarid southern California, where burned-out chaparral provides poor cover for unstable mountain watersheds.

This wide range of climate makes possible a great variety of vegetable and floral products. Almost every plant, tree, or shrub that grows in temperate zones, and many that are indigenous to the tropics, can be grown somewhere in California. The state also is known for unique forms of vegetation, especially its giant Sequoias, which have their roots deep in the ancient past. Along with the bristle-cone pines of the White Mountains, these monarchs of the forest may well be the oldest living things on Earth. Sequoias that are now standing were mature by the time of Christ. Their age may even be 5,000 or more years. Sequoias are virtually immune to diseases that afflict other trees, and their tannic bark is practically resistant to fire. Most "big trees" that have perished have been the victims of zealous loggers, lightning strikes, or fierce storms.

The gnarled Monterey cypress, a picturesque denizen of the seacoast, grows along a rugged section of the Monterey shoreline. These trees, clinging precariously to promontories like Cypress Point, are totally exposed to Pacific storms. Over the years heavy winds have twisted them into fantastic forms, and yet they survive. Similar in tenacity are the rugged Torrey Pines hugging the coastline above San Diego.

California's skies were once darkened by flocks of geese, ducks, and other migrating birds that wintered there. Although the indigenous wildlife has been seriously depleted, 400 species of mammals and 600 varieties of birds still make the state their home. From the horned toad and desert tortoise to the bobcat, weasel, and black-tailed deer, California's fauna is as diversified as its other natural features. In the wilderness, coyotes, mountain lions, and wolverines still roam. Once common, Bighorn mountain sheep and Wapiti (commonly known as elk) are now rare, and the grizzly bear is extinct. The California condor and sea otter have barely escaped extinction.

Geologically, California is still young. The 400-mile-long Sierra scarp, formed by processes known as uplifting and faulting, and the Cascade and Klamath mountain ranges in the north are all in youthful stages of development. The California coastline, pushed up out of the Pacific's depths at Points Pinos and Lobos, as well as at Cape Mendocino, is a rocky one, with headlands jutting out to sea. This coastline, unlike the eastern shore of the United States, is geologically one of emergence, rather than submergence; in fact, the entire Pacific shoreline is sharply uplifted. This geologic

Joshua Tree National Monument. Courtesy Lynne Blanton.

pattern has produced few navigable rivers or harbors comparable to those of Boston, New York, Philadelphia, or Baltimore. With the exception of San Diego Bay in the south, San Francisco Bay in the middle, and Bodega and Humboldt Bays (both lesser estuaries) in the north, California has few natural harbors.

In past geologic ages, stupendous changes, frequently abrupt, sometimes gradual, have shaped the face of California. The two principal mountain chains, the Sierra Nevada and the Coast Ranges, resulted from titanic upheavals beneath the Earth's ever-shifting crust. The fiery origin of the Cascade Mountains in the state's northeast is revealed by their lava formations and extinct cinder cones. One supposedly dead volcano, Lassen Peak, came back to life in 1914, spouting out a mass of hot mud and ash that devastated everything in its path. At intervals, Lassen floats a menacing pennant of smoke from its summit, as if to warn that its inner fires still smolder. Seething geysers and hot sulphur springs—safety valves for subterranean heat and pressure—testify that underlying fires are far from extinguished at Calistoga and Geyserville in the Napa Valley.

Glaciers, changes of weather and temperature, volcanic and chemical action, running water, and successive earthquakes—have all shaped the mountains of California. The Yosemite Valley is a symbol of California's vanishing wilderness. Its glacial U-shaped chasm is lined with perpendicular walls, out of which cascade the magnificent Bridalvale Waterfall.

Continuous earth tremors have also altered geography. The sheer precipice of the eastern Sierra, facing Owens Valley and Nevada, drops 10,000 feet below Mount Whitney. It provides a striking example of a vertical fault caused by earthquakes. Ancient seashells, whale bones, and beach boulders are to be found on mountaintops far above the present level of the sea, proof that ages ago ocean waves washed against the base of the Sierra Nevada range.

Prehistoric California went through numerous transitions of climate, including both arctic cold and tropical heat. A few small glaciers still exist in the Sierra range as mementos of the last ice age. As for the distant tropical past, it is locked into the asphalt beds at Rancho La Brea, now a municipal park in Los Angeles. During the Tertiary Age, the quaking, sticky surface of this prehistoric swamp became a death trap for animals and birds since extinct. The blackened skeletons of creatures caught in these tar pits furnish evidence of the kinds of animal and plant life that once existed in the region. Museum dioramas can only suggest an era of strikingly large mammoths, camels, horses, saber-toothed tigers, and ground sloths that once roamed through primeval forests. Carbon-dating has established the age of animal and mineral remains taken from La Brea at more than 28,000 years.

California's remoteness long kept it isolated. Visitors had to cross the Pacific Ocean, only to risk a dangerous landing on the craggy shore, or traverse an unexplored continent, unfordable rivers, waterless deserts, and rugged mountain peaks covered with snowfields. When the explorer John Charles Frémont entered the remote province in 1844, his expedition narrowly escaped death in the icy Sierra Nevada. Two years later a group of overland emigrants known as the Donner Party lost half its members in these same mountains. Similarly, Death Valley acquired its name from desperate overlanders who perished in that unforgiving inferno.

California's actual "discovery" by Europeans came by sea. That event occurred relatively late in human history, partly because, as mentioned, it was not that easy to reach California's shores by boats. In 1542, Spain's mariners, after repeated voyages, finally sighted that distinctive and still unexplored "terrestrial paradise at the left hand of the Indies."

The region's human story actually begins with the indigenous peoples whom the invading Spaniards encountered.

SELECTED READINGS

For descriptions of the geologic and natural wonders of California see Roderick Peattie, ed., *The Pacific Coast Ranges* (1946) and Peattie's *The Sierra Nevada* (1947); Allan Schoenherr, *A Natural History of California* (1992); Alfred Runte, *Yosemite, The Embattled Wilderness* (1989); John McPhee, *Assembling California* (1993); Jeffrey F. Mount, *California Rivers and Streams* (1995); David Hornbeck and Phillip Kane, *California Patterns: A Geographical and Historical Atlas* (1983); Warren A. Beck and Ynez D. Haase, *Historical Atlas of California* (1973); David W. Lantis, Rodney Steiner, and Arthur E. Karinen, *California: Land of Contrast* (1963); G. H. Geschwind, *California Earthquakes* (2001) and Robert Tacopi, *Earthquake Country* (1964).

Early histories include Hubert Howe Bancroft, *History of California* (7 vols. 1884–90); Theodore H. Hittell, *History of California* (4 vols. 1885–97); Zoeth S. Eldredge, ed., *History of California* (5 vols. 1915); Charles E. Chapman, *History of California: The Spanish Period* (1921); Robert Glass Cleland, *History of California: The American Period* (1922), which preceded his *From Wilderness to Empire* (1944) and *California in Our Time* (1947).

CHAPTER TWO

THE
NATIVE AMERICANS

Over the course of thousands of years, California's original inhabitants had fashioned a harmonious adjustment to their environment. Yet, nineteenth-century observers claimed that they did not compare favorably with other tribal groups in North America. Nevertheless, their routine included the production of baskets with intricate designs, acorn-leaching operations, and the skillful chipping of flint into useful tools. Furthermore, some of the groups, among them the Hupa and Yurok, practiced sophisticated rituals.

It is difficult to generalize about California's many different tribal groups. Isolated from other North American Indians by rugged mountains and bleak deserts, Native Californians lived close to the soil within an uncomplicated culture. Favored by ample supplies of acorns and abundant game and seafood, but lacking metal tools, they never developed organized agriculture. Similarly, their fine basketry work may explain why they rarely made pottery, with the exception of groups in the Owens Valley and along the lower Colorado River. In such a culture, one's livelihood revolved around gathering food as well as hunting and fishing, as opposed to sowing, planting, and harvesting crops. Therefore, instead of labeling the lifeways of California Indians as simplistic, it is more accurate to speak of their traditional cultures as realistic. Theirs was a practical social system adapted to their environment that functioned successfully and remained intact for thousands of years.

Today's anthropologists maintain that the first Americans (perhaps hunting mammoths) crossed from Siberia over a land bridge in the Bering Sea. Some 20,000 years ago, the terrain, exposed during low sea levels, may have made this approach possible The ancient bones of Laguna Man are about 17,000 years old. Flint chips from a site near Calico have been

Major Native Linguistic Groups in California

Adapted from A. L. Kroeber, *Handbook of the Indians of California* (Bureau of American Ethnology Bulletin 78, Washington, DC, 1925), Plate I.

dated at about 20,000 years in age. A link between California's Indians and Asian natives has been verified. Recent DNA studies match those of the coastal Chumash with ancient remains from Alaska to Tierra del Fuego at the tip of South America!

More than 10,000 words and grammatical forms used by California natives resemble those employed in remote parts of Siberia. These language linkages suggest that the first humans to reach the Pacific coast of

North America were Mongolians. California's Penutians, who lived north of Monterey, appear to have arrived only 3,000 years ago. In addition to Asian linguistic similarities, their domestic practices and religious beliefs resembled those of tribal societies in far-off Siberia.

Most of California's Indian natives were of sturdy stock and they lived long lives as well. Chief Solano of the Suisunes, for whom Solano County is named, was six feet seven inches tall. Sam Yeto, Mighty Hand, as he came to be called, was hardly dull-witted. His followers speedily picked up the Spanish language from the missionaries. They also quickly learned how to read music and even to sing complex religious chorals in Latin. They were, however, generally resistant to working in the fields, having no background in organized agriculture.

California's missions were built by Indian laborers under the direction of the Franciscan friars. Controversy has arisen among historians over the missionaries' treatment of natives as if they were children who needed to be punished for their sins. Yet the missionaries also taught the natives new trades, including carpentry and weaving. In a short time, the Indians also became excellent horseback riders and cattle herders, even though they had not previously possessed domesticated livestock, including horses.

Traditionally, basketmaking lay largely in the hands of the women, who were also experts at dressing skins and fashioning rushes into bedding mats. Coastal Indians built dugout canoes with no better tools than wedges of elk horn and axes fashioned from mussel-shell blades. The natives' household utensils included stone mortars with which they ground acorns and other seeds. They employed horn knives and flat spoons or paddles to stir acorn gruel. The Indians used looped sticks for cooking meat in baskets lined with red-hot stones, as well as nets made of vegetable fiber to catch fish or carry small objects. They also made attractive wooden trays and bowls.

The first sound one likely heard upon approaching an Indian village might be the pounding of pestles in mortars. Natives sometimes mixed pulverized acorns with bits of dried salmon and whole nuts, which became basic provisions during winter. Before acorns could be consumed, they had to be hulled and parched, with the tannic acid leached out in a basket-pot or a sand basin. Next, they boiled the sweetened ground acorn meal. The Shastas roasted moistened meal, while the Pomo and other groups mixed red earth with their meal and baked it; the resultant product could be eaten immediately or stored for later use. These original Californians also ate the boiled green leaves of certain plants and roasted roots. The Indians distilled no intoxicating beverages, but they induced inebriation by smoking or chewing wild tobacco. Jimson weed was their equivalent of marijuana.

The Indians generally constructed simple dwellings, the designs of which varied in accordance with the local climate. In northwest and central California, some homes lay halfway below the ground, their sides and roofs consisting of broad slabs of wood. These dwellings kept the inhabitants warm in cold weather and cool on hot days. The Klamath River tribes sometimes constructed shelters out of bark and redwood planks. The Chumash constructed houses of poles drawn together in a semicircle and tied at the top with reeds. These the natives thatched with grass, foliage, or wet earth, making their dwellings well suited to the mild climate of the Santa Barbara coastline.

Along the Pacific coast, its natives had few weapons other than small bows and arrows and flint-tipped lances. When hunting large animals, they made up for a lack of better armament by employing clever strategies. In order to draw near enough to big game to kill it, the natives donned disguises fashioned from the heads and upper parts of skinned animals. They purposely set out decoys to attract birds within arrowshot. Coordinated game drives also were organized, wherein Indians herded animals past their hunters lying in ambush. They also employed the less common practice of running down deer in human relays, until the quarry fell to the ground from exhaustion. Indians constructed pits and traps to catch even larger or more dangerous game. Nevertheless, they relished as foodstuffs small animals such as wood rats, squirrels, coyotes, crows, rabbits, lizards, field mice, and snakes. Cactus apples and wild berries too formed part of the diet.

Some tribelets ate snails, caterpillars, minnows, crickets, grubs (found in decayed trees), slugs, fly larvae (gathered from the tops of bushes in swamps), horned toads, earthworms, grasshoppers, and skunks (the latter killed and dressed with all due caution). Seafood and shellfish formed an important part of the diet of coastal inhabitants. Other natives fished inland along northern rivers in which great schools of salmon once spawned. Nature, in addition to furnishing the Indians with food, also provided them with basic clothing. When weather permitted, the men went naked except for their moccasins and crude sandals. Further north, they fashioned snowshoes from animal skins. If temperatures plummeted, the Indians donned rabbit or deerskin cloaks and skin blankets. Some women wore skirts made of tule grass or aprons of animal skin. In cold weather they employed capes of deerskin or rabbit fur or simply covered their breasts with furs, including those of the otter and wildcat. Some groups painted their faces and bodies in intricate patterns; others braided decorative seashells into their hair. For ceremonial occasions both sexes donned elaborate headdresses of feathers and beads. Northern peoples wore basketry hats, while those of the central region bound their heads with hairnets.

Another source of pride among certain groups was the craftsmanship of their watercraft, which the males handled with dexterity and skill. Small boats included tule balsas, or reed rafts, made out of woven river rushes. The natives poled these or paddled them along inland waters, as they did plank canoes, the burned- or chopped-out trunk segments of large trees. While the men engaged in hunting and fishing, the women and older children hunted small animals, gathered acorns, scraped animal skins, fashioned robes, hauled water and firewood, wove baskets, barbecued meat, and even constructed dwellings. Yet it is misleading to label the men as lazy; they simply became specialized in their roles. Hupa males made bows, arrows, nets, and pipes, dressed hides, and used dry sticks to start fires.

A Mono home. In front of this typical winter shelter is an assortment of burden-baskets and winnowing trays. All the utensils pictured were used by the inhabitants of this home alone. Northwestern University Library, Edward S. Curtis's *The North American Indian: The Photographic Images,* 2001. Library of Congress, LC-USZ62-49232.

Dancing was not only a social amusement but an important part of highly structured Indian ceremonies. There were special dances to honor the newborn child, the black bear, the new clover, the white deer, and the elk. Other dances were intended to welcome visitors. Additionally there was a dance of peace and one of war, for which young men painted themselves and dressed in plumes and beads. Dancing also took place during puberty rites, separate for boys and girls. The Yurok held a first-salmon dance at the mouth of the Klamath River. The Hupa, in addition to staging a first-eel ceremony, also celebrated an autumnal first-acorn feast.

Singing became spirited when a group celebrated by chewing or smoking narcotic jimson weed. Some religious rituals, such as those of the Toloache cult, used music as an adjunct to narcotics. Accompanied by the hum of the bull roarer (a slat of wood swung at the end of a thong), chanting and singing might go on late into the night.

Among other types of celebrations were those during which participants boasted about the fine huts they had built or the victories their warriors had won. All such achievements were intoned aloud by wizened elders in lengthy orations, to which onlookers listened in solemn silence. Celebrating crowds did not gorge themselves, usually eating abstemiously.

Some tribes held a special ceremony each summer to memorialize the dead. This ritual included building a large fire into which clothing, baskets, and other possessions were thrown as offerings to the departed. Young men then danced in a circle around the fire, accompanied by the rattle of a melancholy chant of mourning. A few tribes buried their dead, while others practiced cremation. Organized mourning for the dead by close relatives was practiced by nearly all tribes. This entailed smearing one's face with a wet paste mixed from the ashes of the deceased. The mourners usually kept this facial covering on until it wore off, perhaps as long as a year.

Many Indian customs might seem strange to us today. In northwestern California, for example, a wife could be purchased for strings of shell money or deerskins. In fact, a man was disgraced if he secured a wife for little or nothing. Polygamy was practiced by males who could afford more than one wife. Some of the men were inveterate gamblers who would risk their last possession, including their wives. A guessing-game was popular, as were other games of chance involving the placing of stone pebbles under seashells. In ball games, and in leaping, jumping, and similar matches, the contestants accepted defeat with the same good sportsmanship that they displayed in victory.

Governed by lineage and precise social patterns, each family was a judiciary system unto itself. The bodies of adolescent boys and girls were

CALIFORNIA'S NATIVE POPULATION[1]

Pre–1542	300,000[2]
1769–1822	100,000
1870	30,000
1880	16,277
1890	16,624
1900	15,377
1910	16,371
1920	17,360
1930	19,212
1940	18,675
1950	19,947
1960	39,014
1970	91,018
1980	198,275
1990	285,270
2000	308,571[3]

1. Population census statistics are muddled by changing criteria. Indians were not included in census data before 1890. Early data are approximate. Later figures include in-migration from other areas.
2. Only 133,000 to 150,000 according to A. L. Kroeber. The larger figure is based upon Sherburne F. Cook's estimate of 310,000.

painted by shamans who acted as their temporary guardians, or "spirit helpers," during their rites of passage into adulthood. At all times natives stressed obedience to elders. There was no systematic punishment for crime. Although atonement for injuring another was expected, some offenses could be excused by recompense. A murderer might buy himself off by paying the family of the deceased in skins or shells.

Because the local natives spoke some 135 different dialects, there was no strict universal political or tribal system. One should, therefore, avoid use of the term *tribe*. Except for a minority of well-defined tribes or tribelets, including the Yumas and some of the Indians of California's northwest coast, the Indians' basic political unit was the village community settlement. The Spanish called these village units *rancherías*, which were loosely knit confederations of several hundred persons, within each of which were smaller clans identified by individual totems. A ranchería had a leader who received a strict deference. One can apply the term *chief* to such leaders only loosely. The child of a male or female chieftain stood to inherit a family's power, but only if he or she demonstrated similar leadership talents.

California's Indians were not generally nomadic, unlike those who lived on the western plains. A clan's boundaries were quite well defined. If one passed beyond a local boundary line, the trespasser might pay with his or her life. Mothers, therefore, were careful to teach their children the specific landmarks of their family or tribal areas. These lessons were often imparted via a singsong enumeration of certain stones, boulders, mountains, trees, and other landmarks beyond which it was dangerous for a child to wander. Controversies between families, sometimes over the abduction of women, or concerning access to food sources, were occasionally severe. Rock fights might break out over access to acorn groves or salmon streams. One of California's northern counties, Calaveras (or skulls) was named after a river along the banks of which the Spanish explorer, Gabriel Moraga found whitened skulls.

Natives revered their "medicine man," for he claimed the ability to cure illnesses. One method which he employed was to recite an incantation before placing the end of a hollowed-out wooden tube against the body of the patient. After pretending to suck out the "cause" of the disease—a sliver of bone, a sharp-edged flint flake, or a dead lizard or other small animal that he had previously secreted in his mouth—he spat it out for all to see. His success, in fact, depended partly upon his ability to fabricate entertaining, sometimes fantastic, stories. Notwithstanding the pretenses of these practitioners, the medicine men did have a working knowledge of the medici-

Top: Hupa Indian in ceremonial white deerskin dance costume. Library of Congress, LC-USZ62-101260.
Bottom: Hupa female shaman from northwestern California. Library of Congress, LC-USZ62-101261. Both images: Northwestern University Library, Edward S. Curtis's *The North American Indian: The Photographic Images*, 2001.

nal properties of herbs, roots, and other natural remedies, which they used to the benefit of their patients.

Even the Spanish consulted the Indian medicine men, or shamans, when they failed to cure the scourge of dysentery through other means. Until the coming of the Spaniards the Indians seem not to have suffered from smallpox, influenza, or measles. Tuberculosis and venereal diseases were unknown to the natives. Their constant scratching from lice and fleas, however, bloodied their bodies, and they were kept awake many a night by the vermin living in the animal skins they used as bedclothes.

In colder areas one of the natives' favorite treatments of illness was a visit to the local *temescal*, or sweathouse. This was a mound-like structure, usually made of timbers hermetically covered with earth, with only one small opening. A large fire was built inside the sweathouse. There, nestled among steaming hot stones, patients remained until dripping with perspiration. Then they rushed out of the sweathouse and leaped into the nearest lake or stream. This icy "kill or cure" remedy resembled a Finnish sauna.

Natives sought freedom from pain by having a medicine man engage in a "doctors' dance." There were also rain, rattlesnake, and bear clairvoyants who allegedly possessed curative powers. Various tribal groups practiced shamanism and animism to cure disease and for religious needs. Indians used healing rituals involving dream interpretation similar to those practiced in ancient Greece.

Religious cults explained the creation of the world and its first devastating flood. One tradition held that at a remote time in the past a billowing sea rolled up onto the plains to fill the valleys until water covered the mountains. All living beings were destroyed in this deluge, except for those who remained on the highest peaks. These were creatures chosen by a supreme being. In eternity, worthy persons would pass over to a happy land beyond the water. When the coming of the new moon was celebrated, an old man would dance in a circle, saying, "As the moon died and cometh to life again, so we also, having to die, will live once more."

The native languages were certainly not monolingual. No less than twenty-two linguistic families, with 135 regional dialects, have been identified. All but one of sixty tribal groups (the Yukian) extended beyond the state's present borders. This wide range of dialects proved difficult for the Spanish missionaries. Some native groups, though separated by only the width of a stream, could not understand one another's speech. Among the better-known linguistic classifications are the Hupa, Pomo, Modoc, Maidu, Mono, Yurok, and Yuma. Some smaller local dialects have been lost forever.

The names of nine California counties—Colusa, Modoc, Mono, Napa, Shasta, Tehama, Tuolumne, Yolo, and Yuba—come from tribal group names. Two more county names—Inyo and Siskiyou—are of probable Indian origin. These place names remain an enduring monument to the first lords of California's remote past. One estimate places the original number of Native Americans there from 100,000 to 300,000 persons. But a mild climate and plentiful food supply could not ward off the onslaught of devastating European diseases against which they had no immunity

By the 1790s, only 8,928 Indian *neophytes* were housed at California's nine missions. Over a period of sixty years, these persons were overseen by some 142 Franciscan priests. The *padres* controlled Indian relations by use of a four-volume *Recopilación*, translateable as "The Laws of the Indies." When the Indians entered the confinement of the missions, they gave up the old practice of periodically burning down their dwellings as well as use of the sweathouse. This removed a major protection against vermin, decreasing sanitation, and making the Indians even more susceptible to the diseases carried by the Spaniards. Soon after the Europeans arrived, the average life expectancy of Indians fell to only forty years. The brutal murders of Indians by the newcomers also decreased their numbers.

Shortly after California's American period began, mining operations depleted the Indians' traditional food sources. As toxic metals and chemicals filtered into the ecosystem, fewer salmon, once so important to the existence of the northern Indians, swam upstream to spawn. In addition, vital acorn groves were leveled by miners seeking firewood. By 1800, the Indian population still numbered between 200,000 and 250,000 persons. On the eve of the Gold Rush, that number had been reduced to approximately 100,000. In 1869, only twenty years after American occupation began, the Indian population of the new state was a meagre 30,000 persons. By the start of the twentieth century, the Indian population had decreased further, to an estimated 16,000. The record of this tragic decline is examined in a later chapter.

Only in recent decades has the American Indian population of the state been partially restored. Today most Indians have white, and sometimes black, ancestors after decades of intermarriage.

SELECTED READINGS

Basic to an understanding of California's aboriginal peoples is Alfred L. Kroeber, *Handbook of the Indians of California* (Bureau of American Ethnology, Bulletin 78, 1925); and Frederick W. Hodge, *Handbook of the American*

Indians North of Mexico (2 vols. 1959). Also useful are Kroeber's monographs in the *University of California's Publications in Archaeology and Ethnology,* especially his "California Culture Provinces," in volume 17 (1920). See also *Aboriginal California: Three Studies in Culture History* (1963), the combined work of Kroeber, James T. Davis, Robert F. Heizer, and Albert B. Elsasser. Consult Sherburne F. Cook, *The Conflict Between the California Indian and White Civilization* (1943), and his *The Population of the California Indians* (1976); C. Hart Merriam, *Studies of California Indians* (1955); Brian Fagan, *An Archaeologist Looks at Our Earliest Inhabitants* (2003) and M. Kat Anderson, *Tending the Wild: Native American Knowledge... of California's Natural Resources* (2005).

A recent analysis of missionization is in James Sandos, *Converting California: Indians and Franciscans in the Missions* (2004); see also Joel Hyer, *We Are Not Savages: Native Americans in Southern California* (2001) and Kent Lightfoot, *Indians, Missionaries and Merchants ... on the California Frontiers* (2005) as well as C. Alan Hutchinson, "The Mexican Government and the Mission Indians of Upper California, 1821–1835," *The Americas* 21 (April 1965), 335–62, and Daniel Garr, "Planning, Politics, and Plunder: The Missions and Indian Pueblos of Hispanic California," *Southern California Quarterly* 54 (Winter 1972), 291–312.

Another summary is Lowell J. Bean, "Indians of California: Diverse and Complex Peoples," *California History* 71 (Fall, 1992), 302–23. Consult also Robert H. Jackson, *Indian Population Decline: The Missions of Northwestern New Spain* (1994); Robert F. Heizer, "The California Indians, Archaeology, Varieties of Culture, Arts of Life," *California Historical Society Quarterly* 41 (March 1962), 1–28, and Heizer's *Languages, Territories and Names of California Indian Tribes* (1966).

Other sources include Galen Clark, *Indians of the Yosemite Valley and Vicinity* (1904); R. F. Heizer and M. A. Whipple, *The California Indians: A Source Book* (1951); R. F. Heizer, *California Indians* (1978); R. F. Heizer and J. E. Mills, *The Four Ages of Tsurai* (1952) as well as C. D. Forde, *Ethnography of the Yuma Indians* (*University of California Publications in Archaeology and Ethnology* 31, 1928) and, in the same series, P. E. Goddard, *Life and Culture of the Hupa* (1903). On the Hupa tribe see David Rich Lewis, *Neither Wolf nor Dog: American Indians, Environment, and Agrarian Change* (1994).

Religion is discussed in James R. Moriarty, "A Reconstruction of the Development of Primitive Religion in California," *Southern California Quarterly* 52 (December 1970), 313–34. See also Edward W. Gifford and Gwendoline H. Block, *California Indian Nights Entertainment* (1959);

Theodora Kroeber, *The Inland Whale* (1959) and her *Ishi in Two Worlds: A Biography of the Last Wild Indian in North America* (1961). See also Karl and Clifton Kroeber, eds. *Ishi In Three Centuries* (2003) as well as Richard Cunningham, *California Indian Watercraft* (1989), and, more recently, Herbert W. Luthin, *Surviving Through the Days . . . A California Indian Reader* (2002).

For the origin of place names, consult Erwin G. Gudde, *California Place Names* (1960, revised in 1998 by William Bright). See also Bright's *1,500 California Place Names* (1997); Phil Townsend Hanna, *The Dictionary of California Land Names,* as well as Barbara and Rudy Marinacci, *California's Spanish Place Names* (1980); A. L. Kroeber, *California's Place Names of Indian Origin* (1916) and David Durham, *California's Geographic Names* (1998) which includes more than 50,000 entries.

See also George H. Phillips, *The Enduring Struggle: Indians in California History* (1981); James J. Rawls, *Indians of California: Their Changing Image* (1984); Robert H. Jackson and Edward Castillo, *Indians, Franciscans and Spanish Colonization* (1995); William McCawley, *The First Angelinos, The Gabrielino Indians of Los Angeles* (1996); Diana Bahr, *From Mission to Metropolis: Cupeño Indian Women in Los Angeles* (1993); and Albert L. Hurtado, *Indian Survival on the California Frontier* (1988).

CHAPTER THREE

EXPLORING
BAJA AND ALTA
CALIFORNIA

The name *California* was derived from a sixteenth-century Spanish novel, *Las Sergas de Esplandían* (The Exploits of Esplandían) by García Ordóñez de Montalvo. The narrative was one of those impossible romances of chivalry that grew out of the crusades of the eleventh century. Its protagonist, Esplandían, is a knight bound to vows of courage and chastity as the conquistador of all his enemies. The hero visits "California," a wonderful island inhabited by tall, bronze-colored, and tempestuous Amazons. Their powerful queen is named Calafía. Even though she repelled all male suitors, these strong and beautiful women excited the lustful imagination of many a Spanish soldier who read the book.

The *Las Sergas* saga was popular at the time when the Spanish conquistador Hernando Cortés arrived in New Spain. Following his conquest of Mexico (1519–21), Cortés wrote to the Spanish king about a rumored island of Amazon women purportedly "abounding in pearls and gold." At the time, the Spaniards still believed that the peninsula of Baja California was an island. By the mid–1530s, mariners dispatched north by Cortés had landed in *Baja* (Lower) California. Most historians, however, have given credit for the first official use of the name *California* to Francisco de Bolaños, who explored the Baja peninsula in 1541. Whoever first named the province anticipated finding pearls, gold, and other riches mentioned in Montalvo's fantastic tale.

Asian contact with *Alta* (Upper) California possibly occurred before 1542, when the first Spanish navigator, Juan Rodríguez Cabrillo, arrived there. Junks sailing from Asia via the North Pacific Ocean could have utilized the Japanese current to propel them as many as one hundred miles per day. (The longest distance between the Commander and Aleutian Is-

20

lands is about 150 miles.) Some experts in Chinese language and history maintain that the earliest mariners traveled eastward to a mysterious land known as "Fusang" along the Pacific Coast of North America.

In 1972, a huge doughnut-shaped stone, supposedly of Chinese origin, turned up in California off Point Conception. In ancient times such stones were used to clear seaweed from anchor chains. Other artifacts found over the years in California include a Chinese bronze fan and some ancient Chinese coins. In addition, glass globes, long used by Japanese to hold up fishing nets, have regularly washed ashore in California. As late as 1697, Francesco Giovanni Gemelli–Careri, an Italian merchant who traveled in a Manila galleon along the coastline, believed that California "bordered upon Great Tartary," an extension of the Far East. Despite such conjectures, the first effective discovery of Alta California by Cabrillo occurred in 1542.

Rumors continued to circulate that rich cities lay on the banks of a northern strait that led to a distant and mythological Cathay. These legends included tales of the Seven Cities of Cíbola, the Kingdom of La Gran Quivira, and a great hoard of gold called El Dorado. During the

Cabrillo National Monument, dedicated to Juan Rodríguez Cabrillo, is located on Point Loma's east shore near the site where Cabrillo's flagship, the *San Salvador*, is believed to have anchored. The monument commemorates the first European expedition to explore what is now the west coast of the United States. Photographed by Nate Foman, copyright 2006.

1530s dramatic reports led the Spaniards into a futile search in the North American interior for the villages of the Zuñi Indians, which were said to be the fabled Seven Cities. According to Spanish lore, at La Gran Quivira everything, even kitchen utensils, was made of gold.

After Cortés completed his conquest of Mexico, he was commissioned by King Charles V to search for the Strait of Anián, the legendary body of water connecting North America directly with the Far East. In 1532 Cortés sent a party of explorers from the west coast of Mexico to Baja California; this expedition ended in mutiny. The mutineers who went ashore at La Paz in order to get fresh water were killed by fierce Indians. Nevertheless, two sailors who had remained aboard the ship returned to Mexico with news of pearl beds lying off the Lower California cape. The report stimulated further exploration. In May of 1535, Cortés personally entered the bay in which the massacre had occurred.

Although discouraged by the aridity of the land surrounding the bay, Cortés in 1539 ordered Francisco de Ulloa to undertake a voyage farther north. In command of three small vessels, Ulloa turned up into the Sea of Cortés, or the Vermillion Sea, as the Gulf of California had come to be called. Following the mainland shore, Ulloa then made his way to the head of the gulf. He expected to find there a passage around the "island" and into the open sea. After failing to find the mythical waterway, he returned to the south, this time hugging the eastern shore of Baja California. While attempting to round the long peninsula, Ulloa met a violent tempest on the open sea. For eight days his ships beat up and down the Baja coast. Finally they reached the tip of Lower California and, rounding it, turned northward into the Pacific Ocean.

On January 5, 1539, Ulloa's expedition sighted Cedros Island, its summit bristling with tall cedars. After landing there, he and his men encountered Indians who attacked them with sticks and stones. Later, while battling opposing winds, Ulloa, at 30° north latitude, was compelled by lack of provisions to turn around, thereby missing the chance to be the first white person to land in Upper California. As a result, the misrepresentation of California as an island continued to appear on maps made as late as 1784.

These earliest expeditions in and around Baja California extended only slightly Spain's vague knowledge of North America's Pacific shore. Therefore, the Viceroy of New Spain, Antonio de Mendoza, in a further attempt to discover the Strait of Anián, decided to send one more exploratory party north by sea. He gave this group orders to explore the coast beyond the latitude reached by Ulloa. Its captain was Juan Rodríguez Cabrillo, the real discoverer of Alta California.

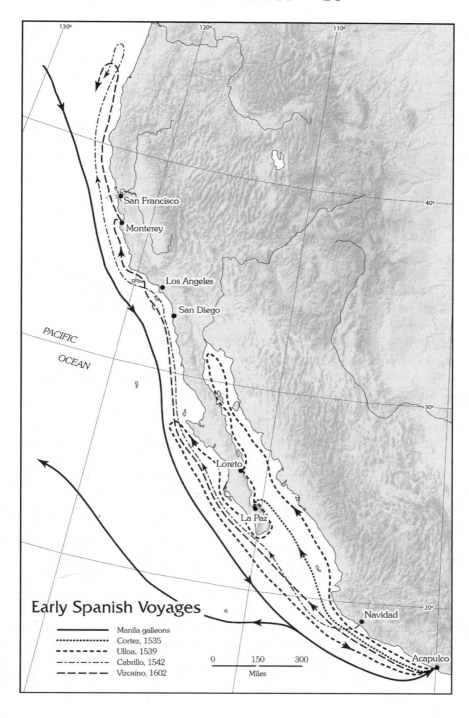

Early Spanish Voyages

————————	Manila galleons
··················	Cortez, 1535
– – – – –	Ulloa, 1539
–·–·–·–	Cabrillo, 1542
— — —	Vizcaíno, 1602

San Francisco

Monterey

Los Angeles

San Diego

Loreto

La Paz

Navidad

Acapulco

PACIFIC

OCEAN

130°   120°   110°

40°

30°

20°

0   150   300

Miles

Cabrillo's two small ships unfurled their sails on June 27, 1542, leaving the port of Navidad on the west coast of Mexico. These vessels were poorly built and badly outfitted; their anchors and ironwork had been carried overland across Mexico to the Pacific shore. Their crews, made up of scarcely provisioned conscripts, were soon wracked by scurvy, the dread disease so feared by all sailors.

This voyage took seven-and-one-half months, during which Cabrillo explored the coast as far as 41° and 30' north latitude. His tiny fleet, beaten back by northwest winds and becalmed, rocked idly on the waves for days, unable to make a "northing." The captain, the documents say, paced the deck, peering anxiously into the dense fog ahead. He did not realize that he was about to make a great discovery, and to lay down his life in so doing.

On September 28, 1542, after three emaciating months at sea, Cabrillo's ships entered the future harbor of San Diego. This formally marked the discovery of Alta (Upper) California. When the party landed, they learned from the local Indians that people like themselves, bearded and wearing clothing, had apparently been seen toward the interior. The Indians made gestures to show how the white men they had seen threw their lances. By galloping along the ground in imitation of a horse, they further suggested that the strangers had been on mounts. We shall never know if the Ulloa maritime expedition of 1539 or the Coronado land party of 1540 could possibly have met these same Indians.

When Cabrillo and company reached what was later called Santa Catalina Island, they encountered another group of astonished Indians. Along the shoreline opposite present-day Santa Monica, the captain noted an indentation on the mainland that he called "the Bay of Smokes." Even in the days long before smog, Indian campfires covered the bay near today's Los Angeles with spirals of smoke. Farther northward, the shoreline of the Santa Barbara Channel teemed with a dense Indian population.

Above Santa Barbara, heavy gales forced Cabrillo to land his ships at Cuyler Cove on San Miguel Island. It too was populated by Indians. The crew was astounded by their unruly hair, intertwined with daggers made out of flint, bone, and wood. The natives also wore no clothing and painted their faces in square designs, resembling a checkerboard.

As Cabrillo beat his way northward, he skirted Monterey Bay and the narrow opening that the American explorer John Charles Frémont later called "the Golden Gate," without spotting San Francisco Bay. From offshore, the Berkeley Hills blend in with the coastline, obscuring the entry to that vast body of water. Cabrillo next drifted northward and on November 16 sighted what became known as Drake's Bay. Because of heavy seas, he set sail to the south once more, again missing the Golden Gate. Unable to make a landing on the rocky coast north of Point Conception, and buffeted by high winds, the expedition was compelled to winter at San Miguel Island.

On January 3, 1543, an exhausted Cabrillo died, probably as the result of a violent fall during which he had broken his arm. After his men laid their commander to rest, they renamed the island La Isla de Juan Rodríguez in his honor. Drifting sand and falling cliffs later obliterated his gravesite. Today, not even the name of the island commemorates the true discoverer of Alta California. As the explorer lay dying, he charged his men to explore the coast as far northward as possible. His pilot, Bartolomé Ferrer (or Ferrelo), took command, and the expedition again set sail to the north. Scudding before a breaking storm, Ferrer possibly reached the Rogue River area on the Oregon coast. At this point the crews, crazed from the effects of scurvy, forced Ferrer to turn back southward.

This first voyage to Alta California had, of course, failed to find the fabled Straits of Anián. Furthermore, Cabrillo had seen no cities with gold and silver walls—indeed no civilization nearly as rich as the Aztec or Inca empires. Yet, he and his men had opened the sea route to a remote province at least vaguely familiar to all the world.

In 1564, King Philip II, seeking to protect Spain's claims to California against those of other European nations, ordered a fleet sent from Mexico to the Spanish-held Philippine Islands. The king felt that finding a new route across the Pacific could be entrusted only to New Spain's most skilled navigator. This was Andrés Urdaneta, chief cartographer and sailing master of the king's fleet. On November 24, 1564, Urdaneta left the port of Acapulco bound for the Philippines. He returned after a voyage of only 129 days, having established a landfall in Alta California at the latitude of Cape Mendocino.

For two and a half centuries, from 1565 to 1815, Spain's famed Manila galleons carried silver bullion from Acapulco to Manila, Spain's Philippine colony. There these lumbering vessels were reloaded, returning eastward to California, sailing before the prevailing trade winds and laden with prize silks and spices, as well as precious jade and amber, musk, aromatic resin, porcelains, inlaid chests, and even exotic birds that talked and did tricks. Back in New Spain (today's Mexico), these Asian rarities were snapped up by buyers enriched from mining Mexican and Peruvian silver. Traded for silver coins called "pieces of eight," various luxuries from Asia

Captained by Sir Francis Drake, The *Golden Hind* circumnavigated the world between 1577 and 1580. Of the five original vessels which set out from England, this was the only one to return. *Golden Hind,* 1927, by Montague Dawson, the Mariners' Museum, Newport News, VA.

were reshipped to Spain and sold all over Europe. Indeed, partly due to the Manila galleons, Spain became a power on a scale not seen since the Roman empire.

Mariners in Spain's Philippine trade risked their lives on the cumbersome and insecure galleons. More than forty of these vessels failed to make it back to the Americas. Ordinarily, the outward trip from Acapulco required only sixty to ninety days. But the return voyage to the west coast of Mexico took from seven to nine miserable months, during which a ship's foodstuffs usually became rancid, its water supply often failing. This compelled the eastbound crews to hoard scarce rainwater, which they caught both in sails and barrels. Whenever a crew experienced scurvy, a serious vitamin deficiency, corpse after corpse was thrown into the sea. Sadly, many crews were afflicted. By the time they sighted the California coastline, there were often not enough able-bodied men to go ashore for fresh water, or even to raise anchor once dropped. Some ships, therefore, limped on to Mexico, in sight of the California coast but unable to stop there. Despite leaky hulls, spoiled provisions, and putrid water, the occasional sick and dying crew reached Acapulco. Most did not.

Spain's viceroy in New Spain eventually realized the need to find a safe landing place for the battered returning galleon crews in need of wood, water, meat, and a place to make repairs. Such a haven, he ascertained, lay somewhere along the coast of California. Meanwhile, in the late sixteenth century, the intrusion into Pacific waters of the English privateers Francis Drake and Thomas Cavendish rudely shocked the Spaniards. Little more than licensed pirates, these buccaneers braved passage through the dangerous Straits of Magellan in order to reach the west coast of the Americas, where they lay in wait for Spain's overloaded galleons returning from Manila. Though armed with small cannons, muskets, and catapults for hurling stones, the scarcely maneuverable galleons were helpless against raids by fast English corsairs and pirates.

In 1577, Drake, armed with a secret commission from Queen Elizabeth I of England to "annoy the King of Spain in his Indies," set sail from Plymouth, England, on a voyage that would last several years. His 100-ton schooner, the *Golden Hind*, made its way through the Magellan Straits and swooped down upon unsuspecting Spanish outposts like a hawk among barnyard fowl. After he anchored at the ports of Lima, in present-day Peru, and at Guatulco in today's Mexican province of Oaxaca, Drake's men sacked both towns. Under sail on the high seas, Drake also attacked Spain's ships, looting their cargoes of gold and silver.

Drake's *Golden Hind* was loaded almost to the sinking point with treasure. Fearing that Spanish ships might intercept him if he returned toward the Straits of Magellan, he sought a northward passage back to England. We do not know exactly how far north Drake sailed along the California coast. On June 17, 1579, his lookout sighted a "convenient and fit harborough," at 38° and 30' north latitude. He entered a sandy bay in order to repair its hull, previously damaged on some rocks. The crew pushed their vessel onto its side, caulking and mending a bad leak. The exact location of Drake's anchorage in California has long been a matter of controversy. Arguments have been advanced for the bight under Point Reyes, known today as Drake's Bay, a white-cliffed harbor then inhabited by the Miwok Indians. Others believe that Drake anchored at Bodega Bay. One historian maintains that Drake never even landed in Alta California. As to San Francisco's spacious bay, no firm evidence has been produced that Drake or any of his men ever laid eyes on it. Only as late as 1775 did the Spanish ship *San Carlos* become the first verifiable vessel to enter San Francisco Bay.

Drake established friendly relations with the local Indians. He exchanged gifts with them and staged a ceremony in which the Indians supposedly accepted England's sovereignty over them. These symbolic acts corresponded to the smoking of a "peace pipe." After scraping the barnacles off the bottom of their ship, Drake's party held religious services, during which the Indians mumbled incantations led by their medicine men. Before he departed, Drake claimed title to the country for his queen by leaving behind "a plate of brasse, fast nailed to a great and firm poste."

In 1934, a badly weathered metal plate was reportedly found near the Laguna Ranch on Drake's Bay. After having been discarded, it was "rediscovered" in 1936 under circumstances that led skeptics to question its authenticity. For more than forty years, however, most historians considered this artifact genuine. At San Francisco's Drake Hotel, Professor Herbert Bolton of the University of California, Berkeley, foolishly pronounced it "one of the world's long lost historical treasures." But the popular professor had been duped. In 1977, Oxford metallurgists reexamined the plate, pronouncing it a modern forgery. It contained too much zinc and too little copper or lead to be genuine sixteenth-century brass. Historians had also been suspicious about the quality of the lettering, believing that Drake's gunsmiths would have done a far more elegant job. The metal plate, most concluded, had been crudely cut by machine tools.

The first English chroniclers who described Drake's contacts with the California Indians also possessed a vivid imagination. Their accounts made a princely personage out of an Indian chieftain, who actually would have been attired in rabbit skins; his rude basketwork hat was transformed into a royal crown, and his every gesture into a courtly English mannerism. Accounts of the Drake voyage were set down by writers who embroidered descriptions of California's geography and inhabitants. Drake's own account was never printed; it was probably suppressed lest he cause England diplomatic complications with Spain. He claimed the area for Queen Elizabeth and named his landing place New Albion.

By 1584, Spain's viceroy at Mexico City, aroused by the threat of such foreign interlopers, ordered the mariner Francisco de Gali to sail down the California coast on his return trip from the Philippines. Gali was to look for a new landing place. Instead, he reported finding a "very fair land, wholly without snow and with many rivers, bays, and havens." Ten years later, a Portuguese navigator, Sebastián Rodríguez Cermenho (sometimes Cermeno), recharted Gali's course. On November 4, 1595, Cermenho's galleon, the *San Agustín* out of Cavite in the Philippines, entered the same bay in which Drake had anchored sixteen years earlier. Cermenho was driven ashore by a squall that wrecked his ship's cargo. Fortunately the crew was able to free a launch into which seventy men crowded, their principle provision being acorns obtained from the local Indians. On this remarkable trip, Cermenho noted the entrance to Monterey Bay, thereby qualifying as its real discoverer. On January 7, 1596, he finally arrived at his home port of Navidad. By then, almost his entire crew had died at sea. Cermenho's disastrous voyage awakened New Spain's viceroy to the folly of conducting explorations in such unwieldy galleons. Indeed, these undertakings risked the loss of precious cargoes and the lives of too many crewmen.

Future expeditions to California would travel in ships of lighter draught. In 1602, Viceroy Monterey sent out one more exploratory party. On May 5 of that year, under the spiritual protection of Our Lady of Carmel, Captain Sebastián Vizcaíno, commanding three tiny vessels, headed out of Acapulco. He was ordered to identify potential new ports for the Manila Galleons. The group reached and renamed many of the points visited in 1542 by Cabrillo. To the Vizcaíno expedition we owe such familiar place names as San Diego, Santa Catalina Island, Santa Barbara, Point Conception, Monterey, and Carmel. On December 16, 1602, Vizcaíno sailed into Monterey Bay. As he looked about him at the ring of hills, dark with the growth of pines, he became enamored of what he saw. His report to the viceroy was so misleading that the next Spaniards to see Monterey, in 1769, failed to recognize the place. On their way back down the coast, forty–five members of Vizcaíno's crew died, mostly from scurvy. The ailing men, because of their ulcerated mouths and even the loss of their teeth, could not eat the coarse moldy food on board.

After Vizcaíno returned to Acapulco, a new Viceroy, the Marques de Montesclaros, was reluctant to send future expeditions toward Alta California. In the years from 1602 to 1769, no ship entered California waters from the south. The Manila galleons also passed by Alta California during that time. By 1815, Spain's galleon voyages were finally discontinued. Thus, for more than a century and a half, little was added to Vizcaíno's knowledge of California. The colonization of New Spain's far northern province still lay in the future.

SELECTED READINGS

About the origin of the name *California*, see Herbert D. Austin, "New Light on the Name California," *Historical Society of Southern California, Publications* 12 (1923); Ruth Putnam, *California, The Name* (1917); Irving Berdine Richman, *California Under Spain and Mexico, 1535–1847* (1911), especially pp. 362–66; and George Davidson, *The Origin and Meaning of the Name California* (1910). See also Donald C. Cutter, "Sources of the Name 'California,'" *Arizona and the West* 3 (Autumn 1961), 233–43, and Dora Polk, *The Island of California: A History of the Myth* (1991).

Discussion of Asian contact with California is in Charles Chapman, *A History of California* (1921); Edward Payson Vining, *An Inglorious Co-*

lumbus; or Evidence that Hwui Shan and a Party of Buddhist Monks from Afghanistan Discovered America (1885); Naojiro Murakami, "Japan's Early Attempts to Establish Commercial Relations with Mexico," in *The Pacific Ocean and History* (1917); and Zelia Nuttall, "The Earliest Historical Relations Between Mexico and Japan," *University of California Publications in Archaeology and Ethnology* 4 (1904). See also Douglas S. Watson, "Did the Chinese Discover America?" *California Historical Society Quarterly* 14 (March 1935), 47–57; Charles Leland, *Fusang, or the Discovery of America By Chinese Buddhist Priests in the Fifth Century* (1875); C. W. Brooks, "Report of Japanese Vessels Wrecked in the North Pacific Ocean From the Earliest Records to the Present Time," *Proceedings, California Academy of Sciences* 6 (1876).

On the exploration of California, see Henry R. Wagner, *Spanish Voyages to the Northwest Coast of America in the Sixteenth Century* (1929), as well as Wagner, *Juan Rodríguez Cabrillo, Discoverer of the Coast of California* (1941) and his *Cartography of the Northwest Coast of America to the Year 1800* (2 vols., 1937); Robert R. Miller, "Cortés and the First Attempt to Colonize California," *California Historical Quarterly* 53 (Spring 1974), 5–16. Also see Juan Paez, "Relation of the Voyage of Juan Rodríguez Cabrillo," trans. and ed. by Herbert E. Bolton in *Spanish Exploration in the Southwest* (1916).

Other references regarding exploration are: Maurice G. Holmes, *From New Spain by Sea to the Californias, 1519–1668* (1963); Jack D. Forbes, "Melchior Díaz and the Discovery of Alta California," *Pacific Historical Review* 27 (November 1958), 351–57; Harry Kelsey, *Juan Rodríguez Cabrillo* (1985), and Kelsey's "Mapping the California Coast: The Voyages of Discovery, 1533–1543," *Arizona and the West* 26 (Winter 1984), 307–26. See also R. V. Tooley, *California As An Island: A Geographical Misconception Illustrated by 100 Examples from 1625 to 1770* (1964).

On the Spanish advance by land see Herbert E. Bolton, *The Spanish Borderlands* (1921) and Philip W. Powell, *Soldiers, Indians and Silver: The Northward Advance of New Spain, 1550–1600* (1952). About the Manila galleon trade, the key source is William L. Schurz, *The Manila Galleon* (1939).

Regarding Drake, consult Edward von der Porten, "Who Made Drake's Plate?" *California History* 81 (2002), 116–33. Norman Thrower, ed., *Sir Frances Drake and the Famous Voyage, 1577–80* (1984); Henry R. Wagner, *Sir Francis Drake's Voyage Round the World: Its Aims and Achievements* (1926) and Wagner, *Drake on the Pacific Coast* (1970); C. G. Fink and E. P. Polushkin, "Drake's Plate of Brass Authenticated," *California*

Historical Society, Publication No. 14 (1937); R. B. Haselden first questioned the plate's authenticity in "Is the Drake Plate of Brass Genuine?" *California Historical Society Quarterly* 16 (September 1937), 271–74; Robert F. Heizer, *Francis Drake and the California Indians* (1947) and his *Elizabethan California* (1974). See also Francis P. Farquhar and Walter A. Starr, "Drake in California: A Review of the Evidence and the Testimony of the Plate of Brass" in *California Historical Quarterly* 36 (March 1957), 21–34. See also Adolph S. Oko, "Francis Drake and Nova Albion," *California Historical Society Quarterly* 43 (June 1964), 135–68. Warren L. Hanna, *Lost Harbor: The Controversy over Drake's California Anchorage* (1979); Edward Von der Porten, *Drake and Cermenho in California: Sixteenth Century Chinese Ceramics* (1993) and his *Porcelains and Terra Cottas of Drake's Bay* (1968). Most important are several Bancroft Library publications: *The Plate of Brass Reexamined* (1977) and *Supplementary Report* (1979), both of which found the plate a fake. See also N. B. Martin, "Portus Novus Albionis: Site of Drake's Pacific Sojourn," *Pacific Historical Quarterly* 49 (August 1979), 319–34; *Early California: Perception and Reality* by Henry J. Bruman and Clement W. Meighan (1981); as well as Harry Kelsey, "Did Francis Drake Really Visit California," *Western Historical Quarterly* 21 (November 1990), 455–62; and his *Sir Francis Drake, The Queen's Pirate* (1998). For other buccaneering in Pacific waters, see Peter Gerhard, *Pirates on the West Coast of New Spain, 1575–1742* (1960).

CHAPTER FOUR

COLONIZERS
OF THE FRONTIER

New Spain's northern border extended in an arc from present-day Louisiana to a remote chain of Jesuit missions. These desolate adobe edifices were spread throughout northern Mexico as well as in Upper and Lower California. Mining camps, cattle ranches, and crude forts also dotted the vast frontier.

Three Jesuit clerics contributed to the Spanish colonization of Upper California. Foremost among these was Eusebio Francesco Kino (sometimes spelled Chino or Chini), a native of Trento in what is now northern Italy. As an explorer, cartographer, and mission builder, Father Kino was responsible in the years 1678–1712 for the founding of missions on New Spain's northern frontiers. It was Father Kino, also an astronomer, who proved in 1702 that California was not an island. Aiding him in his work was another Italian Jesuit, the flinty and square-jawed Juan Maria de Salvatierra, who in 1697 founded the first of what would become a chain of missions in Lower California. A third major "black robe," a term used by Indians to refer to the Jesuit missionaries, was Father Juan de Ugarte. He labored for years among Indians newly converted to Christianity.

In 1763, after the defeat in North America of France by the British in the Seven Years' War, Spain feared more than ever that England might attempt to extend its New England colonization farther west, possibly into Spanish territory. To prepare for any such incursions, in 1765 Charles III, one of Europe's enlightened monarchs, appointed José de Gálvez *visitador-general*, or inspector general, of New Spain. In 1768 Gálvez, commissioned to reform colonization procedures, sailed to Lower California on an inspection tour of the peninsula's scraggly frontier missions.

While in Baja California, Gálvez, an avid expansionist, was ordered by King Charles to expel the Jesuits from the Spanish colonies. All over Europe a keen distrust of that order's political power had spread. Fearing that the Jesuits might eventually control Spain's colonial settlements, the king ordered the Jesuits replaced, even in distant Baja California. Thereafter, gray-robed Franciscan friars arrived at La Paz to continue the work begun earlier by Father Kino and his fellow Jesuits. These Franciscan priests would, in time, become the key colonizers for Gálvez in Alta California.

In the meantime, the Russians began to encroach upon California from the north. The voyages of Vitus Bering and Alexei Chirikof in 1741 deeply disturbed officials in New Spain. Furthermore, Russian sea otter–hunting ships were extending their poaching farther southward each year. Gálvez, therefore, felt a pressing need for Spaniards to occupy Alta California, although he personally would never see an outpost in the province.

In his capacity as inspector general, Gálvez next arranged a vital four-pronged expedition into Alta California. Two divisions were to go by sea and two more by land; if one party of either set should fail, the other might succeed. If all went well, however, all four groups would convene at San

Diego before pressing onward to Monterey, the place so highly praised long ago by Vizcaíno. Religious supervision of the expeditions into Alta California was entrusted to the Franciscan missionaries. The peninsular (Baja) missions contributed to the exploring parties all the horses, mules, dried meat, grain, cornmeal, and dry biscuits they could spare.

Gálvez took great care to select a strong cleric to lead the Franciscans northward into the new land. His choice was the fifty-five-year-old Fray Junípero Serra. The selection of Gaspar de Portolá to head the military branch of the expedition proved equally shrewd. Serra, the religious zealot, and Portolá, the dutiful soldier, were to become the first colonizers of Alta California. Father Serra, originally from the Mediterranean island of Majorca, had come to the New World in 1749 to labor among its natives. Before he was called to take charge of the missions of both Californias, he served for nine years among the Pamé Indians in the Sierra Gorda mountains of Mexico.

Serra brushed aside obstacles that would have stopped lesser men. These included a lame leg, from which he suffered pain nearly all his life. He applied manure to it as a poultice to hold the heat in. When Serra set out on the 1769 expedition to Upper California, he was in such poor shape that two men had to lift him onto the saddle of his mule. Yet, when his friend and fellow cleric, Fray Francisco Palóu, bade him a sad farewell, Serra insisted that, with the aid of a merciful God, he would make it to Alta California.

Serra's military companion, Portolá, had served the king as a captain of dragoons. In addition to occupying San Diego and Monterey, Portolá and Serra hoped to establish five missions. Church ornaments and sacred vessels did not constitute all of Serra's cargo. He also brought along seeds and farm tools with which to plant future mission gardens. The two land parties also herded along 200 head of cattle, the descendants of whom would roam the hills and valleys of Alta California and become the chief source of the province's pastoral wealth for several generations.

Meanwhile, two tiny vessels, the *San Carlos* and the *San Antonio*, were rigged out to transport the sea expedition. On January 9, 1769, the *San Carlos*, with its billowing sails unfurled, left La Paz in Lower California. Added to its crew were twenty-five Catalan military volunteers. They were instructed to overcome any resistance the Indians might offer after the party's landing. Five weeks later, the *San Antonio* left the same port, sailing northward toward San Diego.

By the latter part of March, Captain Fernando Rivera y Moncada, in command of the first land division, was ready to start northward. His force

Monterey coastline along northern California first explored by Cabrillo.
© Photographer: Cathy Figuli/Agency: Dreamstime.com.

was bolstered by two dozen leather-jacketed soldiers and forty-two Christianized Indians, Rivera was also accompanied by the Franciscan priest Juan Crespi. On March 22, 1769, their small army began to march up the spiny Baja peninsula. They would become the first overland party to reach Alta California. The other land contingent, the bronzed and bearded Portolá riding at its head, also set out for San Diego on May 15 of that year.

The *San Antonio*, though it had set sail a month later than its sister ship, was the first to arrive at the rendezvous in San Diego, on April 11. When the ship sailed into port, the stunned Indians mistook the *San Antonio* for a great whale. On April 29, to the great joy of those aboard the *San Antonio*, the *San Carlos* nosed alongside and dropped anchor. The 110-day voyage of the *San Carlos* had caused severe scurvy among the crew. There were not enough able bodied men aboard even to lower a shore boat. A third ship, the *San José*, had also been dispatched by Gálvez but was never again seen.

Ashore, tents made out of sails sheltered the crew. Many members suffered from dysentery. Pedro Prat, who had sailed on the *San Carlos* as its surgeon, searched for herbs with which to heal the sick. Because so many had died, all hands were busy caring for the remaining survivors. Any further voyage northward toward Monterey had to be postponed. The deceased were buried at a place the party named *La Punta de los Muertos*, or Dead Men's Point.

On May 14, 1769, the party's gloom was lightened by the arrival of Captain Rivera's land group from Baja California. To assure a better supply of fresh water, Rivera moved the entire camp nearer a stream at the foot of today's Presidio Hill. At the end of June his camp was joined by the arrival at San Diego of the second land party led by Portolá and Father Serra.

More than one-third of the 300 men who had set out for Alta California, by land and sea, failed to survive the trip. Half of those still alive were physically weakened by hunger, dysentery, and scurvy. After the founding of Mission San Diego de Alcalá, Portolá left behind a small garrison of soldiers to care for those who were still too ill to travel. Then, with the least emaciated of his soldiers, he pressed on farther north. The sixty-four

Colonnades of Mission San Juan Bautista, shown about 1866. Library of Congress, LC-USZ62-27205.

members of the expedition included men later prominent in California. Their surnames included Ortega, Amador, Alvarado, Carrillo, Yorba, and Soberanes. All wore leather jackets of thick deerskin and carried bull-hide shields. Lances and broad swords were among their weapons, as were short muskets.

Portolá made frequent stops to rest his men and animals. Their route may be traced by the place names they dispensed, all of which Father Crespi carefully recorded in his daily journal; they include Santa Margarita, Santa Ana, Carpintería, Gaviota, Cañada de los Osos, Pajaro, and San Lorenzo. Portolá pressed on until he reached the shallow Salinas River.

Nearing Monterey Bay, the commander stood atop a hill from which he saw an open *ensenada* (gulf). But the place he beheld hardly matched Vizcaíno's enthusiastic portrait of "a fine harbor sheltered from all winds." Indeed, Monterey was hardly a protected port. Instead, the little company gazed at a long, curving beach. Where was the grand landlocked harbor that Vizcaíno had described? Great swells from the ocean rolled in upon sandy beaches without obstruction, the only refuge from the wind provided by a small indentation in the shoreline. Thus, for good reason, Portolá failed to recognize the Bay of Monterey.

He now concluded that his only hope of finding Monterey or Point Reyes or any other of Vizcaíno's landmarks, was by continuing farther north. Portolá's party, therefore, moved up the coast past today's Santa Cruz. By this point, eleven of his men were so ill that they had to be carried in litters swung between mules. Near Soquel they had their first sight of some "big trees." Portolá named them *palos colorados* (or redwoods) because of the rich color of their wood. At one stopping place they saw a particularly big tree of this species, which they called *Palo Alto* (or the high tree). It remains the name of the university town located there.

As Portolá's advance party continued northward, their path was hindered by deep *arroyos* (gulches) that had to be bridged. Eventually an advance party reported seeing a "great arm of the sea." This was San Francisco Bay, which the group viewed for the first time on November 2, 1769. Astonished by the sight of so magnificent a body of water, the explorers concluded that Monterey Bay must actually be behind them. This splendid sight surely was a different estuary. For decades ships had bypassed San Francisco Bay. Ironically, a land expedition had stumbled upon the greatest harbor on the entire Pacific coast.

All around this grand estuary, waterfowl were so abundant and tame that they could be knocked down with long poles. After his men had feasted on geese, ducks, and mussels, Portolá decided to return southward to Point Pinos. When his party reached Carmel Bay, they erected a large cross near the seashore. At its base they buried a message. It informed any future group who might read it that Portolá's expedition had already claimed this place for Spain. Next the party crossed Cypress Point. Near the area that they still did not recognize as Monterey Bay, Portolá erected another wooden cross. On its arms his men carved these words: "The land expedition is returning to San Diego for lack of provisions, today, December 9, 1769."

On January 23, 1770, Portolá and his party returned to their base at San Diego. Upon their arrival, those who had stayed behind rushed out to greet them. In the years to come, Father Serra and his fellow Franciscans would develop missions near Portolá's camp sites. For the moment, however, survival was at stake. As provisions grew short, Portolá sent the *San Antonio* back to San Blas on the Mexican west coast for supplies. As the ship had not yet returned, on February 10, 1770, he ordered Captain Rivera to lead a small overland party of the strongest men back into Baja California to seek supplies from its missionaries. Instead of hunting wild game, the hungry men at San Diego had to hoard their scarce ammunition in case of Indian attacks.

Each day the missionaries knelt in prayer for the coming of a supply ship. Finally, on March 19, 1770, the encampment spotted a sail in the distance. Then, cruelly, it disappeared. Four days after being sighted, the *San Antonio* reappeared, this time dropping anchor into San Diego's bay. On board were the badly needed supplies.

With the San Diego base more secure, Portolá made another trip north by land. This time he finally recognized Monterey Bay, where he established a garrisoned fort. On June 3, 1770, Father Serra conducted mass at Monterey amid the ringing of bells and salvo of gunfire. Here was founded the second mission in Alta California, dedicated to San Carlos Borroméo. For convenience in obtaining wood and fresh water, the mission was later removed to Carmel, four miles from Monterey. From Carmel, site of his new home mission, Serra wrote his dear friend Father Palóu, "If you will come I shall be content to live and die in this spot."

On July 9, 1770, Portolá turned his brief governorship of both Californias over to Pedro Fages and sailed away on the *San Antonio*. Later he became the governor of Puebla in New Spain. Portolá deserves to be remembered not only as the first governor of both Californias (1767–70) but also as leader of the expedition (over the thousand-mile trail from the Baja peninsula) that discovered San Francisco Bay. Father Serra, Portolá's trail companion, remained in Alta California, where he inaugurated its chain of nine missions.

SELECTED READINGS

A superb new selection of documents that concern California's exploration and colonial governance under Spain and later, Mexico, is: Rose Marie Beebe and Robert Senkewicz, eds., *Lands of Promise and Despair: Chronicles of Early California, 1535–1846* (2001). The best portrayal of Kino remains Herbert Eugene Bolton's *Rim of Christendom* (1936). See also Rufus Kay Wyllys, *Pioneer Padre: The Life and Times of Eusebio Kino* (1935) and Bolton's *The Padre on Horseback* (1932), as well as Frank C. Lockwood, *With Padre Kino on the Trail* (1934). Kino's astronomical activities are discussed in Ellen Shaffer, "The Comet of 1680–1681," *Historical Society of Southern California Quarterly* 34 (March 1952), 57–70. Finally, on Kino, consult Ernest J. Burrus, trans. and ed., *Kino Reports to Headquarters* (1954).

About Salvatierra, see Miguel Venegas, *Juan María de Salvatierra,* translated and edited by Margaret Eyer Wilbur (1929). For other early Jesuit activity in the Southwest, see J. J. Baegert, *Observations in Lower California,* translated and edited by M. M. Brandenburg and Carl L. Baumann (1952); also Father Peter M. Dunne, *Pioneer Black Robes on the West Coast* (1940) and Dunne's *Pioneer Jesuits in Northern Mexico* (1944), and his *Early Jesuit Missions of the Tarahumara* (1948), and *Black Robes in Lower California* (1952). Also consult Theodore Treutlein, ed., *Pfefferkorn's Description of Sonora* (1949).

On Gálvez see Herbert I. Priestley, *José de Gálvez, Visitador-General of New Spain* (1916). See also the translation of Father Javier Clavigero's *Storia della California* (1789) in Sara E. Lake and A. A. Gray, *The History of Lower California* (1937).

Regarding the Russian threat to California see Frank A. Golder, *Russian Expansion on the Pacific, 1641–1858* (1914), and Golder's *Bering's Voyages* (2 vols. 1922–25). Good accounts of the first colonization of California are Charles Chapman, *The Founding of Spanish California* (1916); Irving Berdine Richman, *California Under Spain and Mexico, 1535–1847* (1911); and Douglas S. Watson, (1934).

Missionary activity has been widely chronicled. The diario of Fray Francisco Palóu appears, in translation, in Herbert E. Bolton, ed., *Historical Memoirs of New California* (5 vols. 1926). See also Herbert I. Priestley, ed., *A Historical, Political and Natural Description of California by Pedro Fages* (1937). Lives of Serra include Abigail H. Fitch, *Junípero Serra* (1914) as well as Agnes Repplier, *Junípero Serra: Pioneer Colonist of California* (1933) and Father Zephyrin Engelhardt, *The Missions and Missionaries of California* (4 vols. 1908–15).

The best work on Serra is Maynard J. Geiger's *The Life and Times of Fray Junípero Serra* (2 vols. 1959); see also Geiger, trans. and ed., *Palóu's Life of Fray Junípero Serra* (1955) and Geiger, "Fray Junípero Serra: Organizer and Administrator of the Upper California Missions, 1769–1784," *California Historical Society Quarterly* 42 (September 1963), 195–220, as well as Geiger, *Franciscan Missionaries in Hispanic California, 1769–1848: A Biographical Dictionary* (1969). For Serra's successor, see Francis Guest, *Fermin Francisco de Lasuén (1736–1803): A Biography* (1973).

Regarding Portolá, see Robert Selden Rose, ed., *The Portolá Expedition of 1769–1770: Diary of Vicente Vila* (1911); also Costansó, *The Narrative of the Portolá Expedition of 1769–1770*, Frederick J. Teggart, ed., (1910); Theodore E. Treutlein, "The Portolá Expedition of 1769–1770," *California Historical Society Quarterly* 47 (December 1968), 291–313; Janet R. Fireman and Manuel P. Servín, "Miguel Costansó: California's Forgotten Founder," *California Historical Society Quarterly* 49 (March 1970), 3–19; and *The Costansó Narrative of the Portolá Expedition*, trans. by Ray Brandes (1970).

Spanish claims are analyzed in Henry Raup Wagner, "Creation of Rights of Sovereignty Through Symbolic Acts," *Pacific Historical Review* 7 (December 1938), 297–326; Manuel P. Servín, "Symbolic Acts of Sovereignty in Spanish California," *Southern California Quarterly* 45 (June 1963), 109-21; and Servín's "The Instructions of Viceroy Bucareli to Ensign Juan Pérez," *California Historical Society Quarterly* 40 (September 1961), 243-46.

CHAPTER FIVE

MISSIONS, PRESIDIOS, AND PUEBLOS

The Spanish crown used three institutions to colonize distant California. These were its missions, presidios, and pueblos. The missions became the most important of the three. The other two agencies supported and defended the padres whose purpose was the "saving" of the souls of pagan aborigines. Eventually, however, Spain transformed its converted natives into a labor force. Future missionization would thereby become economically viable and further the expansion of the Spanish empire.

By 1776, Father Serra hoped for an increase in the population of Alta California as well as expansion of its agricultural possibilities. He also wanted to build more missions. Eventually twenty-one of these formed a chain from San Diego to Sonoma. Each mission, some thirty miles apart, was separated by a day's travel on horseback. The so-called King's Highway, or *El Camino Real* of the tourist literature, was little more than a dusty dirt road.

Three requisites determined the choice of each mission site—arable soil for crops, an ample water supply, and a substantial local native population. By the time the twenty-one missions were established, the friars had in their possession much of the choicest land in the province. This would lead to resentment by civilian leaders and settlers.

The first mission buildings were mere huts of thatch and sticks, plastered with mud or clay, and roofed over with tile—not the adobe-brick or cut-stone buildings of today. The stone walls at Mission San Carlos Borroméo, outside today's Carmel, were actually never seen by Serra. Yet his remains are buried there. The California padres, in their isolation, modified Moorish and Roman architectural styles to render structures appropriate to the environment. Thus "California mission architecture" is characterized by open courts, long colonnades, arches, and corridors. The typical red-tiled mission roofs were one way to avoid fires in wooden structures. Destruction of earlier buildings by earthquakes led to the use of thick adobe walls reinforced with occasional buttresses.

At the missions, the padres assumed a paternal attitude toward the Indians, treating them as wards. There were usually two friars at each establishment, the elder of whom had charge of interior matters and religious instruction, while the younger attended to agricultural and outside work. Each mission was subject to the authority of a father-president for all of California. He in turn bowed to the orders of the College of San Fernando, headquarters of the Franciscans in Mexico. Except in the punishment of capital crimes, the friars had control of their native charges. Floggings and other corporal punishments were administered for unacceptable offenses. The missionaries defended their discipline on the ground that it was the only effective means of controlling unruly natives, the souls of whom they were trying to "save."

Some clerical scholars have countered accusations of harshness by the Franciscans toward California's aborigines. Flagellation, or use of a rope *disciplina*, as well as whips and hairshirts, formed part of the clerical mortification of the flesh. Although delinquent natives were whipped, sometimes excessively, and some lost their lives due to poor sanitation conditions in and around the missions, one needs to place both the punishment

Mission San Luis Rey, founded in 1798, from Robinson's "Life in California Before the Conquest," 1846. C. C. Pierce Collection, courtesy of the Huntington Library, San Marino.

and high mortality rates of those at the missions within the context of eighteenth-century medical standards on a distant frontier. Yet, most historians continue to consider treatment of the natives by the Spanish clergy and military as harsh. Those who were missionized did, indeed, suffer high casualty rates from a variety of causes.

The missions were not devoted entirely to religious instruction. Each was also a school in which natives did daily work and were taught trades. Guided by the missionaries, the native peoples proved to be remarkably good students. The friars were also musicians, weavers, carpenters, masons, architects, and physicians.

The friars, putting their own hands to the plow, raised enough food for mission use. They also produced a surplus of wine, oil, hemp, hides, and tallow. These extras were sent southward to New Spain. There they were exchanged for badly needed clothing and agricultural tools. The missionaries transplanted traditional Spanish crops to California. Orange, lemon, fig, date, and olive trees flourished in mission gardens, as did grape vineyards. Even cotton was grown at several of the missions alongside livestock.

Among those who helped assure progress at the missions was the new viceroy, Antonio María Bucareli. He placed great faith in the leadership of Father Serra as well as Fathers Francisco Palóu and Fermín de Lasuén. Palóu had been among the last of the Franciscans to turn over their Lower California missions to the Dominican order, and in 1773 he joined Serra in Upper California. Palóu was also the author of the first book ever written in California, *Noticias de la Nueva California*; this and his *Vida de Junípero Serra* are basic works. Upon Serra's death, in 1784, he and his fellow Franciscans had been in California nearly sixteen years. By then their missions claimed a total of 5,800 native converts. Lasuén, also a cleric of talent and character, filled the post of president with distinction after Serra died.

These priests desired that California's presidios, or frontier fortresses, be strengthened in order to protect the missions against native uprisings. To guard against foreign interlopers, each presidio was located at a strategic position, generally at the entrance of the best ports. Small dwellings, inhabited principally by settlers, traders, and the families of garrisoned soldiers, grew up around the presidios.

The presidial pueblos came to include San Diego, founded July 16, 1769; Monterey, June 3, 1770; San Francisco, September 17, 1776; and Santa Barbara, April 21, 1782. At first they were under military rule. The presidios themselves consisted of a square enclosure, surrounded by a ditch and rampart of earth or brick, within which were located a small church, quarters for officers and soldiers, civilian housing, storehouses, workshops, and cisterns.

With only a few bronze cannons mounted on ramparts, and often without sufficient powder to discharge the weapons, not one of the coastal presidios could have stood up against an attack by a well-equipped ship of war. Indeed, they were maintained more as a symbolic warning against possible enemies, with little expectation of their serving well in a fight. In time the cannons rusted and the presidios took on an air of dilapidation.

The duties of soldiers who manned the presidios included the care of outlying herds and flocks. They also cultivated the soil of nearby fields, utilizing native laborers, who for their hard work received such occasional rewards as a string of beads, an extra dish of porridge, a pair of shoes, or a piece of cloth.

San Francisco's presidio was established largely through the efforts of Juan Bautista de Anza. He was one of the significant trailbreakers and toughest Indian fighters of the West. Anza had long planned to explore and establish a route northwestward from Sonora to the northern California coast. Such a land passage would reduce the delay and perils of sea voyages, on which California still relied for contact with the outside world.

Viceroy Bucareli, wishing to strengthen California's settlements, saw in Anza's proposal an opportunity not only to open a new land route, but also to send colonists north under the protection of a capable leader. Women settlers, as well as provisions, and domestic animals remained in great demand in the new province. Anza, in January of 1774, with the trails-priest Francisco Garcés as his guide, and a band of thirty-four men, set out westward from Tubac in northern Mexico. Theirs was the first sizable crossing by Caucasians into California from the Colorado basin through the San Jacinto Mountains.

A key to the success of this party was Father Garcés. Three years before, he had penetrated into California beyond the junction of the Colorado and Gila rivers, to the walls of the southern Sierra range. Utilizing his expertise, Anza's party, on March 22, 1774, reached Mission San Gabriel in the Los Angeles basin, which had been founded three years before.

Anza had opened up a new overland route some 2,200 miles long. In 1775, Viceroy Bucareli sent Anza with another party to Alta California. This group consisted of colonists recruited throughout Sinaloa and Sonora. On October 23, Anza again left Tubac, leading a group of 240 men, women, and children, along with a herd of 800 cattle, beyond the Colorado River to Mission San Gabriel, and then on to Monterey.

21 7 San Francisco Solano de Sonoma (1832)

San Rafael Arcángel (1817) 20

San Francisco (1776) 3 6 San Francisco de Asís (1776)

Santa Clara (1777) 8 · 14 San José de Guadalupe 3 (1797)

Branciforte (1797) 6 12 Santa Cruz (1791)

15 5 San Juan Bautista (1797)

San Carlos Borromeo (Carmel) (1770) 2 2

13 Nuestra Señora de la Soledad (1791)

3 San Antonio de Padua (1771)

16 San Miguel Arcángel (1797)

PACIFIC OCEAN

5 San Luís Obispo 1 (1772)

La Purísima Concepción (1787) 11

19 Santa Inés (1804)

10 Santa Barbara (1786) 4 Santa Barbara (1782)

9 Santa Buenaventura (1782)

San Fernando 17 Rey de España (1797)

4 San Gabriel Arcángel (1771) 4 Los Angeles (1781)

California Missions
(with order of founding and dates)

● Mission

⬢ Presidio

■ Mission pueblo and civic municipality

7 San Juan Capistrano 2 (1776)

18 San Luís Rey de Francia (1798)

1 San Diego de Alcalá 1 (1769)

0   25   50
Miles

N

A few colonists accompanied him farther north. They settled near the shore of a great bay which they named San Francisco. On September 17, 1776, Anza dedicated the Presidio of San Francisco de Asís. On October 9, Mission Dolores was founded by Father Palóu, the year the American Declaration of Independence was signed.

The viceroy had also sent Captain Juan Manuel Ayala, in command of the vessel *San Carlos*, to explore the area's vast bay, which still had no name. No ship had yet passed through the Golden Gate, and Ayala feared danger along its narrow, rocky shoreline. At nightfall on August 5, 1775, the *San Carlos* moved into the bay, cautiously dropping her lead line until she reached today's North Beach. Ayala named San Francisco Bay's two islands—*Nuestra Señora de los Angeles* (Our Lady of the Angels) shortened later to Angel Island, and Alcatraz or "Pelican," because of the large number of those birds flying over it.

At the Presidio of San Francisco, even its officers lived under primitive conditions. As virtual exiles in a strange land, they waited for the day when they might return to more comfortable quarters in Spain. In 1792, the English visitor, George Vancouver, described the dwelling of the comandante at Yerba Buena (today's San Francisco) as consisting of two bare rooms with earth floors; its windows had no glass, and furniture was sparse.

In addition to presidial and mission pueblos, Governor Felipe de Neve established civilian pueblos. He granted each four square Spanish leagues of land. Facing upon a plaza were a council adobe, church, and a *calabozo*, or jail. The life of the community revolved around these central squares, in which bullfights were also sometimes held.

Spain planned the growth of pueblos in an orderly manner, for this represented the progress of civilization over barbarism. Each settler was entitled to a house lot, livestock, and even an allowance in clothing and supplies. The pueblo also maintained a common pasture. Any surplus agricultural products were to be sent to the presidios. Settlers were to build their own adobes, dig irrigating ditches, cultivate the land, and maintain animals. After five years of exemption from taxes, pueblo residents were to receive final title to their land.

Municipal officers consisted of an *alcalde* (similar to a mayor) and *regidores*, or councilmen. These were members of a local *ayuntamiento*. The alcalde decided all cases of minor importance. But persons charged with high crimes were brought before the governor at Monterey. Anyone had the right to demand trial by "good men" (*hombres buenos*), a jury of three to five members. The powers of an alcalde were respected, for these officials were generally honest administrators. The alcalde was, in effect, the *patrón*, or "little father," of a town, to whom citizens carried their troubles.

The Los Angeles ayuntamiento had jurisdiction over territory as large as the state of Massachusetts. It was a dignified body whose members were attired in black. The ayuntamiento received petitions and complaints from dissatisfied ranchers as well as townsmen. As a badge of office, alcaldes carried a silver-headed cane. They and the regidores were the arbiters of pueblo justice.

California's first civic pueblo was San José de Guadalupe (now San José), founded on November 29, 1777. Originally it consisted of a few mud huts on the banks of the Guadalupe River.

Further southward, Governor Felipe de Neve authorized a settlement that would become the first city of the American West. This second civic pueblo, Nuestra Señora la Reina de los Angeles de Porciuncula, today's Los Angeles, was founded on September 4, 1781, by eleven couples and their twenty-two children—a total of forty-four *pobladores*. It was named after a religious town in Italy. Only two of the Los Angeles settlers were white. Twenty-six of the others had some degree of African ancestry while sixteen were Indian or *mestizo* (mixed Spanish and Indian origin). Not one of Los Angeles's first settlers could write their name. By 1801, however, they were producing enough grain to export a small surplus back to Mexico.

California's third civic community, Branciforte, named after a prominent Mexican viceroy, was established in 1797 near the present Santa Cruz. Its founders were mostly convicts banished to the far north by Mexican legal officials, but Branciforte soon passed out of existence. Along with San José and Los Angeles, these new settlements would eventually form the basis of California's provincial life.

SELECTED READINGS

Basic to understanding the missions is Herbert E. Bolton, "The Mission as a Frontier Institution in the Spanish American Colonies," *American Historical Review* 23 (October 1917), 42–61. More recently, see Steven Hackel, *Children of the Coyote, Missionaries...in Colonial California* (2005); also Harry Crosby, *Antigua California: Mission and Colony on the Peninsular Frontier* (1994); Theodore Maynard, *The Long Road of Father Serra* (1954) and Omer Englebert, *The Last of the Conquistadores: Junípero Serra, 1713–1784* (1956). Also consult Maynard Geiger, ed., *Palóu's Life of Fray Junípero Serra* (1955).

On Anza see Herbert E. Bolton, ed. *Anza's California Expeditions* (5 vols. 1930); also Frederick J. Teggart, ed. *The Anza Expedition of 1775–1776* (1913); Douglas D. Martin, *Yuma Crossing* (1954).

About Los Angeles and other pueblos and presidios, see John Langellier and Daniel Rosen, *El Presidio de San Francisco . . . 1776–1846* (1997); Edwin Beilharz, *Felipe de Neve, First Governor of California* (1972); W. W. Robinson, *Ranchos Become Cities* (1939); Andrew Rolle, *Los Angeles: From Pueblo to City of the Future* (1995); Francis Guest, "The Establishment of the Villa of Branciforte," *California Historical Society Quarterly* 41 (March 1962), 29–50; Theodore Grivas, "Alcalde Rule: The Nature of Local Government in Spanish and Mexican California," *California Historical Society Quarterly* 40 (March 1961), 11–32.

About native relations see Harry Kelsey, "European Impact on the California Indians," *The Americas* 61 (April 1985), 494–511; James Sandos, *Converting California: Indians and Franciscans in the Missions* (2004) and his "Levantamiento: The 1824 Chumash Uprising Reconsidered," *Southern California Quarterly* 57 (Summer 1985), 109–33; William McCawley, *The First Angelinos: The Gabrielino Indians of Los Angeles* (1996).

CHAPTER SIX

CALIFORNIA
AND ITS SPANISH
GOVERNORS

Gaspar de Portolá was followed by two brief interim governors. In 1775, Felipe de Neve became Spain's main authority until 1782. Like Portolá, he was also a military commander who became an innovator. After his arrival at Monterey, he drew up regulations to guide the province's civic and military affairs as well as his newly founded pueblos.

These remote settlements desperately needed colonists. In 1781 Captain Rivera y Moncada received orders to lead a party of settlers bound for Los Angeles and San José. On their way northward, beyond Sonora and Sinaloa, tragedy, however, struck this forlorn group. At the Colorado River, Rivera had fortunately sent some of the colonists ahead, while he and his soldiers stopped to rest. The Yuma Indians were resentful of his men marching clumsily through their cornfields and pumpkin patches. On July 17, the natives suddenly attacked them near Missions Purisma Concepcion and San Pedro y San Pablo, both of which had been established near the river crossing. All the friars in the mission, some male settlers in the area, and Rivera as well as the trails-priest Father Garcés, were shot or clubbed to death. Some women and children, while spared execution, were herded off by the Yumas into slavery.

The natives resented all whites, holding them as their mortal enemies. Yet, the Spanish had previously promised them supplies and good treatment by soldiers and settlers alike. The Yuma Massacre led to the abandonment of this dangerous route to California, originally opened up by Anza. Henceforth, neither pueblos nor missions were established along the Colorado River. As a result, the province of Alta California continued in its isolation from the rest of New Spain.

Later, on August 28, 1784, the province suffered a heavy loss following the death of Father Serra. During his seventy-one years, he had spent thirty-four as a missionary. His successor, Palóu, was President of the California missions for only one year, during which time he prepared several volumes describing local conditions. He was followed by Father Lasuén who labored on for eighteen years, carrying out Father Serra's planned extension of the mission system.

From 1782 to 1791, Pedro Fages served as the governor of California. Fages, a sturdy officer, had also been an Indian fighter and an explorer who (in 1770 and 1772) had led expeditions to San Francisco Bay. He personally had helped keep the Alta California colonists alive during a period when supply ships were delayed. This he did by providing bear meat from Cañada de los Osos (Bear Canyon), near San Luis Obispo. Nevertheless, the governor's brusque manner soon landed him in the middle of disagreements between the missionaries and his young wife, Doña Eulalia Fages, all of which the missionaries recorded in their journals in entertaining detail. Because Doña Eulalia (who had caught her husband sexually involved with an Indian girl) so hated the frontier, the padres eventually solicited Spanish officials for the couple's removal from Monterey, where they had disturbed mission life.

In 1794 another governor arrived. This was a Spanish Basque named Diego de Borica. Like Fages, Borica was a good soldier and administrator. The new governor established a more harmonious relationship with the friars, encouraging Father Lasuén to seek new mission sites. Together they decided that five more such establishments could be founded. Borica believed that conversion of more natives would make it possible to reduce the necessary number of provincial guards. The missions had been isolated units; Borica proposed to link them into one chain, nearer together so that they served the area from San Diego northward to San Francisco and between the Coast Ranges and the ocean. Eventually one could travel safely over a distance of 500 miles and enjoy the hospitality of the missions each night without having to carry along provisions.

Governor Borica also instituted new irrigation works and guarded the provincial revenues. He proved to be a steadfast friend of the local natives. He established California's first education system, however primitive. He also saw to it that Indian lands were not taken and believed that Indians should not face capital punishment, even for the crime of murder.

Upon Borica's retirement in 1800, José Joaquín de Arrillaga served as governor, during which time he tried to mediate between military and religious officials. Meanwhile, back in Mexico City, the viceroy of New Spain was losing interest in the California missions and stopped sending

Mission San Juan Capistrano in the 1920s. Library of Congress, LC-USZ62-92191.

them financial support. He also allowed the presidios and civic establishments of the province to fall into a deplorable state. Buildings deteriorated while ancient cannons rusted from exposure to the weather. Spiritless frontier troops remained badly equipped, going without pay for long periods of time. As for mission expansion, this enterprise came to a halt with the death of Father Lasuén in 1803.

During his administration, one of Governor Arrillaga's principal worries concerned the founding of a Russian settlement in California. The Russians initially had arrived in 1806 to examine fur-trading opportunities. But after they established Fort Ross, north of Bodega Bay, the threat posed by Russian encroachment had become all too real.

California's last Spanish governor was Pablo Vicente Solá. His arrival at Monterey in 1815 was marked by days of feasting and dancing, exhibitions of expert horsemanship, and gory bull and bear fights in the capital's muddy plaza. The vain royalist governor wrongly considered this welcome as an expression of California's loyalty to Spain. Actually, local allegiance was growing ever weaker.

Solá, proud of his Spanish birth, looked with contempt upon colonials whom he considered generally incompetent. He especially objected to smuggling between the Californians and foreigners. Each year increasing numbers of foreign ships arrived offshore. Particularly alarming were vessels sailing under the flag of the new American Union. When these ships landed illegally to take on wood and water, the governor could not rely on his inadequate shore fortifications. Yet, facing severe scarcities of clothing, furniture, and household necessities, the haughty governor managed to rationalize the widespread smuggling.

But Solá's stormy tenure in office would soon be of little consequence. Spain's New World empire was about to crumble. California, though only an appendage of its far-flung colonies, could not escape the revolutionary fervor felt by colonials throughout Latin America.

SELECTED READINGS

The role of each Spanish governor is described in Donald Nuttall, "The Gobernantes of Spanish Upper California," *California Historical Society Quarterly* 51 (Fall 1972), 253–80; see also Herbert E. Bolton, *Outpost of Empire* (1931); Herbert Priestley, trans., Pedro Fages, *A Historical, Political and Natural Description of California* (1937); and Henry R. Wagner, trans., *Letters of Captain Don Pedro Fages and the Reverend President Fr. Junípero Serra at San Diego* (1936).

For the Yuma Massacre, see Douglas Martin, *Yuma Crossing* (1954); Herbert Priestley, trans., *Pedro Fages, The Colorado River Campaign 1781–1782* (1913); Elliot Coues, *On the Trail of a Spanish Pioneer* (2 vols. 1900); John Galvin, ed., *A Record of Travels in Arizona and California, 1775–1776 by Fr. Francisco Garcés* (1965).

Regarding mission architecture see Kurt Baer, *Architecture of the California Missions* (1958) as well as his *Paintings and Sculpture at Mission Santa Barbara* (1955), and Baer, "Spanish Colonial Art in the California Missions," *The Americas* 17 (July 1961), 33–54. See also Norman Neuerburg, *The Decoration of the California Missions* (1987).

Exploration is examined in Herbert Priestley, *Franciscan Explorations in California* (1946); Henry R. Wagner, "Early Franciscan Activity on the West Coast," *Historical Society of Southern California Quarterly* 23 (September 1941), 115–26; John A. Berger, *The Franciscan Missions of California* (1948): Maynard Geiger, *Mission Santa Barbara, 1782–1965* (1965); Clement Meighan, "Indians and the California Missions," *Southern California Quarterly* 69 (Fall 1987), 187–201; Robert H. Jackson, "The Changing Economic Structure of the Alta California Missions, A Reinterpretation," *Pacific Historical Review* 61 (August 1992), 387-415; James A. Sandos, "Junípero Serra's Canonization and the Historical Record," *American Historical Review* 93 (December 1988), 153–69; and Francis Guest, "An Inquiry Into the Role of Discipline in California's Mission Life," *Southern California Quarterly* 71 (Spring 1989), 1–68.

CHAPTER SEVEN

EXPLORATION AND FOREIGN INTERFERENCE

During the long period when Alta California was settled by Spain's priests, soldiers, and colonists, the crown continued to press onward with exploration. In Mexico City, New Spain's Viceroy, Antonio Bucareli, asked his mariners to find out what lay beyond the northernmost California coastline. In March of 1775, he commissioned two explorers, Captains Bruno de Heceta and Juan Francisco de Bucareli, to sail out of San Blas in Lower California. After days of travel, they reached latitude 41° north. There a fine bay's shoreline was covered with wild roses, irises, manzanitas, and tall pines. They took possession of the inviting place in the name of the King of Spain. Since this event took place on the day of the Holy Trinity, they called the bay Trinidad, by which name it is still known.

Far to the north, Captain Heceta also deserves credit for the discovery, on July 27, 1775, of the Columbia River. His achievement is sometimes ascribed to the American sea captain Robert Gray, who arrived on the site only in 1792. Heceta also reached Nootka Sound, on the west coast of cold and damp Vancouver Island. But so many of his crew were ill that he was forced to sail back southward to California.

As for Bodega, although short of food and water and with a crew crippled by scurvy, he pressed on until the cold autumn rains set in. Finally, his men suffering severely from insufficient clothing, he too was compelled to turn around. The southward trip was a stormy one. Great seas rolled over Bodega's ship, carrying away everything movable and filling the hold with water. On October 3, 1775, his vessel drifted into a bay four leagues north of Point Reyes. There he watched bears and deer feeding along the banks. His navigator named the bay Bodega after the captain. The area remained remote for many years thereafter.

Geographic isolation from the rest of the Spanish empire forced colonial Californians to lead calm if rather dull lives. They, of course, knew the names of their king and of the pope but little about events abroad. The decrepit Spanish supply system could not provide sorely needed goods. Hence, California became dependent upon ships flying the flags of other nations. If these foreign visitors had not called attention to its future possibilities, the province may have remained a virtually isolated island.

The profitable fur trade on the northwest coast eventually pushed European and American ships to ports farther south in California. In August of 1785, the French scientist and navigator Jean François de Galaup de la Pérouse arrived from Brest at the head of a geographic, scientific, and commercial expedition. With their two vessels anchored in Monterey Bay, his group of geologists and botanists spent ten days collecting specimens and making careful drawings of what they observed. The hospitable *Californios* supplied the naturalists with cattle, vegetables, milk, poultry, and grain to reprovision their ships. The visitors reciprocated with gifts of cloth, blankets, beads, tools, and seed potatoes from Chile.

The La Pérouse expedition departed after a farewell that turned out to be fatal. Nothing more was ever heard of the party until 1825. That year the wreckage of two French ships were found on the reefs of a remote island north of New Hebrides. Had La Pérouse not forwarded his California journal to France, all record of his voyage would have been lost to posterity.

In September of 1791, the Californios encountered yet another European scientific expedition, this one also from Spain but led by the Italian mariner Alejandro (Alessandro) Malaspina. The captain was on a round-the-world mission with instructions to search for the long-sought Strait of Anián. Malaspina's account of his California stay, while valuable, is not as complete as that of La Pérouse or, later, of the Englishman George Vancouver. But Malaspina did bring to California the body of the first American ever to land on its shores. This was John Green, actually a deceased sailor from Boston who had shipped out as a gunner's mate.

English interest in California remained high during the rest of the eighteenth century. In 1792, Vancouver received orders to examine the extent of Spain's grasp on the province and to seize any unclaimed territory. On November 14, he entered San Francisco Bay in the sloop-of-war *Discovery*. Despite strained relations between Spain and England, Vancouver was given a cordial reception by the local padres and military officials.

Vancouver's party also visited Mission Santa Clara. They were the first non-Spanish foreigners to penetrate into the interior. They also gave the grateful priests at Carmel Mission some scarce table utensils as well as bar iron and church ornaments. Upon his return visit in 1793, however, Vancouver was offended not to receive the same welcome he had enjoyed the year before. His later account grew bitter in tone. Governor Arrillaga had, meanwhile, objected to allowing any more foreign visitors to pass into the province's interior, perceiving all such interlopers as increasing the threat to Spanish authority.

In 1796, the first American vessel anchored in a California port. This was the *Otter* out of Boston. Its master secretly landed ten men and one woman on sandy Carmel beach at night, forcing them from a rowboat at pistol point. They were escaped convicts from Botany Bay, the English penal colony in Australia. Governor Borica put the escapees to work as carpenters and blacksmiths, paying them 19¢ per day.

American ship masters continued to put into California ports, and Spanish officials remained almost powerless to prevent contraband trade between Californios and the masters of the visiting "Boston ships." During 1799 the *Eliza*, yet another Yankee vessel, anchored at San Francisco and obtained supplies on the condition that it would not touch at any other port in the province.

The steady arrival of foreign poachers and traders alike roused the viceroy at Mexico City to issue stricter orders against conducting trade with foreigners. Since, however, he had no means of enforcing such *pronunciamientos*, the Yankee traders continued to defy local regulations. On March 22, 1803, shots were exchanged between the American vessel *Lelia Byrd* and a shore battery at San Diego, after part of the ship's crew had been captured while ashore trading. Although several shots struck the ship's sails, rigging, and hull, no one aboard was hurt. The captain, William Shaler, got his men safely away to the Hawaiian Islands and then to China. The next year saw the *Lelia Byrd* back in California waters doing a flourishing fur business. This time, however, Captain Shaler kept his leaky ship well clear of the refortified ports of San Diego and Monterey.

Although American traders ultimately broke down the restrictions imposed by the Spanish crown, they risked suffering severe consequences. In 1813, Captain George Washington Eayrs of the ship *Mercury* ran into a Spanish longboat. He and his men were captured and interned at Santa Barbara for two long years. Yet, illegal coastal trafficking continued. Ship chandlers traded New England wares for Chinese luxuries. Sea-otter furs, steer hides, tallow, and cow horns (used to make buttons) were also bartered. Though this prohibited contraband was dangerous, the rewards were great. In a single season, 18,000 prime otter pelts were delivered to the China market from California, thereby creating many a New England fortune.

Today Fort Ross is a designated National Historic Landmark. Located in Sonoma County, it served as a Russian settlement between 1812 and 1839, centering around the sea otter fur trade. Its buildings were constructed with California redwood. Photo courtesy of Arthur Verge.

Meanwhile, hardy Yankee whalers, battered by the cold gales of the North Pacific, were grateful to find protected California ports in which they could repair both their ships and spirits. Richardson's Bay, across from today's San Francisco, was an early rendezvous for whalers. There they took on longed-for fresh meat, fruit, grains, and other provisions for the lengthy homeward voyage around the Horn. Whaling ships from Nantucket and New Bedford carried manufactured goods to exchange for coins or local products. Out of their sea chests came needles, stockings, thread, and bolts of cloth. At Monterey, they left behind a sidewalk made out of whalebone in appreciation for the shelter the town had given them. They carried home to chilly New England glowing accounts of pastoral California, which helped popularize the province in the American mind.

The Russians also continued to arrive in California, not with sword in hand but, like their American competitors, but as traders. In the 1740s, Vitus Bering had prepared the groundwork for the Russian-American Fur Company, headquartered in Alaska. Since then the company had accumulated valuable caches of furs at their trading station in Sitka. But the harsh Alaskan climate and the barrenness of the country thwarted nearly all attempts at agriculture in the vicinity. In addition, the abundance of sea otters in California waters proved enticing enough for the Russians to risk confrontation with Spanish local officials.

In 1805, Nikolai Petrovich Rezanov, directly representing the czar, was sent to inspect the Russian colonies in the North Pacific. At Sitka he found emaciated settlers reduced to eating scrawny crows. As Russian supply ships had faltered in provisioning the colony, Rezanov decided to set sail southward to California in search of provisions. His party was courteously received at San Francisco. Then, a novel element was injected into the negotiations between the Russians and the Spaniards: the Russian envoy fell in love with Concepción Argüello, the engaging fifteen-year-old daughter of the comandante of the port. Rezanov, now suddenly a prospective family member, had little trouble persuading Comandante Argüello to furnish supplies for the starving Sitka colony.

With his ship, the *Juno*, loaded up with wheat, barley, peas, beans, tallow, and dried meat, Rezanov sailed away on May 8, 1806, ostensibly to gain Russian permission to marry, having promised to return to San Francisco to claim his bride. Only in 1850, after years of waiting, did Señorita Argüello, who had meanwhile become a nun, finally learn of Rezanov's death in Siberia.

By 1809, another officer of the Russian-American Fur Company, Ivan Kuskov, arrived in California from Alaska. He had been ordered to select a site for a southern outpost. In 1812 Kuskov returned, this time with equipment to set up a trading station along with a group of Aleut Indians whom he had contracted to fish and hunt for the community. Meanwhile Kuskov made no pretense of consulting California officials before constructing his post; he simply chose a strategic shoreline site, eighteen miles north of Bodega Bay, and proceeded to build a sturdy rectangular compound surrounded by a palisade, its corners pierced to emplace artillery. Inside the stockade, a wooden house of six rooms was constructed for the officers. It was furnished with carpets and a piano and boasted glass windows. Granaries, workshops, and huts for the Aleuts were located outside the stockade. The Russians also erected a wharf, a tannery, and a bath house on the site. They named this place "Ross," a derivation of the word Russia. Because of its fortifications, the place became known as Fort Ross.

After 1812, while Kuskov was building his fort, the Spanish officer Gabriel Moraga arrived there to investigate reports of Russian activities. Moraga noted that the Russians at Ross seriously needed food. In January of 1813 he returned with three horses, twenty head of cattle, several *fanegas* (a Spanish unit of measure) of wheat, and permission from Governor Arrillaga to trade with those at Fort Ross.

Although New Spain's viceroy at Mexico City later ordered Kuskov to remove his settlement, Arrillaga's weak garrisons were in no position to enforce the viceroy's order. The Russians, therefore, continued to tan hides, fire bricks and tiles, construct barrels and kegs, and make rope from hemp at their sturdy outpost. They also built and launched four small wooden vessels and even managed to raise delicate plants in a glass hothouse. Indeed, the flowers they planted around the fort gave the place a false look of permanence.

The population of foggy and isolated Fort Ross never exceeded 400 persons, including the Aleut hunters and their wives. Before long, the Russians had cleared most of the sea otters out of the coastal waters between Trinidad and San Francisco Bays. From 1812 to 1840 they also maintained a tiny outpost on the windy Farallones Islands, not far outside San Francisco Bay.

The Russians remained active explorers. During the years between 1808 and 1821, with Spain's colonies in rebellion, Otto von Kotzebue, a Russian sailor-scientist, made two visits to Alta California. On his excellent maps the interior area between the Coast Ranges and the Sierra Nevada was termed *tierra incognita* (or unknown land).

Except for Anza, only Father Garcés had ventured into the southern Sierra near Lake Tulare in the Central Valley. This exposed interior was inhabited by Indians far less tolerant of Europeans than the missionized natives. By 1806, Lieutenant Gabriel Moraga, however, launched forty-six inland campaigns against hostile natives. On his *entradas* (or excursions) into the interior he named the Kings River as well as the Merced and Mariposa Rivers. He called another stream *El Río de las Plumas* (the River of the Feathers) because of wildfowl feathers floating on its surface. The county through which the Feather flows has, however, retained the Spanish name *Plumas*.

After the departure of Governor Solá, local officials could no longer control either the wild interior or the settled portions of California. Furthermore, the remote province would soon be governed by Spain's rebellious colony, Mexico.

SELECTED READINGS

The best appraisal of Spain's influence along the Pacific Coast is Iris Engstrand "The Eighteenth Century Enlightenment Comes to Spanish California," *Southern California Quarterly* 80 (Spring, 1998), 3–30. Regarding Spanish exploration see Donald Cutter and Iris Engstrand, *Quest for Empire: Spanish Settlement in the Southwest* (1996); also Theodore Treutlein, *San Francisco Bay, Discovery and Colonization, 1769–1776* (1968); Francisco Antonio Maurelle, *Journal of a Voyage...* (1781); *Journal of José Longinos Mar-*

tínez . . . 1791–92, Lesley Byrd Simpson, trans. and ed. (1961); and Henry R. Wagner, *The Last Spanish Exploration of the Northwest Coast* (1931).

English explorations are described in George Vancouver, *A Voyage of Discovery to the North Pacific Ocean and Round the World* (3 vols., 1798); Marguerite Eyer Wilbur, ed., *Vancouver in California, 1792–1794* (1953); George Godwin, *Vancouver: A Life, 1757–1798* (1930) and G. H. Anderson, *Vancouver and His Great Voyage* (1923).

Regarding the La Pérouse expedition, see Gilbert Chinard, ed., *Le Voyage de Lapérouse sur les Côtes de L'Alaska et de la Californie* (1937). Malaspina's venture is described in John Kendrick, *Alejandro Malaspina, Portrait of a Visionary* (2004); see also Donald Cutter, *Malaspina in California* (1960) and his *Malaspina and Galiano* (1991).

The *Lelia Byrd* episode is described in Lindley Bynum, ed., *Journal of a Voyage Between China and the Northwestern coast of America made in 1804 by William Shaler* (1935); Roy F. Nichols, *Advance Agents of American Destiny* (1956); Andrew Rolle, "The Eagle Is Seized," *Westways* 46 (December 1954), 16–17.

Regarding the sea otter commerce, see Adele Ogden, *The California Sea Otter Trade, 1784–1848* (repr. 1975) and Ogden's "New England Traders in Spanish and Mexican California," in *Greater America: Essays in Honor of Herbert Eugene Bolton* (1945), 395–415, as well as James Gibson, *Otter Skins, Boston Ships, and China Goods* (1992). Consult also William Henry Ellison, ed., *Life and Adventures of George Nidever* (1937) and Magdalen Coughlin, "Boston Smugglers on the Coast (1797–1821)," *California Historical Society Quarterly* 46 (June 1967), 99–120.

Russian contact with California is in Raymond H. Fisher, *Bering's Voyages* (1977); T. C. Russell, ed., *The Rezanov Voyage to Nueva California in 1806* (1926), and Russell's editing of *Langsdorff's Narrative of the Rezanov Voyage...* (1927); Hector Chevigny, *Lost Empire: The Life and Adventures of Nicolai Petrovich Rezanov* (1937); Otto von Kotzebue, *A Voyage of Discovery in the South Sea* (3 vols. 1821); S. B. Okun, *The Russian-American Company* (1951).

Regarding Moraga and Spanish interior exploration see Donald Cutter, ed., *Diary of Ensign Gabriel Moraga's Expedition of Discovery in the Sacramento Valley* (1957); S. F. Cook, *Expedition to the Interior of California's Central Valley, 1820–1840* (revised, 1962).

CHAPTER EIGHT

ARCADIA

The ancient Greeks wrote of a distant province called Arcadia, a supposedly idyllic land isolated from the rest of the world. Its inhabitants led proverbially happy and natural lives. Was California indeed such a favored place? In the Latino cultures, landowners, whether the *gauchos* of Argentina or California's *rancheros*, were held in high esteem. As local leaders, they helped to loosen Spain's grip on its colonies. A paternalistic royal government had fostered dependence of its colonials by sending them scarce supplies. But the Spanish empire's lines of communication were stretched too thin. Months went by when few ships arrived from the mother country. The Spanish colonists had no choice but to become increasingly self-reliant.

Fortunately the Californios enjoyed abundant pastureland and fresh water in addition to a ready supply of Indian labor. Ranching conditions in the province bordered on perfect. The climate was mild enough to permit animals to live outdoors throughout the year with little shelter. Neighbors were trusted amid a pastoral way of life inherited from the Spanish homeland.

A band of 200 cattle herded north to California by Portolá's expedition, and the few that survived the overland trek with Anza's party, formed the province's original herds. These animals and their progeny would yield hides and tallow in abundance for export. Rancheros did not even bother to fence in their stock. Cattle roamed freely on the large land grants awarded during the Spanish and Mexican eras. Today's U.S. land titles are grounded upon former rancho locations still known by such names as *El Toro* (the bull), *Los Laureles* (the laurels), and *La Sagrada Familia* (the Holy Family).

In 1784, Governor Fages was empowered to make individual grants not to exceed three square leagues. He and his successors ceded less than thirty of such tracts during the Spanish period. But, after the establishment of the Mexican Republic in 1821, the number of land grants increased markedly. By 1830, there were some fifty private ranchos in California. Mexicans of good character, or any foreigner willing to become a naturalized Mexican citizen and to accept the Catholic faith, might petition for as much as eleven square leagues of land, or nearly 50,000 acres. One square league comprised a little more than 4,438 acres. In modern California this would constitute a large ranch. At the time, however, a rancho of four or five leagues was considered small.

The blossoming of the rancho era occurred during the thirteen years between the secularization of the California missions by the Mexican government in 1833 and occupation of the province by the Americans. As late as 1848, the entire white population of California was estimated at only 14,000, divided nearly equally between Californios and foreigners.

Rancho boundaries were loosely defined by such landmarks as a hilltop, a clump of cacti, a streambed, or the whitened skull of a steer. Beginning at a point marked by a pile of stones, called a *mojonera*, a horseman measured out a tract with a fifty-foot-long *reata* (or lariat) trailing behind him. The actual quantity of land comprising most estates was rather vague. The phrase *"poco mas ó menos"* (a little more or less) frequently appears on early land title documents. This vagueness would cause protracted litigation in the American era.

Family fortunes were founded on the great ranchos. For example, Francisco Pacheco owned the Ranchos San Felipe, San Luís Gonzaga, and other properties totaling 125,740 acres. The two ranchos alone supported 14,000 head of cattle, 500 horses, and 15,000 sheep. David Spence, a Scot who married into the Estrada family, counted 25,000 acres in the Buena Esperanza rancho, with 4,000 head of cattle. Henry Delano Fitch of Massachusetts held title to the Rancho Sotoyome of eleven leagues, with 14,000 cattle, 1,000 stallions and mares, and 10,000 sheep. Another American, Abel Stearns, owned thousands of acres on which grazed 30,000 cattle, 2,000 horses and mules, and 10,000 sheep. The Swiss settler Johann Augustus Sutter operated a virtual *hacienda* on eleven leagues of land extending sixty miles in length. The sites now occupied by the cities of Oakland, Alameda, and Berkeley form only a part of what was once the Rancho San Antonio. This was the property of Don Luís Peralta; his lands furnished pasture for 8,000 head of cattle and 2,000 horses. A herd of horses was, incidentally, called a *ramada*. Today's Culver City, near Los Angeles, was the scene of a huge *rincon de los bueyes*, or cattle corral.

During the Mexican era, more than one thousand such ranchos were stocked with an average of 1,500 head of cattle. Cattle were the mainstay of the economy. Leather hides provided harnesses, saddles, shoes, and even door hinges; horns were fastened atop adobe walls to thwart intruders or carved up into shoe buttons. Tallow went into molding candles, a

Young Native American rancho worker. Indian ranch hands were known for their horse riding and roping skills. Courtesy of University of California, Davis, General Library, Department of Special Collections, Eastman's Originals Collection.

vital undertaking in an age before kerosene lamps or electric lights. Hides and tallow became a mainstay of the California economy. Little cash was exchanged. The Californios increasingly obtained much of their clothing and other necessities by bartering hides and tallow with Yankee ship captains and traders. Eventually, a "California bank note," became a dried steer hide valued at approximately $1.

Indian herders and rancho hands, despite a previous lack of experience with stock animals, seemed to take naturally to handling horses and cattle, which they did with great skill. *Vaqueros* (or cowboys) were needed in large numbers. Some ranchos employed more than one hundred Indian workers under the direction of a *mayordomo*, who himself might be Indian. In the absence of fences, stock became so wild that it was unsafe for one to venture among herds on foot or unarmed; in addition, anyone intending to ride the range had to be prepared to defend himself against ferocious grizzlies, then living near the mountains. Indispensable to the rancho lifestyle were horses. A good horse could be bought for $3—less than the cost of a saddle and bridle.

During severe drought years, rancho hands had to "cut out" less desirable stock. Like the cattle, horses sometimes ran wild. When they multiplied to the point that dry local pastures could not support them, some animals were driven over precipices into the sea. The *rodéo* (roundup), the principal means of separating and branding stock, was conducted under a *juez de campo* (field judge) who settled disputes over the ownership of individual animals. Rancheros also held bloody *matanzas* (cattle slaughterings) during which the vaqueros rode through the herds at full speed, quickly ending the animals' lives with a lightning cut of a knife across the neck. Next, skinners moved in to strip the hides off the carcasses and cut the meat into strips for drying. The tallow was melted and poured into bags made of hides, to be floated out to the vessels anchored offshore. Today's Dana Point was their favored trading location.

The American artist Titian Ramsay Peale, who traveled to California in 1841, noted that its hills and valleys were dotted with dry cattle remains. While riding, he encountered so many bleached and brittle bones that Peale was struck by the constant crunching under the hoofs of his horse.

Little planting of crops occurred on the ranchos. But at the missions, where orange trees and grapevines were first raised, agriculture was well organized. At Mission San José, for example, the padres harvested a tract of wheat a mile square. Nonetheless, their farming implements were crude. The Indian workers scratched the ground with a wooden plow, perhaps fashioned from the crooked limb of a tree. Grain was cut with hand sickles and bound in sheaves.

For threshing, a circular piece of ground was usually fenced in. Then its surface was watered and pounded until, after drying, the soil became hard. After wheat was thrown into the enclosure, mules were driven around and around until the grain was trampled out. Next came winnowing by tossing wheat in baskets against the wind. At first, grinding was performed by hand with stone mortars and pestles. But eventually the padres constructed water-driven grist mills. The most common method of grinding became use of the *arrastra*, two circular millstones, one on top of the other. The lower stone remained stationary while the upper stone rotated a cross beam pulled along by a mule. The grain between the stones was crushed, a process used in Spain for centuries.

The Californios never held sheep in the same esteem as they did cattle. Nevertheless, each mission and most ranchos raised small flocks of sheep for mutton and wool. Though coarse and wiry, the wool was strong. The women wove it into cloth and blankets. Hogs were raised mainly for their lard, which was mixed with ashes in the process of soap-making.

Life on the ranchos was carried on within a simple, patriarchal system. The rancho family was a self-sustained unit, of which the ranchero was the unquestioned master. He was to be obeyed by family members and Indian retainers alike. Arising long before dawn, the ranchero might partake of a traditional breakfast of bread and chocolate before mounting his horse to make the daily round of his herds. A strong bond linked parents and children. Yet, the family observed strict internal discipline. A father could administer corporal punishment to sons as old as sixty, and no son dared to smoke in his father's presence. Dances were begun by elders, the young people standing by to wait their turn.

This frontier existence featured a blend of abundance and barrenness. Supplies of clothing and other manufactured articles were always insufficient. But the ranchero and his family had inherited austerity from their Spanish ancestors. When women could not obtain shoes, silk stockings, and other articles of clothing, including *rebozos* (shawls) or *mantillas* (lacy scarves), they simply learned to do without.

The hunting of grizzly bears, elk, and other game was popular. There were also *meriendas* (picnics) to which rancheros rode their best horses, while the women and children might arrive in two-wheeled *carretas* (wagons) pulled by oxen. The meriendas featured *carne asada* (roasted beef), or chicken and turkey, barbecued on spits over a bed of glistening coals. *Enchiladas* and *tamales* were concocted by Indian women who pounded corn in *metates* (stone mortars) to make tortillas in which they wrapped their meat.

It was a rare evening during which there were no guests to join a ranching family in dancing the *jarabe* or *fandango*. The hospitality of the ranchero was a point of pride and was dispensed generously. A host might leave coins in a dish on a table in order to spare an indigent visitor the embarrassment of asking for money before his departure. A traveler who arrived with an exhausted horse often found a fresh one waiting for him in the morning, already saddled up for his use.

Schooling in the province was limited. Among the teachers were discharged soldiers whose only qualification was some knowledge of reading, writing, and "figuring." During the Mexican period the best-known teacher was William E. P. Hartnell, originally an English trader who possessed knowledge of half a dozen languages. He settled near Salinas, where he established a unique schoolhouse. Hartnell would become an important figure in California's shift from Mexican to American rule.

Theft, murder, and other crimes were rare in Mexican California. Visiting sea captains would sometimes sell goods to rancheros on credit.

Months later they might return to receive their pay in hides and tallow. A spirit of trust existed among these early traders. Dishonesty and even banditry, however, would later become more common after the American era began in 1846. The noted bandit Joaquín Murieta ascribed his criminal career to the brutal treatment he had received from American miners.

The padres did much to stabilize provincial life. Baptisms, confirmations, marriages, and other important ceremonies were, of course, performed at the missions. The missions also served as a hospice for wayfarers, who could always count on a night's lodging. Mission accommodations were of the barest sort—usually consisting of a bed of rawhide, scratchy flaxen sheets, and simple meals. But on a stormy night, as the wind whipped across the tile roof, the weary traveler was thankful indeed for the fragrant pine logs burning in the fireplace grate.

Modern California retains many cultural reminders of its pastoral era. Rivers, mountains, and towns are still known by the names given them by the founding Spaniards. In addition to rancho and rodéo, other words grew out of the Spanish heritage. These include *adobe* (sun-dried brick); *arroyo* (creek, or the dry bed thereof); *cañada* (deep valley); *cañón* (narrow passage between high banks); *chaparral* (thicket of brambly bushes); *corral* (enclosure for livestock); *embarcadero* (landing place); *fiesta* (celebration); *placer* (deposit of gold in the loose earth); *plaza* (open square); *pueblo* (chartered town); *sierra* (literally saw, but applied to saw-tooth mountains); *tule* (water reed); and *vaquero* (cowboy).

The prefixes *San* and *Santa*, the masculine and feminine forms of the word *saint*, were used to name missions, which in turn bestowed their names on their home counties, including San Diego, San Luis Obispo, and Santa Clara. Other counties, such as Merced and Sacramento, took the names of their principal streams. Among these is Kings County (from *El Río de los Santos Reyes*, or river of the Holy Kings). The Merced River was first called *El Río de Nuestra Señora de la Merced* (the River of Our Lady of Mercy); it was so named by Gabriel Moraga's exploring party of 1806, which reached its banks after an exhausting march through inhospitable country. Moraga also named Mariposa Creek, after the butterflies he saw on its banks, and the Sacramento River, after the Holy Sacrament.

Fresno (ash) County was named after the abundance of ash trees in the region, and *Madera* (timber) County for the thick forests that covered its valleys. The bay of Monterey was named to honor Viceroy Gaspar de Zúñiga y Acevedo, Count of Monterey. Mendocino was named after Antonio de Mendoza, the first viceroy of New Spain. Some towns and cities bear the names of prominent Californios such as the Martinez's. Vacaville commemorates the Vaca family. Alviso bears the name of one of Anza's colonists; Benicia that of the wife of General Mariano Vallejo, while the town of Vallejo honors that popular general himself.

An Alvarado Street, named after a Mexican governor, can be found in both Monterey and Los Angeles. One of the main arteries in today's L.A., Figueroa Street, honors yet another governor. Dozens of Los Angeles street names also commemorate the Hispanic past. Among these are Pico, San Pedro, Aliso, and Sepulveda. In San Francisco, there is a Junípero Serra Boulevard, as well as streets named Noriega, Pacheco, Ortega, Rivera, Taraval, Ulloa, Guerrero, Valencia, and Palou. Oakland also has two avenues with Spanish names, *Alcatraz* (pelican) and *San Pablo* (Saint Paul).

Place names and architecture, however, are not the only reminders of Spain's past rule. The Anglo cowboy inherited his know-how, horse, equipment (including reata, spurs, chaps, and lasso), and lingo largely from the Spanish. And to this day, California's legal system retains Spanish provisions concerning mining, water rights, trespass regulations, tribunals of conciliation, and the property rights of women.

Pageants and plays that commemorate the Spanish past include the Mission Play of San Gabriel, the Portolá Festival of San Francisco, the "De Anza Days" celebration at Riverside, and a yearly "Spanish" fiesta at Santa Barbara. Finally, there has been persistent exploitation (often inaccurate) of California's Hispanic past by genealogists, artists, architects, ardent promoters of tourism, and even historical societies.

SELECTED READINGS

For a realistic examination of daily life in early California, see Albert Hurtado, *Sex, Gender and Culture in Old California* (1999). Sources regarding Hispanic colonial folkways include William Heath Davis, *Seventy-Five Years in California* (1929); Andrew Rolle, *An American in California: The Biography of William Heath Davis* (1956); Richard Henry Dana, *Two Years Before the Mast* (1840); Richard J. Cleveland, *Narrative of Voyages and Commercial Enterprises* (2 vols. 1842); Samuel Shapiro, *Richard Henry Dana, Jr., 1815–1882* (1961). Later romanticized accounts include Nellie Van de Grift Sánchez, *Spanish Arcadia* (1929); Gertrude Atherton, *Before the Gringo Came* (1894); and Charles F. Lummis, *The Spanish Pioneers* (1893).

Other appraisals include Hubert Howe Bancroft's *California Pastoral* (1888); Alberta J. Denis, *Spanish Alta California* (1927); Susanna Bryant Dakin, *A Scotch Paisano: Hugo Reid's Life in California* (1939) and Dakin, *The Lives of William Hartnell* (1949); George D. Lyman, *The Scalpel Under Three Flags in California* (1925); *The Blond Ranchero: Memories of Juan Francisco Dana, as told to Rocky and Marie Harrington* (1960). See also Antonio Casteneda, "Engendering the History of Alta California, 1769–1848: Gender, Sexuality, and the Family" in Ramón Gutiérrez and Richard Orsi, *Contested Eden* (1997).

For more on place names, see Raymund F. Wood, "Anglo Influence on Spanish Place Names in California," *Southern California Quarterly* 58 (Winter 1981), 392–413. William Mason, *The Census of 1790: A Demographic History of Colonial California* (1998) is a valuable population study. Legal entanglements are described in Paul Gray's *Forster vs. Pico: The Struggle for the Rancho Margarita* (1998).

CHAPTER NINE

MEXICAN CALIFORNIA

After three centuries of neglect by the homeland, the Spanish colonies in the New World grew increasingly restive. Discontent kindled the flame of revolution, which spread throughout Spain's New World provinces between 1808 and the mid-1820s. California remained loyal to Spain partly because so little news reached the province regarding the anti-Spanish revolutionary fervor throughout the rest of Latin America. An aristocrat, Governor Solá, looked upon revolutionary activities south of his capital at Monterey as the work of misguided fanatics.

After 1808, severe discontent arose in California when vessels from San Blas failed to arrive in sufficient number to supply the local populace. Revolutionary attacks against Spanish ships had aggravated the situation, so that fewer and fewer relief vessels made it into California ports. Along with American trading ships that helped fill the supply gap, privateers began to appear in the Pacific, some outfitted in the United States. These vagabond pirates roamed the high seas, menacing shipping lanes as well as the shorelines of Spain's colonies. News of the blockade of the South American Pacific colonial ports of Valparaíso, Callao, and Guayaquil by revolutionists and privateers so worried Governor Solá that he ordered a stricter shore watch for suspicious vessels. Although the Californios registered complaints against the viceroy in Mexico City for his failure to send them sufficient supplies and back pay to the soldiers, they originally had no thought of resisting his authority or that of Governor Solá. They were more concerned with pirates.

In November of 1818, a sentinel at Point Pinos near Monterey sighted two mysterious ships. The larger of the two vessels, the *Argentina*, was commanded by a Frenchman, Hippolyte de Bouchard, who had served in the patriot navy of the new "Republic of Buenos Aires." He was a big, brutal man of fiery temper, a captain who exercised an iron rule over his men. The other vessel was the *Santa Rosa* under the command of an English soldier of fortune named Peter Corney. The Englishman had fallen in with Bouchard in Hawaii, where the latter was trading gold chalices and silver crucifixes looted from churches in Peru and Ecuador. Their crews comprised a motley band of cutthroats and thieves but also ardent revolutionists. Among them were Malays, Portuguese, Spaniards, Englishmen, and Australians—all of whom aimed to profit from the unraveling of the Spanish empire.

The *Santa Rosa* dropped anchor in front of the presidio of Monterey and opened fire. Captain Corney and his crew, expecting little resistance from the dilapidated fort, were surprised at a brisk return of cannon balls from a battery hastily established on the beach by the presidio's forty soldiers. At this point, Bouchard moved in with the *Argentina* and sent ashore, under a flag of truce, a demand for the immediate surrender of Monterey.

Bouchard received a defiant reply from Governor Solá, although the Californians had little means of resisting. The pirate landed several hundred men and a number of field pieces near Point Pinos. Greatly outnumbered, Solá retreated, taking a supply of munitions and the provincial archives with him to the Rancho del Rey, near the present site of Salinas. Back at Monterey, its townspeople fled. Some took refuge at Missions San Antonio and San Juan Bautista. In the meantime, the invaders sacked and burned both the presidio and town of Monterey. Few buildings escaped undamaged. The vandals even destroyed the mission orchards and gardens.

Concerning the conduct of his crew during this pillage, Corney later wrote of them: "The Sandwich Islanders, who were quite naked when they landed, were soon dressed in the Spanish fashion; and all the sailors were employed in searching the houses for money and breaking and ruining everything." The attackers spent something over a week in burying their dead, caring for their wounded, and repairing the *Santa Rosa*. They also made efforts to win over those colonists who had the courage to remain in the pueblo. But, ostensibly promoting the cause of liberty, revolution failed to impress Californians whose homes had just been despoiled.

After the *Argentina* and *Santa Rosa* set sail, the privateers moved down the coast, stopping to burn and pillage Rancho del Refugio in revenge for three pirates who had been lassoed and dragged off by a party of vaqueros. San Juan Capistrano was another of the places sacked and robbed of its store of wines and spirits, much of which immediately went down the throats of the pillagers. After taking two Indian girls aboard, the pirates sailed south from that mission, and California was finally relieved of their presence.

Once Bouchard left the province, life resumed its calmness. Not long thereafter, however, events of great importance to Spain's colonies took place. In February of 1821, Agustín Iturbide, a colonel in the Spanish army in Mexico City, raised a revolutionary flag. He ordered that thereafter New Spain should be called Mexico, an independent nation. Iturbide, who named himself emperor, began to use California as a dumping ground for potential rivals. By 1826, he had exiled more than 10,000 persons.

When news reached California of the seizure of political control in Mexico, Governor Solá convened a *junta* (or political caucus), consisting of officers from the presidios and padres from the missions. These took an oath of allegiance to Iturbide's insurgent government. The friars, however, correctly sensed that withhout Spain's jurisdiction, their mission system was in peril. The California junta chose Solá as its delegate to the new Mexican *Cortés* (or congress). But before the governor could depart for Mexico City, Iturbide sent an official to preside over the transfer of authority from Spain to Mexico. Aware of lingering royalist sympathies, this agent of the new regime sailed into Monterey on a ship boldly flying a green, white, and red flag from its masthead. The eagle in the flag's center, the symbol of a new Mexico, indicated that Spain's sovereignty over California had clearly ended.

Succeeding Solá came a new governor, Luís Antonio Argüello, who was native born and popularly elected. Later, Mexico would impose its own unwanted governors on the province. Argüello, a Californian who had served as comandante of the port at San Francisco, announced that all decrees of the Mexican government would be followed. He also agreed that such designated titles as *nacional* would replace imperial in official documents. Even public and private letters would thereafter conclude with the words: "God and Liberty." The old aristocratic title "Don" was to be changed to *Ciudadano* (citizen). All such Spanish dignities were to give way to an imposed Mexican republicanism.

California, far from the vortex of the revolutionary struggle, luckily became part of an independent Mexico without blood-letting. Yet, the province failed to escape the eruption of personal rivalries. Indeed, scarcely a governor during the entire Mexican period would serve his term in office without facing a disturbing local outbreak against him.

In his election, Governor Argüello, who came from northern California, had been favored by northerners and won out over a prominent southerner, José de la Guerra. Thus began a rift between northern and southern California that has continued—the issues changing with the years—to this day. Argüello established his own *diputación*, or junta. Because of a severe money crunch, he ordered the unprecedented taxation of local crops as well as branded cattle. The padres protested that crops raised by the missions were untaxable, but such claims only earned their establishments increased governmental surveillance. While no direct steps toward mission secularization occurred under Argüello, missionary power was nearing its end. So was the province's willingness to take orders from Mexico City.

During Argüello's governorship, more foreign traders and settlers arrived. Argüello had been friendly with the Russians since the days when Rezanov had courted his daughter. And the Russians had long desired to enter into a partnership for sea-otter hunting and trading with the Californians. Now Governor Argüello signed a contract with Fort Ross that furnished him with his own contingent of Aleut hunters, who in return were to be fed and supplied by the Californians.

Meanwhile, the changing political situation lessened the willingness of the missionaries to cooperate with the governor. In defiance of regulations, the padres signed an agreement with McCulloch and Hartnell, a subsidiary of the English firm of John Begg and Company, today purveyors of Scotch whisky. The firm's representatives in California were Hugh McCulloch and the aforementioned William E. P. Hartnell, who later became a local schoolmaster. Both men were Scots who had arrived from Lima in 1822. They became known as "Macala y Arnel" and were allowed to bring one ship cargo a year to the province. They were also authorized to take out all the hides the missions had for sale at the price of $1 apiece, as well as suet, lard, tallow, wheat, wine, furs, and pickled beef. This launched California into its lucrative "hide-and-tallow" era.

Though illegal, "warm-water Yankee" traders reaped rewards from marketing their sorely needed goods. Some of them settled permanently, including Nathan Spear, William Heath Davis, Jr., John R. Cooper, and Alfred Robinson. Shipmasters eventually were allowed to unload their vessels at designated collecting points, rather than smuggling them in at secret landfalls. Both traders and the Californios profited from the arrival of foreign ships.

One Boston firm, Bryant, Sturgis & Company, maintained a steady chain of ships plying the sea lanes between California, Hawaii, and China. The company's fleet imported hundreds of thousands of California hides for New England's shoe industry. Other Boston shippers included Marshall & Wildes as well as William Appleton & Company. The holds of their ships swelled with hundreds of commodities, from silk stockings to needles and tobacco. The crews of these floating commissaries processed great quantities of hides purchased from interior ranchos. First the skins were soaked in seawater. Then they were stretched on the ground and pegged fast with wooden stakes. Once dried, the hides were sprinkled with salt and scraped. Floated out to ships beyond the breaking surf, the hides were stored alongside cowhide bags filled with tallow.

Some Yankee traders married "daughters of the country" and founded families in California. One of them, John R. Cooper, arrived in 1823 as captain of the American ship *Rover* and settled at Monterey. Along with Cooper came Daniel Hill and Thomas Robbins of Massachusetts, both of whom decided to make their home at Santa Barbara. At Yerba Buena, William A. Richardson, who defected from the ship *Orion*, married the daughter of its comandante. After he was baptized in the Catholic Church, Richardson started a trading post. Thus, a generation of these early American settlers established close relations with the Californios long before the first overland party pushed west across the Great Plains.

California was an appealing place to settle before its Indians learned how to use firearms. In February of 1824, a series of revolts started among the neophytes of Missions Purísima Concepción, Santa Inés, and Santa Barbara. Feeling ill treated because of forced labor, they attacked Mission Santa Inés, setting fire to its buildings. At La Purísima, 400 armed assailants similarly fought a contingent of outnumbered soldiers. Both Indians and whites died in the violent uprising. The natives maintained possession of that mission for nearly a month. By erecting crude dirt fortifications, cutting loopholes in the church walls, and mounting two rusty cannons, they warded off attackers. However, due to their inexperience in handling guns and powder, the occupiers were eventually defeated by Lieutenant José Mariano Estrada and a force of 100 men.

The discontented Indians at Santa Barbara also entrenched themselves in its mission buildings. After Comandante de la Guerra attacked them, they fled into the hills, taking all the church property they could carry. In mid-1825, Governor Argüello reported to the Mexican government regarding the miserable state of the mission Indians. He called attention to the injustice of keeping these people in virtual slavery.

Under Argüello the change to Mexican rule had been quietly accepted by most Californians, and progress was made toward the foundation of a representative government. The sleepy province had, somehow, managed to substitute the paternalistic regime of Spain for the unsettled sovereignty of Mexico. As a result, subsequent governmental instability would fuel further factionalism.

José María Echeandía, Governor Argüello's successor, was a tall, thin, juiceless man apparently possessing little force of character. He was, however, much concerned about the effect of the California climate upon his less-than-robust health. At first Echeandía so feared the foggy weather in chilly Monterey that he came no farther into California than San Diego. Conveniently, Echeandía claimed that Alta California's southernmost town was more centrally located for transacting the business of the two provinces. As nothing in his instructions required this hypochondriac to reside at Monterey, he was acting within his rights in conducting government from the pueblo of his choice. Yet, his move to San Diego made the new governor unpopular from the start.

In 1826, a contest flared up between Echeandía and a young Massachusetts sea captain named Henry Delano Fitch for the hand of Señorita Josefa Carrillo of San Diego. This event suggests that a romantic motive as well as health concerns may have had something to do with the new governor's decision to stay in the south. In fact, lovesick over the sixteen-year-old beauty, Echeandía halted her plans to marry Fitch. At this point Captain Fitch, in command of the U.S. barque *Maria Ester*, sailed his intended to Chile, where the couple wed. Yet their ordeal was far from over. Upon their return to Monterey, the governor charged the captain with abduction and other heinous crimes. Henry and Josefa were jailed, separately, for more than six months. Upon their release, the couple re-

Captain Henry Delano Fitch (1767–1849), reknowned sea captain, merchant and landowner, spent most of his years in San Diego where he successfully ran the only general store and became San Diego's first attorney. He also is credited with creating the first survey of the pueblo lands in 1845. Fitch's personal life was also quite rich and resulted in romanticized retellings of his marriage to the striking Josefa Carrillo.

turned to San Diego, where they started their family of ten children. These were actually ancestors of a future president of the United States, Franklin Delano Roosevelt. In 1840, another Mexican governor granted Fitch the 48,000-acre Rancho Sotoyome near Healdsburg. Ten years later Fitch, who had become a prominent ranchero and merchant, died at the age of forty-eight. Josefa lived on until 1893, dying at the age of eighty-two.

A much more pressing question faced Governor Echeandía. It concerned providing supplies for California's unpaid soldiers and their families. He had to contend with two northern political rivals. Expressing the discontent of the province's frustrated soldiers and suspicious padres, Joaquín Solís, a former convict, and José María Herrera, who had been sent to the province from Mexico as financial agent of the government, issued a *pronunciamiento* accusing the governor of tyrannical behavior toward the populace. In 1828, Solís and Herrera led a local revolt against the governor that began at Monterey and extended as far south as Santa Barbara. Ultimately both dissidents were arrested and shipped off to San Blas. So ended the first of a series of minor uprisings against Mexican authority in the province. These were largely wars of words, not guns.

The practice of deporting criminals to the province also had much to do with the antagonistic feeling between Californians and Mexicans. At approximately the same time as the collapse of the Solís rebellion, Mexican officials sent eighty convicts north to California. They were put ashore at Santa Cruz Island with a few cattle and some fishhooks to sustain themselves. In time, these men made it back to the mainland on rafts of their own construction. In July 1830, another ship from Mexico arrived with fifty more criminals, who were distributed throughout the province. Echeandía was blamed for their arrival. Although Californians asked Mexico not to send any more such reprobates, other convicts entered the province as enlisted soldiers.

In the summer of 1829, Governor Echeandía faced yet another Indian revolt, this one under Chief Estanislao, a former alcalde of San José. Estanislao and a band of angry natives fortified themselves in some dense woods. From there they issued defiant challenges. Forty of the governor's soldiers, armed with muskets and a swivel gun, soon engaged these rebels. The Indians killed two of the soldiers and wounded eight others. The rest of the force abandoned the siege when their ammunition ran out. Echeandía feared that the uprising might become more widespread. So he sent in cavalry, infantry, and some artillery under Mariano Guadalupe Vallejo, commander of California's military. This force ousted the Indians from their entrenchment. Estanislao then fled, taking refuge with Father Narciso Durán, president of the missions, who concealed him until a pardon could be obtained from the governor.

Still, Echeandía's troubles had not ended. His governorship saw the arrival of a new wave of foreign expeditions. On November 6, 1826, the British ship *Blossom* sailed into San Francisco Bay under the command of Captain F. W. Beechey. He, like Vancouver, was struck by the contrast between the natural beauty of the country and Mexico's neglect of its colonists. He commented, for example, on the discontent among all classes and predicted that the Mexicans could not permanently hold onto the land. Many of the friars dreaded the worst, he noted, and would have quit the country. "Some of them were ingenious and clever men," wrote Beechey, "but they had been so long excluded from the civilized world that their ideas and their politics, like the maps pinned against the wall, bore the date of 1772, as near as I could read for fly specks." Beechey's visit is important for the detailed description of the country and its inhabitants. In addition, some remarkable watercolors of California were painted by artists in his crew.

In January of 1827, yet another foreign visitor arrived in California waters: Auguste Bernard Du Haut-Cilly, in command of the French ship *Le Héros*. A close observer and entertaining writer, this Frenchman was accompanied by Dr. Paolo Emilio Botta, an Italian archaeologist who described the peoples and wildlife they encountered. Like almost all such foreign visitors to California, Du Haut-Cilly was critical of both the government and the powerful missionaries.

At this point Mexican officials, still struggling to create a bonafide nation, planned to convert all of the missions into civic pueblos. In California, however, this process of secularization had to be approached cautiously. For one thing, the padres were the only ones who could induce mission neophytes to work. If these priests should ever leave, the province would suddenly be at a loss for sufficient laborers as well as exposed to even more raids by hostile natives from the interior. Because the "missionized" Indians were not generally a threat, on January 6, 1831, Governor Echeandía secularized a number of missions. These were now to become civilian pueblos. As the friars were reduced to the role of mere curates, their power dwindled. No longer would church and state rule California. From now on, local civic leaders would try to dominate political affairs. Furthermore, an interfering Mexico was about to lose control over its most distant province.

SELECTED READINGS

On the Bouchard raid, see Peter Corney, *Voyages in the Northern Pacific* (1896) and Lewis W. Bealer, "Bouchard in the Islands of the Pacific," *Pacific Historical Review* 4 (August 1935), 328–42, as well as Peter Uhrowczik, *The Burning of Monterey: The 1818 Attack on California by the Privateer Bouchard* (2001).

For the transition from Spanish to Mexican control, consult George P. Hammond, ed., *The Larkin Papers* (10 vols. 1951–66); George L. Harding, *Don Agustín V. Zamorano: Statesman, Soldier, Craftsman, and California's First Printer* (1934); Terry E. Stephenson, *Don Bernardo Yorba* (1941) and Robert G. Cleland, *The Place Called Sespe* (repr. 1957).

Regarding early Americans in California, see Robert Ryal Miller, *Captain Richardson: Mariner, Ranchero, and Founder of San Francisco* (1995); Reuben L. Underhill, *From Cowhides to Golden Fleece* (repr. 1946); Harlan Hague and David Langum, *Thomas Oliver Larkin: A Life of Patriotism and Profit* (1990); Adele Ogden, "Alfred Robinson, New England Merchant in Mexican California," *California Historical Society Quarterly* 23 (September 1944), 193–218, and Ogden's "Hides and Tallow: McCulloch, Hartnell and Company, 1822–1828," *California Historical Society Quarterly* 6 (September 1927), 254–64.

See also David J. Langum, *Law and Community on the Mexican California Frontier* (1987); Antonio Ríos Bustamente and Pedro Castillo, *An Illustrated History of Mexican Los Angeles, 1781–1985* (1986); Marion L. Lathrop, "The Indian Campaigns of General M. G. Vallejo," *Society of California Pioneers Quarterly* 9 (September 1932), 161–205; and Albert Hurtado, *Indian Survival on the California Frontier* (1988).

Regarding Beechey and Du Haut-Cilly see August Frugé and Neal Harlow, *A Voyage to California* (1999); Frederick W. Beechey, *Narrative of a Voyage to the Pacific and Bering's Strait* (2 vols. 1831); Auguste Bernard du Haut-Cilly, *Voyage autour du Monde . . .* (2 vols. 1934); Charles F. Carter, ed., "Duhaut-Chilly's [sic] Account of California in the Years 1827–28," *California Historical Society Quarterly* 8 (June-September 1929), 131–66, 306–36.

Family life is the subject of Gloria Miranda, "Hispano-Mexican Child-rearing Practices in Pre-American Santa Barbara," *Southern California Quarterly* 65 (Winter 1983), 307–20, and Miranda, "Racial and Cultural Dimensions in Gente de Razón Status in Spanish and Mexican California," *Southern California Quarterly* 70 (Fall 1988), 265–78.

CHAPTER TEN

INFILTRATION AND REVOLT

By the 1820s, although California was shielded by forbidding deserts and towering mountains, a hardy band of American fur trappers began to enter the province. Long before the U.S. government sought to acquire California, these "mountain men," from points as far east as St. Louis, Missouri, crossed deserts, faced wild animals, scaled rugged peaks, and forded the province's swollen streams.

During Echeandía's controversial governorship, one of these young trappers, Jedediah Strong Smith, blazed the initial overland trail from the Rocky Mountain region into southern California. He can, indeed, be called the first overland American in California history. Smith, at the head of a small band of men, trekked westward in search of beaver and otter pelts, which fetched good prices back east. Along the way, Smith displayed great courage in withstanding Indian attacks, shortages of food and water, as well as other wilderness challenges to his own survival. On one occasion, a ferocious grizzly bear attacked Smith, taking his head between its jaws. Smith somehow managed to escape the grasp of the brute with his life, but the encounter left the trapper with an ear and part of his scalp dangling from a bleeding skull. Incredibly, after one of his men stitched up the lacerations with needle and thread, the indomitable Smith was on his way again.

Guided by two Indians who had fled from Mission San Gabriel, Smith and his party moved southwestward across the deserts in between the Colorado River and the pueblo of Los Angeles. On November 27, 1826, he and his bedraggled men reached Mission San Gabriel, which seemed a luxuriant haven to them. In exchange for food, wine, and lodging, the trappers provided the friars, astonished to behold such strange-looking visitors, with bear traps with which to catch Indians who poached oranges from mission groves. While his men stayed behind with the padres, Smith rode to San Diego to seek Governor Echeandía's permission to trap in the province.

Smith failed to convince the suspicious governor that his men, lost and hungry, had simply stumbled into California. Even worse, Echeandía seized his weapons and placed him under arrest. Smith protested that he was "no Spy," producing a passport and diary that listed the members of his party in order to prove that they were bona fide trappers. Nonetheless, Echeandía considered Smith and his men interlopers and, unable to decide whether to let Smith go, sent to Mexico for instructions.

While confined to a dirty San Diego *calabozo* (jail cell), Smith scrawled a letter in brown ink to the U.S. minister at Mexico City, Joel R. Poinsett. In it, Smith complained: "I am destitute of almost everything with the exception of my Traps (guns which I can not now call mine), Ammunition, etc." The governor finally freed Smith from imprisonment upon the condition that he and his men leave California and promise never to return.

After heading out of San Diego, Smith and his men moved northward, trapping along the Stanislaus and Kings Rivers. On May 20, 1827, Smith left most of his men behind and headed east through the High Sierra toward the Great Basin Country of Utah in order to attend a trading rendezvous with other mountain men. Having failed in an earlier attempt, Smith and his few companions now became the first white persons ever to cross the perilous Sierra crest. They reached the Salt Lake area after about a month of arduous travel.

California, however, had not seen the last of Jedediah Smith. On July 13, 1827, further disregarding the instructions of Governor Echeandía, Smith began the trek back to rejoin the men he had left in the Central Valley. Then, as he and his men approached the Colorado River, they suffered an attack by Mojave tribesmen from the local villages. The warriors killed ten of the Americans and wounded one other.

Despite the loss of more than half his group, Smith eventually reached Mission San José. While attempting to garner supplies there, he was once more detained, this time by Father Narcisco Durán, who accused him of having enticed neophytes under his supervision to desert from the mission. Stripped once more of his guns and placed under heavy guard, Smith made another appearance before an angry Governor Echeandía, who happened to be on one of his rare visits to Monterey. After much argument, Smith was released. In December 1827 he headed out, having promised once more never to return.

Nevertheless, Smith took more than six months to traverse northwestern California on his way out of the province. First he moved up the

Jedediah Smith (1799–1831). Drawn by a family friend a few years after his death, this is the only known image of Smith created by one of his contemporaries.

Sacramento Valley, then parallel to the coastline toward today's Oregon border. On July 5, 1828, while trapping near the Umpqua River of southern Oregon, Smith's group suffered another Indian massacre. Only he and two other men survived. Now the tiny group proceeded as far north as the Hudson Bay Company's post at Fort Vancouver, where the staff of the English firm provided them welcome relief supplies. The classic stovepipe beaver hat had provided handsome rewards for Jedediah Smith and his fellow trappers. Eventually, however, a rage for silk hats almost wrecked their market for beaver furs.

Back in California, Smith's fellow Americans were still regarded suspiciously. Also, resentment toward Mexican rule was increasing, not only because of its neglect, but because of overbearing and mediocre governors. Californios felt contempt for these officials, whom they also viewed as invaders. Yet, as mentioned, successive revolts were halfhearted, bloodless affairs, hardly constituting a movement for provincial independence as had occurred elsewhere in Latin America.

Nevertheless, some political changes in Mexico did resonate in California. Echeandía was supplanted by Lieutenant Colonel Manuel Victoria, a militaristic conservative and an opponent of secularization. Echeandía had already issued his decree of secularization of January 6, 1831, with the purpose of rushing the measure into effect before turning over the government to his successor.

When Governor Victoria arrived in Monterey, his reception was a particularly unfriendly one. He was described as a lean man of such dark complexion (he was half Indian) that he came to be called "the black governor." Convinced that everyone who opposed him was in the wrong, Victoria made no attempt to conceal his contempt for unruly Californios. He ordered the death penalty put into effect, and as some crimes had previously gone unpunished, he boasted that he would make it safe for any citizen to leave a handkerchief or even a watch lying in Monterey's plaza.

Arbitrary by nature, the governor ran roughshod over his political rivals. Victoria considered the American Abel Stearns as well as two local leaders, José Antonio Carrillo and José María Padres, dangerous dissidents. He therefore exiled all three of them to Mexico without so much as a trial. In response, opposition to the governor increased. After having first taken possession of the presidio at San Diego, over fifty rebels marched to Los Angeles and seized control of that pueblo. There they found prominent local leaders in jail, by order of Victoria. Liberated from their cells, these dissidents bolstered the antigovernment forces. Indignant, Victoria marched southward from Monterey with a detachment of soldiers. A few miles from Los Angeles, near the Cahuenga Pass, he was surprised to meet some of his own forces, accompanied by 150 resurgent recruits, arrayed against him. Victoria called upon the soldiers to come over to his side. When they refused, he directed his men to fire a volley over the heads of all "enemies" to frighten rather than to harm them. The southerners replied with a few shots of their own. Then, their courage failing, they turned to flee. Now Governor Victoria was due for another rude surprise.

Among the Angeleños was the popular José María Avila who rode out to face Governor Victoria and a Captain Romualdo Pacheco. He rushed at both men with his lance leveled, while drawing an ancient pistol with which he shot Pacheco through the heart. Avila was, however, thrown from his horse and killed by Victoria, who received a lance wound in the face. Such local quarrels ultimately opened up the province to further foreign intervention. The governor next issued a manifesto stating that he would not allow any further outbreaks. But, after repeated complaints against him were sent to Mexico City, Victoria gave up his office after only a year.

Now Echeandía reassumed the governorship, supposedly temporarily. But when the Californios chose Pío Pico as their candidate, Echeandía refused to relinquish power. He did not want yet another native son as governor. Captain Augustín Vicente Zamorano, formerly the departed Governor Victoria's personal secretary, concluded a truce with Echeandía. The two men agreed to divide California's military command: Echeandía's authority was to extend south of San Gabriel, while Zamorano would rule north of San Fernando. This arrangement came to an end in 1833 with the arrival of yet another newly appointed governor.

This was José Figueroa, the Comandante-General of the Mexican states of Sonora and Sinaloa. So amiable and conscientious was Figueroa that he helped overcome the festering prejudice against imported governors. His first official act was to issue a proclamation granting amnesty to all persons who had taken part in political disturbances. Although Figueroa believed that the missions were not quite ready for full secularization, a sweeping decree of August 1833 came out of Mexico City: the missions were to become parish churches. He, thus, ordered half the mission lands and livestock distributed among their resident natives. This sudden release from mission life would lead to a dramatic decline in the Indian population. Sadly, some confused natives hung about the missions, reluctant to leave the only homes they had ever known. Others joined tribelets in the interior. With the padres no longer overseeing their charges, the Californios steeled themselves for potential Indian violence.

During 1834, Governor Figueroa also ran into trouble when a party of 200 colonists arrived from Mexico under the leadership of José María Padrés and José María Hijar. They planned to establish a new colony that included doctors, lawyers, teachers, and artisans. Because this group was hardly outfitted to survive a harsh winter in the Sonoma Valley, Figueroa, on May 8, 1834, arrested Padrés and Hijar and sent them packing for San Blas, in Lower California. Only a few of the Padrés-Hijar colonists were allowed to remain behind. Most of them settled in northern California.

One of Figueroa's most important acts was a move to establish a firmer possession of the territory to the north. Mexico had inherited from Spain claims based upon two missions: San Rafael and San Francisco de Solano, commonly called Sonoma. Figueroa sent Mariano Guadalupe Vallejo up to the missions to look for a suitable site on which to build a new presidio. Vallejo also established new settlements at Petaluma, near Santa Rosa, and Sonoma, where the general built up his own private estate, Lachryma Montis.

As the process of secularization continued, a worn-out Figueroa died on September 29, 1835. He was among the best of California's Mexican governors, and had he lived longer he might have softened the effects of secularization. Although Figueroa had sought to make the transition as smooth as possible, he was unfairly labeled as the destroyer of the mission system. Ultimately, mission lands intended for the Indian wards passed into the hands of local government administrators and their relatives. Repeatedly, looters stocked their ranchos with animals filched from mission herds. Deeply confused, the Indian converts stood by as the dreams of Junípero Serra vanished. With mission buildings crumbling into dust, an important bulwark of California life had all but disappeared. The ranchos had replaced the missions as the dominant economic and social institutions in pre-American California.

SELECTED READINGS

Regarding Jedediah Smith, consult Maurice S. Sullivan, *The Travels of Jedediah Smith* (1934), and Sullivan's *Jedediah Smith, Trader and Trail Breaker* (1936); Dale Morgan, *Jedediah Smith . . .* (1953); Robert Glass Cleland, *This Reckless Breed of Men* (1950); Harrison C. Dale, *The Ashley-Smith Explorations* (repr. 1941); Donald McKay Frost, "Notes on General Ashley, the Overland Trail and South Pass," *Proceedings of the American Antiquarian Society* 54 (October 1944), 161–312; A. M. Woodbury, "The Route of Jedediah S. Smith," *Utah Historical Quarterly* 4 (April 1931), 35–46; Andrew Rolle, "Jedediah Strong Smith: New Documentation," *Mississippi Valley Historical Review* 40 (September 1953), 305–8, and Rolle, "The Riddle of Jedediah Smith's First Visit to California," *Historical Society of Southern California Quarterly* 36 (September 1954), 179–84; George R. Brooks, ed., *The Southwest Expedition of Jedediah S. Smith* (1977); David J. Weber, *The Californios Versus Jedediah Smith* (1990).

For Mexican rule and turmoil, see Robert Phelps "On Comic Opera Revolutions . . . in Mexican California," *California History* 84 (Fall, 2006), 44–63; also Gerald J. Geary, *The Secularization of the California Missions* (1934); John B. McGloin, *California's First Archbishop* (1966); Madie Brown Emparan, *The Vallejos of California* (1968); Alan Rosenus, *General M. G. Vallejo and the Advent of the Americans* (1995); C. Alan Hutchinson, *The Híjar-Padrés Colony and its Origins, 1769–1835* (1969); also Robert R. Miller, *Juan Alvarado, Governor of California, 1836–1842* (1998).

CHAPTER ELEVEN

ON THE EVE
OF AMERICAN RULE

Governor Figueroa had managed to win the allegiance of the province more by personal charm than by authority. After his death, the *Californios* grew ever more restless. Aggravating local tensions were the many changes of governments in Mexico City. Succeeding Figueroa was Nicolás Gutiérrez, who served as interim governor for four months until the next appointee arrived. This was the Mexican-born Mariano Chico, a political reactionary unpopular from the first. Locally resented, Chico was expelled from office after only three months. Somehow, the Californians avoided open conflict with the national government. Although Chico declared he would return with troops to take vengeance, his threat was an empty one.

Mexican governors were no longer welcome. One after another found the place hostile. Increasingly the provincials referred to themselves as Californios. Upon the expulsion of Chico, the civil and military commands fell temporarily back to Governor Gutiérrez. Though easygoing and inoffensive, he was a Spaniard by birth and regarded as an unwelcome foreigner. A petty quarrel between him and Juan Bautista Alvarado provided the excuse for his overthrow. The Californians seemed determined to secure home rule for their territory. Why should a Vallejo, an Alvarado, a Carrillo, or any other local leader be inferior to an outsider? Contact with visiting foreigners further highlighted the backwardness of Mexico and awakened local ambitions. The Californios had easily expelled Governors Victoria and Chico. This encouraged the most ambitious provincial leaders to act more boldly toward provincial independence.

By late 1836, the twenty-seven-year-old Juan Bautista Alvarado had, by virtue of his education and family ties, made himself prominent as a local patriot. A member of the local disputacíon, he was a vigorous *hijo del pais* (or native son). Endowed with a certain magnetism, Alvarado and an ally, José Castro, assembled a force of seventy-five men armed with antiquated muskets. At Monterey they recruited a Tennesseean, Isaac Graham, a boozy fur trapper, hunter, and a ruffian who ran a whiskey distillery on the Rancho Vergeles. Induced by promises of land and other favors, Graham and some of his rough followers agreed to join the revolutionists. Governor Alvarado would soon regret the day he asked for Graham's help.

Graham headed up a reckless band of about fifty riflemen. These were Indians, pushy Americans, and renegade Mexicans. Alongside Alvarado and Castro's force of 100 Californios, Graham's motley force took possession of Monterey on November 3, 1836, without bloodshed. A lone cannon ball struck the house of Governor Nicolás Gutíerrez. Terrified by such violence, he surrendered immediately. Once again, a governor appointed by the Mexican government was put aboard a homeward-bound ship. This was the third such official expelled by the Californios. Now they proceeded to name their own governor. This was the popular Alvarado.

The new local governor wrote to his uncle, General Vallejo: "It is wonderful with what order our expedition has been conducted. Everybody shouts *vivas*, for California is free." On November 7, 1836, the Californios proclaimed themselves virtually independent of Mexico. Governor Alvarado was then also named the province's military chieftain. Nevertheless, he prudently kept the Mexican flag flying above his headquarters in Monterey. Indeed, a swarm of angry proclamations soon flew out of Mexico City, all of which threatened punishment of California's newly installed leaders.

Soon thereafter, sectional jealousies resurfaced. San Diegans had long wanted the provincial customhouse moved from Monterey to their town in the extreme south. This and other local disagreements resulted in another armed encounter, this one near Ventura, with Castro heading up the northerners and Carlos Carrillo commanding the province's southern forces. Only one man was killed. After another skirmish at Las Flores, in which the two factions met in "a battle for the most part of tongue and pen," Alvarado persuaded Carrillo to disband his forces.

Alvarado would not be recognized as governor by the Mexican government until 1838. Some expressed surprise that Mexico's central government would even confer such an honor upon a local leader lately in rebellion against its edicts. The Mexican authorities, however, cared little who the governor of Upper California was so long as he did not ask for more money or troops.

In the interim, Alvarado had his hands full as chief administrator. One problem concerned the future of mission properties. Because the missions continued to deteriorate, Governor Alvarado appointed a promising native of Lancashire, England, as his inspector of the missions. This honest

Pío Pico (1801–1894), entrepreneur and politician. By the end of his second term in 1864, he had served as the last Mexican governor of California. In the 1850s he was among the wealthiest businessmen and landowners in California but due to bad business decisions and gambling later in life, his final years left him nearly penniless. Courtesy, Anaheim Public Library.

newcomer was William E. P. Hartnell, who soon reported that non-Christianized interior Indians were regularly raiding the most exposed missions, running off horses and mules and killing unguarded cattle. Hartnell would rise to become an important figure in the Salinas area.

Governor Alvarado also faced more threats of local insurrection. At Los Angeles, Pío Pico still sulked over the refusal of Monterey's junta to move the capital southward to his home town. Furthermore, the number of foreigners in and around the northern capital continued to increase. A few of these troublemakers refused to settle down, a list that included Isaac Graham, who made his Monterey cabin a center for dissident American fur trappers and sailors. When Alvarado got wind of a plot to overthrow him, he soon traced its origins to Graham.

Mindful that in 1836 aggressive American immigrants had proclaimed Texas as as an independent republic, in April of 1840 Alvarado rounded up and arrested 120 such malcontents. He then sent Graham and forty-five of his cronies in irons to San Blas. But, not only did Mexican officials release Graham, they even gave him and his followers free ship-passage back to Monterey! This was a clear slap in the face to Alvarado, whose governorship had barely been sanctioned by his superiors in Mexico. Naturally, Monterey's residents were astounded to see Graham and two dozen ragged companions debark from a ship at port. For their part, the returned Americans remained as insolent as ever.

Interest in California from abroad was also clearly mounting. Following upon the previous visits of La Pérouse, Vancouver, Beechey, and Du Haut-Cilly, in 1837 the French frigate *Venus* paid a call. Under the command of Captain Abel du Petit-Thouars, the ship remained at Monterey for a month. The shipmaster's official report included descriptions of the "Alvarado Revolution" and of California's turbulent political climate. In 1840 Governor Alvarado greeted yet another French expedition, this one led by the explorer Eugéne Duflot de Mofras.

These trips were more than pleasure cruises. Foreign governments remained eager to obtain information about California. As if to counter such voyages, in 1841 the United States sent a naval expedition to the Pacific Coast. Its leader, Commodore Charles Wilkes, though pessimistic in his report to Washington, praised what he called the greatest natural harbor in the world, San Francisco Bay. The U.S. Navy clearly wanted this port to remain open.

The joint rule of Alvarado as civil governor and Vallejo as *commandante-general* ended late in 1842. In August of that year a newly appointed executive, Manuel Micheltorena, a haughty Mexican general of brigade, suddenly arrived at San Diego. In appearance he was attractive, with an erect, military bearing. But Micheltorena arrived in the dubious company of 300 toughs, or *cholos*, among them mestizos and ex-convicts. In a state of destitution, these "troops" had been sent northward with Micheltorena, partly to block further entry of foreigners into California. As irregulars, they had not received their pay in a long time and could not resist the temptation to steal kettles, pots, chickens, jewelry, and even clothing. Derided as *rateros* (low-lifes), the new governor's thieves also proceeded to molest the señoritas of San Diego, where they were temporarily billeted. Understandably, the San Diegans grew anxious to send Micheltorena and his thugs on their way northward to the capital at Monterey.

Even before Micheltorena and his band of ruffians left San Diego, the new governor received some startling news. Hostilities between Mexico and the United States had become tense. An American Commodore, Thomas Ap Catesby Jones, while in Peruvian waters, had mistakenly heard that war had been declared between the United States and Mexico. Commodore Jones proceeded to Monterey, where he landed marines and raised the American flag. However, convinced of his error within only a few hours, he restored the Mexican banner and, though embarrassed, quickly sought to make amends.

At Monterey, Micheltorena grudgingly excused the confused U.S. commodore and turned to other internal matters. First, he moved to repay persons whose property had been stolen by his cholos. Next he appeased the friars by restoring properties to their care, even though such action came too late to save the moribund mission system. Then he turned to the foreigners, who pressed the governor for new grants of land. Hoping to secure their loyalty, he awarded some of them tracts in the distant Sacramento Valley.

The governor's troubles were far from ended. Not only did Indian outbreaks continue, but by November 22, 1844, Micheltorena, like others before him, faced a revolt, this one, too, under the leadership of Alvarado and José Castro. Foreign residents landed on both sides of this quarrel. Abel Stearns and Isaac Graham ultimately sided with Alvarado, gratifying their hatred of previous governors, especially Victoria. Johann Augustus Sutter, the Swiss adventurer who had arrived in 1839 and built a fort he named New Helvetia on the Sacramento River, also voiced his opposition to Micheltorena and his unpopular jailbirds.

On February 20, 1845, the opposing forces, each several hundred strong, met at the Cahuenga Pass, outside Los Angeles, and engaged in a two-day artillery duel—at such long range, however, that there was little danger of anyone being hit. Ultimately, Micheltorena, his foreign support vanished, agreed to being deported from California and taking his cholos with him. His departure amounted to the province's virtual independence from Mexico. While there was now no stopping local control, California remained a house divided.

The Californios proclaimed Pío Pico their next local governor. Castro, as powerful in Monterey as Pico was in Los Angeles, became the province's military comandante. Pico proceeded to move the capital to Los Angeles. Backed by Alvarado and other native sons, Governor Pico at last seemed to control the government. Castro, however, remained in the north in possession of both the provincial revenues and the militia. The tension between comandante and governor, north versus south, dragged on during 1845 and 1846. Castro ran everything above Monterey while Pico represented only the pueblo of Los Angeles and its surrounding rancheros.

As local factionalism constantly threatened to erupt into fighting, a number of residents actually began to hope for an American takeover. By 1841 the Russians had withdrawn completely from California, leaving the Americans as the leading foreign group. The *Yanquis* seemed to come from a more stable society than any of the locals had ever known. With the pastoral era receding, most Californios and foreigners alike seemed about to accept American rule. But such a future would hardly be tranquil.

SELECTED READINGS

The last days of Mexican rule are portrayed in J. J. Hill, *History of Warner's Ranch and Its Environs* (1927). See also George and Helen Beattie, *Heritage of the Valley: San Bernardino's First Century* (1939) as well as William Phelps, *Fore and Aft, or Leaves from the Life of Old Sailor* (1871); Thomas Jefferson Farnham, *Travels in the Californias . . .* (1844); and Henry Wise, *Los Gringos* (1849). Some of these early books have been reprinted in modern editions. Also see William Deverell, *Whitewashed Adobe* (2004).

Regarding foreign visitors, see Richard Batman, *The Outer Coast* (1985); Charles N. Rudkin, trans., *Voyage of the Venus: Sojourn in California* (1956); Marguerite Eyer Wilbur, trans. and ed., *Duflot de Mofras' Travels on the Pacific Coast . . .* (2 vols. 1937); Charles Wilkes, *Narrative of the United States Exploring Expedition* (5 vols. 1844); Daniel M. MacIntyre, *The Hidden Coasts* (1953); David B. Tyler, *The Wilkes Expedition* (1968).

On Americanization, see William Barger, "The Merchants of Los Angeles: Economics and Commerce in Mexican California," *Southern California Quarterly* (Summer 2001), 125–44; also Doris Wright, *A Yankee in Mexican California: Abel Stearns, 1798–1848* (1977); Robert Glass Cleland, *The Cattle on a Thousand Hills* (repr. 1951); Judson Grenier, *California Legacy . . . The Watson Family* (1987); and Ronald C. Woolsey, *Migrants West: Toward the Southern California Frontier* (1996).

CHAPTER TWELVE

TRAPPERS, TRADERS, AND HOMESEEKERS

Before the discovery of gold in 1848, the fur trade was the most impor-tant economic stimulus to western development. The overland movement pioneered by Jedediah Smith attracted other trappers. Among these were James Ohio Pattie and his father Sylvester as well as Ewing Young, William Wolfskill, the Sublette brothers, and the famous western scout Christopher (Kit) Carson. They were a mixed lot. Their ranks included eccentrics like the obstreperous Isaac Graham. Nevertheless, this stream of mountain men, traders, and later homeseekers would transform a remote Mexican province into an American outpost.

In mid-1824, James and Sylvester Pattie set out on a lengthy fur-trap-ping expedition southwest from the Missouri River frontier. On June 20, their little party, consisting of five men, crossed the Missouri River sixty miles above St. Louis. There, a larger group joined them. Not all of these would accompany the Patties into the unexplored Southwest. For near-ly two years, the Patties trapped for beavers along muddy streams never before seen by white persons. They reached the Mohave Indian villages near the Colorado River on March 16, 1826, some six months before Jed Smith. They thus became the first Americans to trap in the Arizona-Cali-fornia area. As they assembled many furs, their prospects seemed excellent. Then some Indians stole their pack animals, compelling the Pattie group to cache (bury) their unwieldy furs, most of which they never recovered. Still worse, another of their illegal caches was confiscated by the Mexican governor at Santa Fe, who pocketed the proceeds. For the Americans had been trapping without a proper license.

Late in September of 1827, the Patties and about thirty companions continued westward from Santa Fe in today's New Mexico to trap below the Gila River. By the time they reached the junction of that river and the Colorado, repeated misunderstandings among them caused the party

Kit Carson, "King of Guides." Shown here is the cover of the May 3, 1884 issue of *Beadle's Boy's Library,* a popular dimestore novel of the period. Christopher "Kit" Carson, famed Rocky Mountain scout and subject of many such romanticized stories, is depicted on horseback in front of a wagon train. Library of Congress, LC-USZ62-66371.

to divide. From then on the Pattie group numbered only eight persons. These wandered aimlessly through what is now Arizona. At one campsite, a band of Yuma Indians, under cover of a heavy storm and the blackness of night, stampeded their horses. This left the Patties no choice but to build canoes from some nearby cottonwoods and float them down the Colorado River.

As the Patties approached the Gulf of California, they abandoned their crudely made boats due to "the tumultuous commotion of the water" and cached more furs. Next, they set out further westward on foot in the hope of finding some sort of Mexican settlement. The fierce sun and scorching sand, the almost total lack of moisture, and extreme fatigue, instilled desperation in their little band.

At last, with the assistance of several Indian guides, the Patties reached the Dominican mission of Santa Catalina, east of Ensenada on the Baja California peninsula. But the Patties were considered unwelcome foreigners, and instead of being accorded relief by the padres, they were thrown into the guardhouse. The interlopers were then sent northward under guard to San Diego, the temporary seat of Upper California's Governor, Echeandía. The Patties were amazed at the harsh treatment accorded them by him. Suspicious of such poaching trappers after his dealings with

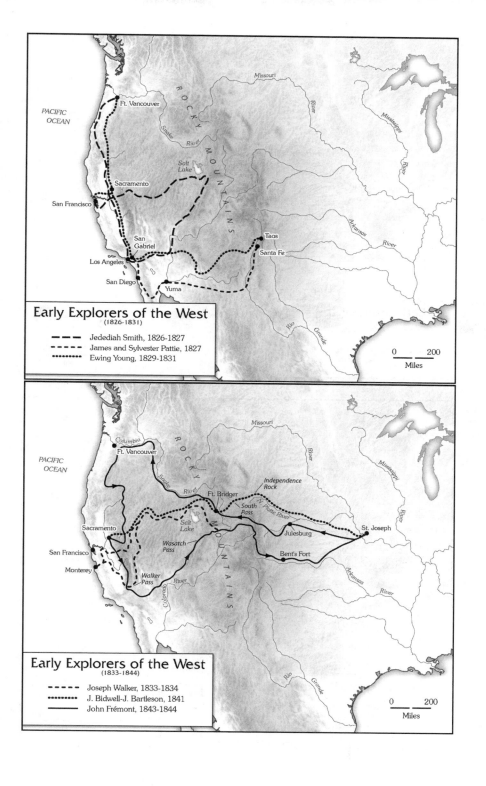

Early Explorers of the West
(1826-1831)

- – – – Jedediah Smith, 1826-1827
- - - - - James and Sylvester Pattie, 1827
- • • • • • Ewing Young, 1829-1831

0   200
Miles

Early Explorers of the West
(1833-1844)

- - - - - Joseph Walker, 1833-1834
- • • • • • J. Bidwell-J. Bartleson, 1841
- ——— John Frémont, 1843-1844

0   200
Miles

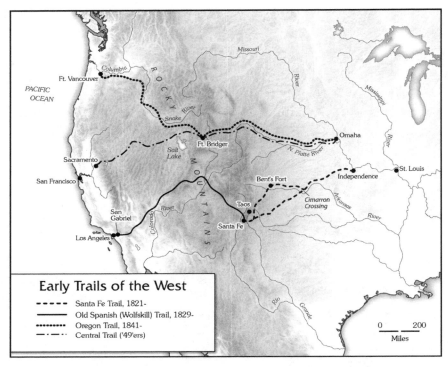

Early Trails of the West

- - - - - Santa Fe Trail, 1821-
────── Old Spanish (Wolfskill) Trail, 1829-
•••••••• Oregon Trail, 1841-
─·─·─·─ Central Trail ('49'ers)

0   200
Miles

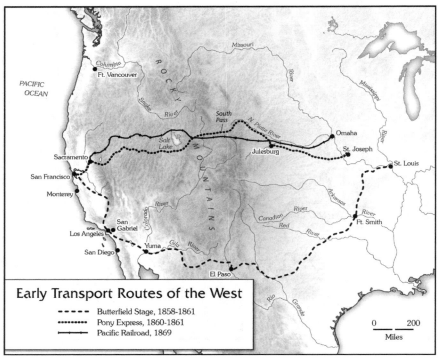

Early Transport Routes of the West

- - - - - Butterfield Stage, 1858-1861
•••••••• Pony Express, 1860-1861
├─┼─┼─┤ Pacific Railroad, 1869

0   200
Miles

Jedediah Smith, the governor remanded the Pattie group to separate cells. In a fit of anger he tore up a document issued by New Mexico's governor which granted the Patties permission to trap beaver.

The impaired health of Sylvester Pattie was not equal to his brutal physical treatment. He soon grew ill and died. After the death of his father, James fortunately got the chance to serve the governor, who needed an interpreter to deal with the increasing number of American intruders. We cannot be sure if James Pattie even told the truth about his exploits. Years later he put together a tall-tale about a smallpox epidemic that allegedly was sweeping through California. When the governor learned that the Patties had brought along some scarce vaccine, he promised James his freedom if he would agree to vaccinate California's population. The story appears fabricated, but parts of Pattie's narrative are verifiable.

In 1830, James Ohio Pattie is said to have made his way back to Kentucky by way of Vera Cruz in Mexico and New Orleans. He left behind one of the most improbable, yet exciting, records of western adventure. His *Personal Narrative,* published in 1831, told the story of how he and his father had pioneered the rugged Gila River route to California.

Pattie was followed by another American trapper, Joseph Reddeford Walker, who opened up a new trail across the Sierra mountain ridge. In August of 1829, one other "mountain man," Ewing Young, headed a party westward from Taos, New Mexico, traveling down the Gila and the Colorado rivers. Kit Carson, originally a protégé of Young, was in this group. The Young party traveled over parts of the "Old Spanish Trail," which crossed the Mohave Desert into southern California. Early in 1830, Young's men reached San Gabriel Mission via the Cajon Pass. The next year Young returned to California to trap river otters and beavers along the Kings River and stretches of the San Joaquin. He also collected furs as far north as Oregon's Umpqua River. Such trappers had to carry on their activities clandestinely, for only Mexican citizens were supposed to possess licenses to trap legally.

Nonetheless, dozens of foreigners subsequently entered California, sometimes under odd circumstances. Milton Sublette had the good fortune to be granted a trapping license after agreeing to teach local residents "the art of trapping." Among the trappers who settled permanently in California was George Yount, who founded the town of Yountville in the Napa Valley, where he is buried. Similarly, J. J. Warner started a ranch in southern California that much later became a tourist attraction known as Warner's Hot Springs. Louis Robideaux, a trapper of French descent, even had a mountain near Riverside named after him, while Joe Walker is remembered as the discoverer of Walker Pass in the Sierra Range.

As the Californios accomodated all these foreigners, the already mentioned Swiss Johann Augustus Sutter would play a unique role in Americanizing the province. Born in the Grand Duchy of Baden on the German frontier, Sutter left Switzerland for America in 1834 to escape a debtor's prison and an angry wife. After tarrying in Indiana and Missouri, and visiting parts of Mexico along the Santa Fe Trail—as well as Honolulu and the Russian colonies in Alaska—he arrived on the Pacific coast. Called "a dreamer with a gifted tongue," the shrewd and wily Sutter achieved a distinct place in California. Sutter brought with him from Hawaii various laborers, then called *Kanakas*. He hoped to build a self-sustaining colony and fort in the Sacramento Valley. By 1839 he had obtained permission from Governor Alvarado to occupy an unexplored 50,000-acre tract of land near the junction of the Sacramento and American Rivers. Sutter had convinced the governor that he could act as a semi-official representative of the government in the interior. Impressed with this proposal, the governor promised Sutter Mexican citizenship.

The early American trader William Heath Davis, Jr., at age seventeen, first guided Sutter's party to the site of the future city of Sacramento, where Sutter planned to build his fort. Sutter took two pieces of artillery with him into the wilderness. When, after eight days, the company reached their destination, they found between 700 and 800 Indians awaiting them. Sutter prepared his party to resist an attack, but the Indians were more curious than hostile. A number of them ventured out on the river in *tule balsas* (raft floats) to greet the foreigners. Reassured, Davis and Sutter landed and pitched tents. When Davis took leave of the group, Sutter fired a salute in honor of his departing guide. Upon hearing the noise of the cannon, hundreds of Indians crowded into Sutter's makeshift encampment. Large numbers of deer, also startled at the sound, ran crazily out of the nearby woods. Davis later recalled that "the howls of wolves and coyotes filled the air, and immense flocks of water fowl flew wildly about over the camp."

In 1840, Sutter began construction of a more permanent outpost. He had since purchased from the Russians departing Fort Ross the bulk of their equipment and supplies. Sutter now saw himself as the virtual guardian of California's northern frontier. He built an adobe wall eighteen feet high by three feet thick to enclose a rectangular fort. The enclosure remains today. Sutter named his colony "New Helvetia," in honor of his Swiss homeland. Here he became a virtual feudal baron. His property was located just below the point at which overland immigrants came down out of the Sierra range. Therefore, he generously provided a welcome respite for exhausted overland parties.

Among them, Sutter attracted a unique but fraudulent neighbor. This was "Doctor" John Marsh, a young Harvard graduate who passed himself off as a physician. He reached California with a company of Santa Fe trappers and settled on a rancho at the base of Mount Diablo. The publication of Marsh's letters in Missouri newspapers stimulated interest in California. Then came the trapper Antoine Robideaux, who in 1840 started yet another publicity campaign on behalf of the Pacific province. Speaking at the little town of Weston, Missouri, the trapper claimed that he had found "a perfect paradise," and "a perpetual spring" in the far west.

Weston's twenty-year-old schoolteacher, John Bidwell, had become excited by the idea of seeing the "Great West" beyond the Rockies. He helped ready a migration party, even though he "had barely the means to buy a wagon, a gun, and provisions." By May 1, 1841, Bidwell's company consisted of forty-seven emigrants, three trappers, a group of Catholic missionaries, their wagon freighters, a lone Methodist minister, and various adventurers. Fifteen women and children were in the party. Paul Geddes was elected its president, John Bartelson its captain, and Bidwell its secretary. Thomas Fitzpatrick (also known by his Indian name, "Broken Hand") had trapped in the Rocky Mountains and was headed for the region again. He was the only person in the group familiar with the country to be traversed.

On May 19, 1841, Bidwell's motley caravan, which would become known as "the first emigrant train to California," started on its dusty way from Sapling Grove in Missouri. First came some missionaries,with four carts and one wagon. Headed by the later renowned Jesuit Peter De Smet, they accompanied Bidwell westward as far as the Rocky mountains. Father De Smet moved into the northwest, where he established a mission among the Flathead Indians. Next in the line of march were eight wagons drawn by horses and mules. Then came the last unit, consisting of five wagons drawn by seventeen yoke of oxen.

By June 22, the party reached Fort Laramie, moving next toward Independence Rock along the Sweetwater River in what is now Wyoming. Then, staggering through the alkali flats near the Great Salt Lake and facing a seemingly endless series of mirages, the weary travelers had no choice but to jettison their heavy furniture, washpans, butter churns, baggage, and lastly their wagons in order to keep going. By September 16, Bidwell wrote that "All hands were busy making pack-saddles and getting ready to pack." Since no one in the group had much experience dealing with pack animals, one can only imagine the caravan of loose packs, saddles, frightened horses, kicking mules, and bellowing oxen that accompanied these tired and aching humans. The footsore group wandered for days through the Humboldt Valley and Carson Sink, their provisions disappearing daily.

One night, John Bartleson, their blundering and selfish captain, deserted the group along with eight other men. They took the best horses in an attempt to find a more direct route westward. Several days later, however, near the Walker River, the disgraced men shamefacedly returned to camp. By that time Bidwell had quietly assumed command of the group. After slaughtering their remaining oxen, jerking, and drying the meat for the trip ahead, they began the ascent of the High Sierra. Traveling through deep snows, the group carefully kept together. Bidwell's wonderful diary recorded on October 28, 1841: "We ate the last of our beef this evening and killed a mule to finish our supper. Distance six miles." Two days later, Bidwell "beheld a great valley," which the group incorrectly estimated to be several hundred miles wide. Almost six months after their departure from Sapling Grove, Bidwell's party had finally reached the Sacramento Valley. They quickly found employment at Sutter's Fort. Bidwell, who ultimately settled on a ranch at Chino, was thereafter called "a prince of California pioneers."

That same year, the Workman-Rowland overland party managed to avoid winter's hardships by taking a southern route into California. Along the Santa Fe trail they drove flocks of sheep for their daily sustenance. As a result, this party's members were in good physical shape when they arrived at Mission San Gabriel. Upon arrival, John Rowland sought out Mexican officials, presenting them with a list of his party's participants. He also declared his intention of obeying all legal requirements for settlement as foreigners. The Workman-Rowland group, thus, were given a welcome not extended to dozens of other parties then entering California. Members of this group also received land grants quite easily.

The members of yet another expedition, the Chiles-Williams party, had faced repeated perils. Fortunately they were led by the experienced trapper Joseph Reddeford Walker and Joseph Chiles, both of whom had accompanied John Bidwell's 1841 group. In 1843, Walker and Chiles left Missouri and headed out toward Fort Boise, from which they proceeded southwestward across the southern Sierra range toward the Owens Valley. There, because of the weakened condition of their animals, the travelers abandoned their wagons. By Christmas, they reached the Salinas River, continuing on to the lower Santa Clara Valley. After their arrival, members of this group, like those of the others, scattered to different points. All became homeseekers.

By word of mouth, as well as through printed journals, pamphlets, and the letters of John Marsh, the uncoordinated publicity campaign continued, coaxing immigrants from all over the nation toward California. Frequently, smaller groups joined forces at prairie junctions, traveling in long wagon trains for weeks on end. It is impossible to list the many groups that traveled westward from the Missouri frontier. Among the better-known parties were the 1844 Stevens-Murphy and Grigsby-Ide groups. The latter reached Sutter's Fort on Christmas Day of 1845. During that season alone, Sutter witnessed the arrival at New Helvetia of more than 1,000 Americans.

Beginning in 1846, increasing numbers of new settlers also reached California by water. Among these were several hundred Mormons headed by Samuel Brannan, who arrived at the Golden Gate aboard the chartered ship *Brooklyn*. Brannan's group originally intended to move on to Salt Lake City, where Brigham Young awaited them. However, enchanted with California, Brannan urged his followers to stay on with him there. Two children had been born during the voyage: a boy named *Atlantic* and a girl named *Pacific*!

Now a new era of exploration by government survey parties was about to begin. The years 1843–44 saw the arrival in California of John Charles Frémont, a young and highly ambitious naturalist-explorer-scientist on his second expedition to the Far West. Frémont's party was sponsored by the newly formed U.S. Topographical Engineers, and his guide was Kit Carson. The publication of Frémont's journals and invaluable maps would induce a flood of homeseekers to emigrate toward the Pacific. Furthermore, Frémont's father-in-law was senator Thomas Hart Benton of Missouri, the powerful chairman of the U.S. Senate Committee on Territories and an ardent expansionist.

After a dangerous, snowy crossing of the Sierra, Frémont's men reached Sutter's Fort in March of 1844. He then moved southward along the San Joaquin Valley to the Kings River, crossing the Tehachapi Pass on his way back to Saint Louis. The explorer's official report, thousands of copies of which were printed, made Frémont a national figure. He had produced accurate maps that induced more overland groups to move toward California with much greater confidence about the routes they chose.

One such party was, however, doomed to play a tragic role in the history of the American West. In the spring of 1846, the Donner group started its fateful journey in Springfield, Illinois. From the very beginning, bad luck and poor judgment plagued the party, although some of its participants would display notable heroism in the midst of the forthcoming disaster.

At Fort Bridger in Wyoming, the Donners decided to follow the foolish advice of Lansford Hastings, author of the *Emigrant's Guide to Oregon and California* (1845), a copy of which they had brought along as a reference. That book described a new route to California, which Hastings alleged was 200 miles shorter than the proven route by way of Fort Hall in today's Idaho. This new trail, called the "Hastings Cut-off" (which Hastings himself had never traveled prior to the publication of his guide), terminated eight miles west of modern-day Elko, Nevada. Running south of the Great Salt Lake via Fort Bridger, the cut-off rejoined the California Trail on the Humboldt River. The decision to take this alleged short-cut turned into a nightmare for the Donner Party.

On July 20, the Donners broke camp and plunged into an unknown wilderness. Along an almost impassable route, they fought their way through the Wasatch Mountains. At times the group was compelled to use ten yoke of oxen to draw a single wagon up the side of a steep gulch. It took the emigrants a month—instead of a week, as they had planned—to reach the shores of the Great Salt Lake. The loss of time proved costly. West of Salt Lake it became apparent that their supplies would give out before the group could reach California. Now two members of the party volunteered to proceed on horseback, procure food from Sutter's Fort, and return to reprovision the weary and hungry group, which included women and children. For a lack of water, the party abandoned thirty-six head of cattle on the desert. Then a mirage, revealing the seemingly blue waters of a lake, turned disappointment into anguish. By this point, return to Fort Bridger was impossible; there was no alternative but to continue onward.

The tension increased when John Snyder inadvertently struck the wife of James F. Reed with a bullwhip. Enraged, Reed stabbed Snyder to death and then used the boards from his wagon to make a coffin for the dead man. The Donner Party passed a severe judgment on the murderer, who cried out that he had acted in self-defense. There on the remote desert floor of western America, miles from the nearest habitation, Reed's companions forced him to leave the wagon train.

With his rifle and only a few provisions, Reed set out alone for California. Each day thereafter his wife and children looked for traces of him along the way, hoping to find the feathers of a bird killed, or perhaps a note pinned onto a bush. They also feared that he might have been scalped by Indians. The Donner Party had foolishly banished one of its most needed members.

In the Sierra, winter was coming on fast. But instead of pressing forward, the disorganized party tarried several days to take a badly needed rest at Truckee Meadows, near present-day Reno, Nevada. The banks of the Truckee River were covered with lush grasses and clover, making it difficult to leave such security behind and proceed toward the unknown.

On October 19, one of the volunteers, having made it all the way to Sutter's Fort, returned with two Indian guides, seven mules, and limited amounts of beef and flour. Three days later the Donners crossed the wind-ing Truckee River "for the forty-ninth and last time in eighty miles." The party moved northward through barely passable canyons. Clouds high on the mountain crest gave a clear indication of approaching bad weather; there was a sharp nip in the air. As they moved into higher elevations, they could not drag their wagons through the early snows that had fallen in the Sierra that year. One wagon broke its axle and tipped over onto little Eliza Donner, three years old, and Georgia, age four; the children were almost crushed by the avalanche of household goods that crashed upon them. There was further delay as the party repacked provisions onto cumbersome oxen.

A particularly early winter quickly descended upon upper Alder Creek. Part of the train became bogged down completely in the snow near today's Donner Lake. Another small remnant sought shelter from the falling snow under brush and canvas sheets about six miles away. There the desperate travelers waited four excruciating months until early spring, sheltered only by snow-covered pines on one of the Sierra's windiest passes. The snow that winter reached a depth of twenty-two feet. Scattered into small clusters, the members of the Donner party made repeated efforts to get out of the mountains. They improvised snowshoes from oxbows and strips of rawhide. In mid-December of 1846, a group known as "The Fifteen" left the rest behind. After weeks of severe suffering, dazed and stumbling about in the snow, seven survivors emerged from the mountains via the Emigrant Gap.

On the nineteenth of February of 1847, those left behind on the Sierra crest were startled by the shouts of approaching men. The strongest of them, climbing to the top of a huge snow bank, beheld the "most welcome sight of their lives"—a reconnaissance party of seven men, reprovisioned by Sutter, composed of formerly snowed-in survivors. Each bore a pack. Then James Reed, whom they had banished what now seemed so long ago, arrived with a second relief group to save some of the very men who had cast him out. Reed was overjoyed to find his wife and four children still alive. Then a third contingent reappeared, but by then George Donner was too weak and sick to travel. His wife refused to leave her husband's side, allowing the rescue party to take her little daughters from her to safety. When the fourth and last relief party arrived in the spring, they found Mr. and Mrs. Donner dead. Only forty-five of the seventy-nine persons in the original Donner Party survived. No one knows the full extent of the harrowing experiences the emigrants endured during their battle against freezing temperatures and starvation. Writers sympathetic to the Donners later denied any allegations of cannibalism. Yet those who survived apparently had eaten the flesh of their dead trail mates. Lieutenant Henry Augustus Wise, an American naval officer in California at the time, recorded what he believed happened in gruesome, if fantastic, detail: "The survivors were found rolling in filth, parents eating their own offspring . . . exchanging limbs and meat—little children tearing and devouring the hearts of the dead, and a general apathy and mania pervaded all. . . . One Dutchman actually ate a full-grown body in 36 hours; another boiled and devoured a girl nine years old in a single night. . . . One [girl] feasted on her good papa, but on making soup of her lover's head, she confessed to some inward qualms. . . . A young Spaniard, Baptiste . . . told me that he ate Jake Donner and the baby."

Members of the Donner Party who lived on for years after the tragedy became popular local culture heroes. Each symbolized the hardiest western pioneers. Such folk were celebrated as a mixture of frontier individualism and religious conviction. Indeed, their sacrifices seemed to embody a popular phrase of the era: "Manifest Destiny." Despite adversity and suffering, such Americans had sought to build a new world beyond the rugged mountains in distant California.

SELECTED READINGS

Regarding the fur trade, see Paul C. Phillips, *The Fur Trade* (2 vols. 1961) and Cleland, *This Reckless Breed of Men*; also Charles L. Camp, ed., *James Clyman: American Frontiersman* (1928); Alpheus H. Favour, *Old Bill Williams, Mountain Man* (1936); Richard Batman, *American Ecclesiastes: The Stories of James Pattie* (1985); Stanton A. Coblentz, *The Swallowing Wilderness* (1961); Clifton B. Kroeber, ed., "The Route of James Ohio Pattie on the Colorado in 1826: A Reappraisal by A. L. Kroeber," *Arizona and The West* 6 (Summer 1964), 119–36; Rosemary K. Valle, "James Ohio Pattie and the Alta California Measles Epidemic," *California Historical Quarterly* 52 (Spring 1973), 28–36; Donald Rowland, *John Rowland and William Workman: Southern California Pioneers of 1841* (1999); Paul Gray, *Forster vs. Pico: The Struggle for the Rancho Margarita* (1998); Iris Wilson, *William Wolfskill, 1798–1866: Frontier Trapper to California Ranchero* (1965) and LeRoy Hafen, ed., *The Mountain Men and the Fur Trade of the Far West* (6 vols. 1965–68).

About Sutter, the latest biography is Albert Hurtado, *John Sutter: A Life…* (2006). Also consult Kenneth Owens, ed., *John Sutter and a Wider West* (1994); Erwin G. Gudde, *Sutter's Own Story* (1936); James Peter Zollinger, *Sutter: The Man and His Empire* (1939); and Marguerite Eyer Wilbur, *John Sutter: Rascal and Adventurer* (1949).

Overland travelers are described in Rockwell D. Hunt, *John Bidwell: Prince of California Pioneers* (1942) and Bidwell, *California Before the Gold Rush* (repr. 1948). Regarding the Donners, consult Henry Augustus Wise, *Los Gringos: Or An Inside View of Mexico and California* (1849); C. F. McGlashan, *History of the Donner Party: A Tragedy of the Sierra* (repr. 1947); George R. Stewart, *Ordeal by Hunger: The Story of the Donner Party* (1936, 1960); Walter M. Stookey, *Fatal Decision: The Tragic Story of the Donner Party* (1950); Eliza P. Donner Houghton, *The Expedition of the Donner Party* (1920); David E. Miller, "The Donner Road through the Great Salt Lake Desert," *Pacific Historical Review* 27 (February 1958), 30–44.

Overland trail details are in J. Gregg Layne, *Western Wayfaring: Routes of Exploration and Trade in the American Southwest* (1954); Arthur Peters, *Seven Trails West* (1996) and George R. Stewart, *The California Trail* (1962). See also Howard Thomas, *Sierra Crossing: First Roads to California* (1998) and Greg MacGregor, *Overland: The California Emigrant Trail of 1841–1870* (1996), which features excellent photos and maps. See also Patricia Etter, *To California on the Southern Route* (1998). First generation pioneers are the subject of Ronald Woolsey, *Migrants West* (1996). Jesuit travelers out west are chronicled in Gerald McKeritt's *Brokers of Culture … 1848–1919* (2007).

CHAPTER THIRTEEN

AMERICAN CONQUEST

American sentiment for the acquisition of faroff California had deep political roots. By the 1820s, Spain's province was being described in the United States as "a plum ready to be plucked." Both its rancheros and missionaries resented the arrival there of a succession of mostly arrogant Mexican governors who enforced Mexico's regulations, including unpopular import tariffs. As early as 1829, U.S. President Andrew Jackson sent Anthony Butler as his envoy into Mexico in order to negotiate the potential purchase of California, Texas, and New Mexico. Butler's arrogant suggestion of a bribe to facilitate U.S. acquisition of the territory deeply offended the Mexicans, and he was forced to return home in disgrace.

The idea of adding California to U.S. territory, however, was never abandoned by President Jackson, nor by his successors, Van Buren, Tyler, and Polk. Lax Mexican control over California made it plausible that the province might fall into the hands of some European power. The strategic location of San Francisco Bay alone, with its matchless harbor and rich surrounding countryside, greatly increased American enthusiasm for the annexation of California.

Although the Russians had, by 1842, withdrawn from their Fort Ross trading post, leaders of other countries, including even far-off Prussia, had expressed interest in the province. The French, after the exploratory voyages of La Pérouse and Duflot de Mofras, spoke of establishing a protectorate over California. England, too, coveted control over Oregon and Texas as well. James Alexander Forbes, the British Consul at Monterey, suggested to his Foreign Office that the province might easily be acquired. The Californians became even more apprehensive at the news that an Irish Catholic priest, Father Eugene McNamara, planned to establish a colony of 1,000 Irish and English Catholics in the San Francisco Bay area. This venture, however, never materialized.

John Charles Frémont (1813–1890), known as "The Great Pathfinder," was a renowned explorer, surveyor, and Civil War general. Library of Congress, LC-DIG-ppmsca-03210.

Increasing U.S. involvement in California stultified all such foreign plans. The year 1844 saw the election of James K. Polk as President of the United States, an executive who already had committed himself to a popular expansionist policy. He had sent John Slidell, yet another envoy, to Mexico in order to renew negotiations regarding the possibility of purchasing what would become the American Southwest. In California, President Polk relied upon an alert consul at Monterey, Thomas Oliver Larkin, to prepare the groundwork for a peaceful American penetration of the province. But on April 15, 1846, following a dispute with Mexico over its border with Texas, President Polk's administration requested a declaration of war from the U.S. Congress. During the next month, U.S. Army General Zachary Taylor boldly led his troops across the border into Mexico.

Meanwhile, the young explorer Frémont, aware that a war with Mexico over territorial conflicts in the Southwest was possible, had left St. Louis in May 1845 on his third western expedition. Its stated purpose, further exploration of the Great Basin and the Pacific Coast, was hardly likely to relieve tension between the two countries. With a party of sixty-two soldiers, scouts, topographers, and six Delaware Indians, Frémont again crossed the Sierra crest to Sutter's Fort, reaching California on December 9, 1845. This time he traveled as far as Monterey, where he held a conference with Consul Thomas Oliver Larkin. José Castro, commander of the garrison at the capital city, was suspicious of the motives that had brought Frémont west. Castro gave the expedition permission to winter in California, with the understanding that Frémont would keep his men away from all coastal settlements.

In early March 1846, Frémont demonstrated his typical flair for the dramatic. He boldly withdrew toward a bluff named Gavilan, or Hawk's Peak, where he built a log fortification overlooking the Salinas Valley, only twenty-five miles from Monterey. Even after a warning from Castro, he raised the American flag, as if to defy his expulsion from the province. At first, Frémont ignored the possibility of trouble. Then the arrival of a warning letter from Consul Larkin, and the realization that Castro seemed

to be preparing to dislodge him by force, persuaded Frémont to vacate Hawk's Peak "slowly and growlingly." He next moved his men northward toward the wilds of Oregon. Frémont's rashness embarrassed Larkin and other American residents, who had hoped for a U.S. annexation of California by quiet, behind-the-scenes contacts. Castro, in particular, was outraged by Fremont's occupation of Hawk's Peak.

On their way north, Frémont's group were overtaken by Lieutenant Archibald Gillespie, a U.S. Marine Corps officer who had crossed through Mexico in disguise. Gillespie produced secret messages from officials in Washington, including Secretary of State James Buchanan, as well as from Frémont's wife, Jessie Benton, and her father, the bombastic expansionist senator, Thomas Hart Benton. Gillespie's dispatches probably warned

Frémont that war with Mexico was likely and directed him to cooperate with land and naval forces of the United States should a conflict break out. About such a volatile situation, Frémont later wrote: "I was to act, discreetly but positively." Yet, most historians have strongly criticized his subsequent actions as lacking in either discretion or tact. His role had suddenly changed from that of explorer to soldier.

As Frémont approached the Marysville (today's Sutter) Buttes north of Sutter's Fort, a number of upset Americans flocked into his camp. Believing that Castro had received orders from Mexico City to burn out such American settlers, they formed a group that came to be called the "Bear Flaggers." These Americans had also heard the rumors of the approaching war between the United States and Mexico. As a member of the U.S. Army's Topographical Corps of Engineers, Frémont had no instructions to support a revolt among Americans in California. Yet his very presence encouraged a plot to capture General Mariano Guadalupe Vallejo at Sonoma. Though Vallejo was a supporter of Americans in California, at dawn on June 14, 1846, a group of "the Bears" smashed their way into his home, routing the general from his bed, and proceeded to help themselves to his brandy. Their boisterous behavior deeply offended the Vallejo household. "To whom shall we surrender?" asked the general's wife, unable to comprehend such commotion. After forcing the humiliated general to sign some vague articles of defeat, the Bear Flaggers placed him under arrest. Next they took him to Sutter's Fort, which further embarrassed its Swiss owner.

Frémont's role in the Bear Flag Revolt was ambivalent, for he uncharacteristically stayed on the sidelines. It was William Ide, a local American, who led this incipient revolt. His followers hastily fashioned a rough flag with a grizzly bear on it to identify their movement. On the day the Bear Flaggers captured Sonoma, they proudly raised their new red and white banner over its central plaza. On that flag a grizzly bear, California'a fiercest animal, faced toward a red star. Under this image the framers of this crude ensign wrote: "A bear stands his ground always, and as long as the stars shine, we stand for the cause." They then pronounced the institution of a nonexistent "California Republic." The Bear Flaggers would have liked to use the Stars and Stripes as their emblem, but Frémont, although sympathetic to their cause, urged them not to do so.

The Bears next fought one short skirmish with native Californios at the so-called Battle of Olompali. This was a relatively unimportant affair that mainly served to bolster the rebels' morale. The Bear Flag Revolt, an extra-legal event, came to a sudden halt when U.S. naval forces captured Monterey on July 7, 1846, and raised the American flag. With the Bear

Flag movement nullified, Vallejo was at last released from imprisonment at Sutter's Fort.

Provincial pride and historical romanticism have created the legend that the Bear Flaggers produced an independent California, which then became part of the United States. Actually, this tiny uprising was of limited significance in the acquisition of California. The province's American conquest would surely have occurred anyway. On July 7, 1846, Commodore John Drake Sloat, commander of U.S. naval forces in Pacific waters, landed 250 marines and sailors at Monterey. A week later, the flag of the United States was flying at Yerba Buena, Sutter's Fort, Bodega Bay, and Sonoma. In fact, Sloat's landing prevented any further military actions by independents.

On July 15, Commodore Robert F. Stockton arrived at Monterey on the *USS Congress* to replace Sloat. Stockton, who threatened to march against "boasting and abusive" dissidents in the interior, was an even more forceful commander than Sloat. Now Stockton issued a proclamation officially organizing Frémont's volunteers into a unit called the California Battalion of Mounted Riflemen. Although himself a naval officer, Stockton suddenly promoted Frémont to the rank of an army major. Frémont then enlisted volunteers from among local settlers into his new unit. "We simply marched all over California, from Sonoma to San Diego," wrote John Bidwell, who had joined the battalion, afterward, adding: "We tried to find an enemy but could not." The California Battalion raised the flag unopposed almost everywhere it went. This was possible because Castro's active forces numbered scarcely 100 men, now disaffected and poorly armed. Despite this, the Californio boasted that if the Americans tried to march on Los Angeles "they would find their grave."

On August 13, 1846, Commodore Stockton's forces entered Los Angeles. Lieutenant Gillespie, the courier who had met Frémont with messages from Washington, was left in command there with a garrison of fifty men. By enforcing an unrealistic curfew, however, he angered the Angeleños. On September 23, the locals surrounded his small garrison on a hilltop in the middle of the pueblo. Besieged and short of water, Gillespie, under cover of darkness, secretly sent a messenger named Juan Flaco to Stockton for aid. The dispatch he carried was written on cigarette papers and concealed in his long hair. Pursued for miles by Californio horsemen, Flaco managed to outride them. After Stockton received the message of distress, he sent 350 sailors and marines to relieve Gillespie's tiny force.

These reinforcements arrived aboard the *USS Vandalia* under the command of Captain William Mervine, which dropped anchor at San Pedro, outside Los Angeles, on October 7, 1846. Mervine was almost too late, for Gillespie's hilltop position had become untenable. He had virtually surrendered to the Californios but, following a sort of truce, was allowed to retreat with his men to San Pedro. Upon reaching the port, Gillespie departed by sea. Before leaving, his men buried their casualties on a small island that came to be known as "Dead Man's Island."

After U.S. forces landed at San Pedro, a strange skirmish followed. This became known as "The Battle of the Old Woman's Gun." On the Dominguez Rancho a number of locals gathered on horseback, armed with sharp willow lances and smooth-bore carbines. Their most damaging weapon, however, was a four-pound cannon, an antique firearm that had been hidden by an old woman during the first American assault on Los Angeles. The cannon was lashed with leather *reatas* (thongs) to a mud-wagon, which the Californios whipped up and down a hillock, firing the cannon effectively enough to force the Americans to retreat to their ships. Though Lieutenant Gillespie had only narrowly escaped, for a time the territory south of Santa Barbara, including Los Angeles, was again temporarily in the hands of Castro's Californio forces.

At San Diego, as Commodore Stockton planned to retake Los Angeles, he received an important message that modified the military situation in California: this was a desperate dispatch from General Stephen Watts Kearny. The War Department had ordered Kearny to proceed overland with an "Army of the West" from Fort Leavenworth, Kansas, to pacify New Mexico and proceed to California to set up a government there. As Kearny moved westward from Santa Fe, he ran into Kit Carson. Carson was at the very moment relaying some dispatches from Commodore Stockton eastward to Washington. He mistakenly told General Kearny that the American flag was already proudly flown throughout California.

Not knowing that renewed fighting had broken out near Los Angeles, Kearny sent most of his force back to Santa Fe, continuing himself onward with only 100 dragoons and two small howitzers. This was a grave mistake. Because Carson was such an experienced guide, Kearny ordered Carson to turn around and return westward with him. The general sent Stockton's dispatches back to Washington with one of his own scouts, the mountain man Thomas Fitzpatrick.

On December 5, 1846, northeast of San Diego, General Kearny ran into a hornet's nest. More than 150 armed Californios under Andrés Pico, Pío Pico's brother, were encamped at San Pascual (near present-day Escondido). During a cold rainstorm, the Californios charged Kearny's forces. The Americans, their ammunition and powder wet, tried to beat off the onslaught by hand-to-hand combat during which twenty-two Americans died. Kearny's tired and bony army mules were no match for the quick

Los Angeles, 1857. From a contemporary print. Courtesy Andrew Rolle.

California ponies whose riders made deadly use of their sharp willow lances. The Americans, armed with only short sabres, could barely defend themselves against their fleet opponents. The general soon found himself on a hilltop near the San Bernardo Rancho surrounded by hostile forces. With their powder still damp and their supplies dangerously low, Kearny's tired dragoons subsisted for four days on half-roasted and smelly mule flesh, their water in scant supply. Though exhausted, their spirits soared after the arrival of 200 rescuing sailors and marines that Commodore Stockton had dispatched from San Diego.

General Kearny had suffered a humiliating defeat at what became known as the Battle of San Pascual. He was grateful indeed that Stockton had relieved his tattered forces. After Pico's men finally withdrew, Kearny resumed his march toward San Diego. After resting there, the general joined Stockton's forces on a northward march. With 600 army dragoons, marines, and sailors, they left San Diego to retake Los Angeles. At the same time, Frémont, on his way down the coast from Monterey with 400 volunteers, was also nearing that pueblo. Hoping to enter Los Angeles from the south, Kearny and Stockton met no real opposition until they reached the muddy banks of the San Gabriel River outside Los Angeles. Meanwhile, General José María Flores hoped to surprise the Americans with a final cavalry charge along the northern bank of the river. Nonetheless, Kearny and Stockton succeeded in fording the stream. Several days later, on January 10, 1847, at the Cañada de los Alisos, near the town's future stockyards, the Americans and the Californios fought a skirmish called the Battle of La Mesa. Although of slight importance, it did confirm the American recapture of Los Angeles. At its plaza, Lieutenant

Gillespie joined in the ceremony to hoist the American flag he had been compelled to haul down the previous September.

On January 13, 1847, Stockton and Kearny were taken aback when Andrés Pico stated that he would prefer to surrender to Frémont, who had moved into the San Fernando Valley just north of the pueblo. Meanwhile, his brother, Pío Pico, the last Mexican governor of California, had fled to the Mexican state of Sonora. Frémont, now being called a lieutenant colonel, clearly acted over the head of Kearny, a brigadier general, when he pardoned Andrés Pico and other Californios. The generous peace treaty that Frémont concluded with them became known as the Cahuenga Capitulation. Frémont was considered a fellow Latino by those Californios caught on both sides of the unwanted conflict.

An American settler whose loyalties were also split was Isaac Williams, who had married a local girl, Maria de Jesus Lugo. Her father, a land baron, had presented the couple with a 22,000-acre rancho. Williams, by purchase, had added another 13,000 acres to the spread. When this property was attacked, he actually begged for help from Mexican forces. During the nearby battle of Chino, part of his hacienda caught fire. Williams and his children climbed onto the roof, waved a white flag, and pleaded for mercy. Both the Americans and Mexicans subsequently labeled him a coward, even a traitor to the United States.

Meanwhile, a conflict in orders from the Navy and War Departments had led to a three-way quarrel over which of California's conquerors commanded the 1,000 or more U.S. servicemen under them at Los Angeles. General Kearny quite rightly considered himself the ranking U.S. commander in California. But Commodore Stockton had confusingly decided to relinquish his authority in favor of Frémont in order to travel back to Washington, DC. This left General Kearny and Frémont to fight it out over who would govern California. Ultimately, the general prepared court-martial charges against the unbending Frémont. Their animosity toward one another led to a long military trial following the War with Mexico.

That conflict officially ended with the signing of the Treaty of Guadalupe Hidalgo on February 2, 1848. A new southwestern boundary now gave the United States all of Upper California as well as New Mexico and a greatly enlarged Texas. Residents thereafter had the option of becoming American citizens. The U.S. government agreed to pay Mexico $15 million for land that had already been conquered.

Although the immediate political future of California remained unsettled, its control was no longer in the hands of Latino leaders. Despite having been conquered by "Los Yanquis," the Hispanic tradition remained so strong that, in some homes, the speaking of English was forbidden.

More than a few Californios were never reconciled to being ruled by their American conquerors. But, having finally expanded across the breadth of the continent, the Americans were in California to stay.

SELECTED READINGS

Regarding the last days of Mexican rule, see George Tays, "Pio Pico's Correspondence with the Mexican Government, 1846–1848," *California Historical Society Quarterly* 13 (March 1934), 99–149. Concerning the acquisition of California, the earliest nonheroic study was Robert G. Cleland, *The Early Sentiment for the Annexation of California* (Austin, 1915). See also Paul Bergeron, *The Presidency of James K. Polk* (1987); Charles Sellers, *James K. Polk* (2 vols. 1957–66); also Allan Nevins, ed., *Polk: The Diary of a President* (1929).

On Frémont in California, see Allan Nevins, ed., *Narratives of Exploration and Adventure* (1956) and his *Frémont: Pathmarker of the West* (1939); Cardinal L. Goodwin, *John Charles Frémont: An Exploration of His Career* (1930) is dated and strongly negative. For an opposite viewpoint by Frémont's powerful father-in-law, consult *Thirty Years View* (1854–56). Andrew Rolle, *John Charles Frémont: Character as Destiny* (1991) is an appraisal of both his strengths and emotional shortcomings. See also *Proceedings of the Court Martial in the Trial of (J. C.) Frémont* (1848).

The Bear Flag Revolt appears in Fred B. Rogers, *Bear Flag Lieutenant: The Life Story of Henry L. Ford* (1951); also see the reprint of Simeon Ide, *A Biographical Sketch of William B. Ide* (1967). General Kearny's march westward is detailed in Dwight Clarke, *Stephen Watts Kearny, Soldier of the West* (1961); William H. Emory, *Notes of a Military Reconnaissance* (1848); Joseph Warren Revere, *A Tour of Duty in California* (1849); Arthur Woodward, *Lances at San Pascual* (1948); Philip St. George Cooke, *The Conquest of New Mexico and California* (1878).

On the War with Mexico, see Neal Harlow, *California Conquered: War and Peace in the Pacific, 1846–1850* (1982); Justin H. Smith, *The War with Mexico* (2 vols. 1919); Glenn W. Price, *Origins of the War with Mexico:, The Polk-Stockton Intrigue* (1967); Edwin A. Sherman, *The Life of the Late Rear Admiral John Drake Sloat* (1902); Gene A. Smith, *Thomas Ap Catesby Jones, Commodore of Manifest Destiny* (2000); Samuel Bayard, *A Sketch of the Life of Com. Robert F. Stockton* (1856); Harlan Hague and David J. Langum, *Thomas O. Larkin: A Life of Patriotism and Profit* (1990); Fred B. Rogers, *Montgomery and the Portsmouth* (1959); Werner H. Marti, *Messenger of Destiny: The California Adventures of Archibald H. Gillespie* (1960). See also Theodore Grivas, *Military Governments in California* (1963).

CHAPTER FOURTEEN

GOLD

The American conquest of California was soon followed by a world-class event that would forever shape the future of the province. On January 24, 1848, James Wilson Marshall, a Scotsman from New Jersey, was busy supervising some day laborers. An impressive figure, dressed in buckskin and a bright Mexican serape, he ordered them to dig a millrace along some mud flats on the south fork of the American River. His plan was to divert water in order to run Johann Sutter's new sawmill. The Indians called this location *Collomah* (today's Coloma). Marshall recalled that "my eye was caught by something *shining* in the bottom of the ditch." He bit into a flake of shining metal. It was soft, even after he hit with a hammer. Instead of fragmenting, the metal flattened out. He gathered up other nugget and flake samples. Back at New Helvetia he and Sutter tested them chemically with Aqua Fortis. This confirmed that they were real gold.

Neither man yet realized that Marshall had discovered a new El Dorado. This was not, however, the first discovery of California gold. Years earlier, some mission Indians had unearthed small quantities of the metal. When they brought the gold to the padres, the friars cautioned them not to divulge the location of their discovery. The missionaries did not want to see the province inundated by money-mad foreigners.

Later, in 1842, along southern California's San Feliciano Canyon, inland near today's Newhall, Francisco Lopez, who lived nearby, used a sheaf knife to dig up some wild onions. When he pulled the plants from the ground, he noticed bright yellow flakes clinging to their roots. It too was gold. After nearby settlers heard the news, several hundred of them headed up the canyon. The American trader Abel Stearns sent twenty ounces of the metal they brought out from Los Angeles to the Phildelphia mint. Unfortunately, the San Feliciano lode "played out" within only a few months.

Then came the greatest of all gold discoveries. The principal figure in this event was clearly Marshall. Back in 1844, equipped with only a flintlock rifle and training as a coach and wagon builder, he had arrived in California by emigrant train. He bought a small plot of land near Little Butte Creek, where he raised a few cattle and also built and repaired spinning wheels, plows, ox yokes, and carts. In 1846, after participating in a campaign against the Mokelumne Indians, Marshall joined the Bear Flag insurgents. He next enlisted in Frémont's California Battalion. After the American conquest, Marshall ended up at Sutter's Fort, "barefooted and in a very sorry plight." Nearly all his livestock had strayed from his ranch or been stolen. Like many former California combatants, Marshall had received no compensation for his volunteer war services.

Meanwhile, Sutter's community, clustered around his fort, had experienced an influx of other American settlers. Demand for lumber increased. Desiring to expand his operations, Sutter had originally sent Marshall out to search for new stands of timber and a suitable location for the saw and flour mill. Then Marshall saw the gold. Once both men realized the enormity of the their find, they hoped to keep it a secret, so as not to upset the routine at Sutter's Fort.

But their discovery was too great, and news of it impossible to contain. Sutter's diary tells us that, by early March, he quite suddenly lost most of his workmen, who "left for washing and digging gold." He complained that "they left me sick and lame behind." His business operations were headed for ruination. Sutter recorded that his Indian workers were "impatient to run" toward the gold streams of the Sierra. An entire year's wheat crop lay unharvested in his fields. Furthermore, Sutter could find no one to operate his new mill.

Meanwhile, Sam Brannan, the apostate Mormon who had refused to join Brigham Young's colony in today's Utah, had become a merchant at Sutter's Fort. Unwittingly, he would further damage Sutter. Hoping to do business with future miners, Brannan galloped off toward San Francisco, clutching a medicine bottle filled with gold dust and nuggets. As he rode along the unpaved streets of the city he shouted "Gold! Gold! Gold from the American River!" He swung his hat wildly with one hand and waved the bright gold bottle in the other.

A great human tide surged toward the icy streams of the Sierra in quest of riches. As labor costs along the California coastline soared, local businesses stopped operating. Some 500 sailing vessels soon lay abandoned in San Francisco Bay; both their crews and passengers rushed inland in search of gold. Soldiers too absconded for the gold fields. Amidst all this hysteria, San Francisco's newspaper, the *Californian*, suspended

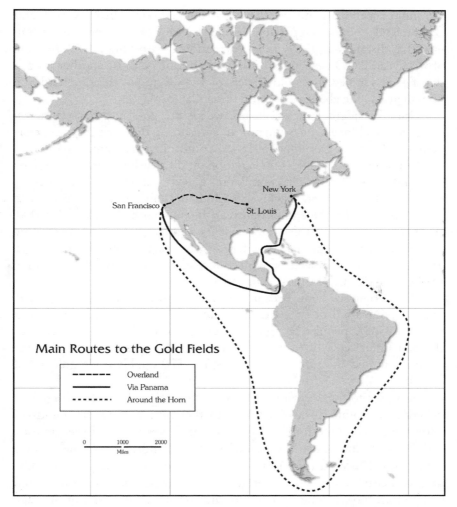

Main Routes to the Gold Fields

- - - - - -	Overland
————	Via Panama
· - · - · - ·	Around the Horn

New York

San Francisco

St. Louis

0   1000   2000
Miles

publication on May 29, 1848, announcing that most of its subscribers had left town, not bothering to pay their bills for lodging or supplies.

At Monterey, Consul Thomas Oliver Larkin bitterly lamented his town's depopulation as well. "Every bowl, tray, and warming pan has gone to the mines," he wrote. Shovels and pick axes were especially hard to find. Walter Colton, a U.S. naval chaplain, wrote that "the gold mines have upset all social and domestic arrangements in Monterey. Even the millionaire is obliged to groom his own horse and wheel his own wheelbarrow."

Within a few months, word of the California gold find reached every part of the globe. Exaggeration of the riches the Sierra held became so feverishly wild that one writer remarked: "A grain of gold taken from the mine became a pennyweight at Panama, an ounce in New York and Boston, and a pound nugget at London." By May of 1848, gold was being mined at distances of thirty miles surrounding Sutter's new mill. By June of that year, 2,000 men were busily digging for gold. In another month that figure doubled. The gold seekers of 1848 were but the vanguard of a human avalanche about to descend upon California.

Once President James Polk learned of the gold discovery in newly conquered California, he could not resist inserting the news into his presidential message of December 5, 1848. Confirming that rumors of gold in California were true, Polk's proclamation set off a rush to San Francisco by land and by sea. California's population quickly ballooned. At the beginning of 1849 there were, exclusive of Indians, only some 26,000 persons in the province. By the end of that year the number had reached 115,000. Approximately half of the adult residents were engaged in mining. Some 20,000 foreign immigrants arrived, mostly by sea, from all over the world. The Chinese outnumbered any other foreign group. They would become the backbone of California's labor force.

San Francisco soon became the fastest growing city in the world. From a population of only 812 in March of 1848, it grew into a boom town of 25,000 people. To process hundreds of small sacks of gold dust, the San Francisco Mint was established. In 1854, its first year of operation, it minted the rarest of all coins, the $20 double eagle gold-proof "S Mint."

Sacramento's waterfront, west of Sutter's Fort, became an agitated debarkation point. Located enroute to the mining areas, thousands of adventurers left there for the diggings. The routes the gold seekers took varied. Most Americans who headed west to California took one of three main routes: "around the Horn" of South America; "by way of the Isthmus" of Central America; or overland "across the plains." The route around Cape Horn took as long as nine months; the actual rounding of the cape being particularly hazardous. Some vessels took weeks to break through the choppy, fogbound Straits of Magellan. Not all of the sailing vessels, especially those of light tonnage, were seaworthy. Passengers had to endure both monotony and seasickness on the trip. On the Fourth of July, aboard the ship *Rising Sun*, its crew boisterously celebrated clearing Cape Horn. They blew bugles, played martial music, and recited the Declaration of Independence. After speeches, a special dinner was served consisting of roast goose, plum pudding, mince pies, figs, and assorted nuts.

Because the lack of exercise on board softened up the thousands of travelers who rounded the Horn, this became known as the "whitecollar sea route." More pointedly, these passengers were often merchants, lawyers, or doctors—not workingmen. Sometimes they were fortunate enough to book a place aboard a ship scheduled to make South American landfalls enroute, either at Rio de Janeiro, Buenos Aires, Santiago, or Callao.

Others arrived in California by crossing the Isthmus of Panama or Nicaragua. This route was the quickest, if not the most comfortable, of the principal routes. The voyage from New York to the Panama Coast was 2,500 miles; the trip across the Isthmus another sixty miles. This is where travel conditions grew unpleasant and even dangerous. Malarial fever was prevalent in all parts of Central America, as were, cholera, dysentery, and yellow fever. Part of the isthmus crossing entailed travel through swamps in long canoes poled or paddled by native boatmen. Some passengers took along a carbine, camping equipment, and a watertight bag in which to stow medicine and clothing. Then these travelers had to go overland, usually on mule back, to reach the Pacific side of the isthmus.

Once there, a shortage of coastal vessels might stretch one's stay in this unhealthy place into months. Now came a second ocean trip, 3,500 miles up the Pacific coast to San Francisco Bay. Most of the vessels providing this service offered wretched accommodations. The food was vile and the water supplies often brackish. Pacific Mail Steamship Company ships, powered by steam, began only gradually to supplement the service offered by worm-eaten and leaky sailing vessels.

About 10,000 persons chose an extreme southern route. Their journey began with a sea voyage of eighteen days from New Orleans to Vera Cruz in Mexico. Then they rode horseback 280 miles to Mexico City, which consumed an additional nine days. Next, the travelers had to continue onward to Mazatlan, some 900 miles, or twenty days of additional travel. The journey concluded with a second sea voyage to San Francisco that took as many as thirty-five days. The total travel time from New York to California frequently lasted a tedious four months.

Even more than the clipper ship or steamer, the covered wagon, or "prairie schooner," symbolized the vast American population movement during the Gold Rush. The favorite overland trail was a northern route leading west from St. Louis through South Pass in the Rocky Mountains. In the year 1849 alone, 30,000 "forty-niners" used this trail. A southern route proceeded over the Santa Fe Trail, which ran from Westport (later Kansas City). This path followed the Gila River to the Colorado River, finally crossing the desert into southern California.

With luck, the 2,000 miles to the gold fields on overland routes could be covered in 100 days. Fortunate parties might trundle along some eighteen miles from sun up to sun down. Caravans included as many as twenty-six covered wagons. Usually each was drawn by five yoke of oxen or a span of ten mules. Regardless of the number of wagons, every overland group faced dangerous river fordings. Scarce food supplies had to be carefully hoarded, and the wagons guarded against Indian attack. Therefore, delays in the trip were inevitable. A wagon had to be unloaded and reloaded several times in a single day to cross rough terrain and swollen streams. Some travelers, overloaded with household belongings, left stores and farm implements behind on the prairies.

Among the most tragic of all pioneer experiences were those encountered by the comparatively few overlanders whose fate led them into torrid Death Valley, 110 feet below sea level, a "seventy-five mile strip of perdition" across which ferociously hot winds drove the stinging sands. The blinding glare of the sun parched the skin and induced in travelers a feverish, half-crazed state.

During 1848–49, a party led by William Lewis Manly from Vermont encountered innumerable delays, making it impossible for them to reach the Sierra in time to avoid the fall snows. Near the Salt Lake, Manly's little band was overjoyed to join forces with another group headed by Asabel Bennett, an acquaintance of Manly. Because it was late in the season, they dreaded facing the same fateful plight as the Donner Party in the Sierra Nevada's winter snows. The Bennett-Manly group, therefore, decided to take a longer and supposedly safer route into southern California. From there they hoped to travel northward to the gold mines. However, the unfortunate group was soon lost, wandering through a seemingly endless sea of hot sand. In the distance the thirteen men, three women, and six children could see the Panamint Mountains, their summits white with snow. Again and again they tried to escape from their camp near Furnace Creek. Although they did find a few brackish water holes, their scarce supplies were fast running out. One after another, their oxen had to be killed for food.

As these pioneers dipped into their last sacks of flour, Bennett proposed that Manly and John Rogers, the strongest of the men, go ahead on foot to seek help. The main party was to await their return from the California settlements with supplies. Manly and his men struck out toward the Panamints. Reaching Walker Pass, they crossed the southern Sierra range. After fourteen days, they luckily reached Mission San Fernando.

There they obtained supplies and pack animals. Twenty-six days later, when they finally returned to the desert camp, the remaining survivors were so weak that Manly and Rogers moved within a hundred yards of the wagons without seeing any sign of life. After they fired a rifle shot, one man crawled out from under a wagon. Manly later wrote: "He threw up his arms high over his head and shouted 'The boys have come! The boys have come!'" But among those huddled under the wagons, Rogers and

The "Devil's Golf Course" is what remains of Death Valley's last lake, which disappeared over 2,000 years ago. The terrain is formed as water rises up through underlying muds and evaporates, leaving pinnacles of salt behind. Devil's Golf Course, Death Valley, California. © Terry Ryder/Dreamstime.com.

Manly found only a few survivors huddled under their wagons. Manly recalled that one of them, Mrs. Bennett, "fell down on her knees and clung to me like a maniac."

About the first of February in 1850, the little band finally escaped from Death Valley. Abandoning their wagons and most of their remaining equipment, they crept along the eastern Sierra slope. They moved through Red Rock Canyon and crossed the bed of the shallow Mojave River. By the time the bedraggled group finally reached Rancho San Francisco in southern California, they had spent an entire year on their journey west, yet were still more than 500 miles from the mines! Their story, as told by Manly in his book, *Death Valley in '49*, remains a classic account of western history.

California's placer camps, however, hardly resembled the paradise envisioned by gold seekers. Mining was dirty, strenuous work, and comforts and conveniences in the field were practically nonexistent. Most "claims" lay along the banks of streams, where thousands of persons crowded in trying to strike "pay dirt." Miners worked both "dry diggings" in flats and gullies and "wet diggings" along sand bars or swift streambeds. In either case, the chances of finding a rivulet laden with gold-bearing gravels were relatively slim.

For washing gold ore, panning was the simplest method. The sifting pan was made of tin or sheet iron, with a flat bottom and sides angled at forty-five degrees. The lonely prospector, gold pan in hand, his meager supplies loaded on the back of a donkey, became symbolic of the Gold Rush. But miners brought a variety of gadgets with them. Some utilized the "Long Tom," or "Rocker," an elongated wooden trough much easier to use than a simple pan. The most effective mining involved the use of elaborate sluice and waterwheel systems, including "flumes," or open ditches constructed of boards, and later of iron pipes. Lighter gravel running through the chutes was washed away by the action of stream water. With luck, the heavier gold was captured, then dried out and bagged in tiny cotton sacks.

California's principal ore-bearing region, known as the Mother Lode, was divided into the Northern and the Southern Mines. This area spanned seventy miles from Mariposa on the south to Amador on the north. The northern mines included the American River and its forks, as well as the Cosumnes, the Bear, the Yuba, and the Feather Rivers. Sacramento was the chief depot for provisioning the north. The Southern Mines, with Stockton as its headquarters, included camps lying below the Mokelumne River and the Calaveras, the Stanislaus, the Tuolomne, the Merced, and mountainous portions of the mighty San Joaquin.

Picturesque place names were applied to the makeshift towns that mushroomed in the mining regions. These included Git-up-and-Git, Lazy Man's Canyon, Wildcat Bar, Skunk Gulch, Gospel Swamp, Whisky Bar, Shinbone Peak, Humpback Slide, Bogus Thunder, Hell's Delight, Poker Flat, Ground Hog Glory, Delirium Tremens, Murderers Bar, Hangtown (later Placerville), and *Agua Fria* (cold water). Hangtown was so named because of a brutal lynching there in 1849.

Miners lived a rough-and-tumble life. As long as a lode held out, those at the mining camps felt few restraints. Nevertheless, charges of claim jumping have been greatly exaggerated, as has the lawlessness of life in the diggings. Most prospectors were law-abiding. While they awaited the arrival of a regular legal system, the miners drew up "district rules," which they themselves enforced. The miners judged criminal offenses individually before makeshift courts, which meted out such penalties as ear cropping, whipping, branding, and even hanging. This extralegal justice involved some abuses, but it discouraged crime. This was the beginning of vigilantism.

The ratio of men to women in the gold fields was approximately twenty to one. Within six months after arrival, one-fifth of the men were dead.

Some perished because of laboring in the frigid rivers and due to deplorable sanitary conditions in the mining camps and shanty towns. Others died as the result of too much liquor or via homicidal disputes. In this predominantly male society, prostitutes were in great demand.

Despite the rowdy environment, miners practiced a certain fellowship in their tents and crude dugouts. Sundays were both a day of rest and the day on which one did the week's washing, baking, or mending. Those with wives and children back home wrote letters. Idle time was enlivened by swapping yarns or drinking and gambling.

The bleak days that prospectors spent grubbing for wealth made them especially appreciative of the traveling performers who stopped in many a mining town. Prominent among them were Lotta Crabtree, Edwin Booth, and the internationally popular Lola Montez. A more frequent means of entertainment for lonesome men was singing in groups from a booklet entitled *Put's California Songster.* The lyrics of mining-camp songs were usually set to such well-known airs as "Pop Goes the Weasel" or "Ben Bolt."

"A Sunday's Amusement in the Mines," 1848–49, from a contemporary print. Robert B. Honeyman, Jr. Collection of Early Californian and Western American Pictorial Material, courtesy of The Bancroft Library, University of California, Berkeley.

No song, however, equaled "The California Emigrant" in popularity. Its chorus was set to the tune of "Oh! Susannah!"

> Oh! California!
> That's the land for me,
> I'm going to Sacramento
> With my washbowl on my knee!

A naughtier aire, sung to the tune of "New York Gals," was retitled "Hangtown Gals":

> Hangtown gals are plump and rosy,
> Hair in ringlets mighty cosy;
> Painted cheeks and gassy bonnets;
> Touch them and they'll sting like hornets.
> CHORUS
> Hangtown gals are lovely creatures,
> Think they'll marry Mormon preachers
> Heads thrown back to show their features.
> Ha, ha, ha! Hangtown gals.
> They're dreadful forty-niners,
> Turn their noses up at miners;
> Shocked to hear them say "gol durn it."
> Try to blush, but cannot come it!
> CHORUS
> Hangtown gals are lovely creatures. [repeated]

Pioneer women were only occasionally acclaimed, as in the song "Sweet Betsy From Pike":

> They swam the wide rivers and crossed the tall peaks,
> And camped on the prairie for weeks upon weeks.
> Starvation and cholera and hard work and slaughter,
> They reached California, spite hell and high water.

Sarah Royce was one of these frontier women. Highly literate, this mother of the future Harvard philosopher Josiah Royce, encountered a hard and scarcely rewarding life in the Far West. In 1849, another pioneer was Mary Bennett Ritter, one of the first physicians and probably the first American woman to come to California via Panama. She recalled that when she arrived, "there were from ten to forty men to be cooked for, beside the general housework, the washing and ironing, the churning, bread making and sewing for four children—plus making my father's shirts and

Broadside advertisement of the Mormon Island Emporium in the California mines, 1848–49. Such stores also served as mail, express, and banking centers. Courtesy of the Huntington Library, San Marino, California.

underwear." Ritter and her mother heated the water for Saturday night baths and made their own soap and candles. All these workaday chores gave rise to yet another song about women:

> There's too much of worriment that goes in a bonnet.
> There's too much of ironing that goes in a shirt.
> There's nothing that pays for the time you waste on it.

A woman's view of the gold rush was far different from that of men. Sarah Haight, seeing the environmental damage wrought by mining, wrote in her diary: "How unsightly it makes the country appear. How few flowers and how little vegetation there is where there is gold . . . How often its blighting effects are on the human heart."

The small savings of most miners were quickly used up. Each was lucky if he earned $100 in a month. This was a skimpy return for the extreme hardships and high cost of staying healthy amid the dampness. Occasionally a miner struck it rich. One man scooped up two and a half pounds of gold in only fifteen minutes, which he sold for a then astounding $16 per ounce.

Due to the gold boom, however, consumer prices in northern California were fantastically high as compared to those in the eastern United States, where money had many times today's purchasing power. In San Francisco, copies of eastern newspapers were grabbed up at $1 apiece. A loaf of bread, which cost 4 or 5 cents on the Atlantic seaboard, sold for 50 or 75 cents. Kentucky bourbon whiskey leaped to $30 a quart; apples sold for $1 to $5 apiece, eggs for $50 a dozen (one boiled egg in a restaurant cost as much as $5), and coffee for $5 a pound. Sacramento merchants sold butcher knives for $30 each, blankets for $40, boots for $100 a pair, and tacks to nail flapping canvas tents for as much as $192 a pound. Medicine cost $10 a pill, or $1 a drop. In Stockton or Sacramento, a hotel room cost as much as $1,000 per month, then a tremendous sum back home.

Heaps of gold dust, usually stored in doeskin bags, piled up in San Francisco's safes. The eastern journalist Bayard Taylor complained: "You enter a shop to buy something; the owner eyes you with a perfect indifference. If you object to the price, you are at liberty to leave, for you need not expect to get it cheaper; he evidently cares little if you buy it or not." The merchant firm of Mellus and Howard was "so surrounded with piles of gold dust and receiving such enormous rents from their landed property . . . that they consider 10 to 12 thousand dollars for discharging a ship a mere flea bite."

By the early 1850s, much of the loose ore had been panned out of California's stream beds. Miners who had lost their grubstakes headed back home. No longer could penniless diggers hope to wrest fortunes from California's rocks and cliffs with only a few simple tools and the sweat of their brow. Henceforth, technological innovations for more complex mining operations required heavy capital. The technique known as hydraulicking involved the use of canvas hoses and nozzles to wash away topsoil, making gold particles more accessible. Whole rivers were diverted and canyons stripped bare. In time, hundreds of miles of canals and flumes carried water through iron pipes to devices that could extract gold. Stamp mills then reduced tons of rock to powder ore. The days of pick, shovel, pan, and burro were clearly over. Now it was mining companies, rather than individual miners, who tunneled their way through bedrock.

Once the "easy pickings" drew to a close by the middle of the 1850s, discouraged prospectors left makeshift ghost towns behind and flocked into the cities, anxious to find any sort of work. Traveling theater troupes that had been able to charge as much as $55 for stall seats now played to almost empty houses. Merchants found it difficult to sell the expensive

"Long Nine" Havana cigars that had commanded high prices in boom days. In San Francisco and Sacramento, shopkeepers threw sacks of spoiled flour into the streets to help fill muddy holes; unsaleable cast-iron cookstoves were dismantled, their plates used as sidewalks. No longer did miners send out their laundry as far as Hawaii and even China.

A few of those who stayed on in California bought farm land that quickly rose in price. These lucky persons, including none other than John Bidwell, amassed the fortunes that had eluded them in the placers. Henry Mayo Newhall, who started out as an auctioneer on the San Francisco waterfront, bought up a number of ranches. He went on to found a great land company.

One of the worst results of the gold rush was despoilation of the natural environment. Hydraulic mining operations, practiced into the 1950s, wreaked serious havoc. Silted rivers and ruined farmlands provoked legal controversies for years on end. Today, as a result, millions of cubic yards of sediment remain in the Central Valley's streams and reservoirs, as well as in the clogged channels of the San Francisco–Delta water system. Mercury mined for gold recovery operations has since produced acidic drain waters loaded with heavy-metal deposits. These toxic pollutants include zinc, copper, lead, and cadmium.

Although California's first bonanza was seemingly over, the exciting gold rush had forever altered its future.

SELECTED READINGS

On mining in general, see Rodman Paul, *California Gold* (1947); Andrew Isenberg, *Mining California: An Ecological History* (2005); John Caughey, ed., *Gold Is the Cornerstone* (1948); Erwin Gudde, *Bigler's Chronicle of the West: The Conquest of California, Discovery of Gold, and Mormon Settlement* (1962); Kenneth N. Owens, ed., *John Sutter and the Wider West* (1994), also see Owens, ed., *Riches For All* (2002); also Alonzo Delano, *Life On the Plains and Among the Diggings* (1854); William Lewis Manly, *Death Valley in '49* (1924); Elza Edwards, *The Valley Whose Name is Death* (1940); Roy and Jean Johnson, eds., *Escape From Death Valley* (1987).

Recent scholarship includes books by Malcolm Rohrbaugh, *Days of Gold: The California Gold Rush and the American Nation* (1999); Mark Eifler, *Gold Rush Capitalists* (2002); Brian Roberts, *American Alchemy: The California Gold Rush and Middle Class Culture* (2000); Mary Hill, *Gold: The California Story* (1999); H. W. Brands, *The Age of Gold* (2002) and J. S. Holliday, *Rush For Riches: Gold Fever and the Making of California* (1999).

Ocean routes to the gold fields are described in James P. Delgado, *To California By Sea: A Maritime History of the California Gold Rush* (1990); Raymond Rydell, *Cape Horn to the Pacific* (1952); John H. Kemble, *The Panama Route* (1943); and Oscar Lewis, *Sea Routes to the Gold Fields* (1949). An original diary is Lucy Kendall Herrick, *Voyage to California Written at Sea* (1998).

Regarding overland trail conditions and legality in the diggings see John P. Reid, *Policing the Elephant* (1996); Charles H. Shinn, *Mining Camps: A Study of American Frontier Government* (1885); Bayard Taylor, *Eldorado, or Adventures in the Path of Empire* (2 vols. repr. 1949); Edwin Beilharz and Carlos Lopez, eds., *We Were '49ers: Chilean Accounts of the California Gold Rush* (1976); and Jo Ann Levy, *They Saw the Elephant: Women and the California Gold Rush* (1990).

Under the pseudonym "Dame Shirley," Louise Amelia Knapp Smith Clappe wrote *The Shirley Letters from the California Mines,* Carl I. Wheat, ed. (1949). Other accounts include E. Gould Buffum, *Six Months in the Gold Mines* (1850); Franklin A. Buck, *Yankee Trader in the Gold Rush* (1930); David M. Potter, ed., *Trail to California: The Overland Journal of Vincent Geiger and Wakeman Bryarly* (1945); Irene D. Paden, *In the Wake of the Prairie Schooner* (1943).

Mormons in the gold fields is the subject of Kenneth Owens, *Gold Rush Saints* (2004). See also Ralph P. Bieber, *Southern Trails to California in 1848* (1937) and his "California Gold Mania," Mississippi Valley Historical Review 35 (June 1948), 3–28; F. P. Wierzbicki, *California . . . A Guide to the Gold Region* (1933); George W. Groh, *Gold Fever* (1966) and James S. Holliday, *The World Rushed In* (1982). Finally, Gary Kurutz, *The California Gold Rush: A Descriptive Bibliography* (1997) summarizes scholarship in this field.

CHAPTER FIFTEEN

APPROACHES TO STATEHOOD

During the War with Mexico the invading Americans treated California as conquered territory, subject to the rule of U.S. military governors. Under international law, however, the province was entitled to retain its municipal institutions. Ideally, the American conquerors were to issue temporary laws and regulations, but this occurred only in part and very slowly.

The *alcaldes*, or pueblo mayors, a remnant of Mexican bureaucracy, also acted as principal judicial officers. Although they continued to perform some traditional functions, their authority became increasingly questionable. Walter Colton, the American naval chaplain who temporarily acted as alcalde of Monterey, referred to his position as a "guardian of the public peace." As the Americans succeeded Californio alcaldes, they superimposed upon that Mexican institution the common law brought west with them. United States law then began to supplant past procedures, providing such legal safeguards as trial by jury.

In 1847, American rule became confused over the controversy between Commodore Stockton and General Kearny as to their respective authority. Stockton had continued as military governor until, following the Cahuenga Capitulations, he appointed Frémont, who acted as California's governor for some fifty days. But instructions from Washington designated General Kearny as the senior officer in the newly conquered area. The general stoutly asserted supreme authority over California. When Frémont challenged Kearny's supremacy, the controversy led to Frémont's courtmartial in Washington. He was found guilty of disobedience, conduct prejudicial to military discipline, and even mutiny. Although President Polk set aside part of this verdict, Frémont angrily resigned his army commission. Soon he was back in California.

The state's new American residents now complained about those parts of Mexican law enforced by their military authorities. Frequent murmurings were heard over infringements upon self-government via civilian court procedures. When Colonel Richard Mason became the military governor, he encountered popular discontent. Nevertheless, he prepared a rigorous new code of laws for California. As immigration into the newly conquered province increased, discontent among its settlers grew. The Treaty of Guadalupe Hidalgo, ratified on May 20, 1848, concluded the War with Mexico and resulted in the final cession of California to the United States. Mason hoped that Congress would confer upon the future state's residents constitutional rights as U.S. citizens. Unfortunately, the political machinery for a civil territorial government was slow. Mason, in turn, was succeeded as military governor by General Persifor Smith.

California clearly needed permanent self-government. In San Francisco a rowdy and self-proclaimed "Legislative Assembly" refused to recognize military authority over that former pueblo, and they deposed a corrupt alcalde. A mass meeting also took place at San Jose. General Bennett Riley, yet another military governor, issued a proclamation that called for selection of delegates to a convention in order to form a state constitution and plan a government.

To prepare the transition to civilian government, President Zachary Taylor sent a prominent congressional leader, Thomas Butler King, to California as his personal agent. King was to sound out popular sentiment for the territory's admission into the Union. He stayed on as collector of the port of San Francisco in 1851 and later became its senatorial candidate.

On the opening days of September 1849, the state's first constitutional convention convened at Colton Hall, a newly constructed white building overlooking the town of Monterey. As its delegates met to write a state constitution, California would seek admission into the Union without yet being officially an American territory. Forty-eight men were sworn in as delegates to the constitutional convention. All of them were deeply interested in the future of California. Although none of the delegates was known nationally, they included old-time Californios as well as some of the first American settlers and "forty-niners," reflecting divergent backgrounds. The delegates were mostly young and flexible. Their average age was only thirty-six; the oldest delegate, José Antonio Carrillo, was fifty-three years old. There were few libraries to which the members of the convention could refer for precedent; probably not more than fifty volumes of law and history were to be found in the locality of Monterey. These books, however, included copies of other state constitutions already enacted.

The Californios, who numbered seven out of the forty-eight delegates, were shown special courtesies. General Vallejo, dignified and generally popular, would go on to become a member of the first California senate. Another Californio convention member, Pablo de la Guerra of Santa Barbara, had much in common with Vallejo. Both men had been prisoner of American troops during the conquest period; both were tolerant and reasonably well-educated. Other Latino delegates included Antonio Pico, Jacinto Rodriguez, Manuel Dominguez, J. M. Covarrubias, and a member of the well-known Carrillo family. The Swiss immigrant Johann Sutter had come to be regarded almost as an American. The most influential delegate was William Gwin, a southern politician who would later be elected to represent California in the U.S. Senate. Thomas O. Larkin, "first and last American consul to California," also lent his authority to solving complicated problems as the diverse group grappled to write the new document.

Because some miners refused to have slaves working beside them, they favored admission to the union as a free state. In addition to Gwin, other southerners had migrated to California. Many of these settled near Los Angeles, hoping that, somehow, slaves could be brought into a new American state. Southerners wanted to create two Californias, with slavery being permitted in the southern portion. Most delegates to the constitutional convention, however, were determined to make California a free state. Another debate concerned California's future boundaries, particularly its eastern border. Some thought the new state should embrace the vast desert area beyond the Sierra Nevada, even perhaps the Salt Lake Basin. The convention agreed upon a line of demarcation east of the Sierra crest. This made the state's new constitution more acceptable to the U.S. Congress.

On November 13, 1849, a month after the conventioners had completed their work, Californians cast bilingual ballots to overwhelmingly

The Great Seal of 1849. Containing the state's motto, "Eureka" ("I have found it!"), the design shows Minerva the goddess of wisdom surveying a California scene that includes a miner at work, ships in port, and a grizzly bear next to a luscious bunch of grapes. Shown is the original design by Robert S. Garnett, introduced to the 1849 state constitutional convention by Caleb Lyons. The 1937 version now serves as the state's current official seal.

approve their constitution. A salute of thirty-one guns was then fired at the Monterey Presidio in honor of the future state in the Union. After the cannonade ended, the crowd assembled outside Colton Hall to cheer and toss their hats in the air as California's newly adopted Great Seal was publicly displayed. This seal bears thirty-one stars, representing the states then in the Union. Minerva, sprung from the brow of Jupiter, is the foreground figure, symbolic of California's admission to the Union without having passed through territorial probation. A grizzly bear crouches at Minerva's feet; a miner, with rocker and bowl, depicts "the golden wealth of the Sacramento." Beyond a river, rises the Sierra Nevada range. At the top of the seal is the legend EUREKA, still the state's motto.

The Constitution of 1849 endured for thirty years as the fundamental law of a growing state. After Peter Burnett was elected the first civilian governor, General Riley, resigned his post. California was now in almost every respect a state, though not officially admitted to the Union. To address that issue two leaders were sent to Washington. One of these was the controversial explorer, John Charles Frémont, who had returned to California after his courtmartial. The other was Gwin. When the two men laid copies of the new state constitution before the U.S. Congress, Californians had already declared themselves to be a state. Faced with this reality, southern legislators became concerned over creating a new and large "free state." Northern abolitionists, on the other hand, wanted to exclude slavery from all the lands acquired from Mexico as a result of the war. The process by which California sought admission to the Union added to the ongoing controversy between North and South.

Only after weeks of deadlock did Congress enact its famous "Compromise of 1850." Finally, on September 9, 1850, this agreement authorized California to enter the Union as a free state. This compromise, however, did not put an end to tensions between North and South, nor within California. On October 18, when news of California's admission to statehood reached San Francisco, all local business was suspended. Wild celebration marked that momentous day. Crowds poured into tiny Portsmouth Square as self-proclaimed orators boasted that California had become a full-fledged member of the American Union.

The new state's internal north-south conflict was to affect the choice of its future capital. Several towns vied for selection. In addition to the obvious claims of Monterey and San Francisco, support also arose for San Luis Obispo, Benicia, Stockton, and Santa Barbara. San Jose was the site of the first session of the legislature, dubbed the "Legislature of a Thousand Drinks" due to the late-night carousing of its members. A proposal by General Vallejo to lay out a new capital city along the Carquinez Straits received northern support, and, in June 1851, the government records were temporarily moved from San Jose to a bleak site owned by and named for General Vallejo.

In February of 1853, another resolution adopted by the legislature established Benicia as the third state capital. That town, which consisted mainly of a two-story brick building in the middle of some mud flats, was hardly more suitable than San Jose or Vallejo. Next, Sacramento made such a strong bid for the state's capital that the legislature convened there in 1854. That city had been a major jumping-off point for miners during the gold rush. Though isolated and plagued by sweltering summer weather, it remains California's permanent seat of government.

Selected Readings

The Frémont-Kearny-Stockton controversy is described in *Proceedings of the Court Martial in the Trial of (J. C.) Frémont* (repr. 1973). Statehood issues are in Judson Grenier, *Golden Odyssey: John Stroud Houston, California's First Controller and the Origins of State Government* (1999) and David A. Johnson, *Founding the Far West: California, Oregon, and Nevada* (1992) See also William H. Ellison, *A Self-Governing Dominion: California, 1849-1860* (1950); Cardinal L. Goodwin, *The Establishment of State Government in California, 1846–1850* (1914) and Joseph Ellison, *California and the Nation, 1850–1869* (1927); J. Ross Browne, *Report of the Debates in the Convention of California* (1850); Rockwell D. Hunt, *The Genesis of California's First Constitution* (1895); Samuel H. Willey, *The Transition Period of California* (1901); James A. B. Scherer, *Thirty-first Star* (1942); Peter H. Burnett, *Recollections and Opinions of an Old Pioneer* (1880); and Donna C. Schuele, "Community Property Law and the Politics of Married Women's Rights in Nineteenth-Century California," *Western Legal History* 7 (Summer/Fall 1994), 245–281.

Events at the constitutional convention are recounted in J. Ross Browne, *Report of the Debates in the Convention of California on the Formation of the State Constitution* (1850). See also William Day Simonds, *Starr King in California* (1917).

CHAPTER SIXTEEN

SOCIAL FERMENT

After California finally entered the American Union, it faced serious social problems. The avalanche of persons who arrived there because of the gold rush created a formidable assimilative challenge for its population. Its turbulent society remained in disorder, as too many lawless persons came into the new state.

By 1850, only 8 percent of its 100,000 inhabitants had been born in California. Nearly a fourth had come from foreign countries. Among whites, men outnumbered women by a ratio of twelve to one. African Americans numbered fewer than 1,000. Scattered bands of Indians, bewildered by the American conquest, wandered about in utter confusion. Furthermore, the state's population continued to swell, reaching more than 300,000 by 1860.

At San Francisco, because law enforcement was so weak, a group of arrogant vigilantes took it upon themselves to stamp out crime. As municipal corruption had become entrenched, they enforced their own morality. Mob justice was condoned due to frustration over the failings of official law and order. Naive amateurs with no legal background devised random punishments against drifters who had filtered back into the city from abandoned mining camps. In the camps also, vigilance committees, animated by passion, were set up as "popular tribunals," acting as "champions of justice and right."

After the discovery of gold, a glut of criminals paralyzed municipal justice in San Francisco. In 1849 a band of toughs, who called themselves the "Hounds" or the "Regulators," terrorized the city. The members of a similar group of hoodlums, known as the "Sydney Ducks," had arrived from Great Britain's prison colony in Australia. They greatly confused law and order at the Golden Gate. Honest residents noted their troublesome presence by saying: "The Sydney Ducks are cackling."

Nativism, a form of racial hatred, became entwined with the sordid activities of antiforeign gangs. On Sunday, July 15, 1849, a rowdy crowd of Regulators held a "patriotic" parade. After touring various saloons, where they demanded liquor and smashed windows, they began to assault Chilean families who lived in makeshift tents on San Francisco's sand dunes. Although a citizens' court ultimately disciplined the Regulators, murderers and thieves continued to roam the city's streets. Indignant city elders arrested and sought to try offenders, supposedly in order to stop a kind of criminal delirium. By May of 1851, after a prominent merchant was assaulted and his safe burglarized, more formal charges were brought against such marauders.

That year, 200 members of a "Committee of Vigilance of San Francisco" organized to eradicate public disorder. At the head of the committee to purge the city of vice was William Tell Coleman, a wealthy young merchant and importer who came to be called the "Lion of the Vigilantes." This new-found status made him one of San Francisco's future nabobs. Scarcely had the Committee of Vigilance formed when the city's fire bell rang out, beckoning its members to the Monumental Fire Engine House to consider the case of John Jenkins, a convict from Sydney, Australia, who had robbed a shipping office, making off with its strongbox. Jenkins boldly defied anyone to stop him. When several vigilantes sought to do so, he threw the box into San Francisco Bay. Within a few hours the vigilantes took Jenkins to Portsmouth Square. There, on a scaffold, a noose was draped round his neck and he was hanged until his eyes bulged out. San Francisco's "best citizens" heartily approved the guilty sentence. Sam Brannan and other vigilantes were charged by the coroner with too hasty an execution. But most San Franciscans approved of their harsh justice.

On the morning of July 11, 1851, the bell on the firehouse again summoned the vigilance committee to judge another Sydney Duck, "English Jim" Stuart, a self-confessed criminal. Through mistaken identity, the committee had been prepared to execute an innocent man. After they realized their error and found Stuart guilty instead, he was led to the Market Street Wharf, where he was hanged aboard the deck of a ship. Two other criminals, Samuel Whittaker and Robert McKenzie, were also brought to trial. A crowd of 6,000 persons witnessed the execution.

The Vigilance Committee of 1851 ordered four hangings, one whipping, five deportations out of the state, handing over to the sheriff fifteen men and discharging forty others. Apologists for such "do-it-yourself justice" have cited the remoteness and corruption of the police and courts. But the distinction between vigilance activity and lynching was often lost sight of and grave abuses were obviously committed. Walter van Tilburg Clark's book *The Ox Bow Incident* splits sharply with the glorification of vigilantism, stressing the arrogant dangers of the presumption of guilt. This did, indeed, sometimes result in the execution, ear cropping, or whipping of the accused. Some vigilance committees did act responsibly, freeing suspects they found not guilty.

Foreigners, however, were likely to bear the brunt of mob fury, as in the lynching of Juanita, a so-called "evil" Mexican woman. On the evening of July 4, 1851, at Downieville, a town on the Yuba River, a group of American Independence Day celebrants smashed in the door of Juanita's shack. After she brutally knifed one of her assailants, a vigilante jury speedily sentenced her to be "strung up" from a wooden bridge that spanned the river. Juanita, alas, was a defenseless Latina.

Some of the persecution of foreigners had an economic motivation. Immigrant miners, among them Chileans, Frenchmen, and Hawaiian "Kanakas," were frequently chased out of the best diggings. Yet these foreigners were too valuable a source of cheap labor to exclude permanently. After 1850, Mexican laborers could be obtained in the mines for as little as $1 per day. When restrictions became so severe as to drive foreigners out of California, some employers tried to shield foreign laborers against mobs. A few landowners went so far as to advocate repeal of a foreign-miners tax that had been enacted by 1850. This unfair state legislation failed to produce anything like the estimated $2.4 million in potential revenue. The law was eventually repealed in favor of a small head-tax levied on foreign workers entering California.

In April of 1850, California's governor signed into law "An Act For Better Regulation of Foreign Miners." It came to be known as the Foreign Miners' Tax and imposed a charge of $20 per month on all non-U.S. citizens at work in the diggings. French and Chilean miners unfurled banners protesting the regulation. Local merchants supported the protestors, fearing that the tax would drive away foreign workers who had become valuable customers. By 1852, Chinese immigrants poured into the Sierra range in large numbers. Although Americans fired bullets into foreign flags, the state legislature next levied a lesser foreign miners' tax. It was designed to add money to the state treasury without driving away foreigners.

In the 1850s, self-imposed guardians of respectability also turned their wrath upon suspected prostitutes, thieves, and drifters. At Sacramento, 215 citizens formed themselves into a committee to police that city. At Marysville, after seventeen homicides occurred within one week, another vigilance committee took "prompt steps" to punish suspects. Some hang-

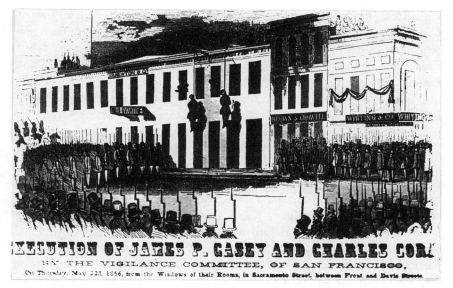

EXECUTION OF JAMES P. CASEY AND CHARLES CORA
BY THE VIGILANCE COMMITTEE, OF SAN FRANCISCO,
On Thursday, May 22d, 1856, from the Windows of their Rooms, in Sacramento Street, between Front and Davis Streets.

Vigilantes in San Francisco execute James Casey and Charles Cora as James King's funeral cortège passes below. Contemporary print, H. G. Hills collection, courtesy of The Bancroft Library, University of California, Berkeley.

ings were actually popular events. At the Mokelumne Hill mining camp, an alleged thief was executed in the presence of nearly 1,000 witnesses.

Only five years after San Franciscans dissolved their first vigilance brigades, another vigilance committee formed there. This became the most reputable and orderly of all such groups. It actually regularized its proceedings, having regrouped only because crime had again increased. Indeed, the hangman's noose had faded from memory. About 1,000 unpunished murders had shocked San Franciscans from 1849 to 1856 alone.

By stuffing unsecured ballot boxes and using toughs at polling places, corrupt officials had also become entrenched in San Francisco's municipal posts. Political lawlessness was related to the murder of James King of William, the gadfly editor of the *Daily Evening Bulletin*. In his editorials, King had openly attacked prominent politicians, including James P. Casey, an unsavory and opportunistic local office-holder. When Casey demanded an apology, he was ordered out of the newspaper's editorial room. He then vowed he would kill King, who scoffed at this threat in his column of May 14, 1856. That evening, Casey approached the newspaperman on the street, drew a revolver, and pulled the trigger. As King breathed his last, Casey was locked up in the city jail. Three days later several thousand vigilantes, enraged over this latest homicide, stormed the jail, and seized Casey and another accused murderer, Charles Cora. Both were then sentenced to death before a vigilante tribunal. On May 22, 1856, as King's funeral cortege moved through the city streets, the vigilantes hanged both Casey and Cora.

Within a fortnight, nearly 10,000 outraged men had rejoined the vigilantes. This reactivated San Francisco Vigilance Committee of 1856 appointed its own chief of police and twenty-five policemen to supplement local law enforcement. But its roster remained secret, each member identified only by a number. Their leader once again was William Coleman, who organized them into squads of 100 men. Mass meetings at Sacramento, Stockton, and San Francisco showed how determined Coleman was to stamp out municipal crime.

A new state "Law and Order" party, however, objected to the harsh verdicts of this latest vigilance committee. California's Supreme Court Justice, David S. Terry, lent his support to the Law and Order faction. Unfortunately for Terry, he became involved in a knifing fracas with one of the vigilantes and was indicted by the vigilance committee. Fortunately, the man he had stabbed did not die from the injury. After almost a month of embarrassing hearings, Judge Terry was acquitted.

Meanwhile, Governor John Neely Johnson asked William Tecumseh Sherman, commander of the second division of the California militia, to aid him in the regularizing of the state's criminal punishments. The governor did not trust the vigilantes. But Sherman, who later became a prominent Civil War general, could hardly cope with the volunteer forces he now faced. Some 6,000 of the vigilantes had personally taken up arms. Their headquarters, called "Fort Gunnybags," was fortified by bags of sand piled ten feet high and six feet thick. Strongly armed, the vigilantes holed up in the building and produced a "black list" of offenders whom they wished to deport. Beginning on June 5, 1856, the committee sent three men off to Hawaii and three others to Panama. Only slowly did the avenging group dissolve itself on August 18, 1856, ending three months of virtual control over San Francisco.

Both vigilante activities and filibustering were typical of mid-nineteenth-century life on an unpoliced frontier. The term *filibuster*, today's prolonged speechmaking to delay legislation, once had a far different connotation. In the late nineteenth century, rootless filibusterers took it upon themselves to go abroad ostensibly to "free" unprotected territory from foreign control. Filibustering was the product of a restless and youthful America, one convinced of its "manifest destiny" to expand toward the country's "natural frontiers." Southerners, in particular, were attracted to filibustering as a way of spreading their cherished institution of slavery beyond the American South. Apologists for filibustering professed admiration for the courage of adventurers willing to shoulder rifles in foreign fields, seeing them as patriotic soldiers of fortune.

Unsettled conditions in California in the 1850s stimulated filibustering as disillusioned gold seekers looked covetously beyond American territory for adventure. However, the filibustering expeditions that originated from California after its admission to statehood were uniformly unsuccessful. The first one, in 1851 under the leadership of Alexander Bell, was foolishly undertaken to reinstate a deposed president of Ecuador. That same year Sam Brannan, the apostate from Mormonism who had by now become a prominent Californian, led a party of adventurers to Hawaii. In his crazy attempt to capture those islands, Brannan was lucky to escape incensed Hawaiian pikemen who threatened to run their spears through him. Other adventurers used San Francisco as a base to raise small groups of filibusters who mostly feuded among themselves. In 1851, Joseph Morehead's plan to take the spiny peninsula of Baja California proved equally futile. Most of his men deserted him in the field, and he was lucky to escape Mexican imprisonment.

California's foreign population included other footloose adventurers. Among these were various Frenchmen who had fled their country as a result of the revolutionary movements of 1848. These failed aristocrats were captivated by plans to colonize Mexico. Three independent freebooters left their mark upon the history of both California and northern Mexico: the Marquis Charles De Pindray, Lepine De Sigondis, and Count Gaston De Raousset-Boulbon, known as "Little Wolf." During the 1850s all three men led hopeless expeditions from California into Mexico, having been promised land there.

In 1852, at the head of 260 men, Raousset-Boulbon returned to Mexico. He unfortunately ignored warnings that he must placate local rivals. After seventeen of his men were killed and twenty-three others were wounded, he left Mexico. In 1854, he courageously returned, this time with 500 recruits. After some of them were killed, he was tried on conspiracy charges and, at his own request, faced a firing squad without a blindfold.

De Pindray, also a minor French noble, was skilled at handling weapons. He accepted an offer from the Mexican government to raise volunteers in California to protect the Sonora mines from raids by Apaches. But, after his party landed at Guaymas on the west coast of Mexico, De Pindray was suddenly shot in the head, murdered by Indians or perhaps by one of his own renegades. The survivors hastily departed for San Francisco, where most of them had been recruited.

The best known of all California filibusters, however, was William Walker. A restless native of Tennessee, Walker arrived at San Francisco in June 1850. Following a short venture into journalism, during which his caustic pen landed him in jail, he entered into law practice at Marysville. Called "the gray-eyed man of destiny," Walker wanted to bring about the independence of the Mexican states of Sonora and Baja California, where he also hoped to extend slavery.

In 1854, Walker left the Golden Gate by ship with forty-eight followers and landed at La Paz. There he met another 200 seemingly sympathetic Mexicans. He then recklessly proclaimed the independent "Republic of Lower California." He quickly abolished the short-lived "government" in order to launch the "Republic of Sonora," with himself as its president. Even local Mexicans resented Walker's harsh punishment of deserters. By May of 1854, his group had been reduced to a paltry thirty-five adherents. When they finally returned to the United States via San Diego, they surrendered to American authorities. Although tried for violating U.S. neutrality laws, Walker was acquitted by a sympathetic jury.

On May 3, 1855, Walker again set sail, this time for Nicaragua, with a force of sixty men. After landing there, he declared himself as president. Two years later, following a series of revolts, he again fled back to the United States. Still undaunted, Walker launched one last enterprise that involved a landing in Honduras, where he was finally killed in 1860.

Henry Crabb, a schoolmate of Walker, led the last of California's filibustering parties. In 1855 he enlisted swashbucklers for an expedition to Nicaragua. After that plan soured, he married into a prominent Sonoran family. Crabb next organized the Arizona and Gadsden Colonization Company, hoping to take over part of the Mexican state of Sonora. His planning and leadership were poor. Facing an impossible goal, in 1857 he too was executed. His assailants tacked his bloody head and that of his brutally murdered men onto wooden poles. These faced northward as a warning to other Yanqui adventurers. Filibustering had become an outmoded stepchild of manifest destiny. But the problem of public disorder had hardly been brought under legal control in California.

SELECTED READINGS

Vigilante activities are recounted in Hubert Howe Bancroft, *Popular Tribunals* (2 vols. 1887); Mary Floyd Williams, ed., *History of the San Francisco*

Committee of Vigilance of 1851 (1921); William T. Coleman, "San Francisco Vigilance Committees," *Century Magazine* 43 (November 1891), 133–50; Stanton A. Coblentz, *Villains and Vigilantes* (1936); George R. Stewart, *Committee of Vigilance: Revolution in San Francisco* (1964); Robert Senkewicz, *Vigilantes in Gold Rush San Francisco* (1985) and Alan Valentine, *Vigilante Justice* (1956).

Condemnations of vigilantism appear in Walter Van Tilburg Clark's novel, *The Ox Bow Incident* (1942); see also John W. Caughey, *Their Majesties the Mob* (1960) and Leonard Pitt, "The Beginnings of Nativism in California," *Pacific Historical Review* 30 (February 1961), 23–38. See also John Stanley, "Vigilance Movements in Early California," in Gordon Bakken, ed., *Law in the Western United States* (2000).

Legal matters are in Paul Kens, *Justice Stephen Field: Shaping Liberty From The Gold Rush to the Gilded Age* (1997); Gordon Bakken, *Practicing Law in Frontier California* (1991); John Boessenecker, *Badge and Buckshot: Lawlessness in Old California* (1988); also Bakken and Christian Fritz, "California Legal History: A Bibliographical Essay," *Southern California Quarterly* 70 (Summer 1988), 203–22; Kevin Mullen, *Let Justice Be Done: Crime and Politics in Early San Francisco* (1989); Ronald C. Woolsey, "Crime and Punishment: Los Angeles County, 1850–1856," *Southern California Quarterly* 61 (Spring 1979), 79–98, and Woolsey, "Rites of Passage? Anglo and Mexican-American Contrasts," *Southern California Quarterly* 69 (Summer 1987), 81–95; Lawrence E. Guillow, "Pandemonium in the Plaza: The First Los Angeles Riot, July 22, 1856," *Southern California Quarterly* 77 (Fall 1995), 183–97; Jacqueline Barnhart, *The Fair But Frail: Prostitution in San Francisco, 1849–1900* (1986).

Regarding filibustering, see William O. Scroggs, *Filibusters and Financiers* (New York, 1931); Laurence Greene, *The Filibuster* (1937); Andrew Rolle, "California Filibustering and the Hawaiian Kingdom," *Pacific Historical Review* 19 (August 1950), 251–63; and Rolle, "Futile Filibustering in Baja California, 1888–1890," *Pacific Historical Review* 20 (May 1951), 159–66.

CHAPTER SEVENTEEN

A NEW CULTURE
AT THE GOLDEN GATE

California's gold rush was a defining American epic. From many parts of the world, fortune-hunters flooded into the newly conquered province. In 1849 alone, more than 36,000 immigrants arrived in San Francisco by sea. In the next twenty years it became California's first cosmopolitan city. But before "Frisco," the city by the bay, could shed its cultural primitiveness, pressing problems demanded action. The fire hazard continued to grow because of its large number of flimsy wooden structures. Six conflagrations swept over the city in a period of eighteen months. The first great fire took place in December 1849. A second blaze occurred in May of 1850. After scarcely a month, came a third fire. Most damaging of all of was the inferno of May 4, 1851, which destroyed a large part of the town. Eventually San Francisco rebuilt itself in brick and stone.

After the gold rush, prices dropped sharply. Pickled beef and pork went from $60 to $10 per barrel; flour decreased from $800 to $20 per barrel. Surplus imports piled up at the wharfs. Bankers and traders had rushed into speculations that were to prove their financial undoing. From 1849 to 1855, the steadily declining yield of gold from the placers caused a reversal in property values. Housing sites that had cost only $15 before the rush reached $8,000 during its height, only to plummet to less than $100 a year later.

Decorated with their plush furniture, chandeliers, and mirrors, the city's saloons and gambling parlors were the most profitable. The "El Dorado," with its eight gaming tables, velvet upholstered chairs, and long bar, attracted crowds. Upstairs there were convenient rooms for prostitution. Customers were, however, supposed to keep their derringers out of sight to avoid gambling disputes. A few of the city's wealthiest merchants got their start as faro dealers and card men.

Among the most fortunate investors, who began a worldwide business, was Levi Strauss. A Bavarian Jew, he arrived in 1853 with some bolts of brown hemp cloth in his luggage. Originally, he hoped to make tents and awnings for those miners still left in the gold fields. He quickly saw that they also needed sturdy trousers. His brother in New York sent him some blue denim cloth with which Levi, by 1860, began to produce pants. They came to be called "jeans." (At an auction in the year 2002, a pair of jeans, allegedly the oldest in existence, fetched an amazing $46,532. They had been found stashed away in a Nevada mining site.)

San Francisco's interconnected settlements made the administration of law and order difficult. By the winter of 1850, a sheltered enclave called "Happy Valley" still contained about 1,000 canvas tents. Another sand lot zone, "Pleasant Valley," sat in the middle of town, stretching toward a raw beachfront. "Sydney Town," near Telegraph Hill, became a hangout for Australian convicts and castaways. That community was targeted by several vigilante groups, as were "Little Chile," "Spring Valley," and a neighborhood called "St. Ann Valley." All of these tiny settlements harbored criminals.

San Francisco was still predominantly a city of young and rootless men, far away from home and removed from family restraints. Among them there were persons who hated the place, such as the authors of the following couplet:

> The pioneers came in '49.
> The whores in '51.
> Between the two they
> Soon begot the native son.

For too many persons, gambling, dueling, and ostentatious living held more appeal than attending church. Others, however, sought spiritual guidance. In 1849, the Reverend Albert Williams organized the First Presbyterian Church of San Francisco. Mission Dolores served as a place of worship for Catholics until 1849, when the first secular church, named for St. Francis, was organized.

Despite its turbulent social conditions, all was not sin in early San Francisco. Education became a major concern of the citizenry. In 1849, John C. Pelton arrived from Boston to open a municipal school on Portsmouth Square, one based upon New England traditions of instruction. By 1851 the city had installed a superintendent of schools and a board of education. Two years later, the first Academy of Science in the West was begun.

California's first English-language newspaper, the *Californian*, had appeared at Monterey on August 15, 1846. This weekly was printed in two columns, English on one side and Spanish on the other. It had to be printed on any stock available, even wrapping or tissue paper, because newsprint was in short supply. Only a few months after this paper appeared, Sam Brannan founded the *California Star*. In 1849 the two papers merged as the *Alta California*. Eventually, that paper dropped use of the Spanish language.

Midcentury California, with San Francisco as its busy cultural center, also welcomed reminiscences written by pioneers who had come to California by sea. Richard Henry Dana's *Two Years Before the Mast* (1840) was one of the first books to introduce pastoral California of hide-and-tallow days to a wide reading public. A less-well-known chronicle by a Yankee sea trader was Richard J. Cleveland's *A Narrative of Voyages and Commercial Enterprises* (1842).

Starved readers clamored for every sort of literary fare. San Francisco's *The Golden Era*, founded in 1852, was California's first weekly of any literary pretension. It was followed by the *Pioneer* (1854), Hutchings' *California Magazine* (1856), and *The Hesperian* (1858). *The Golden Era*, longest-lived of these early journals, remained in publication until 1893.

The best-known magazine was the *Overland Monthly*, which began publication in 1868. Bret Harte, its editor, encouraged other authors to write for the *Overland* and gained a national audience for them. In 1868 Harte attracted attention to the magazine with "The Luck of Roaring Camp." This was followed by "The Outcasts of Poker Flat," in which he created a stereotype of the western miner as a bearded, red-shirted, romantic figure. Harte also helped to introduce a national school of "local color" writers.

A crude literature of burlesque was then fashionable. One of the exponents of this jokester style was an army officer, Lieutenant George Horatio Derby, known under two pen names, "The Veritable Squibob," and "John Phoenix." In 1856, he wrote a salty book, *Phoenixiana*, which became immensely popular. Readers roared at such Derby epithets as "Absinthe [or Absence] makes the heart grow fonder," and "They came to cough and remain to spray." Coarse humor also characterized the writing of Alonzo "Old Block" Delano. His *Pen Knife Sketches* (1853), *Life on the Plains And Among the Diggings* (1854), and melodramatic play, *A Live Woman in the Mines* (1857), were favorites of miners. Educated and uneducated alike

North Beach, San Francisco, ca. 1860. H. G. Hills collection, courtesy of The Bancroft Library, University of California, Berkeley.

reveled in the literary horseplay brought into lonely and obscure camps. Local colorists and frontier satirists boasted about the achievements of a proud generation of hardy pioneers and were prone to high-flown exaggeration. Nonetheless, their writings help the historian to understand the otherwise bleak environment of primitive mining camps.

One obscure writer, Samuel Langhorne Clemens, better known later as Mark Twain, took up mining in Nevada. When bad weather kept him from work in the diggings, he amused himself by writing burlesque sketches. Signed "Josh," he sent these vignettes to the *Territorial Enterprise*, a newspaper at Virginia City in today's Nevada. In 1862, Twain walked 130 miles from a bleak mining site to take a job on the *Enterprise* for $25 per week. Two years later Twain drifted into San Francisco, where he became a reporter for its *Morning Call*. In California, in a cabin near Angel's Camp, Twain wrote "The Celebrated Jumping Frog of Calaveras County." The short story made him famous almost overnight, and he went on to write an entire book of mining tales, *Roughing It*. His piercing satire of human failings out West remained at the heart of his almost instant success. Twain's later books applied what he had learned in California. His light touch, combined with fast-paced narration, captivated readers. After

The residence of Mrs. Mark Hopkins and Governor Stanford, San Francisco. H. G. Hills Collection, courtesy of the Bancroft Library, University of California, Berkeley.

The Crocker and Colton mansions. San Francisco. Located on Nob Hill, renamed "Snob Hill" by jealous San Franciscans. H. G. Hills Collection, courtesy of the Bancroft Library, University of California, Berkeley.

writing *Innocents Abroad* (1869), he lost touch with California as he became internationally famous.

San Francisco also nourished a notable artistic colony. Among its foreign-born artisans was the skilled German etcher and printmaker Edward Vischer. He traveled throughout California making sketches of its missions, which he described as "noble ruins." Another foreign artist who depicted the decaying missions was the Scottish painter William Keith. But it was Keith's watercolors of the Yosemite Valley that made him one of the most appreciated artists in the West. The bear symbol on the masthead of the *Overland Monthly*, drawn by Keith, was due to his friendship with its editor, Bret Harte. In 1866, Keith also painted an Overland Stagecoach poster that became known all over the nation. He was also an early photographer.

John W. Audubon, son of the noted naturalist, toured the California diggings, of which he made hundreds of pencil and watercolor sketches. Because his portfolio was too bulky for overland travel, he decided to ship it to the East Coast. He entrusted his artwork to the care of a friend traveling eastward in 1857 on the ship *Central America*. Unfortunately, both Audubon's friend and the sketches composing his California porfolio went down with that ship.

San Francisco's Bohemian quarter stretched from North Beach across Telegraph Hill. There, Albert Bierstadt, a German artist like Vischer and Charles Nahl, first set up a studio in 1858. Bierstadt had traveled across the plains to California with a government exploring party. His canvases idealized the natural wonders of North America. Unfortunately, some of his best oils, like those of William Keith, were destroyed in the city's great fire of 1906.

Descriptions of the city of the "golden fifties and champagne sixties" stress its opulence as revealed in architecture. There was uniformity in the buildings constructed for the wealthy in those decades. The same Italian artists who painted the interiors of future railroad magnate Mark Hopkins's baroque castle on Nob Hill also decorated theaters, saloons, and brothels along the city's Barbary Coast. Gilt-edged Victorian residences, like that of Hopkins's associate Charles Crocker, overlooked hilly lawns sprinkled with cast-iron animals. Popular legend has it that in the vicinity of the Hopkins mansion there were so many brass fences that a man was employed year round to polish them.

In this atmosphere of opulence, varied entertainment flourished. At the Jenny Lind Theater, Lola Montez's fans flocked to see her perform an exotic "Tarantula Dance," whereas on the East Coast she had been treated as a mere strumpet. Montez was known as a notorious woman who had taken many lovers, including the mad King Ludwig of Bavaria. But it was her exquisite figure, flashing eyes, and raven-black hair that captivated male audiences. Montez capitalized on the title given her by Ludwig as the Countess of Landsfeld. At the mining camp of Grass Valley, she charged $100 per admission. Brandishing a whip on stage, her gyrations drove lonely miners into a sexual frenzy.

A flaming redheaded companion of Lola Montez, named Adah Menken, clad in flesh-colored tights, was showered with gold nuggets and diamond brooches thrown onto the stage by admirers who had struck it rich. Her specialty was acting out a romantic tone poem by Lord Byron. During 1863, at the Tivoli Theater, the shapely Adah so drew the admiration of the St. Francis Hook and Ladder firefighters that they made her the first honorary member of their organization.

Lotta Crabtree, another home-grown chanteuse and dancer who had charmed many a lonesome miner during the gold rush, remained popular in San Francisco through midcentury. Unattached males hungered for appearances by such female performers. Still later, Lillian Russell and the tragedian Sarah Bernhardt captivated San Francisco theater audiences.

Writers, artists and actors all found the city congenial. In the decade after 1850, some 1,100 dramatic productions were staged in San Francisco. Especially popular were two Shakespearean troopers, Junius Brutus Booth and his son Edwin. Audiences raved about their performances of *A Midsummer Night's Dream* and *Romeo and Juliet*. Literature, art, and drama had made the city by the Golden Gate the cultural mecca of the American West.

By 1860, San Francisco ranked fifteenth in population among American cities, but still only fifty-first in manufacturing output. Scarce coal and iron resources, prohibitive interest rates, and lucrative jobs in mining, transportation, and land speculation delayed the city's industrialization.

SELECTED READINGS

Social turbulence is treated in William B. Secrest, *Lawmen and Desperadoes . . . 1850–1900* (1997). See also Bayard Taylor, *Eldorado, or Adventures in the Path of Empire* (repr. 1949); T. A. Barry and B. A. Patten, *Men and Memories of San Francisco* (1873); Robert E. Cowan, *Forgotten Characters of Old San Francisco* (1938); William Drury, *Norton I: Emperor of the United States* (1986); John H. Kemble, ed., *San Francisco Bay* (1957). Julia Altrocchi, *The Spectacular San Franciscans* (1949); William M. Camp, *San Francisco, Port of Gold* (1947); Julian Dana, *The Man Who Built San Francisco* (1936);

George D. Lyman, *Ralston's Ring* (1937); Roger W. Lotchin, *San Francisco, 1846–1856: From Hamlet to City* (1974); Gunther Barth, *Instant Cities: Urbanization and the Rise of San Francisco* (1975); and Peter Decker, *Fortunes and Failures: White Collar Mobility in Nineteenth Century San Francisco* (1978).

Education is discussed in Nicholas C. Polos, *John Swett: California's Frontier Schoolmaster* (1978). For literature, see Franklin Walker, *San Francisco's Literary Frontier* (1939). The theater is the subject of G. R. MacMinn, *The Theater of the Golden Era* (1941). Biographies include Ivan Benson, *Mark Twain's Western Years* (1938); Edgar M. Branch, *The Literary Apprenticeship of Mark Twain* (1950); George R. Stewart, *Bret Harte: Argonaut and Exile* (1931) and Stewart, *John Phoenix, Esq.: The Veritable Squibob* (1937).

An entire issue of *California History*, 71 (Spring 1992), concerns California artists in the nineteenth century. See also Eugen Neuhaus, *William Keith: The Man and the Artist* (1938); Brother Cornelius, *Keith, Old Master of California* (1942). Sketches of John W. Audubon, Albert Bierstadt, William Keith, Charles C. Nahl, and Victor Prevost are reproduced in *California Centennials Exhibition of Art* (1949); also Carl Dentzel, ed., *The Drawings of John Woodhouse Audubon* (1957). For distinctive local views see Gary Kurutz, *California Pastoral, Selected Photographs, 1860–1925* (1998).

Regarding arson in San Francisco, see John Stanley, "Burning Bagdad by the Bay . . . ," in Gordon Bakken, ed., *Law in the Western United States* (2000). James Varley has written about California's most notorious courtesan in his *Lola Montez* (1997). An account of the sinking and later rediscovery of the gold-laden *SS Central America* can be found in Gary Kinder's *Ship of Gold in the Deep Blue Sea* (1998).

CHAPTER EIGHTEEN

POST–GOLD RUSH COMMERCE

As California's richest ores grew scarcer, the pan and cradle were giving way to expensive quartz-crushing and ore-pounding machinery. Some miners settled down to run hardware stores, livery stables, and saloons. The miner partnered with the chemist, pulverizing quartz and treating it with mercury to form an amalgam. This new technological development accompanied the discovery of big silver deposits east of the Sierra range.

By 1853, new prospectors poked about the brush-strewn slopes of the Washoe area. This region, not yet officially part of Nevada, was an extension of California, financially and technologically. The Washoe miners unearthed a bluish-tinged ore that, at first, they cast aside. In 1859, an assayer found that this "blasted blue stuff" was actually sulfide containing high percentages of silver and gold.

For more than fifteen years, the region around today's Carson City, Reno, and Virginia City, Nevada, was gripped by rampant speculation. By the 1860s, thirty mills were in operation. William C. Ralston and his Bank of California invested heavily in what came to be called the Comstock Lode. Thousands of feet of timber and tons of machinery came over the Sierra from California to shore up tunnels amid rich veins of silver. The San Francisco financiers who made up "Ralston's Ring" turned the Comstock into a honeycomb of conduits and shafts propped up by wooden beams, the lode coming to be called the tomb of the Sierra forests.

In 1873, Adolph Sutro, a Prussian-born mining engineer, had enriched himself in Nevada. He began to build a tunnel into the heart of the dangerous Comstock lode. This engineering feat would make him so famous that he later became a powerful San Francisco landowner and that city's mayor. His tunnel provided "hot sumps" below the ground with ventilation and drainage. However, its completion in 1878 took so long that Sutro's stockholders failed to reap its promised benefits.

Placer miner on the Colorado River, ca. 1890. C. C. Pierce Collection, courtesy of the Huntington Library, San Marino, California.

Like Sutro, other millionaires got their start in the Comstock. The pooled investments of George Hearst, E. J. ("Lucky") Baldwin, John W. Mackay, James Fair, James C. Flood, William S. O'Brien, John P. Jones, and Alvinza Hayward financed the uncovering of huge hidden bodies of ore. Half of the new mansions in San Francisco were constructed with silver and gold earnings from the Washoe area.

"The King of the Comstock," William Sharon, who controlled vital lumber and rail interests from California, had coaxed Ralston into sinking millions into the "Washoe Madness." Then, during the national panic of 1873, the failure of Ralston's Bank of California set off a string of financial bankruptcies. In 1875, Ralston, distraught at the prospect of ruin, met his death—either by suicide or accident—in the icy waters of San Francisco Bay.

Probably as much capital was put into the Comstock Lode as was ever mined. Once its "blue stuff" gave out, failed speculators limped back into San Francisco. There they found more promising pursuits. After becoming its mayor, Sutro founded a noted library. Mackay lent his energies and capital to a cable and telegraphic system. James Fair's family name remains perpetuated in today's Fairmont Hotel on Nob Hill.

California's two great mining rushes also stimulated staging and freighting operations. As early as 1849, James E. Birch established the California Stage Line Company, which connected Sacramento and Coloma. Miners paid Birch a fare each way of two ounces of gold, or $32. In 1850 John Whistman inaugurated stage service between San Jose and San Francisco. The forty-five-mile run took nine hours to make.

Delivery service was so poor that for six weeks during the winter of 1852–53, Los Angeles received no mail. Eventually two eastern staging firms, Adams and Company Express and Wells, Fargo and Company, absorbed much of the local mail service. Wells Fargo, a firm with national connections, transported $58 million worth of gold into San Francisco alone in a five-year period. In time both companies also took on banking functions.

It was no easy job to drive the large teams of mixed mustangs hitched to heavily loaded stages over the steep grades of the Sierra. A good driver communicated with his mules or horses through gentle movements of the reins. Tough as saddle leather, and inured to the dust and heat of the trail, these drivers, sometimes called "whips" or "jehus," raised stage coaching almost to an art form.

Nonetheless, most stagecoach travelers endured bone-jarring rides. Although the introduction of lighter, faster stages shrank travel time, a week of travel spent through clouds of dust and in the rain and snow so upset some passengers that they actually stopped the stages to duel with one another. At outlying stations, drivers obtained fresh horses while passengers took the opportunity to rest from their journey.

The fastest stage lines used light Concord carriages, manufactured by Abbott, Downing and Company in New Hampshire. The coaches rode on a heavy leather cradle of "thorough braces" that cushioned passengers against the buffetings of the road. Constructed of New England ash wood and the finest Norwegian iron, the Concord coaches were ornately paneled. Though considered "light," the 2,500-pound carriages required three spans of good horses to pull them. Some stage lines, however, merely modified old mud-wagons used on almost every California ranch. These heavier, springless vehicles, fitted out to carry only twelve passengers, were slow and hardly comfortable vehicles.

In 1858, with a federal financial subsidy, John Butterfield began to carry the mails cross-country. By using relays of horses exchanged at ten-

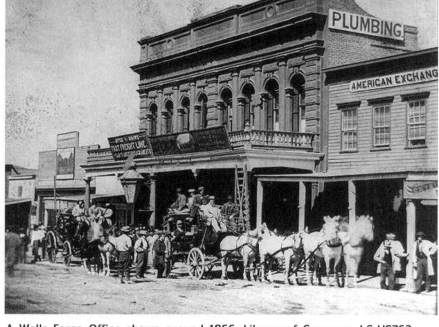

A Wells Fargo Office shown around 1866. Library of Congress, LC-USZ62-11055.

mile intervals, his coaches could cover the 2,800 miles between Missouri and San Francisco in twenty-four days, eighteen hours, and twenty-six minutes. The schedule called for an average speed of five miles an hour, both day and night. Eventually Butterfield employed more than 1,000 men across the country, drivers as well as way-station attendants.

As the Civil War approached, Butterfield began to transfer equipment northward. In 1861, his Overland Mail service offered passengers a connection from St. Louis to California via Salt Lake City. Meanwhile, sectional tension kept the nation from settling upon a future transcontinental railroad route.

In 1855, a picturesque episode in the story of southwestern transportation had also begun. This was the appearance of the army's "Camel Corps." The short-lived "lightning dromedary express" completed its first trip from Arizona to California in fifteen days, the camels swimming the Colorado River en route. Three years later, in January of 1858, the population of Los Angeles turned out to witness the appearance of the first camel caravan to reach their city. It was on its way to Fort Tejon, where Lieutenant Edward Fitzgerald Beale supervised subsequent trips between that fort and Albuquerque, New Mexico. These freight-carrying "ships of the desert" developed sore legs from cacti, prickly pear, and sagebrush. Eventually the army gave up their use.

Still another innovation in western transportation involved young single riders using relays of fresh horses to carry mail more quickly between distant points. The Pony Express had begun to function on April 3, 1860, with the departure of its first rider from St. Joseph, Missouri, for California. The westward route of the Pony Express was much the same as that taken by overland wagons. After reaching Sacramento, both rider and horse went from the capital by steamboat down the Sacramento River and across the bay to San Francisco. The run of 1,966 miles was completed in nine days and twenty-three hours, less than half the time required by the best stages to California from Missouri.

The Pony Express utilized 80 riders, 190 relay stations, 400 station men, and 400 fast horses. Only young and light riders were selected, each sparsely armed only with a six-shooter and a knife. Each man changed horses every ten miles, but one of them, "Buffalo Bill" (William F. Cody), is credited with a continuous ride of 384 miles. Letters, transported in leather pouches, were written on the thinnest of paper in order to keep the loads light. With the Express in place, the rate of postage fell from $5 per half ounce to $1. Completion of a transcontinental telegraph line in 1861 ended the Pony Express. Though operated for only sixteen months, and failing to make a financial profit, the Pony Express had demonstrated the practicality of a central transcontinental route, the forerunner of the track beds of the Central Pacific Railroad.

Another pre-transcontinental railroad entrepreneur was Ben Holladay, a boisterous and coarse buccaneer. He moved from Kentucky to Missouri, where he operated a general store and saloon. During the War with Mexico he also freighted supplies westward for the army. At war's end, he purchased surplus wagons and oxen from the government at bargain prices. Holladay's trans-Missouri state line earned him the titles "King of Hurry" and "Napoleon of the Plains." In addition to operating 3,300 miles of stage routes as far west as Placerville, California, he financed steamboat and rail services throughout America's middle west. Eventually, Holladay sold his staging operation to Wells Fargo.

Few stages traveled at night for fear of dangerous potholes, Indians, or bandits, who could suddenly appear at a coach door. Masked and armed, bandits quickly relieved passengers of their valuables and the stagecoach of its strong box. Resistance meant instant shooting. Among local banditti was Joaquín Murieta, whose name struck terror from one end of the state

Going into the Southern California mines by stagecoach, 1904. Diggings are in the canyon and can be seen in the background. C.C. Pierce Collection, courtesy of The Huntington Library, San Marino, California.

to the other. He has been called the super bandit of California's past. He became such a problem that the legislature took extraordinary measures and offered a $1,000 reward for his capture. Texas Ranger Harry S. Love was hired to track Murieta down. In 1853, Captain Love finally captured and killed a man alleged to be Murieta, whose head was then exhibited at freak shows preserved in a jar of alcohol.

Equally feared was the bandit Tiburcio Vásquez, who became the most romanticized criminal in nineteenth-century southern California. For three years he regularly robbed ranches and stagecoaches. Finally captured in 1874, after having evaded the law for years, a sheriff's posse blasted Vásquez out of a hideout in the Cahuenga Hills and hanged him. In northern California, another road robber, "Black Bart," wore a white flour sack over his head to hide his identity. He achieved renown because of the doggerel verses, which he mockingly left at the scene of his crimes. He also barked out a terse four-word phrase upon stopping a stage: "Throw down the box!" From 1875 to 1883, twenty-eight different drivers readily complied and threw down their express boxes to Black Bart. During one such robbery he inadvertently dropped a handkerchief; its laundry mark led detectives to San Francisco, where the infamous Black Bart turned out to be Charles E. Bolton, a mining engineer. He was sent to San Quentin Penitentiary, served his sentence, then promptly disappeared from recorded history.

In 1853, accompanying transportation developments, were the beginnings of telegraph service via a connection between the lighthouse at Point Lobos and San Francisco. By 1860, Los Angeles was also linked telegraphically with the Bay area. The next year the first telegraphic message arrived on the East Coast from California, addressed to President Lincoln.

Banking was another enterprise related to communication. Some frontier bankers began as saloon keepers or stage coach operators who kept strong safes on their premises. On their visits to town, miners entrusted their hard-earned treasure to these men for safekeeping. In contrast with modern banks, which pay interest to their depositors, western merchants charged depositors interest for storing their money. Indeed, early western bankers considered safeguarding a miner's doeskin bag of nuggets or "poke" of gold dust as a risky venture. Only the large national express companies possessed the facilities for the safe transportation of money.

By the mid-1850s, travel by water entered a new era. Upon finally arriving at the Golden Gate, river boats took passengers to interior ports. These included Marysville, Sacramento, and Stockton. The fastest steamboats, among them the *Senator, Cornelia,* and *New World,* sometimes foolishly engaged each other in dangerous races. On several occasions passengers on riverboats moving under high steam felt the explosion of iron boilers as decks buckled beneath them.

Steamboats and barges along California's inland rivers irregularly serviced outlying ranches. These lighter vessels continued up the Sacramento and San Joaquin Rivers, trading supplies en route. The smaller vessels were able to reach shallow bodies of water, including the Mokelumne River and Lake Tulare, which was once linked to the turbulent lower Kern River and the new town of Bakersfield.

After the Civil War, San Francisco remained California's major port. By 1870, an increasing number of ships entered its waterfront, sometimes in ballast, to load grain, lumber, wool, quicksilver, and flour. In and around the city, nearly 100 flour mills were in operation, as were scores of lumber and textile mills and foundries. Among these were the Risdon and Pacific

Iron Works, the San Francisco chocolate factory of Domenico Ghirardelli, the sugar-beet refineries of the Oxnard Brothers and Claus Spreckels, several cigar and boot factories, tanneries, ship-repair yards, and even gunpowder works. San Jose, Stockton, Sacramento, Marysville, and Merced each started woolen mills.

California also needed more blacksmiths, harness and saddle makers, wheelwrights, and carpenters. Almost every sizable town acquired a brewery or distillery and a metal or iron shop; soon canneries would also make their appearance. John Studebaker at Placerville and Phineas Banning at Wilmington began to build excellent wagons and carriages. After 1867, Banning operated a stage line into Los Angeles and eventually a railroad that reached San Pedro's harbor.

As the state's population grew, fishing and whaling became important industries. In 1855 alone, 500 whaling vessels visited the California coast. That same year, firms as far north as Sacramento were smoking and salting salmon. As canned salmon production increased, Monterey emerged as a terminus for anchovy and sardine fleets while San Pedro became a tuna-packing center. San Diego too was processing tons of mackerel, sole, sand dabs, skipjack, albacore, rockfish, and barracuda. In order to meet the demand for shellfish, clams, crabs, and abalone were increasingly harvested all along the California coast.

The building of a transcontinental railroad would greatly expand manufacturing, commercial fishing, and produce marketing. The state was on its way to becoming a provider of what would become nationally known products. But, California sorely needed steel rails over which to ship its agricultural products and merchandise.

SELECTED READINGS

Regarding the Comstock Lode, see George D. Lyman, *The Saga of the Comstock* (1934) and his *Ralston's Ring: California Plunders the Comstock Lode* (1937). Also see Lucius Beebe and Charles Clegg, *Legends of the Comstock Lode* (1950); Oscar Lewis, *The Silver Kings* (1947); Grant H. Smith, *The History of the Comstock Lode* (1943), reissued with new material by Joseph Tingley (1998); Robert E. Stewart and Mary Stewart, *Adolph Sutro: A Biography* (1962) and Rodman Paul, *Mining Frontiers of the Far West* (1963). On women in mining, see Sally Zanjani, *A Mine of Her Own . . .* (1997).

For staging and freighting, see Oscar O. Winther, *Express and Stage-coach Days in California* (1936); Le Roy R. Hafen, *The Overland Mail, 1849–1869* (1926); Frank A. Root and William Elsey Connelley, *The*

Overland Stage to California (1901); William Tallack, *The California Overland Express: The Longest Stage Ride in the World* (1935); William and George H. Banning, *Six Horses* (1930); Ernest A. Wiltsee, *The Pioneer Miner and Pack Mule Express* (1931); Roscoe P. and Margaret B. Conkling, *The Butterfield Overland Mail, 1857–1869* (3 vols. 1947); Walter Lang, ed., *The First Overland Mail* (2 vols. 1940–45); M. H. B. Boggs, *My Playhouse Was a Concord Coach* (1942); Noel Loomis, *Wells Fargo* (1969); Ellis Lucia, *The Saga of Ben Holladay, Giant of the Old West* (1959); J. V. Frederick, *Ben Holladay the Stagecoach King* (1940); and Edward Hungerford, *Wells Fargo: Advancing the American Frontier* (1949). See also Martin Ridge, "Reflections on the Pony Express," *Montana, The Magazine of Western History* 46 (Autumn 1996), 2–13; Samuel H. Adams, *The Pony Express* (1950); William Lightfoot Visscher, *A Thrilling and Truthful History of the Pony Express* (1908); Raymond W. Settle and Mary Lund Settle, *Empire on Wheels* (1949) and their *Saddles and Spurs* (1955) as well as his *War Drums and Wagon Wheels: The Story of Russell, Majors and Waddell* (1966). The camel experiment is in Lewis B. Lesley, *Uncle Sam's Camels* (1929) and Harlan Fowler in his *Camels to California* (Palo Alto, 1950). More on transportation is in A. C. W. Bethel, "The Golden Skein: California's Gold Rush Transportation Network," in Rawls and Orsi, eds., *A Golden State* (1999).

Descriptions of travel include William H. Brewer, *Up and Down California in 1860–1864* (1930) and W. Turrentine Jackson, *Wagon Roads West* (1952). The telegraph is the subject of Robert L. Thompson, *Wiring a Continent* (1947).

Regarding outlaws, consult William B. Secrest, *Lawmen and Desperadoes . . . 1850–1900* (1997); Joseph Henry Jackson, *Tintypes in Gold: Four Studies in Robbery* (1939) and Jackson, *Bad Company* (1949); Ben C. Truman, *Life, Adventures and Capture of Tiburcio Vásquez* (1874); and Walter Noble Burns, *The Robin Hood of El Dorado* (1932).

Early banking is in Ira B. Cross, *Financing an Empire* (4 vols. 1937); Robert G. Cleland and Frank B. Putnam, *Isaias W. Hellman and the Farmers and Merchants Bank* (1965); Robert G. Cleland and Osgood Hardy, *The March of Industry* (1929); Harris Newmark, *Sixty Years in Southern California* (repr. 1930); and J. A. Graves, *My Seventy Years in California* (1929).

CHAPTER NINETEEN

THE MESSY LAND PROBLEM

Under Hispanic law, landownership had been the basis for measuring a person's wealth and status. Actually, land in the New World theoretically belonged to the crown. The Spanish king, however, had authorized a few California land grants to deserving colonists. Later, under the Mexican colonization law of 1824, the number of these grants increased to more than 800. By the time of the American conquest, almost 14 million acres had been granted to rancheros by both Spanish and Mexican officials. A few of these claims were gargantuan; one covered nearly 1.8 million acres.

In 1846, the last year of the Mexican era, eighty-seven rancho grants were made by Governor Pico alone, mostly to personal friends. Although the U.S. and Mexican Treaty of Guadalupe Hidalgo guaranteed protection and security to landowners, invading American land seekers were appalled at the sheer size of such grants. Two different legal traditions, the Spanish and the American, were about to collide. Old-time Californios suddenly came under extreme pressure to change their languid way of life. Rancheros had, perhaps for too long, clung to their silver-trimmed saddles and horsemanship. The times were changing, and swiftly.

After 1850, rancheros were stuck with herds of stunted cattle on overgrazed pastures. These animals had to be sold at prohibitively low prices because of rising costs. The rancheros also faced fierce competition from American cattle drovers who herded stronger Texas Longhorns into the new state. Land-hungry American squatters also challenged virtually any ranchero's right to hold huge grants intact. These avaricious newcomers, oblivious to personal property rights, roamed about the countryside, moving their covered wagons onto rancho tracts, using up scarce water and grazing areas as they pleased. They even rounded up unbranded stray calves and cattle to claim their ownership.

Ranchos located near a creek or on a lake frontage were especially targeted by poachers. Overland cattle drovers stopped at such places to

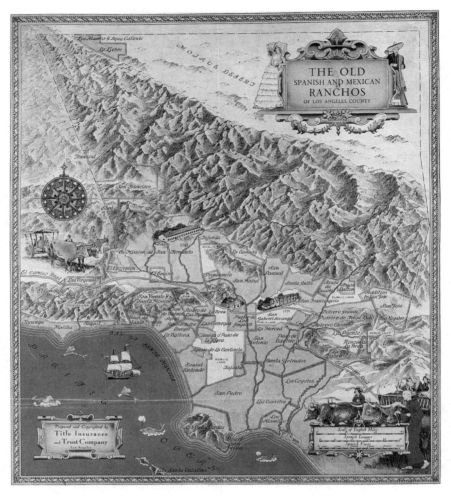

Created in 1919, this map marks the supposed boundaries of old Spanish and Mexican ranchos of L.A. County. The scale is given in English miles and Spanish leagues and varas. Photo credit: Title Insurance and Trust Company, Los Angeles (CHS-13060), collection of California Historical Society.

water their stock. These invading American homesteaders simply became permanent squatters. They asked what right had the Vallejos, the Argüellos, or the Swiss Captain Sutter to their seemingly regal estates of eleven or more square leagues? This, despite the fact that both Commodore Sloat's Proclamation and the subsequent Treaty of Guadalupe Hidalgo guaranteed the Californios their existing grantee rights.

Incoming Americans justified seizures of rancho lands by pointing out that, unlike in other areas of the United States, California had practically no arable free land that was readily available. Therefore, squatters looked upon all noncultivated land as public property.

In 1849, the U.S. Secretary of the Interior appointed William Carey Jones, like Frémont a son-in-law of the powerful Senator Benton, to investigate California's messy system of land grants. Jones and Frémont had lost no time buying up several ranchos, so Jones was certainly not an unbiased party. Yet, he did find the majority of existing land titles to be valid. An earlier study of these titles had been made by an army captain, Henry Wager Halleck. He had doubted the validity of claims that had been granted, especially during the late Mexican era. This had encouraged American arrivals to claim California land. Having faced overland dangers—deserts, mountains, and hostile Indians—these emigrants felt that they deserved western land.

A congressional act of March 1851 created a U.S. Land Commission to examine the validity of California's Mexican titles. Land claimants who failed to appear before the commission in San Francisco within two years would forfeit rights to their lands. These then would be considered "a part of the public domain of the United States." The Land Commission was mostly framed by Senator Gwin, whose sympathies lay with the invading land seekers. Indian landowners were subjected to complicated legalities, especially after fraudulent claims were uncovered.

One of the most astounding frauds was perpetuated by José Limantour, who asserted that he owned 600,000 acres, including several islands and four square leagues within and adjoining San Francisco Bay. He demanded that residents pay him "quit-claims" or get off his land. Because this was regarded as blackmail, Limantour was ultimately arrested. While awaiting trial for embezzlement, he deposited a $30,000 bond. He then fled San Francisco, forfeiting the bond and was never again seen in California.

Meanwhile, nothing but superior force could dislodge determined squatters. Some seized vacant lots in the middle of the night, erecting flimsy shanties. On December 14, 1850, forty armed squatters attempted to regain possession of a Sacramento lot from which one of them had been ejected. In the ensuing riot the mayor was injured. He then declared martial law and mobilized a force of 500 volunteers to face the squatters. In the hectic days that followed, Sacramento's sheriff was killed. So were several squatters. Meanwhile, in the mining regions outside the town, a prospector dared not leave his claim untended and then expect to find it still unoccupied upon his return. "Claim jumping" occurred precisely because notice of ownership had not been established.

In San Francisco, scarcely any land parcel was exempt from seizure by squatters. There were, in fact, "professional squatters" who hired themselves

A makeshift squatters camp in Arroyo Seco in Pasadena. Courtesy of The Security Pacific Collection, Los Angeles Public Library.

out to hold possession of coveted land. During the city's fire of 1851, especially nervy squatters fenced in disputed lots while the ashes of the city were still hot, ostensibly to prevent their claims from being "jumped" by newcomers!

Not all squatters were scoundrels. Some honestly believed that the grants on which they settled were not actually the legal possession of anyone else. They took on in good faith the backbreaking job of developing a plot of land. Accurate surveys of grants did not yet exist, and most original boundary marks had disappeared or become unrecognizable. For example, the original title to Rancho San José read: "A large oak was taken as a boundary, in which was placed the skull of a beef, and some of the limbs chopped." Such primitive tract markings sometimes included burning the owner's cattle brand onto a tree. Further confusion arose because of duplication in the names and boundaries of the earliest grants. Rancheros were at the mercy of American squatters. The Californios seldom built fences, yet hardly ever quarreled over rancho boundaries. Land was abundant and shared by all.

As squatters increased in number, politicians eagerly sought their votes. By 1854, Governor John Bigler's annual state message referred glowingly to squatters as "that enterprising and useful portion of our people." A federal Land Commission to adjudicate conflicting claims stayed in session at San Francisco until 1856. During a four-year period, rancheros diligently searched their adobes for original grants issued by Mexican governors. At great cost, lawyers looked for early maps in the state surveyor general's archives in order to confirm asserted land titles.

Desperate rancheros called neighbors and relatives to testify regarding how long they had lived on their land, for the burden of legal proof remained on the rancheros. Many of them were forced to mortgage their lands, usually at high interest rates, to pay for legal fees and expensive trips to San Francisco and Washington in order to appeal to federal officials. Making matters worse, none of the land commissioners spoke or read Spanish.

American attorneys charged large retainers for unraveling complicated land-title snarls that involved vaguely defined or overlapping boundaries. The partners in the early San Francisco law firm of Halleck, Peachy, and Billings rather quickly enriched themselves while their clients patiently waited for the results of one costly legal appeal after another. Bankers too profited from all this chaos, lending money at high interest rates to rancheros strapped for cash.

Supposedly "final" decisions of the Land Commission were, furthermore, repeatedly contested in both lower and upper courts, sometimes culminating in appeals to the United States Supreme Court. Legal delays lasted for many years. Confirmation of the patent to the San José de Gracía de Simi Rancho took fourteen years. In one case a claimant had to wait thirty-five years before he could officially call his land his own. From 1865 to 1880, the owners of Rancho Palos Verdes underwent seventy-eight separate lawsuits, six partition suits, a dozen suits over the ejection of squatters, and three condemnation proceedings. Some rancho titles were not "proved up" until the 1870s. Not all of the rancho owners lost their titles, despite all the hazards of offering evidence of ownership, as well as repeated appeals. Bernardo Yorba, by keeping good records, avoiding debts of any kind, and paying attention to his daily ranching business, retained title to his property.

Landowners, however, continued to experience angry squatter confrontations, including knifings and shootings outside the courts. Some rancheros spoke not one word of English and therefore could not understand the rigidity of U.S. land-title examinations. Meanwhile, politicians

helped squatters to become better organized, even leading to the formation of a new Settlers' party.

Confusion, however, continued for years over the legality of all land
titles. Even pueblo land claims became subject to complicated litigation.
This retarded municipal settlement of both San Francisco and Los Angeles. San Francisco, under Spanish legal tradition, was, like every pueblo,
entitled to four square leagues of land. At Los Angeles, however, its city
fathers voraciously staked out claims to four leagues squared (an area larger than four square leagues). This claim was, however, eventually whittled
down.

The 1860s were especially difficult years on California's ranchos and
farms. Insolvent landowners received only temporary relief through the
forced sale of land parcels. To make matters worse, a grasshopper invasion was followed by severe flooding. Then, in the middle of the decade, a
drought settled on California. The year 1864 saw the worst of this bone-
dry aridity. That year, 5,000 head of cattle had to be marketed at Santa
Barbara for only 37¢ per animal!

During this time, the annual income of Los Angeles land baron Abel
Stearns fell to only $300. Desperate rancheros did almost anything to
avoid bankruptcy. They sold whole corrals of horses and sought to rent
out their remaining animals for plowing. Proud rancheros were reduced
to cutting up cordwood for sale in nearby towns. As if all this misfortune
were not enough, livestock in the state began to suffer from a deadly new
cattle disease—anthrax.

California's colorful rancho tradition—that "Arcadia" so celebrated
by today's chambers of commerce—could not withstand overwhelming
Americanization. Not only did more efficient agricultural techniques replace past rancho methods, but an entire way of life quickly retreated into
history.

SELECTED READINGS

Regarding the complicated land problem, see W. W. Robinson, *Land in
California* (1948) and Robinson, *Ranchos Become Cities* (1939). Paul Wal-
lace Gates has written the following key articles: "Adjudication of Span-
ish-Mexican Land Claims in California," *Huntington Library Quarterly* 21
(May 1958), 213–36; "Pre–Henry George Land Warfare in California,"
California Historical Society Quarterly 46 (June 1967), 121–48; "The Fré-
mont-Jones Scramble For California Land Claims," *Southern California
Quarterly* 56 (Spring 1974), 13–44; and "Carpetbaggers Join the Rush for

California Land," *California Historical Quarterly* 56 (Summer 1977), 98–127. Other Gates essays are handily reprinted in his *California Ranchos and Farms* (1967).

Three early land authorities were William W. Gwin, *Private Land Titles in the State of California* (1851), *Treaty of Guadalupe Hidalgo and Private Land Claims* (1891) and William Carey Jones, *Report on the Subject of Land Titles in California* (1850). The philosopher Josiah Royce, concerned about land abuses, wrote *California From the Conquest in 1846 to the Second Vigilance Committee . . .* (repr. 1948), 367–87. Also see Henry George, *Our Land and Land Policy: National and State* (1871). Though this book is dated, it remains an important source.

A novel of conflict, reflective of land differences between Hispanic and U.S. law, is Muriel Elwood, *Against the Tide* (1950). Similar in theme is William McDonald, *California Caballero* (1936). See also Charles Outland, *Sespe Gunsmoke: An Epic Case of Ranchers versus Squatters* (1991).

Also see Gordon Bakken, "Mexican and American Land Policy: A Conflict of Cultures," *Southern California Quarterly* 75 (Fall, 1993), 237–62, and Bakken, "Rancho Cañon de Santa Ana," in Kenneth Pauley, ed., *Rancho Days in Southern California* (1997), 207–23; also Donald Pisani, "Squatter Law in California, 1850–1858," *Western Historical Quarterly* 25 (Number 3), 277–310. Finally, consult Paul Gray, *Forster vs. Pico: The Struggle for the Rancho Santa Margarita* (1998).

CHAPTER TWENTY

CALIFORNIA
AND THE UNION

California's rapid growth underlay its quick transition into statehood. By the end of its first decade as a state, population growth continued to increase at a prodigious 310 percent. In 1860, the state had reached 380,000 residents. Those born outside the state outnumbered the native-born by two to one.

With General Zachary Taylor's election to the presidency in 1848, the Whig party took over many existing governmental positions. This created a flood of unemployed Democrats, some of whom moved westward. Among them was an unusual Irish politico named David Broderick. Once in California, he quickly sought to transfer New York City's ward system to San Francisco city government.

Another new leader was William M. Gwin of Tennessee, one of California's first U.S. senators. Gwin and Broderick, in an age of political simplicity, quickly attained power. Newly arrived settlers, absorbed in mending leaks in cabin roofs, lining wells with bricks, and fencing property boundaries, showed limited interest in politics.

After the ratification of California's constitution, the first legislature met at San Jose in December 1849. Peter H. Burnett, a pioneer from Oregon, was sworn in as governor. Burnett, a Democrat, was succeeded in 1851 by another Democrat, John McDougal. Among the first tasks facing these politicians was the organization of new counties. The former military governor, General Bennett Riley, had divided the state into ten districts to be represented at the constitutional convention of 1849. These districts were subdivided by the first legislature into twenty-seven counties. By 1907, the number of counties had grown to fifty-eight.

Equally important were the beginnings of party organization in California. The functioning of the local Democratic party began after its first meeting in March of 1851 at the temporary capital of San Jose. Later that year, a Democratic convention at Benicia nominated a new candidate for governor, John Bigler, who had worked at Sutter's Fort before the discovery of gold. Bigler received the backing of his fellow Democrat Senator Gwin, won the election, and was inaugurated governor on January 8, 1852.

The legislative practices of the time were actually quite venal. Corruption generally went unquestioned. Individuals rather than parties dominated the political scene. For more than a decade there was but slight change in the relative strength of California's political parties, the state usually continuing Democratic.

In 1851, the legislature failed, after 142 ballots, to elect a successor to Senator Frémont, leaving Gwin for the better part of a year the only accredited representative at Washington. The proslavery southern viewpoint that Gwin represented stood in contrast to California's "free state" admission into the Union back in 1850. Under Gwin's tutelage the next session of the state legislature was marked by persistent efforts to promote sentiment in favor of slavery. After passage of a notorious U.S. fugitive slave act, Gwin's proslavery forces were bound to be challenged.

The campaign of 1853–54 saw a serious split in California's Democratic party. Broderick faced Gwin's prosouthern cohorts head-on. In Sacramento, at the state Democratic convention of 1854, the tension was high enough that delegates of both groups attended with both pistols and bowie knives concealed. When the two factions failed to settle their differences, two separate Democratic Party conventions were convened. Each wing selected its own candidates.

By the mid-1850s, the nativist Know-Nothing party had spread to almost every town and mining camp. Its platform was anti-Catholic as well as antiforeign. Members of this secret fraternal order, when asked about their activities, were urged to reply: "I know nothing." This party, with its secret handclasps and passwords, pushed for Asian exclusion in California. By 1856, a tide of "Americanism" swept a Know-Nothing racist candidate named J. Neely Johnson into the governorship.

Meanwhile, a hostile Gwin and Broderick were about to split the new state's Democratic party as they sought to dominate the fight over its two U.S. senatorial posts. In California's political history, their rivalry has never been exceeded in intensity. These two Democrats clashed not only politically, but personally as well. Gwin was the picture of the courtly southern gentleman. His avid followers, who held strong proslavery views, were known as the Chivalry Wing of the Democratic Party, or "Chivs." In sharp contrast, the volatile Broderick, a bold and bitter Irish Catholic northerner, was unequivocally opposed to slavery and its extension.

In March of 1857, both Gwin and John B. Weller, who had succeeded Frémont as senator in 1851, faced reelection. Gwin was especially anxious to retain his seat. In those years, the state legislature chose senators and the state's congressional representatives. The incessant partisan bickering over the selection of Gwin and Broderick followed the pair to Washington. The feud crested when Broderick denounced Gwin on the floor of the Senate, even charging him with misappropriation of government funds.

By the summer of 1859, Judge David S. Terry, a close friend of Gwin and a southern hot head, became irritated by Broderick's abusive public statements toward Gwin. After the angry brawler turned his caustic tongue on Terry as well, the judge demanded a retraction from Broderick. Both men had fierce tempers; Terry was a onetime Texas Ranger, gold prospector, and ex-Confederate. After Broderick refused to apologize, a duel was inevitable in an age when "affairs of honor" were in vogue. On September 13, the principals met in San Mateo, outside San Francisco. Judge Terry took off his court robes and loaded his pistol. Broderick's first shot went awry. Terry's shot lodged in his adversary's chest and Broderick fell dead. Although he was charged with murder, a friendly judge dismissed the case. Later, Terry, as a private attorney, was involved in several scandalous cases. In 1889, en route for a court hearing, he was himself shot dead.

After the Terry-Broderick duel, Senator Gwin's prosouthern views became a political liability to the Democrats, especially during the election of 1860, in which Abraham Lincoln rode a Republican ticket all the way to the White House. Following the outbreak of the Civil War, Gwin was arrested as disloyal to the Union cause. In the last year of that conflict, both he and Terry temporarily went into exile in Mexico along with other disgruntled Confederates.

As California had entered the Union as a free state, relatively few blacks had been brought in from the South. Among the former black slaves were Jacob Dodson, who walked west with Frémont on his 1842 expedition. James P. Beckwourth, a scout and trapper also came west in 1844, naming Beckwourth Pass. William A. Leidesdorff, vice consul to Mexico at Yerba Buena, was of African American and Danish parentage. During the gold rush, Fritz Vosburg, Abraham Holland, Gabriel Simms, and other black miners operated the Sweet Vengeance Mine profitably. Another African American man, Alvin Coffey, used gold dust mined in the High Sierra to purchase his freedom for $1,000; subsequently he paid equal amounts for the manumission of his family members. Tragically, after accepting his money, Coffey's unscrupulous master took him back to St. Louis and sold him to a new owner. In 1854 Coffey, duped and re-enslaved, returned to the California mines. Only after several more years did he earn the $7,000 with which he purchased his freedom for a second time!

The Census of 1850 listed about 1,000 African American residents of California. By 1852, this number had grown to 2,200. Legally, none of these people was a slave. The terms of California's admission to the Union prohibited slavery within its borders. But the California Fugitive Slave Act of 1851, had provided that slaves brought into California before it became a state might be forcibly returned to slave states.

Darius Stokes, an African American pastor who, by 1856, had founded fourteen churches in California, claimed that the assessed valuation of property owned by the black population of San Francisco that year was $150,000—a large sum of money at the time. Three-quarters of a million dollars had been sent back to the South by California blacks to purchase freedom for their families. Stokes remarked that "men had paid as high as $2,000 each for their companions who were enslaved, to gain their freedom, and bring them to this State."

"Andy," an African American placer miner, at a sluice. Courtesy of the Huntington Library, San Marino, California.

Among those who boldly purchased the freedom of slaves were mining engineer Moses Rodger and mine owners Gabriel Simms, Freeman Holland, and James Cousins. Another African American man purchased eight of his own children for $9,000, having earned the money by washing clothes. Mifflin Wistar Gibbs also helped his people with money he gained as a merchant. So did Mary Ellen Pleasant, known as "Mammy" Pleasant, in addition to running an affluent house of prostitution, donated $30,000 to buy rifles for John Brown's famous raid at Harpers Ferry, Virginia. She also helped various African Americans escape from slavery. In 1855, a "Convention of Colored Citizens of California" was convened in San Francisco to push for repeal of restrictive ordinances against African Americans. Their own newspaper, *The Elevator*, became the voice of the "Colored Convention."

As national disagreement between North and South grew, a majority of Californians remained loyal to the Union. An antislavery group within the state included Collis P. Huntington, Cornelius Cole, Mark Hopkins, Charles and Edwin B. Crocker, and Leland Stanford.

Meanwhile pro-South sympathizers tried to kindle the fires of secession. Among southern residents of California was Kentucky-born General Albert Sidney Johnston, U.S. Army commandant at the presidio of San Francisco. To him, the "coercion" of California into a state of war by the North was flagrantly unconstitutional. When General Johnston's loyalty came into question, he gave up his California command to join the

Confederate Army. Various southern officers from the state's Sixth Army Regiment followed him into the Confederacy.

There was other opposition to the Union. Before Lincoln's inauguration discussion arose of a "Pacific Republic" by Representative John C. Burch. This fiery legislator urged Californians, in case of a fratricidal war, to "call upon the enlightened nations of the earth to acknowledge our independence, and to protect us." John B. Weller, who became governor in 1858, also advocated that California, instead of siding with North or South, should establish on the shores of the Pacific "a mighty republic, which may in the end prove the greatest of all." In January of 1861, a resident of Stockton hoisted a flag to represent a Pacific Republic. This touched off the raising of the Stars and Stripes throughout the city. It was clear that Union feeling remained strong.

Later in 1861, once hostilities had begun, California's legislature debated whether it would support President Lincoln. That year, the lawmakers resolved that "the people of California are devoted to the Constitution and the Union now in the hour of trial and peril." They allocated funds to train volunteers for the Union Army at Drum Barracks in San Pedro.

Paradoxically, nearby Los Angeles became a hotbed for secessionists. The *Los Angeles Star* was banned from the mails for its seditious editorials. Its Bella Union Hotel on Main Street was out of bounds for Union troops because the hotel's bar was a gathering place for Southern sympathizers. They toasted Robert E. Lee with tumblers of bourbon and referred to Abraham Lincoln as "that baboon in the White House." The *Los Angeles News*, a pro-Union paper editorialized: "Los Angeles County is disloyal, double-eyed in treason, and the inhabitants break out in broad grins upon hearing the news of a Confederate victory."

Secretive supporters of the Confederacy included the Knights of the Golden Circle, Knights of the Columbian Star, and the Committee of Thirty. The members of these organizations avoided meeting in large groups, seeking not to draw attention to themselves. During the war, advocacy of secession sometimes broke out in public speeches, sermons, and prayers from the pulpit, and at covert celebrations of Confederate victories. Newspapers that urged independence for California included the *San Francisco Herald, Sacramento Standard, Alameda Country Gazette, Marysville Gazette,* and *Sonora Democrat.* The *Visalia Equal Rights Expositor,* which repeatedly printed inflammatory editorials, saw its printing press smashed by the state militia. The operation of five other "disloyal" newspapers was wrecked by mob violence.

To counteract growing secessionist sentiment, the California legislature enacted severe emergency measures. One such law made it a misde-

168 CALIFORNIA: A HISTORY

meanor "to display rebel flags or devices." Illegal behavior also came to include "adherence to the enemy" by "endorsing, defending, or cheering" the subversion of United States authority. Other state laws were enacted "to exclude traitors and alien enemies from the courts of justice in civil cases." Secessionist dissension at El Monte, Visalia, San Luis Obispo, Santa Barbara, San Bernardino, and Los Angeles was discouraged by the presence of federal troops.

During the great conflict, Californians were spared actual warfare at home. Pro-Union demonstrations took place in all parts of the state, with resolutions of loyalty adopted at mass meetings in various towns and counties. San Francisco Home Guards promoted enlistments in the Union Army, kept an eye out for conspiracy, and worked vigorously for the election of a pro-Union war governor. Californians, having cast their vote for Lincoln in 1860, chose Leland Stanford, one of the builders of the Central Pacific Railroad, as their wartime governor. Meanwhile, Lincoln's popularity remained so great that in 1864 he would again receive the state's vote for the presidency.

California provided indispensable financial strength for the Union cause. As a "hard-money" state, it did not at first gracefully accept national laws making paper greenbacks legal tender. Californians, accustomed to trading in real gold and silver, did not trust greenbacks as a stable currency. Yet California gold flowed into the federal treasury, bolstering the nation's economy during the stressful wartime period. The state also helped to supply the Union armies with wool, wheat, and other raw materials.

The war hastened California's integration into national life in other ways as well. Passage of the Pacific Railroad Bill of 1862 by Congress was facilitated by the absence of Southern legislators who previously had blocked adoption of a northern railroad route. During 1863, work on the Central Pacific Railroad began at Sacramento. As that project's principal advocate, Governor Stanford joined national party leaders in temporarily abandoning the name "Republican." They sought the support of all citizens under a Union party label. Nevertheless, anyone who deviated from expressions of Northern loyalty was apt to feel the whip of public censure.

Californians were moved to new heights of patriotism for the Union cause by Thomas Starr King, a popular Unitarian preacher. As many as 40,000 persons came to hear him speak at mass meetings. Although King lived in California for less than four years, he was an extraordinary figure in the history of the state. After his arrival from Boston in 1860, he became a major spokesman for the Union cause and raised funds for the Sanitary Commission, forerunner of the Red Cross. Over one-fourth of its donations came from California. King's eloquence was so great that his supporters claimed he "saved California for the Union."

Relatively few of the state's residents saw active service, for conscription was never enforced. Only some 15,000 Californians enlisted in the Union army. Some of these volunteers spent the war years pacifying Indians in Arizona and New Mexico. The "California Column," under the command of Colonel James H. Carleton, marched to Yuma, then into New Mexico. But they were too late to forestall a Confederate invasion there. Stranded amid whirling winds and itchy desert sands, their only fight seemed to be what derisively came to be called "the battle of the fleas."

Because Massachusetts paid large bounties for volunteers out of a special fund earmarked for recruiting, a company consisting mainly of native-born Californians was organized at San Jose. They were actually equipped with lassoes, which they used expertly. Another unit, the "California Hundred," sailed through the Golden Gate on December 11, 1862, leaving cheering crowds behind at dockside. Five weeks later, after a trip around Cape Horn, these troops reached Boston for service in the Union Army. Finally, during 1865, Californians rode with General Philip H. Sheridan in the defeat of Robert E. Lee's Army of Northern Virginia. Some were even present for Lee's surrender to Ulysses S. Grant at Appomattox Court House.

Once the war ended, Governor Stanford was elected to the U.S. Senate from 1885 to 1893. A railroad builder and skillful politician, Stanford created one of the largest personal fortunes in the West. Also repeatedly reelected to the Senate was George Hearst, father of the well-known publisher, William Randolph Hearst. Another senator was a geriatric wonder. Cornelius Cole, during his 102 years from 1822 to 1924, lived within the life spans of every U.S. president from John Adams through John F. Kennedy—who was already born when Cole finally died.

In the years after the Civil War, both of the major political parties remained relatively conservative, both in California and nationally. Not until the Progressive Era would voters move toward embracing needed political and economic reforms.

SELECTED READINGS

Regarding early state politics, see Arthur Quinn, *The Rivals: William Gwin, David Broderick and the Birth of California* (1994); A. R. Buchanan, *David S. Terry of California: Dueling Judge* (1956); David Williams, *David C.*

Broderick: A Political Portrait (1969); Jeremiah Lynch, *A Senator of the Fifties: David C. Broderick of California* (1911); William H. Ellison, ed., "Memoirs of Hon. William M. Gwin," *California Historical Society Quarterly* 19 (1940), 1–367; Earl Pomeroy, "California, 1846–1860: Politics of a Representative Frontier State," *California Historical Society Quarterly* 32 (December 1953), 291–302; H. Brett Melendy, "Who Was John McDougal?" *Pacific Historical Review* 29 (August 1960), 231–43.

Civil War California is chronicled in Percival Cooney, "Southern California in Civil War Days," *Historical Society of Southern California Annual* 13 (1924), 54–68; Helen B. Walter, "Confederates in Southern California," *Historical Society of Southern California Quarterly* 35 (March 1953), 41–55; Benjamin F. Gilbert, "The Confederate Minority in California," *California Historical Society Quarterly* 40 (June 1941), 154–70; Jay Monaghan, *Civil War on the Western Border* (1955); Oscar Lewis, *The War in the Far West, 1861–1865* (1961); Aurora Hunt, *The Army of the Pacific* (1951); Gerald Stanley, "Civil War Politics in California," *Southern California Quarterly* 54 (Summer 1982), 115–32, and Stanley, "Slavery and the Origins of the Republican Party in California," *Southern California Quarterly* 50 (Spring 1978), 1–16; John W. Robinson, *Los Angeles in the Civil War* (1977); Leo P. Kibby, "Some Aspects of California's Military Problems During the Civil War," *Civil War History* 5 (September 1959), 251–62; Milton H. Shutes, *Lincoln and California* (1943); Edward A. Dickson, "Lincoln and Baker: The Story of a Great Friendship," *Historical Society of Southern California Quarterly* 34 (September 1952), 229–42.

About Civil War politics, see Richard H. Peterson, "Thomas Starr King in California, 1860–64," *California History* (Spring 1990), 12–21; Ronald C. Woolsey, "Disunion or Dissent? Southern California Attitudes Toward the Civil War," *Southern California Quarterly* 66 (Fall 1984), 185–205; George T. Clark, *Leland Stanford* (1931); Ann Casey, "Thomas Starr King and the Secession Movement," *Historical Society of Southern California Quarterly* 43 (September 1961), 245–75; Russell M. Posner, "Thomas Starr King and the Mercy Million," *California Historical Society Quarterly* 43 (December 1964), 291–307; George Upshur, *As I Recall Them: Memories of Crowded Years* (1936); Carl B. Swisher, *Stephen J. Field, Craftsman of the Law* (1930, 1969); and John Higham, "The American Party, 1886–1891," *Pacific Historical Review* 19 (February 1950), 37–46.

Regarding early African Americans in California, see Douglas Henry Daniels, *Pioneer Urbanites: A Social and Cultural History of Black San Francisco* (1990); Eugene H. Berwanger, *The Frontier Against Slavery* (1967); J. Max Bond, *The Negro in Los Angeles* (1972); Delilah Beasley, *Negro Trail*

Blazers of California (1919); Rudolph M. Lapp, *Blacks in Gold Rush California* (1977); Sue Bailey Thurman, *Pioneers of Negro Origin in California* (1952); Lionel U. Ridout, "The Church, the Chinese and the Negroes in California, 1849–1893," *Historical Magazine of the Protestant Episcopal Church* 28 (June 1959), 115–38; William E. Franklin, "The Archy Case," *Pacific Historical Review* 32 (May 1963), 137–54; Mifflin Wistar Gibbs, *Shadows and Light: An Autobiography* (1902); and Charlotta Bass, *Forty Years: Memoirs From the Pages of a Newspaper* (1960). Shirley Ann Wilson Moore, "African Americans in California: A Brief Historiography," *California History* 75 (Fall 1996), 194–8. In the same issue of this journal are articles about early blacks in California by Clarence Caesar, Susan Bragg, and Rick Moss. See also Quintard Taylor, *In Search of the Racial Frontier: African Americans in the American West* (2000).

A useful bibliography covering this period is Richard Quebedeaux, *Prime Sources of California and Nevada Local History . . . 1850–1906* (1992).

CHAPTER TWENTY-ONE

SHIPS AND RAILS

Before the building of a transcontinental railroad, maritime transportation flourished. By the mid-1850s, the California Steam Navigation Company controlled traffic in and around San Francisco Bay and along the inland rivers. So powerful was "California Steam" in setting freight and passenger rates that smaller shipping companies actually welcomed the arrival of the transcontinental railroad. The expense of getting from the East Coast to California by sea averaged $400, the trip taking as long as 120 days. Such a trip might be made by transcontinental rail for as little as $150. But critics maintained that the cost of construction of the railroad would be both risky and prohibitive without huge government land grants and loans to the builders.

Nevertheless, the idea of building a railroad all the way to the Pacific gradually gained acceptance. The deeply rutted wagon trails were clearly inadequate. The country was straining to expand: moving mail, passengers, and freight more quickly was essential. While no one disagreed that a cross-country railroad should traverse the shortest possible distance, the exact route was debated for years. Washington legislators had no experience with such questions as: Should construction and operation of a transcontinental railroad be administered by the government? Or should a system be built and operated privately? How far should federal and state governments go toward providing subsidies to railroad construction companies?

As early as 1852, one suggested route swung southward from the American Midwest through Texas, moving westward by way of Arizona's Gila Valley to Yuma, then on to San Diego. The next year, Congress appropriated funds to sponsor four western survey parties to recommend overland railroad routes. But, when their specific suggestions came in, northern and southern congressmen clashed over future rail routes. As noted, the outbreak of the Civil War brought an end to any prospects of a southern route.

Finally, on June 28, 1861, three California merchants founded the Central Pacific Railroad Company at Sacramento. These were Leland Stanford, who acted as president, Collis P. Huntington as vice-president, and Mark Hopkins as treasurer. These three men, along with Charles Crocker, who joined them later, became known as the "Big Four." Originally, their plans relied less on their own efforts than on the determination of a talented young civil engineer named Theodore D. Judah.

He had already laid out rails for a projected Sacramento Valley Railroad to serve mining regions along the slopes of the Sierra Nevada. Judah's small railway consisted of only twenty-three miles of track. In an age of widespread skepticism, some called him "Crazy Judah." Others accused him of promoting the construction of railroads purely for personal gain. Nevertheless, Judah had considerable construction experience, which gave his bold engineering concepts credence. Traveling to Washington, he personally lobbied Congress for passage of a transcontinental railroad bill. Ultimately Judah became the chief engineer of the powerful Central Pacific Railway Company.

On July 1, 1862, Congress finally passed the long-awaited Pacific Railroad Bill. This legislation authorized two construction companies to begin laying the tracks that would eventually link both coasts of North America. The Union Pacific Company was to build 1,006 miles of track westward from Omaha, Nebraska, while the Central Pacific's crews moved eastward out of California. In addition to a 400-foot right of way, each construction company claimed huge land grants. These stretched off in checkerboard fashion on either side of the track, along the length of their lines. The two construction companies were also entitled to 1.28 million acres of public land for every hundred miles of track they laid, plus $3 million in credit, supported by government bonds.

Judah had induced Congress to subsidize a loan to the Central Pacific of $16,000 per mile of track laid across level land, $32,000 per mile in the foothills, and $48,000 per mile across mountainous areas. As if the deal were not generous enough, the "Big Four" connived to collect twice the prescribed subsidy on some hundred miles of track that the Central Pacific laid. They did this by convincing Congress that the foothills of the Sierra Nevada began farther west than government maps specified! Such reasoning, written into the federal bill, "moved" the Sierra range within only ten miles of Sacramento—near the center of the great valley of California.

Who were the "Big Four?" Stanford was a grocer; Crocker owned a dry-goods store, while Huntington and Hopkins operated a hardware business. All had made their money selling to miners in the gold rush. They were willing to risk their small fortunes in a highly speculative venture. In 1863, Judah, the most vocal of these railroad advocates, would never be credited with having originated their risky project. He went eastward via Panama to seek loans with which to buy out his partners. En route he was stricken with yellow fever and died.

The generous provisions of the Pacific Railroad Act were further increased in 1864. An amendatory act doubled the land grants and other financial inducements to the two railroad companies. The original intention of Judah's partners was to amass the lucrative federal subsidies by laying down the roadbed and track as quickly as possible. Crocker, who supplanted Judah as the Central Pacific's construction manager, not only wanted to build cheaply, but he also wished to get out quickly by selling the company to other investors, who would take over actual operation of the road.

Building eastward from Sacramento, the Central Pacific had to ship machinery and building supplies around Cape Horn, or via Panama, at great expense. In addition, the Sierra Nevada presented a more formidable obstacle to the engineers of the Central Pacific than the Rocky Mountains did to their counterparts employed by the Union Pacific. The Sierra, however, did supply the Central Pacific with timber for ties, trestles, and the long snow sheds required to move heavy items in midwinter. Meanwhile, the Union Pacific's crews worked their way across the treeless Great Plains.

In the Sierra, Central Pacific track workers used hundreds of picks, axes, blasting powder, and dumpcarts. Some 15,000 Chinese workers made up the C.P.'s track crews. They were not well treated and were assigned dangerous tasks. These "Celestials," a name taken from "the Celestial Empire" of China, were tied by ropes around their waists as they chipped away at the sides of steep cliffs. After they had chiseled out a footing along canyon walls, other Chinese laborers made use of this toehold to blast out a roadway for the track. Despite repeated delays, the Central Pacific crossed the Sierra summit in December of 1867. Further eastward lay less rugged terrain.

As the rail lines stretched toward one another, a rivalry developed between the two railway companies. This became intense when Crocker announced a back-breaking schedule of a mile of track for every working day. His patient Chinese labor force—patronizingly referred to as "Crocker's Pets"—amazingly responded to every new demand management made upon them. By June 1868 they had reached Reno. After the Union Pacific reported laying six miles of track in one day, Crocker's Chinese labor force countered with seven miles, ultimately setting a record with ten miles and fifty-six feet of track laid in under twelve hours. Crocker took per-

Chinese construction workers on the Central Pacific Railroad at "Cape Horn," a strategic point in the crossing of the Sierra crest. Courtesy Andrew Rolle.

sonal pride in his workforce's more than successful competition with the U. P.'s Irish track-layers.

Because the government's payments were based on the number of track miles laid, each railroad company was eager to cover as much ground as possible. Therefore, as the distance between the rival construction crews lessened, their competition grew keener. For a time, grading crews of the respective railroads worked within a few hundred yards of each other along parallel lines, their employers unable to agree as to where the tracks should join. Early in 1869, federal railroad commissioners settled the matter decisively, ruling that the two lines must meet in northern Utah Territory, 56 miles west of Ogden, 1,086 miles from Omaha, and 689 miles from Sacramento. There the construction gap between the railroads closed.

Eventually, it remained only to drive the ceremonial last spike. On the tenth day of May, 1869, near Utah Territory's desolate Promontory Point, the ceremony was performed, uniting Atlantic and Pacific with bands of steel. Two bonnet-stacked, wood-burning locomotives faced each other on the shining new tracks, one headed east, the other west. Several hundred witnesses were present, including the Twenty-first Infantry Regiment of the U.S. Army, officials of both railroads, a photographer, and nearby settlers. Following the symbolic driving of Arizona's spike of gold, silver, and iron, and Nevada's spike of silver, the final tie, crafted of California laurel, was put in place and the final spike, forged of California gold, was readied. Each blow of the silver sledge that drove the final spike home was announced via telegraph to both distant coasts.

San Francisco gave itself up to three days of celebration after the telegraph announced: "The last rail is laid! The last spike is driven! The Pacific Railroad is completed!" At Sacramento the bells and whistles of thirty different locomotives joined in a chorus with the bells of the city's churches and fire houses. Completion of the largest engineering job yet undertaken in North America was, indeed, a decisive event. Exactly one hundred years after California's settlement by the Portolá-Serra expedition, its frontier isolation had come to a close.

After completion of the Central Pacific line, the "Big Four" obtained a charter for a second railroad to be called the Southern Pacific. This new line extended their north-south routes through California's Central Valley and along the coast from Oregon to southern California. The S.P., as it came to be called, also reached out from Los Angeles to Yuma on the Arizona border, then on to Tucson and into New Mexico Territory. By 1882, the S.P. met the Texas and Pacific Railroad in Texas. The next year the Southern Pacific's "Sunset Route" reached New Orleans.

Not only did its Palace Sleeping Cars carry thousands of excursionists and new settlers westward, but long lines of boxcars transported wheat, gold, silver, and lumber. This brought the "Big Four" wealth undreamed of by their late engineer, Judah. The Southern Pacific Railroad Company ultimately serviced thousands of miles, with steamship connections linking California with New York and Havana.

The Southern Pacific Company was granted over 11 million acres of government land within California alone. The railroad also demanded possession of a great deal of county and city lands; indeed, the extent of a particular city's generosity helped the "Big Four" decide whether to provide railroad service to it. The governments of California towns, large and small, soon realized that enticement of the railroad required money, with which a community would buy construction bonds. When the S.P. was repeatedly accused of extorting funds from towns along prospective routes, the "Big Four" retorted that the company needed this seed money to build bridges, overpasses, and to grade track beds. Among the interior towns that mushroomed because the railroad had come to them were Fresno, Merced, Tulare, Modesto, and Bakersfield. Some communities which the railroad bypassed were left to slumber and ultimately died.

Not until the 1880s was the S.P.'s monopoly challenged. Building westward, the Atchison, Topeka and Santa Fe Railroad reached El Paso in 1881. It then crossed New Mexico and Arizona, sending its wood-burning locomotives into California at Needles, where it bridged the Colorado River. Next the Santa Fe purchased and rented a series of short lines, entering Los Angeles in 1887. With a new track northward from Bakersfield to Stockton, the Santa Fe also bought or negotiated its way into San Francisco. Although the Southern Pacific would wield its mighty economic and political power in California for many years to come, there was no denying that a new competitive railroad age had arrived.

SELECTED READINGS

Inland water transportation is described in Stan Garvey, *King and Queen of the River . . . Paddlewheel Steamboats Delta King and Delta Queen* (1999); also in Jerry MacMullen, *Paddle Wheel Days in California* (1944); and in Andrew Rolle, "Turbulent Waters: Navigation and California's Southern Central Valley," *California History* 75 (Summer 1996), 128–37.

Regarding railroads, the most recent scholarship is Richard Orsi's *Sunset Limited: The Southern Pacific Railroad* (2005). Also see George Albright, *Official Explorations for Pacific Railroads* (1921); Creed Haymond, *The Central Pacific Railroad Company: Its Relation to the Government* (1888); John Moody, *The Railroad Builders* (1921); Robert E. Riegel, *The Story of the Western Railroads* (1926); Wesley S. Griswold, *A Work of Giants* (1962); Carl Wheat, "A Sketch of the Life of Theodore D. Judah," *California Historical Society Quarterly* 4 (September 1925), 219–71; John H. Kemble, "The Big Four at Sea: The History of the Occidental and Oriental Steamship Company," *Huntington Library Quarterly* 3 (April 1940), 330–58; John D. Galloway, *The First Transcontinental Railroad* (1950); Neill C. Wilson and Frank J. Taylor, *Southern Pacific: The Roaring Story of a Fighting Railroad* (1952). Glenn C. Quiett, *They Built the West: An Epic of Rails and Cities* (1934); Gilbert H. Kneiss, *Bonanza Railroads* (1941); Glenn D. Bradley, *Story of the Santa Fe* (1920); James Marshall, *Santa Fe: The Railroad That Built an Empire* (1949); L. L. Waters, *Steel Trails to Santa Fe* (1950).

Recent scholarship includes William Deverell, *Railroad Crossing: Californians and the Railroad* (1994); Donovan Hofsommer, *The Southern Pacific* (1986); David Lavender, *The Great Persuader [Collis P. Huntington]*

(1970); Ward McAfee, *California's Railroad Era, 1850–1911* (1973) and Keith Bryant, *History of the Atchison, Topeka, and Santa Fe Railway* (repr. 1982). The absorption of only one of many small railroads by the Southern Pacific Company is recounted in Andrew Rolle, *Henry Mayo Newhall and His Times* (1991).

CHAPTER TWENTY-TWO

AGRICULTURAL
AND URBAN GROWTH

The economy of most agricultural states depends heavily on a single crop, such as corn, tobacco, cotton, meat or dairy products. California produces more than 200 different farm commodities. The garden and field planting that went on at the missions was later complemented by cattle ranching and sheep grazing. By the early 1860s, more than 3 million cattle roamed California's hills and valleys while several hundred thousand sheep roamed the state's ranges. Trouble was bound to flare up with sheep herders when cattle ranchers erected barbed-wire fences for their stock. Lambs give off a particularly noxious odor, and they also overcrop cattle ranges, which partially explains the animosity between the two groups.

Conflicts sometimes became violent. The sheepherders seldom emerged victorious as cattle ranchers were better organized. Among them were two aggressive German immigrants, Henry Miller and his partner Charles Lux. They established a ranching empire that covered more than 800,000 acres. Their lands stretched from the Mexican border northward into Oregon and eastward to Nevada. Miller and Lux, by rigidly controlling water rights, became the largest ranchers on the Pacific Coast. In addition to raising more than a million head of cattle, they also herded sheep and grew crops on many thousands of acres. These wealthy cattle barons drove small ranchers and farmers out of business, particularly in drought years. Some land monopolists were backed by eastern, English, and Scottish capital.

Ranching, however, was a risky investment. During the devastating drought of 1863–64, the dust on the ranges was so dense that it killed animals by clogging their nostrils. The bleached skeletons of thousands of cattle, sheep, and horses dotted the hillsides. Abel Stearns alone lost 30,000 head of cattle on his ranchos near Los Angeles. By the late 1860s, range land sold for as little as ten cents an acre.

Vicente Lugo ranch house and some of its landlords and neighbors, 1892. C. C. Pierce Collection, courtesy of the Huntington Library, San Mariano, California.

Meanwhile, California's cattle herds, roaming the ranges without proper care, had markedly deteriorated. Because of inbreeding, they had become scrawny and bony. Their numbers had also been drastically reduced by the rough conditions of the drought years. Large ranchers began to import heavier, meatier strains of cattle into California. They adopted new techniques of stock feeding, breeding, and land management. While such efforts sometimes rescued the cattle industry, they also spelled the end of small ranchers without enough capital to compete.

Neither California butter nor milk had been marketed aggressively during the Mexican period, the chief value of cattle being their hides and tallow. In the new American era, however, the production of dairy products grew steadily. The breeding of Holstein and Jersey cattle (breeds known for the quality of their milk) transformed Stanislaus and San Joaquin Counties into important dairy centers. Dairies close to large centers of population moved California beyond Wisconsin as first in the nation in dairy production.

Before and after the Civil War, a mechanical revolution in agriculture produced iron and steel plows, as well as mowers, reapers, and threshers.

Wheat and corn were increasing in demand on international markets, and California's climate and soil were splendidly suited to growing these and other grains. Whereas the state had previously imported most of its grain, vast new ranches in the Central Valley made that region a major exporter of oats, barley, and corn. The state produced a hard, dry wheat that was popular with British millers. In fact, grain exports to Liverpool, England, were controlled by Isaac Friedlander, the "Grain King." He skillfully managed his own production, shipping terminals, and global marketing, shipping durum wheat in burlap bags to Australia and China as well as to Mediterranean countries.

By 1890, annual wheat production in California reached 40 million bushels and the state ranked second among all states in its growth. As the profits on wheat rose, fierce competition developed between large growers and small farmers. The big landowners, however, could make more favorable deals with middlemen, railroad agents, and steamship owners, eventually buying out those farmers who could not stay solvent.

Among the new crops put into expanded production during and after the Civil War was cotton. But not until the second decade of the twentieth century did cotton production boom, when irrigation projects in the Imperial and San Joaquin Valleys increased markedly. The quality of California cotton was superior even to some grown in the American South, and the yield per acre frequently higher. No such success story can be told concerning efforts to produce silk in the state. Although the legislature had offered a bounty for silkworm cocoons in 1862, sericulture in the Golden State never amounted to much more than a passing fad.

Far more important was the development of citriculture. From the days when the padres first introduced fruit trees into mission gardens, horticulture expanded but slowly. Before the development of the refrigerated railroad car, California fruit growers, remote from large markets, could not market their perishable crops in the East. After its advent, however, some growers prospered by raising and marketing one unique crop—citrus fruits.

California's citrus exports included lemons, tangerines, and grapefruit. But the real symbol of the citrus industry became the orange. In the mission period, orange groves were small and undeveloped, the trees producing a pithy, thick-skinned, and sour fruit. One of the earliest groves was planted at San Gabriel Mission. In 1834, the French Luís (or Louis) Vignes, transplanted thirty-five of these trees to his residence in Los Angeles, near today's Union Station. In 1841 another Angeleño, William Wolfskill, expanded his orange grove to seventy acres. His son sent the first trainload of oranges eastward to St. Louis in 1877.

California orange pickers about 1895. Library of Congress, LC-USZ62-78372.

Substantial experimentation in the cultivation of oranges occurred at Riverside. There, in 1870, Judge John Wesley North bought 4,000 acres of barren land on credit. In cooperation with the transcontinental railroads, North was successful in introducing new growers to California from Michigan and Iowa. Among the settlers in North's agricultural colony were Luther Calvin Tibbets and his wife Eliza, who in 1873 introduced the Washington Navel variety of oranges to California. Two tiny cuttings that the couple brought to California grew to maturity and produced a juicy, flavorful, and seedless orange. California's climate and soil was especially suited to the Washington Navel. The two Tibbets trees became the parent stock for planting throughout the 1880s.

In the early days of the orange industry there was no crop-inspection or fruit-quarantine system. Trouble came when destructive insects were introduced in California through imported nursery stock. The cottony cushion scale arrived from Australia in 1868. So injurious was this pest that, for a time, California's fledgling orange industry was threatened with extinction. Then a small ladybug (also from Australia) that attacked the scale was purposely introduced in the state, and eventually this species checked the spread of the scale. The black scale also seriously damaged the citrus industry, as did a sooty mold that caused decay among individual trees. To fight the mold and the black scale, growers had to spray tree trunks thoroughly. Fumigation also offered protection against diseases affecting orange trees.

Another hazard to the orange industry was frost. To protect their crops from extreme cold, citrus growers used oil heaters that burned a cheap crude fuel. Nearby city dwellers, whose house furnishings, draperies, and rugs were soon covered with soot from oil burners, complained bitterly. Eventually, growers protected their orchards against cold-weather damage by the use of wind machines, which keep air currents in motion to prevent frost from settling on the fruit.

Growers who marketed their own fruit remained easy prey to speculative commission agents who bought citrus in large quantities, securing rebates from railroad companies. Paradoxically, the larger the individual grower's crop, the more indebted he became to middlemen and packers. As a result, in 1893 growers formed the cooperative marketing California Fruit Growers Exchange. Its trade name, "Sunkist," inaugurated a nationwide advertising campaign.

Indeed, the California citrus industry now set about to change the American breakfast diet. Decorated trains, which dispensed oranges at whistle stops across the Midwest, gaudy advertising billboards, free orange wrappers (to prevent mold), spoons, and essay- and poetry-writing contests all helped carry the message of California's "golden fruit" eastward. As a result of this campaign, orange juice, or sliced oranges and grapefruits, became substitutes for such morning staples as buckwheat cakes, bacon, ham, porridge, and waffles. A new slogan read "Oranges for health and California for wealth." Chambers of commerce and real estate boosters joined the advertising campaign begun by the citrus industry.

California has long produced nearly all of the lemons grown in the United States. Introduction of the Eureka and Lisbon varieties rounded out the development of its citriculture. The Eureka lemon tree from Sicily is an early-bearing variety. The heavy foliage of Lisbon lemons protects its fruit from sunburn. Among those attracted to California citrus groves were retired businesspeople from the East and Midwest, some of whom had lost their health. A new life in California's sunshine and dry air proved restorative and rewarding. Often these older immigrants brought needed capital to the state, and some of them built fine residences amid their groves.

Other unique crops flourished there. The Santa Clara Valley became the world's chief producer of Italian prunes, while Sylmar developed into an olive-growing area. In 1867, at Santa Barbara, the soft shell walnut was planted commercially, and at Los Angeles, in 1873, Wolfskill and Vignes replanted the English walnut. Today that variety, once called the Madeira or Persian walnut, accounts for almost 100 percent of the nation's walnut production. California also produces virtually all the almonds grown in the United States.

The pioneer botanist Luther Burbank, from 1875 until his death in 1926, carried on experiments with garden crops at Santa Rosa. Burbank's efforts made possible increased competitive production of tomatoes, lettuce, cauliflower, carrots, alfalfa, sugar beets, celery, and potatoes. Accompanying California's burgeoning agricultural productivity was the development of a canning industry; such trade names as Del Monte, Iris, and (in the case of sugar packaging) Spreckels became familiar names in American households.

A fortunate combination of climate and soil, particularly in northern California, also gave viticulture a propitious start. Today, some 90 percent of the U.S. grape crop, and most of its wine, comes from California. Vines of the European *Vitis vinifera* stock were originally planted at the missions, where they bore grapes for more than 100 years.

In 1857, a group of Germans formed the Los Angeles Vineyard Society on lands located thirty miles southeast of Los Angeles. They gave their tract the name Anaheim, from its site in the Santa Ana Valley and the German word for home, or "heim." Around their property the Germans built a fence five and one-half miles long, consisting of 40,000 willow poles. The poles took root, forming a living wall around the colony. Such "fortifications" were constructed mainly to keep out roving herds of cattle. Using water from the Santa Ana River, the colonists planted more than 400,000 grapevines.

Among other European wine makers was Agoston Haraszthy, a Hungarian credited with the introduction, in 1851, of Zinfandel grapes at his Sonoma vineyard. Others included Étienne Thée and Charles Lefranc, two French vintners who founded the Almaden Vineyards at Los Gatos. In 1860, Charles Krug founded the Napa Valley winery that was later acquired by the Mondavi family.

By the 1880s, no organization planted quite so many grapes as did the Italian-Swiss Agricultural Colony. Located at Asti, it was founded by northern Italians who had settled in the Napa and Sonoma Valleys. The

Harvesting in the San Fernando Valley, ca. 1900. Library of Congress, LC-USZ62-53885.

colony's 1897 vintage was so large that there was insufficient cooperage in all California to hold the wine. A reservoir had to be chiseled out of solid rock. This became the largest wine tank in the world. When empty, its floor could accommodate 200 dancers.

New wineries appeared not only in Sonoma and Napa but in the Livermore Valley and the San Joaquin–Sacramento Valley. At Cucamonga, in southern California, the Secondo Guasti family owned what they billed as "the largest vineyard in the world." The area became known for the production of such fortified dessert wines as ports, sherries, and muscatels. Despite increasing urban development, the California wine industry has become a world-class enterprise. At Fresno, Modesto, Madera, and other interior towns, Italian and French immigrants established even more vineyards. The Inglenook Cellars at Rutherford, the Paul Masson winery at

Saratoga, and the Beaulieu vineyards of Georges de Latour, also at Rutherford, became internationally important.

Although America's Prohibition Era of the 1920s would temporarily put an end to wine making, the industry flourished again as soon as Prohibition was repealed. During this period the Louis M. Martini and Mondavi families began to produce quality table wines near St. Helena in the Napa Valley. Ernest and Julio Gallo, also Italians, formed the largest winery in the world, later acquiring even the smaller Martini enterprise.

Extensive land reclamation saw the planting of such new commercial crops as artichokes, asparagus, and watermelons. One of the first regions to undergo reclamation was the triangle of land formed by the Sacramento and San Joaquin Rivers. On this half million acres, originally consisting of a group of islands and swampy plains, were built dykes, canals, conduits, and check dams to protect new farms from floods. The "Delta" has since become known for its output of rice, sugar beets, asparagus, spinach, celery, and other vegetables.

Eventually irrigation projects had to be devised to ensure California's agricultural future. The Imperial Valley is a notable example. Sometimes called the "American Nile," this fertile valley is located in the hot southeastern part of the state. Much of the soil is sandy and alluvial. George Chaffey, a Canadian who in the mid-1880s had founded an irrigation colony at Ontario, also planned to transform the Imperial Valley. By diverting the waters of the Colorado River, which ran unchecked into the Gulf of California, Chaffey made it possible for the Imperial Land Company to bring a large number of settlers into the valley by 1900. However, in 1905 a flood began that lasted almost two years, creating the Salton Sea. This torrent could not be stopped until the breach in the banks of the Colorado was sealed.

With flood damage repaired, by 1913 the Imperial Valley's canal system covered more than half a million acres, extending below the border into Mexico. This operation was then the largest irrigation project in the United States. The number of acres planted in barley, alfalfa, and other crops expanded rapidly, and the Imperial Valley, equally famous for its cantaloupes and other melons, became known as the "Winter Garden of the World." Farther north, the once arid Coachella Valley was also transformed by artificial irrigation.

As rancho holdings were broken up by controversies over legal titles, the lands fell into the hands of urban promoters, and the communities that sprang up on these sites took the names of the former ranchos. William Heath Davis converted part of Rancho San Leandro (acquired by marriage from the Estudillo family) into the central California community of San Leandro. He urged a neighboring native family, the Peraltas, to do likewise. Their claims covered the present sites of Berkeley, Oakland, and Alameda. The ownership of such vast holdings was disputed in the courts for years. Little profit was gained by the original owners from urban development of their ranchos.

At first, towns were little more than country crossroads, which became farm supply centers. In the 1850s, long before railroad connections with the outer world had been provided, Davis and other town founders strained their financial resources to the breaking point. They built houses, paved streets, constructed wharfs for visiting steamers, and provided hotels for exhausted overland travelers. In short, new developers tried to transform a community of crumbling adobes into a real city. At San Diego, Davis, however, was doomed to failure. He was not a good businessman, especially as compared to his competitors. By the 1860s, the real estate promoter Alonzo Erastus Horton constructed a "New San Diego." Even he lost a fortune there. But some town developers succeeded from the start. Among these was Phineas Banning, founder of Wilmington. This community was located on an estuary providing maritime access to the expanding pueblo of Los Angeles. Banning's Wilmington wharf and warehouses, built between 1851 and 1858, were sheltered by a rock jetty between Terminal and Dead Man's Islands, near what was to become "New San Pedro." The harbor's channel was dug deep enough to float barges and steam tugs carrying freight and passengers from ocean-going vessels anchored offshore. During the Civil War the U.S. Army established Camp Drum and Drum Barracks near Banning's home at Wilmington. This government installation helped to assure the future of a new port for Los Angeles.

Later in the nineteenth century, former ranchos became almost instant towns once litigation over land titles was finally settled. Pasadena mushroomed out of the sprawling Rancho San Pasqual. Benjamin D. Wilson, who had come to California with the Workman-Rowland party, enticed a group of colonists from Indiana to the area. By 1874, the group had laid out a community complete with irrigation conduits leading into new orchards and grain fields. This town, once dotted with small stands of oak trees and fields of poppies, became a winter playground of eastern millionaires.

Fortunate factors contributed to the rapid growth of towns such as Pasadena. Among these was the low cost of land; the energy of speculators in providing water as well as transportation facilities; and population pressures caused by the railroads. The Santa Fe Railroad Company alone platted twenty-five towns in the L.A. area. Other developers laid out seventy-five more. An arid countryside was quickly turned into prosperous towns. In a place his wife named Hollywood, Horace Henderson Wilcox carved out 100 acres for homesites. He could not have imagined that his land would become the future home of a new movie industry.

A flood of population descended upon the state. Flocking into southern California were unemployed cowboys and fruit pickers, farmers, engineers, health seekers, and real estate promoters. On March 7, 1886, the *Los Angeles Times* reported that cross-country passenger fares, which had formerly been as high as $125 from the Midwest, reached as low as $1. The next year 200,000 persons arrived in California by railroad. New towns sprang up, accompanied by new colleges, banks, and business institutions. Within less than two years, 100 communities had been "platted" inside Los Angeles County, which experienced prodigious growth—the result of effective advertising, the lure of the climate, and railroad competition.

Promoters familiar with Italy exploited romantic similarities between California and ancient Tuscany or Campania. The San Diego and Riverside chambers of commerce issued brochures that advertised "their" Italy of America. California soon had its own Hesperia, Rialto, Tarragona, Terracina, and Verona. At one such Italianate namesake, Venice, the real estate boom of the 1880s saw the building of imitation lagoons and piazzas along an open beach. Real estate speculators stopped at nothing as the state moved from agriculture to urbanization.

In northern California, at Senator James D. Phelan's elegant Villa Montalvo, near Saratoga, rococo porticoes, cypress hedges, stone gryphons, and classical statues sustained the mood. The facade of Stanford University's chapel framed a mosaic similar to that of a church in Rome called St. Paul Outside the Walls. These ornate architectural achievements were among the permanent results of California's real estate boom.

SELECTED READINGS

Recent scholarship concerning land and agriculture includes Richard Street, *Beasts of the Field: A Narrative History of California Farm Workers* (2004); Mark Arax and Rick Wartzman, *The King of California...The Making of a Secret American Empire* (2003); Stephanie Pincetl, *Transforming California: A Political History of Land Use and Development* (1999); David Vaught, *Cultivating California: Growers, Specialty Crops, and Labor, 1875–1920* (1999); and Steven Stoll, *The Fruits of National Advantage: Making the Industrial Countryside in California* (1998).

Regarding the orange industry, see Douglas Sackman, *Orange Empire: California and the Fruits of Eden* (2005); Matt Garcia, *A World of Its Own: Labor and Citrus in the Making of Los Angeles* (2001); Richard Sawyer, *To Make a Spotless Orange: Biological Control in California* (1996); also Minnie Tibbets Mills, "Luther Calvin Tibbets, Founder of the Navel Orange Industry of California," *Historical Society of Southern California Quarterly* 25 (December 1943), 127–61.

On cattle raising, see David Igler, *Industrial Cowboys: Miller and Lux...1850–1920* (2001); Edward Treadwell, *The Cattle King* (repr. 1950); L. T. Burcham, *California Range Land* (1957); James M. Jensen, "Cattle Drives From the Ranchos to the Gold Fields of California," *Arizona and the West* 2 (Winter 1960), 341–52; Dane Coolidge, *Old California Cowboys* (1939).

On agriculture and Indians see Dennis Alward and Andrew Rolle, "The Surveyor General: Edward Fitzgerald Beale's Administration of California Lands," *Southern California Quarterly* 53 (June 1971), 113–22; Sally Miller, "Changing Faces of the Central Valley: The Ethnic Presence," *California History* 74 (Summer, 1995), 175–89. Regarding "the father of the California wine industry," see Brian McGinty, *Strong Wine: The Life and Legend of Agoston Haraszthy* (1998); also Joan Marie Donohoe, "Agostin Haraszthy: A Study in Creativity," *California Historical Society Quarterly* 47 (June 1969), 153–63; Mildred Yorba MacArthur, *Anaheim: The Mother Colony* (1959). Iris Wilson, "Early Southern California Viticulture, 1830–1865," *Historical Society of Southern California Quarterly* 39 (September 1957), 242–50; Vincent Carosso, *The California Wine Industry, 1830–1895* (1951).

For grain production, see Rodman W. Paul, "The Great California Grain War: The Granger Challenges the Wheat King," *Pacific Historical Review* 27 (November 1958), 331–49, and Paul, "The Wheat Trade Between California and the United Kingdom," *Mississippi Valley Historical Review* 45 (December 1958), 391–412; Robert L. Kelley, *Gold vs. Grain: The Hydraulic Mining Controversy in California's Sacramento Valley* (1960). Irrigation is in Frederick D. Kershner, Jr., "George Chaffey and the Irrigation Frontier," *Agricultural History* 27 (October 1953), 115–22; also J. A. Alexander, *The Life of George Chaffey: The Story of Irrigation Beginnings in California and Australia* (1928). On growing silk see Nelson Klose, "California's Experimentation in Sericulture," *Pacific Historical Review* 30 (August 1961), 213–27.

Local histories include Gordon S. Eberly, *Arcadia: City of the Santa Anita* (1953); William Martin Camp, *San Francisco: Port of Gold* (1947); Works Progress Administration, *Berkeley: The First Seventy-*

Five Years (1941); Chester G. Murphy, *The People of the Pueblo: or The Story of Sonoma* (repr. 1948); Clara H. Hisken, *Tehama: Little City of the Big Trees* (1948); Hallock F. Raup, *San Bernardino, California: Settlement and Growth of a Pass-Site City* (1940); Donald H. Pflueger, *Glendora* (1951) and Pflueger, *Covina: Sunflowers, Citrus, Subdivisions* (1964); L. J. Rose, Jr., *L. J. Rose of Sunny Slope, 1827–1899* (1958); Andrew Rolle, *William Heath Davis and the Founding of American San Diego* (1953); Joseph J. Hill, *The History of Warner's Ranch and Its Environment* (1927); Robert G. Cleland, *The Irvine Ranch of Orange County, 1810–1950* (1952); W. W. Robinson, *Ranchos Become Cities* (1939); R. Louis Gentilcore, "Ontario, California and the Agricultural Boom of the 1880's," *Agricultural History* 34 (April 1960), 77–87.

On the migration after 1887, consult Glenn S. Dumke, *The Boom of the 'Eighties in Southern California* (1944); Richard W. Barsness, "Iron Horses and an Inner Harbor at San Pedro Bay, 1867–1890," *Pacific Historical Review* 34 (August 1965), 289–304; Robert C. Post, "America's Electric Railway Beginnings . . . at Los Angeles," *Southern California Quarterly* 69 (Fall 1987), 203–19; Joseph S. O'Flaherty, *An End and a Beginning* (1972) and O'Flaherty, *Those Powerful Years* (1978).

CHAPTER TWENTY-THREE

DISCRIMINATION AND ACCOMMODATION

Foreign immigrants were at the heart of building the transcontinental rail-road. Without Chinese and Irish laborers, its construction would not have been possible. California's growth was also furthered by Japanese farmers in the Central Valley, Italian and French wine growers in the Sonoma and Napa region, as well as Swiss and German dairymen along the Coast Ranges. This key foreign influx, accelerated by the gold rush, quickly made California a cosmopolitan society.

The state's history, however, involves a record of discrimination and violence toward certain minority groups. Paradoxically, the first Chinese immigrants to arrive were treated with consideration. This was partly due to a need for dependable labor. Otherwise, during the nineteenth cen-tury, Asians faced tough battles for acceptance. Their mistreatment was summed up in the popular phrase of the day: "He doesn't have a China-man's chance." Yet, Chinese workers seemed content with the meager wages they earned.

By 1850, after a few Chinese miners actually managed to accumu-late more gold than did whites, jealous Californians enacted the Foreign Miners' License Law. This imposed a monthly tax of $20 on immigrant miners. The legislation had the effect of driving a horde of penniless for-eigners away from the mining. This was followed up in 1855 with a head tax of $50 levied on each foreigner upon entry into the state. Meanwhile aggressive whites simply barred the Chinese as well as other immigrant groups from the diggings. Chinese miners became the victims of ground-less accusations and unprovoked violence.

Increasingly the cry "California for the Americans!" was heard throughout mining camps and cities alike. Influenced by rising public an-tipathy, Governor Bigler, who in 1852 succeeded John McDougal, stig-matized the Chinese as "coolie" laborers. He called upon the legislature to prohibit contract immigration, the practice of bringing in groups of laborers as virtual indentured servants. Bigler thereby became the first important official to display anti-Chinese prejudice. When the financial panic of 1854 brought prices down with a crash, ruining some businesses and causing public unrest, anti-Chinese sentiment reached new heights. Miners by the thousands drifted back to San Francisco, only to find the labor market glutted. Now the large numbers of Chinese in "the City" were held responsible for the distressingly high rate of unemployment. White workers complained that "Orientals," by undercutting wages, deprived them of work. They were seen as "human leeches," sucking the very lifeblood of this country.

Governor Bigler, capitalizing on the prevailing public temper, loudly rebuked the legislature in 1854 for its negligence in not passing new laws to restrict Asian immigration. Prejudice among whites now extended even to little children, who were encouraged by bigoted elders to practice disrespect toward and insult the Chinese. Mistreatment of the "pig-tail," or "Almond-eyed Celestial," had become an almost daily occurrence by the late 1850s. The Chinese, sharply set apart by their physiognomy, dress, religion, mores, and exotic food choices, were in no position to retaliate. The nadir of indignity was reached in San Francisco's notorious 1855 "Pig-Tail Ordinance," a regulation requiring Chinese men to cut off their queues one inch from the head. When the Chinese fiercely protected their right to wear long hair, the practice being culturally important to them, it contributed to the belief among antagonistic whites that Asians were unassimilable.

In spite of prejudice and persecution, from 1850 to 1900 a "Little China" grew steadily on upper Sacramento Street and along Dupont Street in San Francisco. The mysteries of Chinatown held a great attraction for city residents and tourists alike. Smoke-filled gambling dens flourished, back-room saloons, secret passages, deep basements, and hidden recesses all teemed with hive-like activity, day and night. Opium smoking in filthy dens both fascinated and revolted Americans. Some accused the Chinese of importing prostitutes for the use of white customers and of keeping these women in human bondage.

By 1915, some Chinese founded their own community at Locke. Located along a Sacramento River levee, this was the only all-Chinese town in the United States. But there were also several dozen other Chinese enclaves located in rural areas. These were inhabited by first- and second-generation immigrants who had come looking for gold, only to end up as day laborers on farms and railroads.

Back when the Central Pacific was under construction, Mark Hopkins had founded his "Six Companies" to recruit, transport, and utilize Chinese laborers on a large scale. This enterprise, operated by Hopkins's agents, was responsible for much of the Asian immigration in the early 1860s— roughly 9,000 Chinese in all. Included among "Crocker's Pets" were undernourished, sometimes sickly, laborers bound to the "Six Companies" by contract. These came chiefly from southern China, where devastating poverty existed. They were in no sense free laborers; rather, they were the tools of speculators who paid them a few pennies per hour. Shrewd brokers cooperated with railroad and steamship agents to exploit the Asians. In contrast, Governor Stanford later called the Chinese "peaceable, industrious and economical, apt to learn and quite as efficient as white laborers." Since their labors made a vast fortune for him, he probably could not have said anything less.

The pattern in the mining camps was repeated elsewhere. When the Chinese came into economic competition with other laborers in various trades, resentment exploded into violence. In 1859, Governor Weller sent a company of state militia into Shasta County to put down riots by northern miners. By 1867, vigilante-style "anti-coolie clubs" had grown strong enough to dictate punishment for the misbehavior of Asians. Sheriffs, courts, and juries generally looked the other way in the face of such action. In December of 1867, one such group drove various Chinese out of French Corral, a settlement in Nevada County, then proceeded to destroy their cabins. Out of a total of twenty-seven Caucasians arrested for this mob violence, only one was tried. The rest were set free. Found guilty, the single accused man was fined $100. On October 23, 1871, nearly a score of Chinese were massacred in a Los Angeles race riot that originated in a quarrel between competing Chinese groups. This bloody episode was ignored by the legal system. Indeed, Los Angeles earned an early notoriety due to lawlessness in its Chinatown and what unfortunately came to be called "Nigger Alley."

Such racial hostility involved economic, social, and religious factors. The press charged the Chinese with intolerable competition in mining, construction work, cigar making, and in the lesser trades. Moreover, critics accused the Chinese of draining the state of substantial sums of money, which they sent back to relatives in China. Now the Chinese were called the "yellow peril," allegedly living on inferior food in crowded, unsanitary dwellings, a threat to "Christian values and Republican government." They were said to be pagan, depraved, and vicious. It was commonly believed that the Chinese practiced a mysterious quasi-government among them-

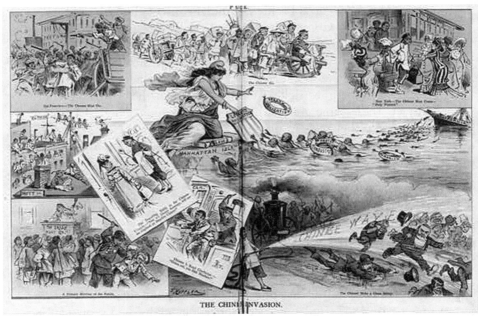

THE CHINESE INVASION.

Nine anti-Chinese cartoons on the "Chinese Invasion" of the United States, published about 1880. Library of Congress, LC-USZ62-103143.

selves that encouraged internecine wars. Their accusers found the Chinese lack of assimilation inexcusable. Yet these same critics seemed oblivious to the fact that they had made it virtually impossible for the Chinese to function as American citizens.

Although numerous Californians favored the exclusion of Chinese immigrants, a treaty negotiated in 1868 by Anson Burlingame eased the passage of Asians into the state. One clause in the agreement actually encouraged further Chinese immigration. Burlingame, formerly the U.S. Minister to China, was so tactful that the emperor hired him to visit foreign countries in order to negotiate similar amicable treaties. Regardless of widespread racial prejudices, cheap labor remained in high demand in California, where the railroad kings continued to expand their extensive network.

Nevertheless, public sentiment continued to flow in the opposite direction. Agitation against the Chinese continued at both local and state levels. In 1871, Governor Newton Booth was elected to office on an anti-Chinese platform. Almost every time the state legislature convened, nativists proposed an "immigrant tax." Eventually, strong feeling arose for repeal of the Burlingame Treaty, which had guaranteed free immigration. Such pressures were bound to affect legislation at the national level. In

Chinese butcher shop in San Francisco, ca. 1890. Wyland Stanley Collection, photograph by I.W. Taber, courtesy of The Bancroft Library, University of California, Berkeley.

1878 Congress passed the "Fifteen Passenger Bill," restricting the number of Asian immigrants on any ship entering the United States to fifteen. Although President Rutherford Hayes vetoed this law, an inflamed press in California pushed for a treaty with even stronger exclusionist provisions. In 1882 the California state Democratic convention passed a sweeping resolution against all further Asian immigration. Both major parties were, in fact, anti-Chinese, on a national as well as a state level.

By the mid-1890s, the country was moving toward absolute racial exclusion. On April 30, 1902, despite a stiff complaint from Chinese Minister Wu Ting Fang to Secretary of State John Hay, Congress pushed a new federal bill, "to prohibit . . . and to regulate the residence within the United States of persons of Chinese descent." This restrictive legislation was approved by President Theodore Roosevelt.

California can take little pride in its history of exclusion. Bigotry, race prejudice, and chauvinism were prime factors in national agitation against Asians. On the other hand, the U.S, unlike leading European powers, refrained from carving up the Chinese Empire after the Boxer Uprising of 1900. It actually returned an indemnity fund levied against China for the education of young Chinese in America. But such a tardy manifestation of good will could not eradicate American guilt for past treatment of the Chinese.

The state still has sizeable Chinese communities in San Francisco and Los Angeles. At the turn of the century, Fresno's Chinatown boasted 5,000 inhabitants and even had its own Chinese opera house. Today, except for celebration of the Chinese New Year and the annual moon festival, Chinese activity in California's interior towns is not to be compared with that of earlier times. Yet, a former *joss* house (Chinese temple) in Weaverville still functions as a state historical monument and as a bona fide Taoist temple. Its altar, imported from China during the gold rush, is an ancient artifact. Also, Chinese *tongs*, or welfare and fraternal organizations, continue to be strong in both Los Angeles and San Francisco. Chinese in these large centers have remained a relatively homogeneous group, partly because of their restaurants and shops in artificially maintained "Chinatowns" frequented by tourists.

Significant numbers of Japanese also began to enter California in the late nineteenth century. Like the Chinese, they experienced reasonable treatment at first. But after the Civil War, renewed hostility surfaced toward all foreigners. "The front door has been off its hinges long enough," one California xenophobe of the 1870s declared. In this atmosphere, the Japanese posed a new cheap labor threat, and Californians began to apply the term "yellow peril" to them as well. In the 1880s a second nativist "American Party" was formed. In the tradition of the Know-Nothings, its members routinely attacked Asians.

Not until 1891 did Japanese immigration into the United States for a single year exceed 1,000 persons, but from that time on it increased markedly. Acquisition of Hawaii by the United States in 1898 was followed by a heavy two-year influx of Japanese and Chinese from these islands, and public opinion was aroused anew against all "Orientals." Yet, they still came. In 1900 alone, 12,626 Japanese entered the United States. Ten years later, the number of Japanese in the country had swelled to more than 40,000 persons.

The first anti-Japanese exclusion meeting was held in May of 1905 at San Francisco, resulting in the organization of a body known as an Asiatic

Exclusion League. The next year, the San Francisco Board of Education recommended establishment of special schools for Chinese and Japanese, separate from those for Caucasians. Before action on this proposal could be taken, the city experienced the great earthquake of 1906, which disrupted all civic activities except those devoted to recovery. Then the school board issued a "separate school order," which required the transfer of a majority of San Francisco's ninety-three Japanese pupils to an existing Asian school. This aroused indignation in Japan, from which diplomatic protests were promptly lodged with the U.S. government. The Japanese objected as much to the forced inclusion of their children in a school with the Chinese as to discrimination against them by whites. President Roosevelt subsequently insisted that the national government become a party to the controversy.

In accord with the president's view, the San Francisco school board's order was rescinded. But, following a recommendation by a newly organized Japanese and Korean Exclusion League, the board passed a second resolution. On October 11, 1906, it again announced that Japanese children would be received only at an "Oriental" public school, along with the Chinese. Exasperated, U.S. Secretary of State Elihu Root stated that the federal government "would not allow any treatment of the Japanese people other than that accorded the people of other nations." Next, the attorney general of the United States started legal action to enforce immigration agreements with Japan. However, since a previous Supreme Court decision (*Plessy* v. *Ferguson*) had become the law of the land, this federal suit could affect only alien Japanese children who had treaty rights.

Meanwhile, the mayor of San Francisco and members of the city school board journeyed to Washington to confer with President Roosevelt. As a result, all federal suits against Asians were dismissed, but only after the local board of education rescinded its objectionable orders.

Nonetheless, the arrival of Japanese laborers in ever larger numbers led to continued agitation against them. In 1908, following further public demonstrations, Japanese Ambassador Aoki protested once more to President Roosevelt, who in turn telegraphed California Governor James N. Gillett that further restrictive measures before the California legislature would strain relations with Japan at a time when his administration was negotiating for the exclusion of immigrant laborers. State anti-alien bills were therefore withdrawn.

Obviously the major way to cut down further Japanese immigration was by diplomatic means. In order to avert an international crisis with Japan, President Roosevelt called for further negotiations, which resulted in the well-known "Gentlemen's Agreement" within the Root-Takahira accords that took effect in 1908. Under these new provisions, Japanese and Korean laborers who surreptitiously entered the United States from Mexico, Canada, and Hawaii were deportable. Furthermore, the Japanese government agreed to restrict the issuance of passports. California officials hoped this agreement would prevent the smuggling of Japanese into the United States. It did not. Immigrants subsequently entered the country illicitly in large numbers.

By 1913, the state legislature passed an Alien Land Law. Known as the Webb Act, this legislation prevented aliens ineligible for citizenship from holding land. Property acquired by them would be returned to the state, and agricultural lands could not be leased to aliens beyond a three-year period. One way to evade the Webb Act, however, was to register land in the name of a U.S. citizen. By leasing and subleasing land in this manner, the Japanese came to control large truck-farm acreages. Californians continued to fear the efficiency of the Japanese and the possibility that they might somehow come to dominate the state's economic life. Further resentment arose because some Japanese refused to work for whites who offered daily wages, preferring to bargain for a share of the crops they helped grow.

By 1920, because of loopholes in the "Gentlemen's Agreement" and the Webb Act, an "Anti-Alien Initiative Measure" prohibited the *Issei*, or first-generation Japanese immigrants, to hold an interest in any company owning land. After World War I, as thousands of young Japanese women came to the United States, the Native Sons of the Golden West, the California State Grange, and other exclusionist organizations demanded even tighter immigration laws. The federal Immigration Act of 1924 sought to put an end to Asian immigration to the United States.

As compared to Asians, African Americans, and Mexicans, European immigrants to California encountered fewer barriers to acceptance. In the Far West, Caucasian foreigners were able to cast off their immigrant origins more quickly than their counterparts in the large cities of the East. In rural environments the folkways and customs of Basque sheepherders, Swiss dairy farmers, and Armenian fig growers merged with those of their neighbors. Europeans who came to pick crops became owners of the very land they once worked as field hands.

Italian and French workers entered the restaurant trades and, along with the Portuguese, the fishing industry. At San Francisco's North Beach, Italians formed the majority of the population after 1890. One of their shrewdest leaders was Amadeo Pietro Giannini, founder of the modern

Bank of America. Earlier called the Bank of Italy, his loans contributed much to the rebuilding of the city after the fire of 1906.

Irish and German tradesmen, merchants, and farmers too became known for their thrift and industry. Among California's Germans were Adolph Sutro and Henry Teschemacher, both mayors of San Francisco. Theodore Cordua and Charles Weber became founders of Marysville and Stockton, respectively, just as the German-Swiss Sutter had earlier settled in what became Sacramento. Claus Spreckels became the "sugar king" of California, and Edward Vischer and Charles Christian Nahl were among the state's acclaimed artists.

Too much of California's immigrant past has been obliterated. Few issues of local foreign-language newspapers have been preserved. And little remains of the French utopian colony of Icaria Speranza, organized in 1881 near Cloverdale, or of the original German colony at Anaheim. However, the Danish immigrants at Solvang, above Santa Barbara, turned their community into a prosperous tourist center.

The immigrant contribution was a lasting one. Indeed, California would become America's leading multiethnic state.

SELECTED READINGS

Regarding the Chinese, see Elmer C. Sandmeyer, *The Anti-Chinese Movement in California* (1939); Gunther Barth, *Bitter Strength: A History of the Chinese in the United States 1850–1870* (1964); Ping Chiu, *Chinese Labor in California, 1850–1880: An Economic Study* (1963); Kwang Ching Liu, *Americans and Chinese* (1963); and Thomas W. Chinn, ed., *A History of the Chinese in California* (1969); Luther W. Spoehr, "Sambo and the Heathen Chinese: California's Racial Stereotypes in the Late 1870's," *Pacific Historical Review* 42 (May 1973), 185–204; also Sucheng Chan, *Asians in California* (1991) and her *The Bittersweet Soil: The Chinese in California Agriculture* (1986). Also see Liping Zhu, *A Chinaman's Chance* (1997); Charles J. McClain, *In Search of Equality: The Chinese Struggle against Discrimination in Nineteenth-Century America* (1994); Lucy E. Salyer, *Law Harsh as Tigers: Chinese Immigrants and the Shaping of Modern Immigration Law* (1995); Sucheng Chan, "A People of Exceptional Character: Ethnic Diversity, Nativism, and Racism in the California Gold Rush," in Starr and Orsi, eds., *Rooted in Barbarous Soil* (2000) 44–85. On Chinese women see Benson Tong, *Unsubmissive Women* (1994) and Judy Yung, *Unbound Feet* (1995).

For other Asian groups, consult David Yoo, *Growing Up Nisei: Generations and Culture Among Japanese of California* (2000); Roger Daniels and Spencer Olin, eds., *Racism in California* (1972); D. S. Thomas and R. S. Nishimoto, *The Spoilage* (1946); D. S. Thomas, *The Salvage* (1952); Jacobus ten Broek, Edward N. Barnhart, and Floyd W. Matson, *Prejudice, War, and the Constitution* (1954); Roger Daniels, *The Politics of Prejudice: The Anti-Japanese Movement in California* (1962); and Yuji Ichioka, *The Issei: The World of the First Generation of Japanese Immigrants, 1885–1924* (1989).

As to the Italians, see Andrew Rolle, *Westward The Immigrants* (2000); Dino Cinel, *From Italy to San Francisco* (1982) and Felice Bonadio, *A. P. Giannini: Banker of America* (1995). On the Germans see Erwin G. Gudde, *German Pioneers in Early California* (1927); Charles G. Loomis, *The German Theater in San Francisco, 1861–1864* (1952). About the French see Gilbert Chinard, ed. and trans., *When the French Came to California* (1944); Abraham P. Nasatir, *French Activities in California* (1945). On the Irish, consult Hugh Quigley, *The Irish Race in California and the Pacific Coast* (1878); Thomas F. Prendergast, *Forgotten Pioneers: Irish Leaders in Early California* (1942); and R. A. Burchell, *The San Francisco Irish, 1848–1880* (1980).

Regarding California's Jews, see I. Harold Sharfman, *Nothing Left to Commemorate* (1969); Robert Levinson, *The Jews in the California Gold Rush* (1978); as well as Max Vorspan and Lloyd P. Gartner, *History of the Jews of Los Angeles* (1970).

CHAPTER TWENTY-FOUR

CRUSHING OR SAVING THE INDIANS?

As California became more Americanized, white assaults on its Indian population increased. Ranchers, miners, and the military regularly overran native lands. Also, the same squatters who threatened rancheros began to invade traditional Indian campsites. They sought legal ownership under American law. Arrogant whites even demanded that the Indians change their way of life or get out of the way altogether.

In the last half of the nineteenth century, the U.S. War Department ordered infantry and cavalry units in California to deal sternly with Indians involved in violent confrontations with settlers. But decimation of the natives had relatively little to do with military operations. Starvation, disease, and liquor conspired with bullet and knife against the Native Americans. Pulmonary and venereal infections, smallpox, and other Caucasian-imported disease altered even the marginal lifestyle the Indians had experienced under Mexican rule.

American settlers cared little about the rights of natives. Harassed by Indians while crossing the Great Plains, most whites were scarcely in a conciliatory mood. Although California's natives were hardly as fierce as the Plains tribes, local tribelets did raid the property and livestock of settlers. After the Gold Rush, whites turned from mining to ranching, staging devastating raids on tribal villages. Ishi, who became a fabled native, hid out in the mountains for fifty years. Most of his Yahi clan had been massacred by white settlers. Anthropologists would proclaim Ishi "America's last Stone Age Indian."

In the prereservation era, those Indians who wandered into various towns fared worst of all. If they found work, their wages were miserable. More harmful were the disastrous effects of addiction to gambling or liquor. Finally, anyone willing to pay the fine of an Indian arrested for a minor offense, such as public drunkenness or vagrancy, could pick up a laborer who was required by law to work off the amount of the fine.

Meanwhile, whites continued to complain to the government about the "Indian problem," and the officials responded with a new policy. In 1850, a federal Indian Commission, with a meager appropriation of $50,000, was charged with setting up California's reservation system. Contrary to the designs of the commission, most Indians did not want to move out of their mountain homesites onto the flat lands of the Central Valley. While miners continually griped that the Indians interfered with mining operations, it was sheer hunger that eventually forced Indian tribal leaders to negotiate with government commissioners.

In the 1850s, the latter concluded 18 treaties with 139 native bands. Each tribelet was forced to recognize the sovereignty of the United States and to refrain from retaliation against settlers. The treaties also bound the tribes to accept 18 reservations. These consisted of 7.5 million, mostly arid, acres in compensation for the rights to vast lands seized by the government. The commissioners, in addition, promised to supply each reservation with agricultural implements and food, and to provide instruction in farming, blacksmithing, and carpentry.

Satisfied, the commissioners sent the treaties back to Wasington for ratification. However, the U.S. Senate, responding to repeated complaints of California residents, deemed these agreements too costly and refused to confirm them. Although the Indians justly countered that they had complied with the terms imposed by the commission, the compensatory acreages promised them were, for the most part, not forthcoming. Only a few tribelets secured a minute portion of their former ancestral lands. Most of the others were forced, by presidential executive orders, onto marginal plots. There, in an environment of shacks and shanties, the Indians henceforth endured a life that was neither native nor American. For years, only half a reservation system existed, and a mismanaged half at that.

Indeed, with few exceptions, white management of California's Indian reservations is hardly a matter of white pride. Some officials in charge of reservations were clearly unfit for their posts. Too often, whenever valuable land was at stake, Indian agents stood by as avaricious whites swooped in, driving the natives onto rocky or sandy terrain unfit for farming. Frustrated and sometimes desperate, Indians left their reservations to become unskilled laborers on ranches or farms. To make their plight worse, municipal ordinances as well as local officials continued to encourage a system of virtual peonage. Indians seldom understood federal or state regulations which suited white settlers.

The federal policy of administering Indian matters was as unsuccessful in California as elsewhere. There was, however, one startling positive achievement. In 1853, Edward Fitzgerald Beale, a thoughtful young naval officer who had taken part in California's conquest, returned to the new state. He now held an appointment as its first Superintendent of Indian Affairs. On a tract of 75,000 acres at Fort Tejón in the Tehachapi Mountains, Beale began to convert a wild region into an Indian preserve that he hoped would become a self-sufficient model for reservations throughout the West. Beale, a compassionate man, met with the local natives daily to discuss ongoing operations. He never hesitated to criticize whites or to take disciplinary action against subordinates who treated Indians unjustly. This resulted in complaints to Washington about Beale's administration. Charges of malfeasance forced him, in 1855, to relinquish his superintendency. Instead, he was appointed Surveyor General of California with no Indian jurisdiction. Finally, in 1863, his promising Tejón enterprise was abandoned. Herded into other reservations, most tribelets further deteriorated.

Mismanagement of Indian affairs occurred partly because the U.S. War Department and the Department of the Interior quarreled over how to manage the reservations. "Pacification by feeding," which forced too many Indians into shameful dependency, and closely regulated "supervision" formed the basic policy of the Interior Department. When, however, Indians escaped from inhospitable reservations, the War Department ordered out the army to bring them back onto approved sites, where they could be controlled.

It is remarkable that Indians displayed so little hostility toward white settlers. In southern California there had been only one significant uprising. This was near Warner's Ranch in 1851, led by a chieftain named Antonio Garrá. Skirmishing also took place in northern California, especially along the Humboldt, Eel, and Rogue Rivers. Fearful whites (both civilian and military) sought to drive Indians into remote locales where they would be rendered harmless to white settlements.

One particular expedition against retreating Indians led to a remarkable geographical discovery. The members of Joseph Reddeford Walker's trapping expedition may have been the first whites to see the Yosemite Valley, though its first recorded discovery occurred in 1851. That year, Major James D. Savage, leader of a volunteer company of whites known as the Mariposa Brigade, was pursuing marauding Yosemite and Chowchilla Indians. Savage's posse chased about 350 Yosemites into their Sierra hiding place, high above the Merced River. There he stumbled upon one of the world's most beautiful valleys, which had become a potential Indian stronghold. After a stubborn military campaign, the proud Chief Tenieya,

Wi-ne-ma, or Tobey Riddle, standing between a federal agent and her husband, Frank, on her left. Four more Modoc women sit in front. Taken at an army camp near Tule Lake, 1872. These natives were not part of the warring band. Courtesy of the National Archives, NWDNS-165-MM-1624.

saddened by the death of his favorite son, surrendered. Now he and his followers were forced to leave their native grounds forever.

The last and most violent of California's Indian clashes was the localized Modoc War, the culmination of two decades of native-white conflict. The first bloodshed took place in 1852, when some warriors attacked a small party of whites en route to California, the Modocs killing nearly half of the would-be settlers. Outraged, miners and other whites in the area demanded the extermination of the Indians who had participated in the raid. Throwing the Modocs off guard by proposing a "peaceful" meeting to settle the dispute, local armed Americans moved in and took bloody retaliation against the Indians. The Modocs never forgot what they considered an infamous butchery. For the next ten years hostilities continued intermittently.

By 1864, most of the Modocs had been seriously reduced in number. Ongoing pressures against them were relentless. Eventually U.S. Indian agents persuaded the remaining Modocs to relocate on the Klamath Reservation in southern Oregon. But this northward migration forced the Modocs directly through the hunting lands of the Klamaths. Because the Klamaths then threatened to repulse the unwanted Modoc trespassers, Chief Kientepoos (also known as Captain Jack) led his band back southward to their ancestral preserves.

Indians sometimes had only tenuous tribal connections with each other. Yet, the U.S. government had tried to crowd two autonomous groups into the same area. The Klamaths saw this as a violation of ancient territorial rights and clearly would not permit it. Nonetheless, late in 1869 the Superintendent of Indian Affairs for Oregon persuaded Captain Jack to return to the Klamath Reservation with 200 Modocs. When, however, the outraged Klamaths resisted the Modocs for a second time, the chief and his followers returned once again to their old camping grounds in present-day Modoc County.

By coming back to California, the Modocs defied U.S. authority, an act that invited military intervention. Disturbed settlers, in an atmosphere of confusion, spoke of organizing a force to protect themselves against the Modocs. By the winter of 1872, the U.S. Army moved in an observation force. On a November day in that year a Modoc girl named Wi-ne-ma caught sight of the military strength of the whites. Anxious to prevent bloodshed, she mounted a bay mare at Yreka and rode seventy-five miles to warn her people and to urge them not to resist. She suddenly became a hero of her tribe. An unfortunate clash, however, occurred when an Indian known as Scar-Faced Charley refused to give up his pistol to U.S. authorities. In the aftermath of this incident, marauding Modocs killed eleven settlers. The American cavalry then closed in on the Indians, who, at the order of Captain Jack, retreated with their ponies toward the lava beds to the southwest of Lake Rhett. There they sought the safety of caves guarded by jagged rocks and ledges.

Though cut off from supplies, the Indians survived by eating field mice and bats found in the caves and by drinking water from underground springs. Captain Jack announced that he would not molest incoming settlers unless they entered his winter camp. He claimed that it was not his men but the whites who were warlike. Nevertheless, the army was determined to force the Modocs back onto the Klamath reservation. The cost of dislodging this small band of Indians, secure in their lava fortress and supplied with old muzzle-loading rifles and other antique firearms, proved high indeed. Confusion quickly set in on both sides of this needless struggle.

On January 17, 1873, the army advanced on the Modocs, firing cannon volleys into their lava beds. Concealed behind rock breastworks, the Indians returned fire. U.S. losses in the exchange compelled retreat. At this point General E. R. S. Canby, commander of the Modoc operation, and several commissioners decided to meet with Captain Jack. With 1,000 men surrounding the Modoc position, General Canby moved his camp to the edge of the lava beds and pitched a council tent. During the peace conference of April 11, 1873, the chief was unfortunately goaded by some young tribesmen into committing a fatal act. The chief and the white emissaries had agreed to negotiate unarmed. However, not only did the Modocs wear concealed weapons to the talks, but several young warriors lay hidden in nearby bushes, armed with rifles. After Captain Jack gave the

McKay, the *San Francisco Bulletin* correspondent, taking notes on the California lava beds. At left are two partially hidden Warm Springs scouts on the lookout for Modocs, 1872. Courtesy of the National Archives, NWDNS-111-SC-82307.

signal for attack, he personally shot and killed General Canby, also stabbing and shooting a peace commissioner.

Following a prolonged struggle, Canby's troops finally captured Captain Jack and two of his accomplices. They were tried and hanged at Fort Klamath. All told, the Modoc War had cost the federal government half a million dollars, and ended the lives of a general and about seventy-five servicemen. All this might have been avoided if the Modocs had simply been allowed to occupy their remote lava beds and the nearby marginal grazing lands.

The virtual disappearance of California's Indian population is a tragic story. The condition of the formerly missionized natives had become truly pitiable. Cut off both from their land and cultural foundations, some were virtually auctioned off as private laborers. The semi-enslavement that many Indians endured was complicated by a high incidence among them of addiction to grape-based alcohol. Scattered about in small rancherias, without support, the dispossessed faced elimination. Between the beginning of the American period and the opening of the twentieth century, the number of natives in California declined from 100,000 to only 15,500.

After General Ulysses S. Grant became president of the United States in 1869, he replaced Indian agents with army officers. Still later, various churches were allotted Indian agencies to supervise. That policy, too, gave way, as had the military superintendencies, to appointees of the Commissioner of Indian Affairs. Responding to the pleas of the Native Americans themselves, Grant in 1875 authorized nine small reservations in San Diego County and created additional reserves. These were, however, mostly brush-strewn acreage that whites did not want.

Thereafter, the novelist Helen Hunt Jackson was appointed a commissioner to investigate the conditions under which the remaining California Indians lived. Her two influential books, *A Century of Dishonor* (1881) and *Ramona* (1884) called attention to the mistreatment of these peoples. Charles Fletcher Lummis, the southwestern author, joined Jackson's public-awareness campaign, soliciting funds to relocate several tribelets onto more fertile land.

Under the 1887 Dawes General Allotment Act, which formally marks the end of the U.S. government's reservation policy, each Native American family was given the right to own 160 acres of land, to be held in trust for twenty-five years—in which time, in theory, Indian landowners would learn to become self-sufficient farmers on the Anglo model. After that, the holders were to receive legal ownership of the land tract and full American citizenship. These so-called allotments, mostly of five to ten acres, were made under separate acts passed by Congress from 1890 to 1910. All remaining non-allocated tracts were held in a tribal trust. But the decline of tribal autonomy had begun long before the start of the allotment process. Those Indians who remained on reservations relied heavily upon the government food-ration system.

Meanwhile, Indians lucky enough to be awarded good land usually fell prey to unscrupulous whites who tricked them into selling it. With only a partial understanding of American concepts of land ownership and little experience in managing land, Indians often made a poor adjustment to American society. The Dawes Act had come too late to benefit a people who needed charity as much as a governmental definition of their status.

Now white "authorities," government agents as well as well-meaning but paternalistic private citizens, claimed that the remaining Indians would function best if back within a tribal group. Hence, in 1934, the Dawes Act was repealed. From that date until 1953, the government tried to restore tribal life, encouraging Indians to earn a reservation-based livelihood through production of traditional handicrafts. But by that time, large numbers of California's Indians had already left their reservations for good. Some simply disappeared, as measured by census statistics.

"Indians Welcome, Indian Land" logo is partially hidden under the U.S. Penitentiary sign at the entrance to Alcatraz Island. The graffitti is a reminder of the island's 1969–71 occupation by activists emphasizing the need for American Indian self-determination. © Alessandro Bolis/Dreamstime.com.

Occasionally, private, state, and national organizations made solid contributions to the betterment of Indians in California. One such institution was the Sherman Institute, near Riverside, founded in 1901 to afford Indian children industrial and handicraft training. With a few such exceptions, however, efforts to help the Indians have failed. Some tribal groups did win favorable land-tenure legal decisions.

Beginning in the 1930s, the Indians finally encountered somewhat better governmental understanding. Two California attorneys general, Earl Warren and Robert Kenny, sought to remedy past injustices. The state asked for a recompense of $1.25 per acre from the federal government for lands that had been taken away from several tribelets. During the ensuing proceedings, these lands were appraised at $17.5 million. In 1944, after fifteen years of litigation, the state's Indians were awarded only $5,165,863.46. This sum, however, was placed in the U.S. Treasury. The money became available only after protracted congressional struggles over its appropriation.

After 1948, the U.S. Supreme Court awarded a mere 3,337 acres of Palm Springs land to seventy-one surviving members of the Agua Caliente band of the Cahuilla Indians. In 1959, because this remnant remained unsatisfied with that allotment, Congress passed another law on their behalf. The Palm Springs Indians eventually achieved a commanding position in real estate ownership at the popular desert resort town, receiving in excess of 30,000 acres.

Hearings before a federal Indian Claims Commission during the 1950s and 1960s determined that California's natives held title to 64 million acres for which they were entitled to a further $29 million in compensation. Although the federal government eventually paid this sum, the aggrieved ancestors of the Agua Calientes were long since dead.

California's Indians have been forced to make a difficult adjustment to the society that has overwhelmed their traditional way of life. In recent times, Indian activists staged several powerful "media events." Among these was the 1969–71 occupation of the abandoned federal prison on Alcatraz, a rocky twelve-acre island in San Francisco Bay. During their siege the occupiers issued a proclamation that asserted:

We the native Americans, reclaim the land known as Alcatraz Island in the name of American Indians by right of discovery. . . . We feel that this so-called Alcatraz Island is more than suitable for an Indian reservation. . . .

    1. It is isolated from modern facilities and without adequate means of transportation.

2. It has no fresh running water.

3. It has inadequate sanitation facilities.

4. There are no oil or mineral rights.

5. There is no industry and so unemployment is very great.

6. There are no health care facilities.

7. The soil is rocky and non-productive, and the land does not support game.

8. There are no educational facilities.

9. The population has always exceeded the land base.

10. The population has always been held as prisoners and kept dependent on others.

(Indians of All Tribes Newsletter, January, 1970.)

In 1998, California voters passed Proposition 5, a hotly contested ballot issue that provided for casino gambling on Indian reservations. Opposed by conservatives and Nevada gaming interests, the Indians were led by Luiseño tribal leader Mark Macarro. Calling themselves "California Indians for Self-Reliance," they mounted a TV ad campaign that cost $70 million. The passage of Proposition 5 not only protected the pre-existing California Indian casino industry, but also opened doors for its expansion.

The argument for Indian casinos was that natives had finally found a way to reduce their need for public support. One casino alone, on the Pachanga Reservation, installed 2,000 slot machines! The Cabazon Band of the Cahuilla Indians, which numbered only thirty-five adults living on sixteen square miles of desert, established an even larger $200 million casino called "Fantasy Springs." Gleaming in the sunlight of the California desert, this resort complex included a twelve-story, 250-room hotel tower, convention center, and golf course. Down the road, the Morongo tribe floated bonds with which they opened a rival $250 million casino that offered blackjack and roulette as well as slot machines. It included a twenty-seven-story hotel. The Agua Caliente Band of the Cahuillas, which owns chunks of downtown Palm Springs, opened similar facilities.

Critics pointed out that congress never intended to authorize such tax-free bond issues for gambling. Yet, these establishments provided jobs, and financed new roads as well as sorely needed health facilities, police, sewers, and schools. Even the seventy-six tribes without casinos receive a share of the earnings. The Soboba Band of Mission Indians, the Redding Rancheria of Wintu, the Pit River as well as the Yana (or Win-River tribelet) have all profited from gaming establishments. Annually this has amounted to $22.5 million, or almost $300,000 per tribal group. As a result of the casino gambling industry, some triblets have gone from virtual destruction into affluence. California's Native Americans have also achieved real political power by contributing heavily to congressional and gubernatorial campaigns. These donations have given formerly impoverished natives a status that is national in scope. Their downtrodden ancestors would not have considered such a status miracle possible.

SELECTED READINGS

A basic work is R. F. Heizer and M. A. Whipple, eds., *The California Indians: A Source Book* (1951). See also Sherburne Cook, *The Population of the California Indians 1769–1970* (1979); Helen Hunt Jackson, *A Century of Dishonor*, Andrew Rolle, ed. (repr. 1965); George E. Anderson, *Treaty Making and Treaty Rejection by the Federal Government* (1978); William H. Ellison, "The Federal Indian Policy in California," *Mississippi Valley Historical Review* 9 (June 1922), 37–67. Avowedly emotional over the mistreatment of the American Indian is Rupert and Jeanette Costo, *Natives of the Golden State: The California Indians* (1995).

On reservation problems, see Imre Sutton, *Indian Land Tenure* (1975) and Sutton's *Irredeemable America* (1986); Stephen Bonsal, *Edward Fitzgerald Beale: A Pioneer in the Path of Empire, 1822–1893* (1912); Helen S. Giffen and Arthur Woodward, *The Story of El Tejón* (1942); Richard E. Crouter and Andrew Rolle, "Edward Fitzgerald Beale and the Indian Peace Commissioners in California, 1851–1854," *Historical Society of Southern California Quarterly* 42 (June 1960), 107–32; John W. Caughey, ed. *The Indians of Southern California* (1952); Lafayette H. Bunnell, *Discovery of the Yosemite and the Indian War of 1851* (1911); Annie R. Mitchell, *Jim Savage and the Tulareno Indians* (1957); and C. Gregory Crampton, ed., *The Mariposa Indian War, 1850–1851* (1958).

Other titles include William Edward Evans, "The Garrá Uprising: Conflict Between San Diego Indians and Settlers in 1851," *California Historical Society Quarterly* 45 (December 1966), 339–49; Keith A. Murray, *The Modocs and Their War* (1959); Max Heyman, *Prudent Soldier* (1960), a biography of General E. R. S. Canby; Erwin N. Thompson, *Modoc War: Its Military History and Topography* (1971); C. T. Brady, *Northwestern Fights and Fighters* (1907); Kenneth Johnson, ed., *K–344, Or the Indians of California vs. the United States* (1966); David G. Shanahan, "Compensation for the Loss of the Aboriginal Lands of the California Indians," *Southern California Quarterly* 57 (Fall 1975), 297–320; George H. Phillips, *Chiefs and Challengers: Indian Resistance and Cooperation in Southern California*

(1975); also Phillips, *Indians and Intruders in Central California (1993)* and his *Indians and Indian Agents: The Origins of the Reservation System in California, 1849–1852* (1997). See also William F. Strobridge, *Regulars in the Redwoods: The U.S. Army in Northern California* (1994); Joan Weibel-Orlando, *Indian Country: Maintaining Ethnic Community in a Complex Society* (1991); and Clifford E. Trafzer, "Native Sovereignty and the Northwest," in *"They Made Us Many Promises": The American Indian Experience, 1524 to the Present*, Second Edition, Philip Weeks, ed. (2002).

Recent scholars have placed the work of Helen Hunt Jackson and Charles Fletcher Lummis in a regional perspective and located their impact in a gendered context. See Margaret D. Jacobs, *Engendered Encounters* (1999); Sherry L. Smith, *Reimaging Indians: Native Americans through Anglo Eyes, 1880–1940* (2000); Valerie Sherer Mathes, *Helen Hunt Jackson and Her Indian Reform Legacy* (1997).

CHAPTER TWENTY-FIVE

LABOR, THE FARMERS, AND THE NEW CONSTITUTION

In 1873, a nationwide economic panic severely affected California society. Unemployed workers without shelter slept in abandoned barns and crowded dusty roads in search of employment. The luckiest among them were paid $2 a day. The dry winter of 1876 ruined the state's grain harvest and added to the travails facing ranchers. Then, in 1877, a great railway strike plunged the country into violence and turmoil. Labor riots in large cities like New York and Chicago encouraged discord out West as well.

In San Francisco, a forceful labor leader arose to take advantage of widespread dissatisfaction. Denis Kearney, a native of County Cork, Ireland, had arrived during 1868, having followed the sea from boyhood. He was industrious and frugal. Short and stout, with coarse features and dark probing eyes, his appearance was formidable. Clothed in a sweat-stained waistcoat, Kearney became a dynamic speaker who shouted at crowds with vile and intemperate language. His San Francisco freight-draying business, purchased in 1872, prospered until Kearney's incendiary utterances caused merchants to withdraw their patronage.

A rabid exclusionist, Kearney harangued his followers with the slogan "The Chinese Must Go!" As unemployment increased, 22,000 Chinese laborers suddenly arrived in the year 1876 alone. Their presence fanned the flames of social unrest that the unruly Kearney had lighted. Meanwhile, his followers, called "shoulder-striking hoodlums," had been recruited among disgruntled workers. They were more than ready to physically attack Chinese dock workers.

Below the palaces of San Francisco's Nob Hill millionaires, unemployed workers prowled the streets looking for hapless Chinese to abuse. In July of 1877, anti-Chinese riots broke out, posing an emergency that the understaffed police could not possibly handle. As a result, a new Committee of Safety was formed under the leadership of William Tell Coleman, the former vigilante chieftain known as the "Lion of the Vigilantes." Coleman's new law-enforcement group equipped itself with 6,000 hickory pick handles with which to quell rioters along the turbulent waterfront. At the docks, one fight raged for two hours before Coleman's vigilantes could subdue laborers who wanted to prevent the landing of more Chinese.

Amid these violent conflicts, Kearney founded the Workingmen's Party of California. With 15,000 men unemployed in San Francisco, he easily stirred up disgruntled workers with talk of violence in open-air gatherings. The meetings were held on a windswept sand lot that fronted San Francisco's city hall. There the fiery Irishman suggested "a little judicious hanging" of employers whom he labeled "robber-capitalists." One of Kearney's largest meetings took place during October of 1877, with 3,000 workers forming the crowd. Days later, Kearney and six of his cronies were arrested. His incarceration served only to strenghten Kearney's following. After spending only two weeks in prison, he resumed his unrestrained attacks, this time focusing on public officials.

In January of 1878, the unemployed of San Francisco took to the streets demanding "work, bread, or a place in the county jail." As the number of marchers swelled to 1,500, the beleaguered mayor pleaded that he was powerless to help them. At another packed gathering disaffected workers threatened to "blow up the Pacific Mail Steamship Company's dock and steamers," bomb the Chinese quarter, and use firearms and "infernal machines" to destroy any "marked men." In this charged atmosphere, Coleman's militia reassembled and a U.S. Navy man-of-war arrived to protect the government mail docks. More of Kearney's firebrand followers were then thrown into prison. They were charged with having committed violent acts, for an alarmed legislature had made it a felony to incite a riot.

On January 21, 1878, the noisy Workingmen's party held its first formal convention, inveighing against a government that "has fallen into the hands of capitalists and their willing instruments." By this time the Workingmen had become a force in state politics. Suggesting relatively modest reforms, by 1879 they had elected a mayor of San Francisco, several state supreme court judges, eleven state senators, and sixteen assemblymen.

But disintegration began to appear in the labor party's ranks after a rumor spread that Kearney had accepted railroad money and was personally corruptible. Both his integrity and loyalty to his workers continued to be impugned in a whispering campaign that led to his removal from leadership of the Workingmen. By dismissing Kearney, his opponents within the party, which also acted as a labor union, thereby hoped to combat charges of recklessness that had tarnished organized labor under his leadership.

In an age when capitalists like the "Big Four" felt no need to apologize for their abuses, the Workingmen were considered dangerous radicals. Although Kearney was well outside the social mainstream, he lived to see some of his reform measures become law. These included the eight-hour workday, a statewide public school system, reform of a corrupt banking system, and restrictions upon land monopolists.

Accompanying the Workingmen's demands, Californians moved toward an even more major revision. The 1849 constitution had barely met the needs of a frontier area anxious for admittance to the Union. That document contained outmoded provisions for public finance, the safeguarding of public lands, and improving labor conditions. Furthermore, it offered Californians no real public controls against violence at a time when discontent of both farmers and workers was rising. Both had become fed up with the abusive practices of railroad management.

On September 28, 1878, California's second constitutional convention convened with 152 delegates assembled. Among the largest group of delegates were lawyers. Farmers had the next sizeable representation. Thirty-five delegates were of foreign birth. No Native Americans were represented. As the state desperately needed more revenue, the subject of taxation took on great importance. Some favored a poll tax. Others advocated a tax on all property, a state income tax, a graduated tax on the largest estates, and suspension of taxes for citizens already in debt. Two delegates representing an Independent Taxpayer party assumed a prominent position in the debates over taxation. They alleged that the bulk of future taxes would be shouldered by the poor unless the tax burden was equalized. The Independent Taxpayer Party, joined by the Workingmen and other reform groups, achieved adoption of a California State Board of Equalization. This new body was to "equalize the valuation of taxable property in the several counties, and also assess the franchise, roadway, roadbed, rails and rolling stock of all railroads. . . ."

Other delegates held the railroads responsible for racial and labor conflict by their importation of thousands of Chinese. Among the most vocal critics were the state's farmers. They were represented at the 1879 convention by "farmer clubs," or Granges. The Grangers charged the railroads with hurting small farmers by corrupting elections, fixing high freight rates, and favoring large shippers through secret rebates. The Grangers, aided by the reformist writer Henry George, charged that such monopolies were seriously hurting the poor. Dissatisfied farmers charged that

California was dominated by monopolies and further plagued by powerful landowners. As early as 1867, the Granger movement had sponsored political forums to protest abuses against farmers. To remove costly middlemen, they also established cooperative grain elevators, mills, and supply centers, The Grangers continued to bristle at commodity schemes that dictated the retail prices charged for their products.

Although the 1879 constitution created a State Railroad Commission, that body never acted as an effective consumer watchdog on the industry. Individual commissioners bowed to the whims of railroad executives, and railroad attorneys, often working with sympathetic judges who spared the companies from paying their full share of taxes. Even when the commission leveled charges against certain companies, their attorneys managed to tie up legal proceedings for years on end. Finally, government reforms were watered down, and abusive railroad practices continued for many years after the 1879 constitutional convention.

On May 1 of the next year, along a dry creek bed called Mussel Slough in Kings County, a dispute broke out between some farmers and the Southern Pacific. These homesteaders had bought some mostly worthless railroad land for $2.50 an acre. But, after improving it, the S.P. claimed it still retained title and wanted to sell it for more than ten times the original sale price. Having improved their land, as well as building an elaborate irrigation system, the settlers encountered repeated delays in the conveyance of titles. Cruelly deceived, the farmers claimed the land had been bought under irrevocable conditions. When the S.P. tried to evict these settlers, they shot it out with some railroad men, a U.S. marshal, and some local toughs. At the end of the gun battle, seven of the settlers lay dead. The S.P., backed by the courts, had five of the surviving settlers imprisoned because they had resisted a federal official who tried to control their outrage.

Although reform-minded delegates at the constitutional convention seemingly united in opposition to railroad abuses, they split over proposals to control the banks. As the credit of local banks was vital to farmers, the Grangers sided with country bankers who opposed too rigorous reform of banking practices. Both the banks and the railroads favored the status quo, which they of course had created.

Agitated by the racist rantings of Denis Kearney, delegates marred the new constitution by clamoring for several anti-Asian clauses. Condemnation of Asiatic "coolieism," or contract labor, described as "a form of human slavery" became part of the document. These prohibitions against employment of Chinese were, however, later ruled unconstitutional. The

Denis Kearney (1847–1907), the volatile founder of the Workingmen's Party, ca. 1880. With 15,000 men unemployed in San Francisco, he easily stirred up disgruntled workers with talk of violence in blustering open-air gatherings in 1877.

1879 state delegates also gave the state's public school system its basic shape. The University of California received the legal status of a corporation. Other legalities concerned the granting of divorces, eminent domain, as well as the state's jurisdiction over its waters and shorelines. The latter would be cited to support state claims to all offshore oil deposits.

The convention continued its deliberations for 157 days, during which lobbying by so many different special interest groups actually hindered the granting of some reforms. Though several delegates pleaded for political equality of the sexes, it met with little immediate success. California was not to achieve women's suffrage until 1911. In the end, after proposed restraints upon corporations were watered down, Henry George complained that the state's land monopolists remained untamed.

The vehemence with which Kearney's Workingmen shouted their demands had scared off potential political allies, especially the farmers. Although unsuccessful in breaking monopolies, what restrictions the new constitution contained had been gained through the energies of the Workingmen. Their demands for an eight-hour day, fixed salaries for government jobs, and the creation of a bureau of labor affairs eventually influenced the two major parties. Unfortunately, most Workingmen had pushed for passage of the Federal Exclusion Act of 1882. This overt racism was clearly aimed at Asian immigrants.

Alas, the Constitution of 1879 remained a catalogued code of laws rather than a working framework of government. California's original constitution could have been revised, with its worst deficiencies fixed by a series of amendments. Instead, today's constitution is still a wordy and unwieldy compendium.

SELECTED READINGS

Regarding labor history, see Daniel Cornford, ed., *Working People of California* (1995); Jules Tygiel, *Workingmen in San Francisco, 1880–1901* (1992); Ralph Kauer, "The Workingmen's Party of California," *Pacific Historical Review* 13 (September 1944), 278–91; J. C. Stedman and R. A. Leonard, *The Workingman's Party of California* (1878); Ira B. Cross, *Frank B. Roney: Irish Rebel and California Labor Leader* (1931); and Cross, *History of the Labor Movement in California* (1935); Arthur N. Young, *The Single Tax Movement in the United States* (1916) and Henry George, Jr., *Life of Henry George* (1900).

About the first constitutional convention, see *Debates and Proceedings of the Constitutional Convention of the State of California* (3 vols. 1880); Winfield J. Davis, *History of Political Conventions in California* (1893); and Carl B. Swisher, *Motivation and Political Technique in the California Constitutional Convention, 1878–1879* (1930).

Criticism of the railroads is in Gordon W. Clarke, "A Significant Memorial to Mussel Slough," *Pacific Historical Review* 18 (November 1949), 501–4; Irving McKee, "Notable Memorials to Mussel Slough," *Pacific Historical Review* 17 (February 1948), 19–27; John A. Larimore, "Legal Questions Arising From the Mussel Slough Land Dispute," *Southern California Quarterly* 58 (Spring 1976), 75–94. Also see Paul Kens, "The Railroad Tax Cases: Corporate Equal Protection and the Creation of the Corporate Person," in Gordon Bakken, ed., *Law in the Western United States* (2000), 454–58.

CHAPTER TWENTY-SIX

CALIFORNIA CULTURE, 1870–1918

By 1870, the pioneer phase of California's history had ended. At San Francisco, easily the state's premier metropolis, wealthy patrons encouraged the arts and education. Other towns also began to establish museums, opera houses, and even symphony orchestras.

Among those who contributed significantly to the new culture were women. A popular author, Helen Hunt Jackson, began her career as a writer of children's stories. Later, she raised public consciousness over the mistreatment of Indians. She was also concerned with neglect of California's Hispanic past. Indeed, her articles in *Century Magazine* and her book *A Century of Dishonor* (1881) stirred up national indignation over the plight of California's abused natives. However, her novel *Ramona* (1884) failed to achieve the same effect. Readers, instead, were entranced by Jackson's romantic portrayal of the love affair between an Indian brave and a Latina maiden. This was taken as a true reflection of California's idyllic mission era. Such an Arcadian stereotyping would later be dramatised by local actors in the town of Hemet, which still stages an annual "Ramona Pageant."

There were other talented women of Jackson's era. Among them was Helena Modjeska, a Polish actress who in 1876 established a short-lived utopian colony near Anaheim. The flamboyant dancer Isadora Duncan, a San Franciscan, went on to world fame. A quite different, yet remarkable, woman was a former Georgia slave named Biddy Mason. In order to reach California, Mason crossed the Great Plains in 1851 with her three daughters, driving along a herd of sheep. In Los Angeles she found work as a nurse at a wage of $2.50 per day. Yet, Mason managed to save enough money to buy several parcels of land. By 1887, property she had bought for $250 had soared in value to $200,000 (then a substantial sum of money) during the state's first real estate boom. She used her hard-earned wealth

Charlotta Bass in her office at the *California Eagle*, circa 1931–40. The African American newspaper was published for more than 85 years. Bass came to work for the newspaper in 1910. Two years later she became managing editor and publisher. She remained the owner until her retirement almost 40 years later. USC Library for Social Studies and Research.Source #scl-mss064-0001.

to found a nursery school. Mason also frequently visited the city jail in order to cheer up inmates that she knew. She paid the delinquent taxes for her church and provided a rest home for indigent African Americans. Mason died in 1891 as one of the most affluent property owners in California.

Another former slave who achieved prominence was the aforementioned Mary Ellen "Mammy" Pleasant, the operator of a San Francisco boarding house in the 1850s. While she has been remembered as a procuress and a blackmailer, as well as a financial backer of John Brown's famous raid, more important were her efforts to help her fellow African Americans. By lending other blacks money at reasonable rates of interest, Pleasant amassed a fortune, which she used to gain African Americans the right of testimony in the courts. That victory was achieved in 1863 through an act of the legislature. That same year, Pleasant successfully sued two San Francisco streetcar companies that barred blacks from riding their cars. Less well known is Charlotta Bass. At a time when female African American literary figures were rare, Bass became the editor of the *California Eagle*, southern California's first black newspaper.

White women writers encountered fewer hurdles to success than did their black counterparts. In 1893 the state legislature named Ina Coolbrith as California's first poet laureate. The eccentric Gertrude Stein, later an expatriate writer and critic, lived in Oakland from 1879 to 1892 before finally settling in

Paris. The oddities of her prose made her a world-renowned figure. In 1903, a young San Franciscan named Alice Toklas joined Stein in Paris, where the two women shared the rest of their lives together, long before Lesbianism became well known.

In 1899, Mary Austin traveled west from Illinois with her family. Austin taught school in the Owens Valley and in her spare time wrote stories and articles for Charles Lummis's magazine. Her best-known book was *The Land of Little Rain* (1903). In it, she sympathetically describes the native peoples, animals, and landscape south of Yosemite and north of Death Valley. In *The Basket Woman* (1904), *The Flock* (1906), and *California, Land of the Sun* (1914), Austin continued to evoke an appreciation of a seemingly barren land of sagebrush and sand.

Among other women writers attracted to California was Gertrude Atherton, who spent most of her life in her native San Francisco. Her heavily romanticized best sellers include *The Splendid Idle Forties* (1902) and *The Californians* (1898). Both books idealized the state's Hispanic past. The autobiographical writer Charlotte Perkins Gilman, who lived and worked in Pasadena, is best known for her intensely personal essay *The Yellow Wallpaper* (1899).

Yet another female author, Kate Douglas Wiggin, combined a life of public service with writing. After training the majority of California's first kindergarten teachers, she went on to New York to pursue her writing career. She remains famous, however, for the free kindergartens she established for poor children. She wrote books for girls, among them *A Summer in a Cañon* (1889). By 1895, a devotee of Mrs. Wiggin, Sarah Brown Cooper, had established 287 kindergartens throughout the United States.

A less orthodox woman of the period was a one-eyed, high-spirited stagecoach driver known as Charley Parkhurst. As a gangly teenager, Charlotte had fled westward from a Massachusetts orphanage masquerading as a man. The tobacco-chewing Parkhurst wore rough trousers and a patch over her left eye. Her skin was tanned and leathery. Out in California, "Charley" Parkhurst became a highly respected "jehu," or stage driver, who expertly guided her coach along the steep grades of the High Sierra. Parkhurst was known to tote a six-shooter, which she did not hesitate to use in order to shoot and kill highway robbers. Upon her death in 1879, an autopsy finally revealed the secret that Charley had kept for most of her life.

In 1875, Caroline Severance, a pioneer reformer, arrived in Los Angeles from Boston with fresh ideas for changing the town's sleepy pueblo environment. It was Severance who established Los Angeles's first book club and, indeed, the city's public library. She also founded a women's organization known as the Friday Morning Club. Its members advocated reform of the juvenile detention system and led a campaign to keep politics out of school-board elections. Severence and her group also sought to save the giant Sequoias from rapacious logging and worked to place "El Camino Real" signposts along the historical route between the missions. They also helped to develop the Los Angeles Philharmonic Orchestra, and worked to bring a branch of the University of California to Los Angeles (UCLA).

During the late nineteenth century, women's clubs captured the attention of many women, giving them the opportunity to step outside their prescribed sphere of church and home. Six hundred women's organizations served in California as social and intellectual centers while encouraging political action. Despite societal limitations, clubwomen repeatedly demonstrated excellent leadership. Their clubs provided a unique atmosphere of mutual support.

One such woman was Harriet Williams Russell Strong. A founder of the Wilshire-Ebell Club in 1894, Strong also became an agriculturist and a civic leader. Her husband, Charles Strong, had purchased the Rancho del Fuerte, near the present-day city of Whittier, from Pío Pico, the last Mexican governor. After Charles died, Harriet studied marketing, as well as irrigation and flood control. From 1887 to 1894 she took out patents on a sequence of storage dams and various farm and household implements. Strong became known as the "walnut queen" and "pampas lady," for she grew both walnuts and pampas grass. She also won election as the first woman member of the Los Angeles Chamber of Commerce, and gained national attention through her agricultural product exhibits at the 1893 Columbian Exposition at Chicago. Mrs. Strong was also a persuasive advocate of scientific flood control and water supply development, supporting a federal program to dam the Colorado River.

Another woman of distinction was Alice Constance Austin. In 1918 she designed and helped to develop a utopian city known as Llano del Rio. Tied to the California "arts and crafts" movement (a back-to-the-basics approach to design inspired by England's William Morris), she devised an innovative architectural scheme in which a central kitchen and laundry facility were connected to outlying homes via an underground railway!

Women also slowly began to enter male-dominated professions. The Los Angeles City Directory for 1890 listed 287 physicians, 27 of whom were women. One woman who had an ongoing effect upon the legal profession was Clara Shortridge Foltz. She studied law on her own and eventually procured passage of a legislative act that permitted women to practice law. Foltz herself was the first female admitted to the state bar as well as the first woman attorney to plead cases before the California Supreme Court. Other women used their skills to enter politics, albeit without having yet secured the right to vote. Among them was Katherine Phillips Edson, who, after the turn of the century, helped transform California into a leading Progressive party center. Still later, Elizabeth Snyder was the first woman to chair a state political party, going on to become a leading force in Democratic-party circles.

The period also witnessed the rise of a second generation of male writers and social reformers, native sons as well as immigrants to California. Among them were Henry George, Frank Norris, Jack London, Josiah Royce, Ambrose Bierce, and Thorstein Veblen, the creator of a "theory of the leisure class" who taught at Stanford University from 1906 to 1909.

British-born Henry George, restless and unorthodox, had held half a dozen jobs along the San Francisco waterfront before turning to economic analysis, for which he became world famous. Having also worked as both a seaman and a printer, he tried to support himself by prospecting for gold. Then, in an atmosphere of labor turbulence and high unemployment, George became a newpaper reporter and editor who strongly voiced the complaints of all working people. While developing his ideas in San Francisco, he wrote for the *Californian* and four other journals. Despite the fact that he had almost no formal schooling, his writings, among which were tracts in support of the eight-hour working day, attracted wide attention. He evolved an appealing "single-tax" theory in his book *Progress and Poverty* (1880), which drew international attention. In that volume, George protested the presence of poverty and wealth side by side in so rich a land, charging that too many absentee land monopolists and speculators were collecting an "unearned increment." He saw this as a malicious form of rent on their vast holdings.

Yet another original thinker who wrote in a reformist vein was Josiah Royce. Born in 1855 at Grass Valley, Royce, like Henry George, published initially in California. Royce too was incensed at abuses of the land monopolists and the railroads. As a member of the Harvard University philosophy faculty, he became both an idealist and nonconformist, as expressed in his book, *California ... A Study of American Character* (1886).

A spiritual ally of Royce and George was Frank Norris, a talented writer impressed by Europe's naturalist authors. His most famous book, *The Octopus* (1901), was based on the Mussel Slough tragedy. It featured the continuing clash between the railroad monopoly and the farmers. Together with Norris's other reform novels, *McTeague* (1899) and *The Pit* (1903), *The Octopus* won him national acclaim.

Norris also influenced Jack London, whose realism combined a strong romantic strain with a social conscience. A prolific writer, London turned out more than fifty books filled with adventure, primitive violence, and class struggle. He became a celebrated author, gaining international fame. His works demonstrated the overwhelming power of nature versus the basic desire to survive against all odds. In *The Call of the Wild* (1903) and *The Sea Wolf* (1904), London celebrates this elemental interaction of humankind and nature. His own struggle to make a living as a writer is the subject of an autobiographical novel, *Martin Eden* (1909). Once a strong supporter of socialism, London would renounce many of his early views, focusing instead on writing, traveling, and working on his favorite ranch property near Glen Ellen, California. There, at the early age of forty, London died of gastrointestinal uremic poisoning (or uremia). Although London was mired in debt, battling alcoholism, and afraid that he was losing his creativity as a writer, his works remain widely read and his ranch was spared. Today, the ranch is the popular Jack London Historic State Park. There, London's ashes, and those of his wife, Charmian, are buried beneath his favorite oak tree.

A writer of a different sort, the acid-tongued Ambrose Bierce, dominated the California literary scene for decades with his spicy diatribes. From the late 1880s onward, he chose many targets, from disreputable politicians to untalented young authors. Bierce delivered contemptuous judgments with gusto in *The Devil's Dictionary*. In his ghost and horror stories, he used satire that was both gruesome and amusing. His criticisms of society also appeared in the columns of young William Randolph Hearst's *San Francisco Examiner*. Bierce's 1913 disappearance, probably into Mexico, remained as mysterious as his controversial writings.

Among the writers of nostalgic reminiscences was William Heath Davis. His *Seventy Five Years in California* gives one an inside view of a provincial society forced to adjust to Yankee urbanism. Such chroniclers highlighted their personal participation in momentous events like the American Conquest and Gold Rush. Harris Newmark's *Sixty Years in Southern California* (1916) presented a view of urban, social, and commercial life through the eyes of a pioneer Jewish merchant.

Enamored with California's alleged Spanish past was Charles Fletcher Lummis, the eccentric Harvard classmate of Theodore Roosevelt. Lummis's *The Land of Poco Tiempo* (1893) and *The Spanish Pioneers* (1893) set the trend for books of adulation about the leisurely existence that supposedly prevailed in early California. Personally, Lummis cut a striking figure, often wearing a green corduroy suit, a sombrero on his head and a red sash wrapped around his middle. He further illustrated his distinctively Bohemian interpretation of Spanish colonial life in El Alisal, the house he constructed from boulders on the edge of Los Angeles's Arroyo Seco. Lummis also championed restoration of the crumbling missions and preserved Indian-Spanish folk traditions in the magazine he edited from 1895 to 1902, *The Land of Sunshine*, which later became *Out West*. On its pages appeared the first English translations of Father Serra's diary, and its literary contributors included many of the writers mentioned in this chapter. Lummis lived out a "cult of Spain," which he extolled to his generation of Californians.

Also writing before World War I were two authors whose works were rooted in ethnology, folklore, and natural history: George Wharton James and Charles Francis Saunders. James was for years employed by the Southern Pacific Railroad, and the books he wrote for publicity purposes praised the wonders of nature, disseminated Indian lore, and promoted California as a unique place to live. Among his most widely read books were *In and Out of the Old Missions* (1905) and *Through Ramona's Country* (1907). Saunders, a Quaker naturalist from Pennsylvania, was fascinated by the southern California backcountry. He wrote charming books about the state such as *Under the Sky in California* (1913), *With the Flowers and Trees in California* (1914), and *Finding the Worthwhile in California* (1916). Saunders's simplicity of expression won him an audience among readers of all ages.

A prolific spinner of narrative yarns was Stewart Edward White, who had spent his boyhood in California. Among White's books, which were serialized in the *Saturday Evening Post* and other national journals, were *The Blazed Trail* (1902), *Gold* (1913), and *The Forty Niners* (1918). White wrote both historical and fictional works that catered to a public yearning for adventurous, if insubstantial, tales about western deserts, mountains, and heroes.

Lummis and White, though incurably romantic, achieved popularity because their picturesque styles suited the taste of the reading public of their time. The theme of California as a pastoral paradise also dominated the writings of John Steven McGroarty, whose *Mission Play* was staged annually at San Gabriel beginning in 1913.

During the same era, a rough-hewn character named Joaquin Miller (Cincinnatus Hines Miller) dubbed himself "Poet of the Sierra." The long-winded Miller was later acclaimed in England, where he appeared at literary soirées dressed in chaps, a sombrero, a red shirt, baggy trousers complete with suspenders, cowhide mining boots, and a sealskin coat.

Miller loved to play the part of an uncouth western rustic, acting out the image of the stereotypical miner.

Two other California poets were Edward Rowland Sill and Edwin Markham. The Connecticut-born Sill graduated from Yale University in 1860, then came to California by sea via Cape Horn. He held a variety of jobs, including post office clerk in Sacramento and professor of English at the University of California. Eventually, he quit teaching to write full time. Both his prose and poetry stressed the California locale, as in his *Venus de Milo* (1883) and *Christmas in California* (1890). Markham, like Sill, bespoke the state's praises, as his *California the Wonderful* (1914) attests. His best-known work is *The Man with the Hoe and Other Poems* (1899). Markham lived to see this protest against the brutalization of downtrodden farmers and laborers translated into forty different languages.

Less serious in tone was the doggerel of Gelett Burgess, originally a surveyor for the Southern Pacific Railroad. By the turn of the century his verse "The Purple Cow" was being recited all over the country:

> I never saw a purple cow
> I never hope to see one
> But I can tell you anyhow
> I'd rather see than be one.

Burgess later wrote, regretfully:

> Oh, yes, I wrote the Purple Cow
> I'm sorry now I wrote it
> But I can tell you anyhow
> I'll kill you if you quote it.

A number of nonfiction writers documented California's natural wonders. The most popular of these naturalists was John Muir. No other writer has shown such feeling for the majesty of the Sierra peaks or the great valley of the Yosemite. Scottish-born but educated in the United States, Muir spent much of his adult life hiking through the California backcountry. He became a vigorous defender of its forests, mountains, and wildlife, founding the Sierra Club in 1892. Partly because President Theodore Roosevelt listened carefully to Muir's advice, government preservation of wilderness areas increased in the state and the nation. Muir left behind works of natural history that are still widely read. Among the best of these are *The Mountains of California* (1894) and *The Yosemite* (1912).

The brothers Joseph and John Le Conte produced attractive geographical essays and Sierra Range sketches. The Le Contes were joined in the writing of natural history by David Starr Jordan, later president of Stanford University, whose *Alps of the King* and *Kern Divide* (1907) rank with Clarence King's *Mountaineering in the Sierra Nevada* (1872). King, a Yale-educated geologist who also loved California's wild places, included John Muir in a circle of friends that numbered John Hay and Henry Adams.

By the end of the nineteenth century, amateur compilers of history were moving toward professionalization. Among these were Zoeth Skinner Eldredge and Theodore H. Hittell. Both authors produced multivolume histories of the state, as did Hubert Howe Bancroft, the best-organized and most prolific of California's amateur chroniclers. Bancroft was originally a San Francisco bookseller and publisher who between 1875 and 1890 compiled thirty-nine stout volumes that spanned the record of the Pacific Coast from Latin America to Alaska. In so doing he set up a virtual "history factory," using an entire staff of assistants to interview early residents and help him compile information. At the heart of the Bancroft series were seven heavily footnoted volumes on California. His invaluable manuscript and book collection was ultimately sold to the University of California at Berkeley, where it forms the core of today's Bancroft Library.

Yosemite's majestic El Capitan. Courtesy of William Doyle.

Market Street, San Franciso, looking east from Third Street before the earthquake and fire of 1906. H. G. Hills Collection, courtesy of the Bancroft Library, University of California, Berkeley.

After World War I, a band of scholars would restructure the history of California in a more systematic manner. At the state university in Berkeley, anthropologist Alfred L. Kroeber turned his enormous talent to the Indian past. Historians Herbert E. Bolton, Charles E. Chapman, and Herbert Priestley dealt with the Spanish period.

A writer who had focused international attention on California was the visiting Scotsman Robert Louis Stevenson. In 1880, he published "The Old Pacific Capital" in London's *Fraser's Magazine*. This story described Monterey and, along with his *The Silverado Squatters* (1884), recalled his short but idyllic stay in California, where he met the woman he eventually married. Some of Stevenson's colorful accounts in local newspapers have recently been reprinted.

California newspapers of the late nineteenth century were typically crude four-page affairs, bearing five to seven columns of small type. On the front page ran several columns of advertisements, including patent-medicine claims—appeals by quack doctors who promised to alleviate severe bodily aches and pains—alongside notices of high-buttoned shoes, canvas sails, pink velvet vests, ten-penny nails, and "long-nine" cigars. The rest of the front page was generally devoted to brief news clippings from the outside world. Before the completion of the transcontinental telegraph in 1861, such "current events" might be weeks, even months, behind the times.

By 1854, San Franciscans published twenty-two different newspapers. The best known of these was the *Chronicle*, founded in 1865 by Michael and Charles De Young. The *San Diego Union* and *Los Angeles Times* were the major papers of southern California. General Harrison Gray Otis acquired the *Times* in 1881, becoming embroiled in the Free Harbor struggle, the Owens River water controversy, and severe labor union confrontations.

At Sacramento, after 1883, Charles McClatchy gave new life to the *Sacramento Bee*, founded in 1857. For several generations it, along with its hive members the *Fresno Bee* and *Modesto Bee*, remained the authoritative voice in the Sacramento Valley. At Santa Barbara, Thomas Storke's *News Press* virtually became the official oracle of that community. Significant "newspaper families" gradually assumed control of most California dailies. The De Youngs, the Hearsts, the McClatchys, the Storkes, and the Chandlers all built powerful newspaper chains, some spreading outside the state.

After 1870, musical performances in California also increased. San Francisco's Tivoli Theater and Opera House offered a year-round schedule of operas. Its 1890 run included the first performance of Pietro Mascagni's *Cavalleria Rusticana*. At the last musical performance to be held in the Tivoli, on November 23, 1913, another Italian composer, Ruggiero Leoncavallo, personally conducted his new opera, *I Pagliacci*.

Before World War I, performers of international stature visited the state. Among them was Adelina Patti, the most celebrated soprano from the end of the Civil War to the turn of the century. Opera singers Ernestine Schumann-Heink and Lotte Lehman liked California so much that they settled there permanently. Other popular divas, including Nellie Melba, Luisa Tetrazzini, and Amelita Galli-Curci, received star treatment in California as well. Tetrazzini became the darling of San Francisco opera fans. On the very night of its devastating earthquake and fire of 1906, the great Italian tenor Enrico Caruso sang in Bizet's *Carmen*, while elsewhere in the city at the same moment the young Shakespearean actor John Barrymore was giving one of his earliest performances.

Drama, like music, was also warmly supported. Shakespearean plays produced in San Francisco after 1870 included *The Merchant of Venice*, *Othello*, and *Macbeth*. The most outstanding actor to appear in California during this period was Edwin Booth, his name synonymous with that of *Hamlet* in the minds of theater fans. In 1876 Booth smashed all attendance records; hundreds of disappointed fans had to be turned away each night from the theater in which he played. That same season, a young San Francisco boy managed to get a walk-on part alongside Booth. His name was David Belasco. With San Francisco as his base, Belasco played more than 170 parts in 100 plays before going on to national prominence.

An entirely different type of performer, Lillian Russell, came to California in 1881. The blond Miss Russell appeared in the revue *Babes in the Woods* attired only in a blouse, purple tights, and high-buttoned shoes. Although women's tongues wagged, men applauded Russell's performances. She was called "the biggest bust on Broadway." Western-born Maude Adams also packed large audiences into San Francisco's theaters with her performances of J. M. Barrie's *Peter Pan* and *The Little Minister.*

In 1872, San Francisco's exclusive Bohemian Club began to admit a select number of actors and artists to its al fresco outings. These events are still held annually on the club's 2,700 acres amid a redwood forest on the banks of the Russian River.

Educational advances accompanied cultural growth . The Jesuits established Santa Clara University in 1851. Later, Catholics established Loyola University, the University of San Francisco, Saint Mary's, and Immaculate Heart College. The College of the Pacific was founded by Methodists in 1851. The next year Mills College opened its Oakland gates for women students. In 1868, the state legislature chartered the University of California, located at Berkeley. It was named for England's Bishop Berkeley who wrote the poetic lines: "Westward the course of empire takes its way." In 1879, the Methodists founded the University of Southern California. At Palo Alto, Stanford University was founded in 1890 as a memorial to Leland Stanford's only son. In southern California the year 1887 saw the founding of Occidental College by the Presbyterians, as well as Pomona College, by the Congregationalists. In 1901 the Quakers established Whittier College, and in 1909 the Baptists founded a college at Redlands. Before midcentury, most of these colleges had officially abandoned their religious connections.

Californians also measured their achievements through a variety of popular celebrations. The Panama-Pacific Exposition of 1915 was a symbolic highlight of the state's pre–World War I era. Although half the world was plunged into war even as its exhibits neared completion, the Pacific Exposition (and another held the same year at San Diego's Balboa Park) trumpeted California's progress since the turn of the century as well as the new sea connection with America's East Coast via the Panama Canal.

Before the great earthquake and fire of 1906 absorbed San Francisco's energies in reconstruction—and before prohibition and civic reform chastened fun-loving San Franciscans—the city hosted Presidents Grant, McKinley, and Theodore Roosevelt. Each enjoyed gold-service banquets in the famed Garden Court of the Palace Hotel. In that same hostelry, the flamboyant "Diamond Jim" Brady once downed six dozen oysters before astonished onlookers. After 1900, in a golden age of *gourmandiserie*, it was possible to obtain a good meal, accompanied by the best Napa Valley claret, at Papa Coppa's for less than 50¢. Diners could find alternative hospitality at other popular restaurants such as Leveroni's Cellar, the Bella Union Saloon, the Bank Exchange Saloon, and Jack's Restaurant, while the Cliff House offered an incomparable view of the Pacific.

The generation that lived in California between the Civil War and World War I possessed an unshakeable faith in progress. Writers, artists, and actors all found the Golden State more than congenial. California's romantic chroniclers had won out over its peddlers of gloom and discord.

SELECTED READINGS

For literature see David Wyatt, *The Fall Into Eden: Landscape and Imagination in California* (1986); Joseph Henry Jackson, *Continent's End: A Collection of California Writing* (1944); Lawrence Clark Powell, *California Classics* (1971); Franklin D. Walker, *A Literary History of Southern California* (1950) and his *San Francisco's Literary Frontier* (1939). Biographers include Jacob Oser, *Henry George* (1974), and Kenneth M. Johnson, "Progress and Poverty—A Paradox," *California Historical Society Quarterly* 42 (March 1963), 27–32; Stephen Fox, *John Muir and His Legacy* (1981). He and other naturalists are in Richard Beidleman, *California's Frontier Naturalists* (2006). See also Walter Neale, *Life of Ambrose Bierce* (1929); Paul Fatout, *Ambrose Bierce: The Devil's Lexicographer* (1967); Franklin Walker, *Frank Norris* (1932); Ernest Marchand, *Frank Norris: A Study* (1942); Earle Labor and Jeanne Reesman, *Jack London* (1994); Joan London, *Jack London and His Times* (1939); Richard O'Connor, *Jack London* (1964); and John W. Robinson, "Charles Francis Saunders: A Quaker Botanist in Southern California," *Southern California Quarterly* 60 (Summer 1978), 143–53.

For women leaders, see Sara Alpern, "Harriet Williams Russell Strong..." in *Southern California Quarterly* (Fall, 2005), 223–268 and Gayle Gullet, *Becoming Citizens: The Emergence and Development of the California Women's Movement* (2000) as well as Elinor Richey, *Eminent Women of the West* (1975); Dorothy Gray, *Women of the West* (1976); Joan Hoff Wilson and Lynn Bonfield Donovan, "Women's History: A Listing of West Coast Archival and Manuscript Sources," *California Historical Quarterly* 55 (Spring 1976), 74–83; Christiane Fischer, "Women in California in the Early 1850s," *Southern California Quarterly* 60 (Fall 1978), 231–54;

David J. Langum, "California Women and the Image of Virtue," *Southern California Quarterly* 61 (Fall 1977), 245–50; Helen Holdridge has written *Mammy Pleasant* (1959); see alsoValerie Sherer Mathes, *Helen Hunt Jackson and Her Indian Reform Legacy* (1997); Ruth Odell, *Helen Hunt Jackson* (1939); Emily Leider, *California's Daughter: Gertrude Atherton* (1991) and Virginia Bouvier, *Women and the Conquest of California* (2001).

Other writers are appraised in Thomas M. Pearce, *The Beloved House* (1940); Mary Austin, *Earth Horizon* (1932); Helen M. Doyle, *Mary Austin: Woman of Genius* (1939); Edwin Bingham, *Charles F. Lummis, Editor of the Southwest* (1955); Turbese Lummis Fiske, *Charles F. Lummis: The Man and His West* (1975); Martin S. Peterson, *Joaquin Miller: Literary Frontiersman* (1937); and Anne Roller Issler, *Our Mountain Heritage, Silverado and Robert Louis Stevenson* (1950).

Historiography is in Harry Clark, *A Venture in History: The Production, Publication, and Sale of the Works of Hubert Howe Bancroft* (1973); John W. Caughey, *Hubert Howe Bancroft: Historian of the West* (1946); and Doyce Nunis, Jr., *The Historians of Los Angeles* (1988), a useful brochure.

Newspapers are the subject of Edward C. Kemble, *A History of California Newspapers* (1927); see also John Bruce, *Gaudy Century: The Story of San Francisco's Hundred Years of Robust Journalism* (1948); and *History of the Los Angeles Star* by William B. Rice (1947); also Marshall Berges, *The Life and Times of Los Angeles, a Newspaper, A Family, and a City* (1984); R. L. Duffus, *The Tower of Jewels: Memories of San Francisco* (1960); and Mrs. Fremont Older, *San Francisco, Magic City* (1961).

For drama, see *Memories and Impressions of Helen Modjeska: An Autobiography* (1910); *Portrait of America: Letters of Henry Sinciewicz,* trans. and ed. by Charles Morley (1959); William Winter, *The Life of David Belasco* (2 vols. 1918); Constance Rourke, *Troupers of the Gold Coast* (1928) and Parker Morell, *Lillian Russell: The Era of Plush* (1940).

Higher education is in William W. Ferrier, *Origin and Development of the University of California* (1930) also his *Ninety Years of Education in California* (1937) and Verne A. Stadtman, *The University of California, 1868–1968* (1970); Albert G. Pickerell and May Dornin, *The University of California, A Pictorial History* (1969); Andrew Rolle, *Occidental College: A Centennial History* (1987); Charles Elliott, Jr., *Whittier College: The First Century* (1986); Helen Raitt and Bernice Moulton, *Scripps Institution of Oceanography: First Fifty Years* (1967); Edith R. Mirrielees, *Stanford: The Story of a University* (1959); Charles Burt Sumner, *The Story of Pomona College* (1914); Manuel P. Servín and Iris A. Wilson, *Southern California and its University* (1969); John R. Thelin, "California and the Colleges,"

California Historical Quarterly 56 (Summer 1977), 140–63 and (Fall 1977), 230–49; *The Memoirs of Ray Lyman Wilbur,* edited by Edgar Robinson and Paul Carroll Edwards (1960); Lester Stephens, *Joseph Le Conte: Gentle Prophet of Evolution* (1982).

Other cultural references include: Judith Raftery, *Land of Fair Promise: Politics and Reform in Los Angeles Schools, 1885–1941* (1992); Robert Griswold, *Family and Divorce in California, 1850–1890* (1982); and Stephen Vincent, ed., *O California! Nineteenth and Early Twentieth Century California Landscapes* (1989).

CHAPTER TWENTY-SEVEN

PROGRESSIVE POLITICS

In California, and throughout the nation, the period between 1900 and the outbreak of World War I featured the growing discontent of farmers. In addition to the railroads, their wrath was directed at the meatpacking, banking, and manufacturing monopolies. City workers, meanwhile, opposed the undue influence of big business over government. They nursed a special anger toward corrupt machine politics. During this period a group of reform-minded journalists, dubbed "Muckrakers" by President Theodore Roosevelt, exposed shady business practices and political graft. They also championed legislation to exercise control over large industrial combinations. California was at the center of all this reformist energy.

But as the new century dawned, no state or national leader had yet stepped forth to head the crusade for reform. In the presidential campaign of 1900, California voted for the conservative Republican William McKinley over Democratic challenger William Jennings Bryan, as did the nation as a whole. By 1904, however, the state and national mood had shifted toward liberalism. In the presidential election of that year, Californians supported Theodore Roosevelt, the standard-bearer of reform. But, in the ensuing gubernatorial campaign, Republican James N. Gillett, a machine candidate, prevailed. He solidified the popular belief that political control of the state lay behind the scenes, rather than with the electorate. The real power in California was the Southern Pacific Railroad.

Beginning with its construction, the political activities of the Southern Pacific shaped California's immediate future. At first, the S.P.'s founders entered practical politics in order to maintain their dictatorship over rates and services. In short order, two railroad lobbyists, William Herrin of San Francisco and Walter Parker of Los Angeles, curried political influence, dispensing large sums of money to politicians throughout the state. At Sacramento, when the legislature was in session, Herrin saw to it each week that a round-trip ticket to San Francisco was left on the desk of every legislator. Furthermore, the railroad annually bribed a sizeable number of the state senators and an even greater number in the assembly.

The railroad also subsidized newspaper editors monthly, to obtain favorable publicity. The S.P. had gained so powerful a grip on the press that opposition to it seemed futile. Independent newspapers, including the *Sacramento Union*, were subjected to relentless criticism by politicians paid off by the railroad. The legislators did not want to read about their own corruption. Hence, any public disapproval of the S.P. was effectively stifled.

The Mussel Slough tragedy added ugliness to the railroad's reputation. The reform writers George, Norris, and Royce described the power of the S.P as free of all regulation. Even earlier the Central Pacific Railroad had been charged as the "third party" in state politics. According to one account, "its leaders, its managers, its editors, its orators, its adherents" were everywhere. None showed allegiance to the people of the state. Few voices dared to speak out against the railroad monopoly.

The new Railroad Commissioners, as noted, proved ineffective in regulating freight and passenger rates. Farmers had long been hostile to the S.P. because of its discrimination against small customers and under-the-table rebates to favored shippers. During 1883, an exposé of railroad politics known as "The Colton Letters," became public knowledge. David Colton had been a close associate of Collis P. Huntington, Leland Stanford, and Charles Crocker back when the three had been lobbying for government subsidies to establish the Southern Pacific network eastward from Yuma, Arizona, toward New Orleans. After Colton died suddenly, his widow was dissatisfied with the meager settlement she received from her husband's selfish colleagues. In retaliation, the unhappy Mrs. Colton released to the public several hundred incriminating letters that Huntington had written to her late husband. These letters provided a sordid picture of backroom political manipulations in Sacramento as well as in Washington.

Long lists of potentially corruptible officeholders came out of Colton's personal correspondence. Huntington had indiscreetly discussed the costs of assuring favorable passage of legislation. The Colton Letters provided an inside view of Huntington's power to influence lawmakers. Their publication bolstered the popular conviction that the railroad had established a government within a government. Furthermore, Huntington was in no mood to apologize. When he boldly appeared before the U.S. Railway

Commission, he stated that it was perfectly proper to pay the salaries and expenses of the entire Arizona territorial legislature in order to get key legislation passed.

After revelation of the incriminating Colton letters, Huntington came in for further notoriety. New federal legislation called for the railroads to repay money loaned them as thirty-year bonds. Even as public awareness increased, Huntington used every means in his power to prevent repayment of the outstanding bonds at the designated rate of 6 percent interest. Instead, he wanted the loans replaced by ninety-nine-year obligations at 1.5 percent interest. Each of the "Big Four" had, meanwhile, amassed great fortunes. Huntington personally owned enough railroad trackage to connect the North and the South Poles; he could travel from Newport News, Virginia, to San Francisco without ever riding on anyone else's rails. He also owned timber sawmills (in which he employed his nephew, Henry E. Huntington), steamship lines, and coal mines.

The *San Francisco Examiner*, owned by the young and ambitious William Randolph Hearst, kept up a barrage of criticism against Huntington. In 1896 Hearst sent the eagle-eyed Ambrose Bierce to Washington to cover Huntington's activities. Bierce wired his paper daily descriptions of the railroad magnate's testimony before congressional committees. Bierce fiercely exposed Huntington's dishonesty, his articles accompanied by cartoons that showed Huntington leading the governor of California around on a leash.

Another controversy that dogged Huntington's career was his involvement in the Los Angeles Free Harbor fight. By 1890 that city, with a population of over 50,000 persons, was on its way to becoming the largest in California. Only one deficiency threatened to halt this grand expansion—the lack of a good harbor. Ships still docked a short distance away at the open roadstead of San Pedro–Wilmington. Only federal funds could build the expensive docks, sea walls, slips, and passages necessary to convert muddy flats into a modern facility.

Two opposing sites, San Pedro and Santa Monica, were proposed. Now a bitter fight developed over which of these would become future L.A.'s harbor. The Huntington interests favored construction at Santa Monica because the Southern Pacific controlled the approaches to that location. Angeleños, however, knew that if Congress should select Santa Monica, it would be a port constructed for the benefit of Huntington and his company.

An aroused Los Angeles public organized a "Free Harbor League" to secure the federal appropriation for San Pedro instead. The term "free harbor" emerged from the sentiment that the new port should not be dominated by the railroad. Critics of the Southern Pacific maintained that if Santa Monica were selected, the hated S.P. would set whatever freight rates it wanted, as well as govern the loading and unloading of ships. Senator Stephen M. White, an influential public figure, allied himself with the Free Harbor Leaguers. So did the *Los Angeles Times* and the city's chamber of commerce. Senator White, a persuasive orator, battled for three years, from 1893 to 1896, to prevent Huntington from having federal funds allocated to Santa Monica. The free-harbor fight ended up with the designation of San Pedro as the site of Los Angeles's future port.

Shortly after Collis Huntington's death in 1900, his nephew, Henry, sold control of the Southern Pacific to E. H. Harriman, builder of the Northern Pacific Railroad Company. Out of seventy-three local lines, Henry Huntington then formed a new interurban railway system to serve the Los Angeles area. He found it difficult to rid himself of the stigma of his uncle's primitive capitalism. Only when he founded the magnificent Henry E. Huntington Library and Art Gallery in San Marino did the memory of the Huntington name begin to reverse negative public opinion.

The S.P. remained a strong power in state politics until reform tide began to swell. After a reform-minded president, Theodore Roosevelt, entered the White House, he helped to force greater railroad regulation. The muckrakers too stepped up their agitation for stricter control of all monopolies. Lincoln Steffens, the best known of these determined journalists, had spent his boyhood in Sacramento. His collected articles, which boldly addressed the corrupt alliance of business and politics, were published in book form as *The Shame of the Cities*.

In 1902, San Francisco proved especially ready for Steffens's hard-hitting investigations. That year a labor-backed political machine, the Union Labor party, installed a theater musician, Eugene E. Schmitz, as the city's mayor. The real power behind the throne, however, was Abraham Ruef, a clever attorney who sported a handlebar mustache. Ruef blackmailed legitimate businesspeople and extorted them through protection rackets. His political machine further forced business owners to purchase licenses to operate liquor, cigar, and gambling establishments and bilked "French restaurants," establishments known to operate prostitution cribs upstairs, out of "hush money."

By 1905, the *San Francisco Bulletin* published a series of articles by Fremont Older, its reformist editor, excoriating the corrupt city regime. Then, just as Older, former mayor James D. Phelan, and sugar magnate Rudolph Spreckels were about to begin a campaign to overthrow Ruef and Schmitz, a disaster of unprecedented magnitude struck San Francisco.

Earthquake damage, San Francisco, April 23, 1906. City Hall from Larkin Street. H. G. Hills collection, courtesy of the Bancroft Library, University of California, Berkeley.

Displaced San Francisco residents wait in a bread line, April 1906. Courtesy of the National Archives, NWDNS-92-ER-15.

At 5:16 A.M. on April 18, 1906, a massive earthquake shook the ground along the San Andreas Fault, running from Salinas in the south to Cape Mendocino in northern California. A menacing rumble, which awakened thousands at San Francisco, was followed by the terrifying sounds of flimsy buildings being twisted off their foundations. As multi-storied brick structures cascaded into the streets, massive fissures opened up in the earth. Almost every chimney in the city tumbled down, putting fleeing residents in danger. In addition, short-circuited electric wires fell onto the city's streets, setting off fires that swept through block after block of residences.

When volunteer firemen attached their hoses to hydrants, little or no water came out. Not only had many pipes burst; in some instances the city's fire hydrants, thanks to the negligence of the irresponsible city government, had never been hooked up to the water mains. Firemen, thus, fought frantically without water to stamp out the advancing flames. General Frederick Funston, the commandant of the Presidio of San Francisco, charged into the city, determined to limit the spread of the fire. His troops proceeded to dynamite more than a quarter mile of mansions along Van Ness Street. The army used black powder in dynamiting buildings to create firebreaks. This made the fires rage worse. Needless explosions fanned a conflagration that raged on for days. Nob Hill and Chinatown were left in ruins.

The northeastern part of the city, extending from the Southern Pacific Depot to Telegraph Hill, lay in heaps of debris. Despite relief shipments sent from all over the world, 300,000 homeless San Franciscans lived for weeks in army tents pitched on vacant lots and in their city's Golden Gate Park. The hapless campers, some still clad in their best Sunday clothes, sadly munched on emergency rations of shredded-wheat biscuits and drank beef tea. Hundreds of tins of corned beef were also distributed by the Red Cross.

Even as the work of rebuilding the devastated city began, the destruction of the Ruef-Schmitz machine became the foremost goal of Older, Phelan, and Spreckels. Joining them was a young attorney named Francis J. Heney, who as a United States prosecutor had indicted fraudulent timber operators in Oregon. By November of 1907, the great "San Francisco graft prosecution" began its indictments of Ruef and Schmitz for extortion. In addition, masses of incriminating evidence piled up, in addition, against executives of the city's public utility corporations. Whereas the bribe takers, Ruef and Schmitz, were condemned for their crookedness, the bribe givers were regarded differently. Newspapers argued that members of the business community had been blackjacked into filtering funds to the politicians who ran the city.

The defense in the great San Francisco graft prosecution, 1906–07. Henry Ach, one of Abraham Ruef's attorneys, whispers to the wily Ruef, San Francisco police chief Bigg is at left. Carl Hoffman Papers, courtesy of the Bancroft Library, University of California, Berkeley.

During the San Francisco graft trials, Fremont Older and his fellow reformers were subjected to repeated indignities, even by their peers—for the city had been penetrated by officials accustomed to graft. In addition to experiencing social ostracism, Older was kidnapped. He was taken by train to Santa Barbara, where he was later "found" and returned to the trial by the police. Next, the house of the principal witness, a San Francisco supervisor, was blown up, and documents intended for use in the graft prosecutions were stolen out of private homes and offices. On November 13, 1907, a prospective juror who had been challenged by the prosecution because of a criminal record, arose in the courtroom during Ruef's trial, drew a gun, and shot the chief prosecutor in the head, nearly killing him. He was succeeded by a then obscure local attorney, Hiram Johnson, then on the brink of a long and famous career.

The graft trials lasted more than two years. The evasive Abe Ruef, although the political boss of San Francisco, was not technically an office-holder. Yet of all the defendants, only he went to the penitentiary, sentenced to fourteen years for bribery. After spending four years and seven months at San Quentin, Ruef was freed.

The spirit of municipal reform, meanwhile, was producing other protests at Los Angeles. In that city an idealistic "good government" movement took shape under Dr. John R. Haynes, a wealthy physician and outspoken critic of the Southern Pacific monopoly. He fathered a "Direct Legislation League" that denounced municipal and state "boodlers," as they called were then called, seeking to replace them in public office with honestly elected citizens. Haynes's ideal was to limit the power of corporations, especially the Southern Pacific, as well as that of wheedling legislators. He also established a foundation bearing his name, with the goal of raising the moral standards of public life.

Through the influence of Dr. Haynes and his civic-minded fellow citizens, Los Angeles became one of the first cities in the nation to adopt initiative, referendum, and recall measures. These three items lay at the heart of the progressive reform program. During 1909 the electorate, using the new administrative recall weapon, forced Mayor Arthur C. Harper to resign after he became involved in a sugar company stock speculation scandal. The fact that Harper had received the support of the Southern Pacific political machine in his bid for office hardly bolstered his popularity.

Reformers also sought the resignation of graft-tainted officials at Sacramento, Oakland, Fresno, and Santa Barbara. On August 1, 1907, a new political alignment within the Republican Party, called the California Progressives, formed the Lincoln-Roosevelt League. The founders of the league were liberal Republicans, who fused the names of their greatest party leaders into a symbol for freeing the Republican Party from domination by corrupt interests.

In 1910, the Lincoln-Roosevelt League ran Hiram Johnson—a stocky little man in a tight vest with the gleam of reform in his eye—as its candidate for governor. Johnson had achieved fame in the last days of the San Francisco graft prosecutions. Only forty-four years old, this stubborn

Hiram Johnson, the popular progressive Republican Governor of California, 1910-17; and United States Senator, 1917-45. Library of Congress, LC-USZ62-78364.

and steel-nerved politician undertook a 20,000-mile automobile campaign over rocky, unpaved roads. He won the governorship against four other candidates and triumphantly led progressive Republican legislators to Sacramento.

The Lincoln-Roosevelt League succeeded in an objective that neither the Republicans nor the Democrats had been able to accomplish. This was the overthrow of one of the nation's most entrenched political systems. The legislature of 1911 racked up a record that was the envy of progressives in every state of the Union. The passage of the direct primary law assured the nomination of candidates by the voters themselves: previously the Republican and Democratic parties had nominated senatorial candidates within politically safe conventions. The state legislature also adopted initiative, referendum, and recall measures. These bills were designed to cut down on the prerogatives of big-city political machines and their bosses.

The 1911 session of the legislature also added twenty-three amendments to the state constitution concerning control of public utilities, workmen's compensation, regulation of weights and measures, conservation of natural resources, income-tax provisions, and women's suffrage. Other progressive measures included a "blue-sky" law for protection of the securities investor, a civil-service law, laws providing for mothers' pensions, and establishment of a minimum wage for women and minors.

Despite the success of the California Progressives, a black spot on their record was an insistence upon Asiatic exclusion. Johnson's retinue were called racists whose liberalism did not extend to minority groups. But this is present-mindedness. Both liberals and conservatives of the Progressive Era would be labeled racists by today's standards. Before World War I, large segments of American society were strongly opposed to unrestricted immigration.

The major achievement of the California progressives was the defeat of the entrenched Southern Pacific political machine. As governor, Johnson worked with the legislature to make sure that the railroads would henceforth become the servants and not the masters of the people. Passage of a cross-filing law in 1913 ensured that progressive candidates could henceforth become the nominees of more than one party. As a result, a candidate's political affiliation need not even be identified on primary election ballots. This allowed progressives to pick up both liberal and conservative votes. They had come closer to controlling the Republican party's future.

By 1912, the California progressives played a role in founding a third national political party headed by former President Theodore Roosevelt. Under this new Progressive party banner, T.R. was again nominated for the presidency. On a "Bull Moose" ticket, with Governor Hiram Johnson as his running mate, Roosevelt carried the state that year. The pair, however, lost the national election. After Johnson's defeat, the state's Progressives lost much of their drive. In 1914, Johnson was, nevertheless, returned to the governorship under the Progressive party banner.

Governor Johnson would play a big role in the presidential campaign of 1916. That year Charles Evans Hughes ran on the Republican ticket against President Woodrow Wilson. Though a Democrat, Wilson's reelection by the slim margin of 3,700 votes was partly due to Johnson's antipathy to Hughes. In August 1916, Hughes visited California but kept in poor contact with Governor Johnson. At one point both men stayed in the same hotel without even meeting. Hughes scarcely realized the extent of Johnson's power in his home state. Johnson felt snubbed by Hughes.

Therefore, Johnson failed to campaign for his fellow Republican. Had he done so, he might have swung the state toward Hughes. Instead, California's electoral votes went to Wilson, leaving Hughes only twelve electoral votes short of the presidency. While some asserted that it was indeed the California vote that had cost Hughes the election, other important "swing" states such as Ohio had voted for Wilson. Johnson's own race for the Senate in 1916 resulted in his victory by almost 300,000 votes. He stayed in the Senate until his death in 1945.

The pioneering progressives not only had cleaned up state and local government, but they had also improved its efficiency. Their primary goal, "to kick the Southern Pacific out of state politics forever," had been attained. Had the Republican Party not split in 1912 into conservative and reform wings, the progressive reform campaigns might have gone even further.

SELECTED READINGS

Labor and railroads are in J. L. Brown, *The Mussel Slough Tragedy* (1958); Irving McKee, "Notable Memorials to Mussel Slough," *Pacific Historical Review* 17 (February 1948), 19–27; David Lavender, *The Great Persuader* (1970); Ralph N. Traxler, "Collis P. Huntington and the Texas and Pacific Railroad Land Grants," *New Mexico Historical Review* 34 (April 1959), 117–33; James Thorpe, *Henry Edwards Huntington* (1994); and William Friedricks, *Henry E. Huntington and the Creation of Southern California* (1992).

Railroad involvement in the free harbor controversy is in Charles D. Willard, *The Free Harbor Contest at Los Angeles* (1899); Edith Dobie, *The Political Career of Stephen Mallory White* (1927); William Deverell, "The Los Angeles Free Harbor Fight," *California History* 70 (Spring 1991),

13–29; Charles Queenan and Stephen Sato, *Long Beach and Los Angeles: A Tale of Two Ports* (1986) and Franklyn Hoyt, "The Los Angeles Terminal Railroad," *Historical Society of Southern California Quarterly* (September 1954), 185–91.

Other references include Norman E. Tutorow, *Leland Stanford, Man of Many Careers* (1971) and his *The Governor...Leland Stanford* (2004) and Ward McAfee, *California's Railroad Era, 1850–1911* (1973); Morley Segal, "James Rolph and the San Francisco Municipal Railway," *California Historical Society Quarterly* 43 (March 1964), 3–18; Judd Kahn, *Imperial San Francisco: Politics and Planning, 1897–1906* (1980); and Philip Ethington, *The Public City . . . San Francisco, 1850–1900* (1994).

One of the great books of its time is J. Lincoln Steffens, *The Autobiography of Lincoln Steffens*, 2 vols. (1931); see also George E. Mowry, *The California Progressives* (1951); William Deverell and Tom Sitton, eds., *Progressivism Revisited* (1994) and Sitton, *John Randolph Haynes, California Progressive* (1992). More about the Progressives is in Richard Lower, *A Bloc of One: The Political Career of Hiram Johnson* (1993); Spencer C. Olin, *California's Prodigal Sons: Hiram Johnson and the Progressives, 1911–1917* (1968); Walton Bean, *Boss Ruef's San Francisco* (1952); Fremont Older, *My Own Story* (1919); Evelyn Wells, *Fremont Older* (1916); Bruce Bliven, "The Boodling Boss and the Musical Mayor," *American Heritage* 11 (December 1959), 8–11, 100–104; and James P. Walsh, "Abe Ruef Was No Boss," *California Historical Quarterly* 51 (Spring 1972), 3–16.

On the San Francisco earthquake and fire, see Philip Fradkin, *The Great Earthquake . . .* (2005); William Bronson, *The Earth Shook, The Sky Burned* (1959); Monica Sutherland, *The Damndest Finest Ruins* (1959); John C. Kennedy, *The Great Earthquake and Fire, San Francisco 1906* (1963) and Gordon Thomas and M. M. Witts, *The San Francisco Earthquake* (1971).

About the Hughes-Johnson misunderstanding see Edward A. Dickson, "How Hughes Lost California in 1916," *Congressional Record* (August 19, 1954); F. M. Davenport, "Did Hughes Snub Johnson?" *American Political Science Review* 40 (April 1949), 321–32, and J. Gregg Layne, "The Lincoln-Roosevelt League," *Historical Society of Southern California Quarterly* 25 (September 1943), 79–101.

As to other elections, see A. Lincoln, "Theodore Roosevelt, Hiram Johnson, and the Vice Presidential Nomination of 1912," *Pacific Historical Review* 28 (August 1959), 267–83; H. Brett Melendy, "California's Cross-Filing Nightmare: The 1918 Gubernatorial Election," *Pacific Historical Review* 33 (August 1964), 317–30; Franklin Hichborn, "The Party, the

Machine, and the Vote: The Story of Cross-filing in California Politics," *California Historical Society Quarterly* 38 (December 1959), 349–57; James C. Findley, "Cross-filing and the Progressive Movement in California Politics," *Western Political Quarterly* 12 (September 1959), 699–711, and Fred Viehe, "The First Recall: Los Angeles Urban Reform or Machine Politics," *Southern California Quarterly* 57 (Spring, 1988), 1–28; Jackson K. Putnam, "The Persistence of Progressivism in the 1920's: The Case of California," *Pacific Historical Review* 35 (November 1966), 395–411; Thomas G. Patterson, "California Progressives and Foreign Policy," *California Historical Society Quarterly* 47 (December 1968), 329–42; Eric Falk Petersen, "The Adoption of the Direct Primary in California," *Southern California Quarterly* 54 (Winter 1972), 363–78; and John L. Shover, "The California Progressives and the 1924 Campaign," *California Historical Quarterly* 51 (Spring 1971), 17–34. Also see John M. Allswang, *The Initiative and Referendum in California, 1898–1998* (2000). On the woman suffrage campaign, the most insightful book is Gayle Gullett, *Becoming Citizens: The Emergence and Development of the California Women's Movement, 1880–1911* (2000).

CHAPTER TWENTY-EIGHT

MATERIAL URBAN GROWTH

The San Francisco earthquake and fire of 1906, among the most cataclysmic events in the history of California, set back the prosperity of that city. The heavy damage, however, produced many years of booming employment, especially in the building trades. Civic leaders demanded a rebuilding of the city on an even grander scale.

Farther south, the citizens of Los Angeles were busy developing a new port. In 1909, consolidation of the coastal towns of San Pedro and Wilmington with L.A. was accomplished through an intricate piece of political gerrymandering. A narrow "shoestring" of land provided an extended harbor district. Originally the harbor was shielded haphazardly from the sea by Point Fermin. Later, U.S. engineers constructed a long protective breakwater. By 1914, this enhanced harbor facility was followed by the opening of the Panama Canal. This made L.A. one of the most important ports in the world. Ten years later, the city had eclipsed San Francisco in the handling of annual cargo tonnage, becoming the busiest port on the Pacific Coast. Situated on the great circle route to Asia, its harbor saw significant growth.

Meanwhile, that city was becoming an urban labyrinth of steel and concrete, expanding rapidly as a population shift occurred from northern California southward. Los Angeles pushed its boundaries over the Hollywood Hills toward the San Fernando Valley. On the west it came to bound Culver City and northward to adjoin Burbank, Glendale, Pasadena, Alhambra, Vernon, Huntington Park, South Pasadena, Torrance, Inglewood, Gardena, Hawthorne, El Segundo, and Long Beach. From the Santa Monica Mountains to the Verdugo Hills, L.A. eventually included more than 450 square miles—and was referred to as "a group of suburbs in search of a city."

Urban transportation was vital to the growth of both San Francisco and Los Angeles. After 1915, as the northern city also increased in size, Francis Marion Smith, "the borax king," developed the Key Route Electric Railway to supplement the city's Peninsular Electric Railway. It was similar to Henry Huntington's network of "big red electric cars" at Los Angeles. His Pacific Electric rail system operated over 1,100 miles of track. Los Angeles County eventually would contain more than forty incorporated cities.

Back in the 1850s, William Heath Davis had wanted to found a "New San Diego." But this nearly forgotten pioneer was hampered by the lack of a reliable water supply system. Also, there were few natural resources in the area, including lumber for the construction of houses and commercial buildings. In the 1870s, profiting from a rail connection, a more successful real estate developer, Alonzo Erastus Horton, built Horton House, a hotel that began to attract tourists seeking a mild climate. Later, John and Adolph Spreckels poured millions of dollars into the development of San Diego, including its renowned Hotel Del Coronado (1887). To this day, the "Del," a national historic landmark, remains a popular resort. After the

The Hotel del Coronado, built in 1887, was designated a historic landmark in 1977. Photo courtesy of David Austin.

turn of the century, California's southernmost city saw still more development. At nearby Point Loma, Katherine Tingley and a group of Theosophists began a utopian colony.

In 1905, along the Los Angeles coastline, transplanted easterner Abbot Kinney opened up his visionary "Venice of America," complete with canals, gondolas, and Italian gondoliers. The heir of a tobacco fortune, Kinney envisioned his seaside community as a place where vacationers and residents alike could enjoy the nearby ocean and take in a wide range of cultural events. Although most of the original canals are gone, Venice Beach draws visitors from around the world to today's oddball shoreline.

San Diego's 1908 welcome of President Theodore Roosevelt's "Great White Fleet" ushered in a new future for the port as a major naval center. By 1915, a Hispanic architectural boom accompanied the opening of the city's Panama-California Exposition. Later, San Diego's Ryan Aeronautical Corporation built Charles E. Lindbergh's renowned airplane, the *Spirit of Saint Louis.*

The prosperity of California was stimulated by World War I. Although the state's location was remote from European zones of combat, it became heavily involved in the national war effort. A few eastern factories were beginning to establish branches there. This attracted new immigration westward, further integrating California into the national economy.

Before World War I, the state's employment had centered around food processing, including packing and canning, as well as lumber, fishing, and mineral and oil production. These activities flourished with renewed vigor as the war encouraged economic diversification. Demand for San Joaquin Valley cotton grew because of use of that fiber in the millions of new uniforms that had to be supplied to soldiers. Taking up the slogan "Food Will Win the War," the state sent huge quantities of grains, fruits, meats, and vegetables into federal government storehouses. California also contributed more than 150,000 soldiers to the Allied forces, especially to the Ninety-first Division, which saw service in the Battle of the Argonne in France. As it had in the Civil War, California also gave generously to Liberty and Victory Loan drives, in each case exceeding a prescribed state quota.

When peace finally came, the economy of California had been lifted onto a new plateau. By the 1920s, the state ranked second in the nation in total mineral production, despite its lack of coal and iron deposits. The war had stimulated demands for gold and silver, as well as for soda, potash, and mercury, known as quicksilver. Unfortunately, hydraulic mining, which had devastated hundreds of square miles of rich agricultural lands, was replaced by yet another environmentally destructive system. This was dredging, which created desolate wastelands by sluicing great quantities of sand and rock out of the earth. The rubble was left alongside the mines in long heaps called tailings.

Meanwhile, the development of new and better roads required increasing quantities of asphalt and cement, virtually creating a new industry. Since 1885, another product, Borax, or sodium borate, had been mined commercially. Used as a cleanser, twenty-mule teams hauled this mineral out of the floor of Death Valley. Far more important was another substance that would change California's economy: petroleum.

From the Mexican period onward, Angeleños had used asphalt, a sticky, low-grade form of petroleum, for roofing. Oil was found at Pico Canyon near San Fernando, but the earliest verifiable oil well in California was drilled in 1861 in Humboldt County. Wildcatters also dug shallow wells all over the Santa Susana Mountains near Ventura, as well as at Santa Barbara and farther north in the Humboldt Bay region.

Meanwhile, the first oil to be marketed west of Pennsylvania was found in California's Ventura County—and without the drilling of wells. This operation had actually begun back in 1859, after a whale-oil mer-

"Spudding-in" ceremonies in Compton, on September 21, 1926. Courtesy of the Historical Collections, Security Pacific National Bank.

chant investigated some curious oil seepages near Los Angeles. On property belonging to Major Henry Hancock, he erected a small pot-still with which he produced semiliquid asphaltum. When he drove speculators off his ranch, the gutsy entrepreneur set up a second still along the Ventura River.

By 1864, a touring professor of chemistry from Yale College, Benjamin Silliman, Jr., after examining the oil seepages in Ventura County, wrote glowing reports on their commercial possibilities. One result of his account was the formation of two companies to exploit California oil resources. Both firms were controlled by the Pennsylvania Railroad. A financial combine, the Philadelphia & California Petroleum Company, drilled a well near the Camulos Ranch and seven other wells in the Ojai region between 1865 and 1867. One of these wells proved to be California's first "gusher."

Not until after the turn of the century were techniques developed for making a satisfactory illuminant from California crude oil, which is heavy and asphalt-based. In the mid-1860s, crude oil was sold as fuel, without refining, as it came from the wellheads. After this initial frenzy of the 1860s died away, the oil industry entered a dormant period that was not interrupted until the mid-1870s, when the California Star Oil Company began drilling in the Newhall Basin. Scores of other small firms followed the lead of the California Star Oil Company. Most of the state's first oil well discoveries were in southern California.

In no industry was competition fiercer than in oil refining. Because so many new wells were dug and refineries set up, the oil market became glutted, causing prices to fall. The frenzied rush to new sites was reminiscent of the gold mania of 1848–49. Few operators survived this experimental and exciting period of speculative enterprise. Despite the production of kerosene for illumination, tar for roofing, and oil for lubrication, the petroleum industry in those years before the invention of the internal-combustion engine still suffered from limited markets and primitive operational techniques. In 1879, California Star became the Pacific Coast Oil Company, corporate ancestor of the Standard Oil Company of California. Pacific was then the dominant oil company of the state. By 1884, many companies had failed or been absorbed by larger operations.

Two oil pioneers were to profit greatly from the state's vast underground reserves. These were Lyman Stewart and Edward L. Doheny. In 1883, Stewart, who had made his fortune in an oil rush at Titusville, Pennsylvania, headed west to begin a new career. By 1890, he formed the Union Oil Company. Two years later that company sank a well in Adams Canyon in Ventura County. This gusher produced 1,500 barrels of oil per day, the output overflowing into the Santa Clara River until the flow could be capped.

Doheny's career is one of the most perplexing in the history of American capitalism. Born in Wisconsin, he started work as a government surveyor. In 1876, as a youth of twenty, he drifted into the Black Hills just as Dakota Territory was experiencing a silver and gold rush. Doheny next headed for Arizona and then Kingston, New Mexico, where another precious metal rush was under way. He also worked as a hard-rock miner along the Mexican border. Later, he found employment as a miner in the Mojave Desert of California. With this experience and some money behind him, Doheny came to Los Angeles in 1892, where he noticed that *brea*, a black tar-pitch, clung to the wheels of carriages and carts. Doheny traced the source of the gooey substance to a seepage near Westlake Park. He then leased a city lot nearby and began to dig, quickly striking a pocket of natural gas. At 600 feet in depth, Doheny's workers next brought in a

Broadway, looking south from Second Street, Los Angeles, June 8, 1889, at the opening of a cable car route. C. C. Pierce collection, courtesy of the Huntington Library, San Marino, California.

well with a capacity of forty-five barrels a day. This started an oil boom. In the next five years 2,300 wells were dug in the Los Angeles basin.

A strange skyline quickly sprang up in the former sleepy pueblo. Wooden derricks stood in both front and back yards, and greasy little refineries were noisily hammered together. Some Angeleños became wealthy. Others got little for their trouble other than expensive drilling bills, uprooted gardens, and dirty clouds of dust that coated their houses and clothing. A rich oil field surrounded La Brea pits where, in 1875, amateur paleontologists found the first remains of prehistoric animals—the skeleton of a saber-tooth cat that had been trapped many thousands of years ago in the tar seeps. By 1897, oil production in the Los Angeles area, including nearby Puente and Fullerton, rose to 1.4 million barrels per year. Five years later the figure increased to 9 million barrels.

But Doheny and his competitors were having trouble marketing surplus oil. They sold some of it to municipalities that sprayed it onto dusty streets to keep the dust down. They also persuaded manufacturers of pipe to use an oil coating to prevent rust. Eventually, however, a new market for oil was created after railroad managers realized that they could save a substantial amount in fuel costs by adapting locomotives from the burning of coal to oil. By 1901, the Southern Pacific Railroad bought 500 tank cars and built fifty storage tanks after converting its locomotives to use oil.

Encouraged by this new market, speculators stepped up efforts to discover new oil reserves. The search was spurred by increasing use of the automobile. During the 1920s, deposits were found in the San Joaquin Valley and in the Midway-Sunset, Lost Hills–Belridge, Elk Hills, Wheeler Ridge, and Kettleman Hills areas. New wells were also brought in at Whittier, Fullerton, Puente, Coyote Hills, Montebello, Richfield, Compton, Torrance, and Inglewood. Along the coast, wells were drilled at Watsonville and Santa Maria, as well as at Coalinga in Fresno County, at Bakersfield, and near the Kern River.

But the greatest oil strikes of all were made after 1920 at Huntington Beach and the next year at Santa Fe Springs and Signal Hill. These three fields contained such vast pools of oil that their discovery upset national prices and glutted storage facilities. By 1922, the Signal Hill fields alone reached a production of 244,000 barrels daily from 265 wells. Two years later California ranked first among the states in the production of petroleum. By the 1930s, there were 15,000 oil derricks in western Kern County alone. Producers sought new markets for petroleum products. Moving beyond kerosene and axle grease, Lyman Stewart encouraged development of an oil burner for marine engines. His Union Oil Company commissioned tanker vessels to transport oil to overseas markets.

Edward Doheny, who also developed oil fields in Peru and Mexico, stirred up a national scandal over some disputed Elk Hills reserves. Charges of corruption led all the way to the cabinet of President Warren G. Harding. Investigators uncovered Doheny's secret operations. In 1921 he had sent a satchel containing $100,000 to Secretary of the Interior Albert B. Fall, "an old prospector friend" who controlled the Elk Hills reserves as well Teapot Dome in Wyoming. Two years later, Fall and Doheny were indicted for conspiracy to corner federal oil resources. Only Fall went to prison.

For the pioneering oil speculators of that generation great opportunities for corruption existed. In 1921, Courtney Julian, an audacious oil salesman, brazenly advertised for investors in Los Angeles newspapers. In two weeks he raised $175,000. He then organized the Julian Petroleum Company. Known as "Julian Pete," his company consisted of only a few wells leased on the edge of Signal Hill. After satisfying a few original stockholders, Julian talked new investors into buying bogus stock in his dummy corporation, a scam through which Julian made several million dollars. In 1925, an audit of his operations was demanded by outraged holders of worthless stock. Julian then jumped prison bail and fled the state. From Canada he ended up in Shanghai, where he committed suicide in 1934.

Other oil producers who continued to curtail production were accused of price fixing. In later years, dwindling reserves encouraged better regulation. Yet, the oil industry was able to maintain tax deductions based on high exploration costs and depletion allowances. The average life of the best-producing wells was only twenty-five to thirty years. As they reached maturity, new and deeper wells had to be drilled. In the 1930s, the quest for oil reserves led drillers to tap offshore pools from rigs anchored onto the ocean floor. The development of the port of Long Beach, which was begun in 1938 and financed in large measure by proceeds from drilling a rich field along its waterfront, created a new legal question: Did the state or the federal government own tideland oil resources? The final answer would have to await future legal decisions. In the meantime, due to over-drilling, sea water began to leak under that city.

From 1900 to 1930, California's oil industry skyrocketed with the discovery of large new pools and the development of better refining techniques. These included the catalytic cracking process, which accompanied increasing fuel demands for factories, automobiles, trucks, and airplanes. By 1919, there had been fewer than 7 million passenger cars registered in the entire United States. Then, in the 1920s, the personal automobile underwent a transformation from a sputtering plaything of the rich, which tended to frighten ladies and horses, to an affordable necessity of the working masses.

Quantity production of the inexpensive but crude Model T Ford, the price of which dropped to only $280, increased the number of cars sold nationally to over 23 million by 1929. Just under 2 million of these cars were the property of Californians. Numerically, this far exceeded that of other western states (Nevada, 31,915; Arizona, 109,013; Utah, 112,661; Oregon, 269,007). On a per capita basis, California's automobile registration already was the largest in the United States. As tractors replaced horses and mules on farms, buses took the place of trolleys in the larger cities. Mechanized transportation of all forms became commonplace.

The family automobile also stimulated roadside enterprise. Service stations sprang up everywhere, providing—in addition to gasoline and minor adjustments—free air for tires, road maps, and restrooms for the convenience of dusty motorists. Repair shops and garages fixed stubborn self-starters, inert spark plugs, and faulty brakes, relieving drivers of such anxieties as the need to know such baffling terms as "carburetor," "magneto," "differential," and "generator." Supply houses installed seat covers, batteries, and side curtains. The growth of tourism led to the development of locally owned motels until national hotel chains arrived in California. The manufacturers of windshields, rubber tires, inner tubes, and automobiles also moved westward.

Filming a movie in the early days. The historic Santa Monica Pier can be seen in the background. Courtesy of the Santa Monica Historical Society.

Along with the phonograph, radio, and movies, the automobile broke down the isolation of those who lived on remote farms and ranches. Automobiles also emancipated city workers, who came to use "the machine" for pleasure trips on weekends and during holiday periods. Gradually, too, autos stimulated the decentralization of cities. This made it possible for laborers to live at some distance from their place of work. In the years from 1910 to 1930, California began to pull itself out of the mud, as rutted country paths were converted into two-lane ribbons of concrete. These, in turn, gave way after the 1930s to four-lane macadamized highways, which remained in use until the advent of still larger freeways in the 1940s. The $18 million appropriation the legislature made for road construction in 1910 seemed like a pittance only a few years later. Highway routes 66, 70, 99, and 101, all major arteries, were built in part with federal funds. These faster highways changed the face of the California countryside, spurring development of raw settlements in sometimes wild and empty deserts.

The automobile virtually created a new type of landscape. Railroad towns were displaced by crossroads with garages, filling stations, hot dog stands, and affordable and convenient tourist bungalows. Gypsy fortune tellers joined concessionaires desirous of doing business with unwary easterners who drove past neon-lighted stucco booths shaped like a half orange. From these stands glared such highway signs as "All the Orange Juice You Can Drink for 10 Cents" and "Palmistry Will Tell Your Future in California."

Favorable climatic conditions, low gasoline prices, and access to desert, beach, and mountain helped to make Californians automobile-minded. Thousands of tourists were brought to the state each year by advertising that emphasized California's constant sunshine. The most popular resorts were the beaches from Santa Barbara to San Diego and Catalina Island. Other attractions included Lake Tahoe, Sequoia and Lassen National Parks, the Yosemite Valley in the High Sierra, the Russian River area above San Francisco, Palm Springs on the Mojave Desert, and Big Bear and Lake Arrowhead in the San Bernardino Mountains. Even the once-dreaded Death Valley became a winter tourist attraction.

Because of the automobile, public transportation suffered a decline. At Los Angeles, the interurban system established by the Pacific Electric Company perished in the interwar years. It was forced to close down branch lines as buses and trucks took advantage of shorter routes between cities. Although the number of automobile accidents and highway fatalities continued to mount, so did the demand for new cars. Whole boulevards, notably Figueroa and Alvarado Streets in Los Angeles and Van Ness Avenue in San Francisco, came to be monopolized by auto dealers.

In the 1920s and 1930s, despite a national economic depression, California's domestic and foreign trade expanded. Increases in tourism and the growth of the mining, hydroelectric power, and film industries all helped to gain prominence for the state. The automobile and its subsidiary industries were largely responsible for all this expansion. The assembly plants of Ford, Chrysler, and General Motors, the tire-production establishments of Firestone and Royal, and such firms as Libby-Owens-Ford Glass and Exide Batteries gave employment to thousands of Californians. Throughout the Great Depression (1930–37), automobile production remained surprisingly stable.

Accompanying a shift of population to such suburbs as Oakland and Long Beach, there arose a greater need to finance new residential and manufacturing construction. Banks were now consolidated into stronger institutions capable of loaning millions of dollars annually. In 1929, a merger created the Security First National Bank of Los Angeles, giving southern California one of the country's largest banks. The largest of all was the Bank of Italy—later the Bank of America—founded in 1904 at San Francisco by Amadeo Pietro Giannini. The son of Italian immigrants, Giannini developed a system of branch banking that came to dwarf other institutions. Geared to the needs of the small depositor, Giannini's system spread beyond the boundaries of the state, and even of the nation. For a time the Bank of America was the largest bank in the world.

The growth of California during the interwar period is mirrored in the record established by its largest city. In 1921 Harry Chandler, who had become the publisher of the *Los Angeles Times*, called a crucial conference to examine ways by which the tourist trade might be increased. Business leaders and real estate boosters who attended that meeting helped him form the "All-Year Club of Southern California," designed to advertise the wonders of Los Angeles in eastern newspapers. In the heady spirit of the 1920s, this organization did much to attract new residents as well as visitors to the Golden State.

By 1930, over 2 million residents lived within a thirty-mile radius of Los Angeles. Yet, only in the early thirties did L.A. develop a genuine civic center, with its Spanish-style Union Station railroad terminal and nearby complex of government buildings. In those years it also hosted the Tenth Olympiad in a new coliseum, saw the arrival of the first streamlined transcontinental trains, built an astronomical observatory at Griffith Park, constructed a metropolitan water system, and laid the groundwork for its future aircraft industry.

San Francisco also improved its metropolitan facilities, strengthening its opera, symphony orchestra, and museums, improving beautiful Golden Gate Park, and building the remarkable Bay bridges to supplant ferry boat

On Nov. 21, 1937 over 12,000 Californians attended the dedication ceremonies at the preview for the 1939 Pacific World's Fair. They took place in front of the $1,000,000 administration building on Treasure Island. Courtesy of the National Archives (SPB) (Control Number: Neg 12775-C).

operations. On May 27, 1939, the day the beautiful Golden Gate Bridge opened, 200,000 people proudly walked across the span. That same year San Francisco was host to the Golden Gate International Exposition, the "World's Fair of the West." Exactly 17,041,999 persons paid the entrance fee for this largest exposition ever held west of Chicago. Treasure Island, in the middle of San Francisco Bay, the site of the fairgrounds, became a naval base during World War II.

San Francisco remained a popular tourist mecca, with its exotic Chinatown, cable cars, restaurants, Coit Tower, and the Golden Gate, through which ships streamed in and out. During the 1930s, the city's shipyards, dry docks, and canneries continued to expand. Captain Robert Dollar made San Francisco the home port of steamship companies, even as the city was becoming a crucial air center. On November 22, 1935, Pan American Airways' *China Clipper* soared off to establish the first air link between North America and mainland China.

The spectacular growth of California's population had proceeded unabated since the Gold Rush. By 1940, on the eve of World War II, the state's population numbered 6,907,387. Los Angeles was then a metropolis of 1,504,277 persons, and San Francisco had reached a population of 634,536. Its commuters sorely needed the new "bedroom communities" that would spring up in the suburbs of Alameda, Oakland, Berkeley, and Burlingame. The contrast between the nineteenth and twentieth centuries was to become even more marked. California was becoming overpopulated while remaining lax in dealing with its complex future problems.

SELECTED READINGS

Regarding religious developments, see Michael E. Engh, *Frontier Faiths: Church, Temple, and Synagogue in Los Angeles, 1846–1888* (1992). The development of urbanism is described in Oscar Osborn Winther, "The Rise of Metropolitan Los Angeles, 1870–1900," *Huntington Library Quarterly* 10 (August 1947), 391–405. See also Spencer Crump, *Ride the Big Red Cars: How Trolleys Helped Build Southern California* (1962); Andrew Rolle, *Los Angeles: From Pueblo to City of the Future* (1995); Charles A. Matson, *Building a World Gateway* (1945); William Issel and Robert Cherny, *San Francisco, 1865–1932: Politics, Power, and Urban Development* (1986) and Issel, "Citizens Outside the Government, Business and Urban Policy in San Francisco and Los Angeles, 1890–1932," *Pacific Historical Review* 57 (May 1988), 117–45; as well as Roger W. Lotchin, *Fortress California: From Warfare to Welfare* (1992) and his "The City and the Sword in Metropolitan California, 1919–1941," *Urbanism Past and Present* 7 (Summer 1982), 1–16; and Michael Kazin, *Barons of Labor: The San Francisco Building Trades and Urban Power in the Progressive Era* (1987). Also see Gary Brechin, *Imperial San Francisco: Urban Power, Earthly Ruin* (2006).

Regarding the development of the petroleum industry see Frank F. Latta, *Black Gold in the San Joaquin* (1949); Frank J. Taylor and Earl M. Welty, *Black Bonanza* (1950); R. G. Percy, "The First Oil Development in California," *California Historian* 6 (December 1959), 29–30; I. F. Marcosson, *The Black Golconda* (1924); Ruth S. Knowles, *The Greatest Gamblers* (1959); Gerald T. White, *Formative Years in the Far West, A History of Standard Oil Company of California and Predecessors Through 1919* (1962); W. H. Hutchinson, *Oil, Land, and Politics: The California Career of Thomas Robert Bard* (1965); and Walker A. Tompkins, *Little Giant of Signal Hill* (1967). More recent studies include Margaret Davis, *Dark Side of Fortune: Triumph and Scandal in the Life of the Oil Tycoon Edward Doheny* (1999); Martin Ansell, *Oil Baron of the Southwest* (1998); James Williams *Energy and the Making of Modern California* (1997); and Thomas Wellock, *Critical Masses: Opposition to Nuclear Power in California, 1958–78* (1998).

Jules Tygiel, *The Great Los Angeles Swindle* (1994) concerns the Julian petroleum scandal. Regarding "the automobile era," see Scott Bottles, *Los Angeles and the Automobile* (1987); Phil Townsend Hanna, "The Wheel and the Bell," *Westways* 42 (December 1960), 41–56; Mark S. Foster, "The Model-T, the Hard Sell, and Los Angeles's Urban Growth," *Pacific Historical Review* 44 (November 1975), 459–84; Fred Viehe, "Black Gold Suburbs: The Influence of the Extractive Industry on the Suburbanization of Los Angeles, 1890–1930," *Journal of Urban History* 8 (1981), 3–26; Bruce Henstell, *Sunshine and Wealth: Los Angeles in the Twenties* (1985); David Gebhard and Hariette Von Breton, *Los Angeles in the Thirties* (1975); Willis Miller, "The Port of Los Angeles–Long Beach, 1929–1979," *Southern California Quarterly* 65 (Winter 1983), 341–78; and Judith Elias, *Los Angeles: Dream to Reality, 1885–1915* (1983).

Health as a factor in migration westward, is the theme of John Baur, *The Health Seekers of Southern California* (1959). Leaders of an emerging business class are the subject of Clark Davis, *Company Men: White Collar Life and Corporate Cultures in Los Angeles* (2000); also see Richard Longstreth, *City Center to Regional Mall: The Automobile and Retailing in Los Angeles* (1997).

CHAPTER TWENTY-NINE

WATER,
CONSERVATION,
AND AGRICULTURE

The new wave of migration into the state, spurred on by the automobile, could not have been supported without water. After the turn of the century, California's cities and counties spent millions of dollars on new dams, reservoirs, and aqueducts to conserve and deliver that precious commodity.

In semi-arid southern California, farmers welcomed the pathbreaking irrigation experiments of a Canadian engineer, George Chaffey, who efficiently diverted streams, created artificial lakes, and stored subsurface water. A growing and thirsty Los Angeles, located amid a dry belt of expanding suburbs, was dependent upon the meager Los Angeles River (an uncertain underground stream) and a shrinking water table. By 1904, its reservoirs were barely able to take in enough water to equal their outflow. The city's chief engineer, William Mulholland, argued that L.A. needed to find a new water source. He recommended tapping the distant Owens River in the southern Sierra range.

A bond issue was subsequently put on the ballot to provide construction of a $25 million aqueduct that would traverse the 238 miles from the Owens Valley to Los Angeles. By 1908, construction of a pipe and flume system across the Mojave Desert, to catch the runoff from the melted snow in the southern Sierra mountain range, began. Utilizing several thousand workers, Mulholland completed his complex network of tunnels and trenches in less than five years. Although it was a highly acclaimed feat of engineering, controversy soon arose. Prior to its construction, avaricious agents for L.A. had quietly bought up Owens Valley farms and ranches for the purpose of obtaining their water rights along the Owens River. That stream drained much of the eastern Sierra. The river was then diverted 200 miles south via canal and pipeline.

Violent criticisms of Mulholland came from ranchers and farmers forced to evacuate their valley homes under threat of eviction. This amounted to a form of eminent domain. Recreationists who loved to fish in the valley joined naturalists in mounting a strong protest. Critics also charged that a Los Angeles elite, who owned big tracts of land in the Van Nuys area, would be the real beneficiaries of water development leading to construction of new urban centers. Displaced farmers alleged that a real estate syndicate had bought up fallow land in order to make a financial killing after Owens River water reached the San Fernando Valley. Residents of the four Owens River towns of Big Pine, Lone Pine, Bishop, and Independence were sure that this syndicate would hoard water looted from the Owens Valley in huge reservoirs outside Los Angeles. Meanwhile, stories in the national press dwelt on the privations inflicted on a pastoral paradise by the beastly aqueduct. Owens Valley residents appealed to the chief forester of the United States, Gifford Pinchot, and to President Theodore Roosevelt. But both men sided with Los Angeles, and in 1913 the city's new aqueduct was completed.

Years later, in 1923, disgruntled ranchers armed with rifles stood guard at the head gate of Big Pine Ditch to prevent further diversion of precious Owens water into the aqueduct. They then dynamited chunks of a concrete spillway near Lone Pine. The next year, other protestors opened up the Alabama water gates north of Lone Pine, temporarily stopping the flow of aqueduct water. Soon thereafter all local opposition collapsed, but bitterness toward L.A. as a looter of water persisted. Finally, in 2006, as a result of legal wrangling, the city rediverted some water into the 62-mile Lower Owens River.

More criticism of William Mulholland arose when a dam he had constructed in San Francisquito Canyon, as part of the Owens Aqueduct, collapsed. On March 12, 1928, an avalanche of water cascaded down the Santa Clara Valley to Santa Paula, fifty miles away. Houses, trees, telephone poles, bridges, and railroad tracks were swept away. Unfortunately, some 400 people lost their lives. Mulholland stoically accepted the blame for having built this dam on a weak clay substratum, thus ending his career of public service.

He alone was blamed for causing Mono Lake to shrivel and for the sucking dry of the Owens River. The resulting dust storms in the Owens Valley posed a serious menace. Yet, Mulholland's defenders pointed to new valley roads, improved in connection with building the Owens Aqueduct. Farmers who once sold alfalfa were able to restart roadside businesses. Furthermore, the city of Los Angeles had reimbursed those whose homes and farms had been confiscated, in addition to paying for the lands of owners willing to sell out.

Although the Owens aqueduct was a major achievement that would provide both hydroelectric power and water to southern California, public demands continued to surface regarding bringing back a 62-mile stretch of river back to life. In 2005, a court order required the powerful Los Angeles Department of Water and Power to restore the flow of the parched Owens River. The DWP was also ordered to reduce groundwater pumping in the Owens Valley by a third.

The burgeoning city of San Francisco also coped with a chronic water shortage in the early years of the twentieth century. Its civic leaders, thus, eyed the pristine Hetch Hetchy Valley near Yosemite National Park as a new source for both water storage and electricity-generation. Naturalists, however, strongly objected to the building of a giant dam that would inundate so majestic a valley as well as divert water from the Tuolumne River. Despite early opposition by John Muir and the Sierra Club, the city of San Francisco finally completed its Hetch Hetchy network in 1931. By then, Muir was long since dead.

As controversy over the Owens Valley Project also raged, Los Angeles too faced severe water shortages. By 1923, the city was gaining 100,000 new residents per year, and its population was approaching 2 million. To solve the disparity between daily intake and the outflow of reservoirs, city engineers went so far as to consult with occult rainmakers, Indian medicine men, and water dowsers before concluding that new dams were the only solution.

Meanwhile, representatives of Colorado, Wyoming, Utah, New Mexico, Arizona, Nevada, and California signed a Colorado River Water Compact. This agreement provided for cooperative development of that river's resources. The project was to be undertaken jointly by the federal government, the participating states, and certain municipalities. Its aims were to protect the Imperial Valley against recurrent threats of flooding, to provide multistate water reserves, and to generate hydroelectric energy for a growing Southwest.

Not, however, until 1928 was the Swing-Johnson Bill passed by the U.S. Congress to permit construction of a high dam in Boulder Canyon. Two years later another federal bill allocated $11 million to begin dam construction. Most of the major cities of Los Angeles County then formed a Metropolitan Water District to coordinate water and power distribution for southern California. In 1931 the district floated a bond issue of over $200 million to complete construction. Since the Great Depression blunted sale of these bonds, the federal government's new Reconstruction Finance Corporation assumed a share of the financing of the huge Boulder Canyon Project.

With Hoover Dam (located in Boulder Canyon) as its dominant structure, this project was one of the largest construction jobs in the world. The dam, 1,282 feet high, required the combined efforts of six construction companies employing 10,000 workers housed in a new town, Boulder City, built expressly for the purpose. Lake Mead, an artificial lake 242 miles long, was constructed in connection with the dam, as well as a complicated system of conduits, reservoirs, and pumping plants to transport water from the lake.

Hoover Dam, with its accompanying storage facility, Parker Dam, was finaly completed on March 1, 1936. Huge generators pumped electrical energy into homes, farms, and industrial plants throughout the Southwest. Piercing its way through six mountain ranges, this new aqueduct provided a lifeline to the communities drawing upon it. The Metropolitan Water District erected a costly diversion dam to deflect water 242 miles to Los Angeles. Water was also diverted above Yuma, Arizona, and transported 80 miles along the All-American Canal, to the Imperial Valley. A 125-mile extension of this canal, built to serve the Coachella Valley, was not completed until 1948.

Hoover Dam was only one federally subsidized water project. Californians, irrigation-based, were dependent upon government largesse outside

Taken in 1941, this photograph shows the lush Imperial Valley nourished by mammoth federal, state, and local irrigation projects of the 1920s–1930s. Courtesy of the National Archives, NRHS-83-ADONPOLI-IMPERIAL V2.

the state for the building of levees and obtaining hydroelectricity. Without the Boulder Canyon Project, southern California could not have expanded commercially and industrially. Hoover Dam, furthermore, safeguards the Imperial Valley and communities surrounding the Gulf of California from spring floods, storing water for release during periods of shortage.

Farther north, the 1930s saw California's farmers increasingly concerned over water supplies. One of the most obvious sources of water was the 400-mile-long Sacramento River, with an average annual runoff of 22,230,000 acre-feet. (An acre-foot of water is the amount that will cover one acre to a depth of one foot—or 43,560 cubic feet.) The Sacramento's drainage area covers almost 30,000 square miles. Many tributaries help swell that river along its way. Among them are the McCloud, Pit, Feather, Yuba, Bear, and American Rivers, which flow out of California's Sierra and northern Cascade ranges.

Because of the damage wreaked by hydraulic mining, the practice had been banned by the courts in 1884. The channel of the Sacramento River had already become so silted that navigation was closed to all but vessels of shallow draft. This situation only worsened whenever the Central Valley's rivers went on a flooding rampage, with the cities of Stockton,

Visalia, Oroville, Yuba City, and Marysville sustaining millions of dollars in damage. It was difficult to harness the San Joaquin River, a twisting stream that flows into the Sacramento out of California's southern Central Valley.

In 1933, the state legislature voted in the Central Valley Project to impound water from the Sacramento, San Joaquin, and lesser streams. When a construction bond issue of $170 million could not be sold, the state appealed to the federal government for assistance under the National Industrial Recovery Act. Congress responded with a Rivers and Harbors Bill of 1935, which authorized starter funds for construction of Shasta Dam as a first step of the Central Valley Project. The Friant and other dams of this project would eventually retain almost as much water as all of California's 600 reservoirs combined. The Friant-Kern Canal and the Delta-Mendota Canal were to carry water throughout the San Joaquin Valley. Completion of the Central Valley Project was repeatedly delayed by controversies over who should build and control its water and power. These struggles involved the Bureau of Reclamation, the Army Corps of Engineers, the state Department of Public Works, municipal water systems, and private utilities. For their part, the power companies branded most public works programs as heady socialistic experiments. Further opposition to government participation in the project also came from large landowners. They fought a 160-acre limit on ownership for anyone receiving water from Bureau of Reclamation projects. Some large farm operators feared the prospect of not qualifying for federal subsidies.

"No state has gained more than California from the artificial application of water, or has more at stake in the extension of its use," wrote Elwood Mead, the pioneer conservationist after whom Lake Mead was named. Irrigation is essentially a form of conservation, Mead believed, as did Theodore Roosevelt and other conservationists. The reclamation of water was accompanied by concern over depletion of the timber and mineral wealth of the Far West.

Although sympathy for conservation had grown by the progressive movement, regulatory steps had yet to be taken. Within only a few generations whole forests had been denuded by fire and axe. A fortunate exception was the Muir Woods. One of the world's great redwood stands, it was spared through the efforts of a nature lover, William Kent. Located on the side of Mount Tamalpais, in Marin County, these majestic trees were about to be logged in 1903, when Kent borrowed money to buy the land and then turned it over to the government as a national preserve.

Lumber companies had been permitted to exploit forest resources, with no provision for replacing trees. By the early twentieth century, the

Giant redwoods. © Photographer: George Wood. Agency: Dreamstime.com.

close connection between overcutting and periodic floods had become clear. Some of the choicest lands already had been ruined by man-made erosion. Meanwhile, whole populations of native animals, including big-horn mountain sheep, had been reduced to a few scraggly specimens in zoos. John Muir and John Burroughs demanded creation of parks to protect the magnificent Sequoias and Coast Redwoods, as well as wildlife.

Only after the creation of the state conservation and water commissions did California begin to enforce advances in scientific forestry. Lumber companies, which long had resisted management of forest preserves, finally came to see the merits of reforestation, if only out of the need to protect their own future. The California Forest Protective Association planted millions of replacement redwoods, as well as Douglas firs, spruce, and cedars, on logged or cutover lands. During the Depression years of the 1930s, the New Deal's Civilian Conservation Corps also carried on extensive replanting along wilderness trails. The National Park Service and the California State Division of Beaches and Parks likewise preserved wilderness sites, as did privately funded agencies like the Sierra Club.

Reclamation helped California's agricultural yield to spiral upward at a time when the acreage of the average farm was decreasing. By 1920, there were 117,670 farms in the state. But huge corporations would gobble up many of these in forthcoming years. A major problem of the inter-war period was finding how to increase consumption of the many crops that California grew. Some of these were plowed under during the Great Depression of the 1930s in an effort to boost prices. All of this took place at the very time when refugees from the Dust Bowl regions of the Midwest were going hungry and thirsty.

California's farmers soak up 80 percent of its water resources. All of this water is paid for at highly subsidized rates. Nearly half of the state's water consumption is provided by seven giant projects: the Los Angeles Acqueduct, the Colorado River Acqueduct, the State Water Project, the Central Valley Project, and the Hetch Hetchy System.

Benefiting from water sources, the central valley towns of Modesto, Stockton, Visalia, Madera, and Merced have become major agricultural centers. More efficient "agribusinesses" have grown apace. In the Napa and Sonoma Valleys, international conglomerates have driven small producers out of business. Yet, the Golden State produces over 90 percent of the grapes grown in the nation. California also grows all of the U.S. commercial almond crop and 80 percent of the world's supply. Fresno and Bakersfield are vegetable, cotton, livestock, dried fruit, and petroleum marketing centers.

Residents of former agricultural centers and of pricey coastal properties have moved to more affordable towns. In southern California, settlers of San Bernardino, Riverside, and Ontario have seen their "Inland Empire" emerge as one of the nation's fastest growing population areas.

SELECTED READINGS

Regarding conservation, see John Muir, *The Mountains of California* (1894) and Muir, *Our National Parks* (1901); Linnie M. Wolfe, ed., *John of the Mountains* (1938); Holway R. Jones, *John Muir and the Sierra Club: The Battle for Yosemite* (1966); Michael S. Smith, *Pacific Visions: California Scientists and the Environment* (1988); Francis P. Farquhar, *History of the Sierra Nevada* (1965) also Farquhar, *Place Names of the High Sierra* (1926); Douglas Strong, *Tahoe: An Environmental History* (1984); W. Storrs Lee, *The Sierra* (1962); Norman Taylor, *The Ageless Relics* (1962), Susan Schrepfer, *The Fight to Save the Redwoods* (1983); and Roderick Nash, *Wilderness and the American Mind* (1967).

Concerning the Owens Valley controversy, see Robert A. Sander, *The Lost Frontier: Water Diversion in the Growth and Destruction of Owens Valley Agriculture* (1994); William L. Kahrl, *Water and Power: The Conflict Over Los Angeles' Water Supply in the Owens Valley* (1982); Abraham Hoffman, *Vision or Villainy: Origins of the Owens Valley–Los Angeles Water Controversy* (1981) and Hoffman, "Origins of a Controversy: The U.S. Reclamation Service and the Owens Valley," *Arizona and the West* 19 (Winter 1977), 333–45.

On water and reclamation, see John Walton, *Western Times and Water Wars... in California* (1992); Catherine Mulholland, *The Owensmouth Baby* (1987); Robert Matson, *William Mulholland, A Forgotten Forefather* (1978); Charles Outland, *Man-Made Disaster: The Story of the Saint Francis Dam* (1962); Doyce Nunis, ed., *The Saint Francis Dam Disaster Revisited* (1995); Joseph Stevens, *Hoover Dam: An American Adventure* (1988); George A. Pettit, *So Boulder Dam Was Built* (1935); David O. Woodbury, *The Colorado Conquest* (1941); P. L. Kleinsorge, *Boulder Canyon Project* (1941); Norris Hundley, *Water and the West: The Colorado River Compact and the Politics of Water* (1975) and Hundley, *The Great Thirst* (1991); Donald J. Pisani, *To Reclaim A Divided West: Water, Law, and Public Policy, 1848–1902* (1992); Philip Ross May, *Origins of Hydraulic Mining in California* (1970); John Upton Terrell, *War for the Colorado River* (2 vols., 1965); Robert de Roos, *The Thirsty Land: The Story of the Central Valley Project* (1948); S. T. Harding, *Water in California* (1961); Kenneth Thompson, "Historic Flooding in the Sacramento Valley," *Pacific Historical Review* 39 (November 1960), 349–60; and Robert Kelley, "Taming the Sacramento," *Pacific Historical Review* 34 (February 1965), 21–49.

A useful compendium concerning California's southern desert area is Diane Lindsay, *Anza-Borrego, A to Z* (2001). More recently, see Robert Righter's *The Battle Over Hetch Hetchy* (2005).

CHAPTER THIRTY

LABOR
IN AN INDUSTRIAL AGE

California's population growth did not occur without serious societal dislocations. The blue-and-gold tourist brochures that urged visitors to spend winters in "the Golden State" never hinted that severe issues were brewing beneath the surface of the state's purported good life. Real estate advertisements that extolled the state's attractions stood in stark contrast to its emerging social unrest.

After the turn of the century, tensions between laborers and employers grew even more pronounced than in Denis Kearney's time. Now workers, through a new Union Labor party, spoke out even more forcefully against powerful financiers and shipping tycoons. Labor had also raised a strong voice of protest during the Ruef-Schmitz scandals in San Francisco. That city became a labor stronghold from which union organizers penetrated the surrounding rural areas.

After 1905, a national labor organization, the Industrial Workers of the World (IWW), turned its attention to California. The IWW sought to organize seasonal and part-time workers into "One Big Union." Among these migratory laborers were field hands, lumberjacks, and cannery workers. They were not welcome to join the powerful American Federation of Labor (AFL), organized along craft lines. New farm machinery had lessened the need for such harvest laborers.

The workday on farms and ranches remained long and the pay extremely low. Furthermore, sanitary conditions in farm labor camps were deplorable. These conditions drew the attention of IWW leaders. From 1908 to 1913, its organizers recruited about 1,000 migratory farm laborers as new members of a dozen local chapters.

The IWW, the first labor group to reach out to migrant workers, urged radical reform of the economy. Its members were referred to contemptuously in rural newspapers as socialist "Wobblies" who belonged to an

"I Won't Work" movement. Frequently local police officials regarded the volatile organization as an outlaw labor group. IWW soapbox orators were arrested at rallies, fire hoses were turned on the members, and fieldworkers were pointedly warned not to join the organization.

In spite of such harassment, the IWW persisted. After labor strife broke out at Fresno and San Diego, these and other municipalities adopted stiff regulations against the IWW. The terror in which municipal officials held the organization was based on its radical ideology. Subscribing as it did to the Marxian concept of class struggle and to syndicalist and anarchist ideas, the organization posed a clear threat to California's status quo.

Some workers distrusted the pushy Wobblies because of their attempts to obtain equal employment status (with whites) for Chinese and Mexican laborers. Most employers also hated the IWW, resenting its on-the-job recruiting and the unannounced strikes that it helped lead. Yet the IWW doggedly persisted. Though its leaders were jailed, clubbed, and even killed, the Wobblies continued their campaign to organize migratory workers.

Violence involving the union peaked on August 3, 1913, at the Durst Ranch, a large hop farm in the Sacramento Valley. In contention were the conditions under which itinerant laborers—including men, women, and children—were forced to work and live on the ranch. Only eight toilets were available for the use of 2,800 itinerant workers. Also, the owners of the ranch had advertised for many more laborers than they could actually use, paying those they selectively hired as little as 75¢ per day. Finally, a ranch-owned store held back 10 percent of these meager wages, forcing field hands to purchase food and supplies at inflated prices. Now the workers, under the leadership of Blackie Ford, the head of the IWW local, called a strike.

When a sheriff's posse sought to arrest Ford, a pistol was fired, and a full-scale riot ensued. The sheriff and the local district attorney, as well as several workers, were killed. Governor Hiram Johnson called out the National Guard to quell the insurrection and brought in private detectives to investigate its cause. As a result of the incident (known as the Wheatland Riot), the IWW organization was virtually dismantled in the Sacramento Valley. Although the actual "shooter" was never found, Ford and a colleague were convicted of murder and sentenced to life imprisonment.

The Wheatland Riot, nevertheless, ultimately improved the welfare of migratory workers. Press coverage of the event had drawn the public's attention to the plight of the field hands, and the California legislature subsequently passed several bills to control labor conditions for seasonal workers, though these measures were not effective. A new Commission on Immigration and Housing also pushed for better working conditions in the fields, but it was hampered by a lack of power to enforce its mandates. Ranchers who continued to import excess workers each season to pick peaches, grapes, cotton, and hops, maintained that they could not afford to furnish individual dwellings to part-time laborers. They argued that, because the harvest lasted only a few weeks, such housing, vacant much of the year, was impractical to maintain. Critics contended that this was a poor excuse for the continued inhumanity with which growers treated the workers.

Depressed labor conditions cried out for new leadership. Late in 1913, a local agitator calling himself "General" Kelley marched an "army" of several thousand unemployed workers to Sacramento demanding better treatment for all pickers. Kelley's adherents resembled Jacob Coxey's ragamuffins, who in 1895 had marched to Washington with similar demands. But Kelley's men were driven off by armed guards after attempting to camp near the state capitol.

In 1910, several years before Kelley's march, the labor movement became involved in another ill-conceived effort. This was the bombing of the *Los Angeles Times* building, an event that set back the labor movement in southern California for many years. The fateful blast occurred at 1:07 A.M. on October 1, just as the newspaper's mechanical force was getting the paper to press. As a result, twenty persons were killed and many more injured. The *Times* building itself was reduced to a mass of rubble.

After the L.A. bombing, mutual suspicion between management and workers increased. The owner of the *Times*, General Harrison Gray Otis, blamed irresponsible labor leaders for the bombing, particularly the International Association of Bridge and Structural Iron Workers, then involved in a local strike. Conversely, labor accused the *Times* management of criminal negligence in operating a plant that union spokesmen described as a gas-leaking firetrap.

In 1911, three labor agitators, Ortie McManigal and James B. and John J. McNamara, were accused of having organized the bombing and brought to trial. Labor retained the defense attorney Clarence Darrow, known for his vigorous opposition to both violence and capital punishment. But the testimony against the McNamara brothers was far too incriminating for Darrow to win their acquittal. Acting on his advice, the defendants changed their pleas from not guilty to guilty and, after a compromise with both prosecution and judge, were sent to the state penitentiary. James McNamara drew a sentence of life imprisonment and John

Destruction by bombing of the *Los Angeles Times* building, 1910. C. C. Pierce Collection, photograph by C. C. Carter, courtesy of the Huntington Library, San Marino, California.

one of fifteen years. McManigal was freed because he had "turned state's evidence." Darrow himself barely escaped conviction over the charge of having bribed the jury.

The *Times* bombing blackened the reputation of all union leaders. Soon thereafter, Samuel Gompers, President of the AFL, backed a reform-minded attorney, Job Harriman, for mayor of Los Angeles on the Socialist party ticket. His chances of winning the election looked promising until the bombing occurred. Harriman lost the election by 34,000 votes. A coalition of powerful business and civic leaders ensured that a socialist associated with labor violence could never control Los Angeles politics. Now Harriman abandoned his political ambitions in order to found a utopian colony which he named Llano del Rio.

After the outbreak of World War I, anti-union sentiment came to be viewed as a lack of patriotism. The war created a heavy demand for both skilled and unskilled workers. This raised wages in urban areas. Apprehensive about the spread of union activity, management urged upon labor the "open shop" as a temporary war measure. This concept of the open shop was a thinly veiled drive against union recruiting and collective bargaining. As public enthusiasm for the open shop increased, so did the antagonism between capital and labor.

In 1916, violence again erupted, this time in San Francisco. President Woodrow Wilson had proclaimed July 22 of that year "Preparedness Day." All Americans were to demonstrate their unity should the U.S. enter the First Word War. At San Francisco, advocates of the open shop helped organize a patriotic parade as a Preparedness Day demonstration. Meanwhile, a serious longshoremen's strike had gotten under way. The combination was enough to make employers and union organizers edgy about their differences. In the midst of this uneasy situation, someone had left a suitcase containing a bomb on a city sidewalk. It exploded at 2:06 P.M., killing nine persons and injuring forty others.

Two San Francisco union leaders, Thomas J. Mooney and Warren K. Billings, were arrested for the crime. Three years earlier, Billings had been convicted of carrying explosives, for which he spent two years in Folsom Penitentiary. Joining in the public outcry over the Preparedness Day bombing and the Mooney-Billings trial, newspapers ran stories dealing with rumor and innuendo. The press circulated a story on January 3, 1917, the day the trial began, that Mooney and Billings, both anarchists, had been part of a conspiracy that plotted to assassinate Governor Hiram Johnson. There was also talk connecting the two men with "Reds" from abroad, who were supposedly converging on California to spread the new doctrine of Bolshevism.

Both Billings and Mooney presented credible alibis. Mooney produced three photographs of himself and his wife on the roof of a Market Street building viewing the parade. In these photos a street-side clock, visible in the background, showed the time to be 1:58, 2:01 and 2:04 P.M. respectively, only minutes before the bombing. Despite such evidence for the defense, Mooney was convicted and sentenced to be hanged. Billings received a life term in the state penitentiary.

The case attracted worldwide attention. A rally was held in support of Mooney and Billings even in Petrograd, Russia, as the White House was deluged by protests to the verdict from world leaders. In response to the international outcry, President Woodrow Wilson appointed an investigative committee to review the case. It concluded that there was insufficient evidence to find anyone guilty of the crime. In the interest of wartime unity, President Wilson requested that Governor William Stephens commute Mooney's sentence to life imprisonment. Nevertheless, during the trial the prosecution had proved Mooney's association with the McNamara brothers—the two convicted earlier of having dynamited the *Los Angeles Times* building.

With Mooney and Billings behind the bars of San Quentin Penitentiary, labor interests embarked upon a determined twenty-year campaign to free the two men. Their sympathizers maintained that the pair had been found guilty only because of their association with anarchistic antiwar exiles. Finally, in 1939, after repeated petitions and appeals, Mooney was released, but he died soon thereafter. Later, Governor Culbert Olson also persuaded the California Supreme Court to commute Billings's sentence to time served, and he too was eventually released.

Partly because of the 1916 bombing, the open shop reigned in California for a number of years. Three years later, during the repressive atmosphere of the post–World War I years, California adopted a Criminal Syndicalism Law to control labor leaders. The act, resulting from the nation's first "Red Scare" (public fear of the spread of communism after the Russian Revolution of 1917), forbade any form of violence in labor disputes. Under the new law, anyone convicted of "labor violence" could be sentenced to as many as fourteen years in prison. Clearly, radical ideas of foreign origin were not welcome in postwar California. Its citizens were deeply suspicious of unions during this period of "100 percent Americanism."

The Criminal Syndicalism Law was repeatedly invoked to discourage union agitators in such tense situations as the 1923 San Pedro waterfront strike, various cannery strikes during the 1930s, and work stoppages in 1933 and 1934 among vegetable, fruit, and cotton pickers of the Imperial and San Joaquin Valleys. At Salinas in 1936, growers recruited a "citizen's army" to put down a strike by migrant lettuce pickers. Equipped with shotguns and pick handles, the angry group "got the lettuce picked," broke the strike, and disbanded offending unions.

The fierceness of California's Criminal Syndicalism Law was illustrated by the arrest of the writer Upton Sinclair for reading the U.S. Constitution aloud in public! A 1923 strike in San Pedro, led by the IWW, had elicited the sympathy of the young, reform-minded Sinclair. His subsequent confrontation with the Los Angeles commercial establishment helped Sinclair launch the American Civil Liberties Union in southern California. The major punitive effect of the law, however, fell squarely where its advocates had intended—upon radical labor leaders. This legislation, as well as municipal ordinances and continuing public pressure, combined in a few years to kill off what remained of the IWW and other extremist groups in California. Labor's strength would not re-emerge for decades.

SELECTED READINGS

Labor struggles are described in Lauren Coodley, ed., *The Land of Orange Groves and Jails* (2005). Also see Anne Loftis, *Witnesses to the Struggle: Imaging the California Labor Movement* (1998). Gregory Woirol, "Men on the Road . . ." *California History* 70 (Summer 1991), 192-204; Carleton Parker, *The Casual Laborer and Other Essays* (1920); William D. Haywood, *Bill Haywood's Book* (1929); Robert L. Tyler, "The I.W.W. and the West," *American Quarterly* 12 (Summer 1960), 175–87; Stewart Holbrook, "The Last of the Wobblies," *American Mercury* 62 (April 1946), 467–68; Louis Adamic, *Dynamite: The Story of Class Violence in America* (1935); William J. Burns, *The Masked War . . .* (1913); also Robert K. Murray, *Red Scare: A Study in National Hysteria, 1919–1920* (1955). The best analysis of the Durst Ranch and the Wheatland Riot is in David Vaught, *Cultivating California: Growers, Specialty Crops and Labor, 1875–1920* (1999).

On the San Francisco bombing, see Ernest J. Hopkins, *What Happened in the Mooney Case* (1932); Thomas J. Hunt, *The Case of Thomas J. Mooney and Warren K. Billings* (1929); Curt Gentry, *Frame-Up: The Incredible Case of Tom Mooney and Warren Billings* (1967) and Richard H. Frost, *The Mooney Case* (1968).

Regarding other labor strife, see Herbert Shapiro, "The McNamara Case, A Window on Class Antagonism in the Progressive Era," *Southern California Quarterly* 70 (Spring 1988), 69–94; Adela Rogers St. Johns, *Final Verdict* (1962); James P. Kraft, "The Fall of Job Harriman's Socialist Party," *Southern California Quarterly* 70 (Spring 1988), 43–68; Louis B. and Richard S. Perry, *A History of the Los Angeles Labor Movement* (1963); Bernard C. Cronin, *Father Yorke and the Labor Movement in San Francisco, 1900–1910* (1943); Grace H. Stimson, *Rise of the Labor Movement in Los Angeles* (1935); Paul S. Taylor, *The Sailors' Union of the Pacific* (1923); Gerald D. Nash, "The Influence of Labor on State Policy: The Experience of California," *California Historical Society Quarterly* 62 (September 1963), 241–57; Norris Hundley, "Katherine Philips Edson and the Fight for the California Minimum Wage, 1912–1913," *Pacific Historical Review* 29 (August 1960), 271–86; David Selvin, *A Terrible Anger: The 1934 Waterfront . . . Strike* (1915) and Selvin, *A Place in the Sun: A History of California Labor* (1981); as well as Alexander Saxton, *The Indispensable Enemy: Labor and the Anti-Chinese Movement in California* (1971).

CHAPTER THIRTY-ONE

THE DEPRESSION YEARS

Americans had never seen an economic collapse of the magnitude that followed the stock market crash of October 1929. With the labor scene in tatters, jobs grew increasingly scarce. Unions could now hardly demand the closed shop, or even bargain for better working conditions. The Republican administration of President Herbert Hoover seemed powerless to stop the country's downward financial spiral.

Californians, therefore, sought more direct political solutions to their economic distress. Across the state, swarms of destitute migrants roamed the city streets and dusty farm roads in search of jobs. In the presidential elections of 1932, the Democratic Party nominated a new type of candidate. This was Franklin Delano Roosevelt, the highly popular governor of New York. His campaign took "FDR" to the major cities of the Far West, which responded to his magnetic appeal.

The unemployed, many of whom were in despair, had tired of hearing that stock-market speculation was the primary cause of the Great Depression. They wanted immediate solutions, especially concerning the weakened local economy. At the Commonwealth Club in San Francisco on September 23, 1932, Roosevelt described in somber terms the concentration of private enterprise in the United States into large business concerns: "Put plainly, we are steering a steady course toward oligarchy, if we are not there already," he said. He went on to speak of every man's right to life and to a comfortable living, declaring that "Our government, formal and informal, political and economic, owes to everyone a portion of that plenty sufficient for his needs, through his own work." When election day came, California voted overwhelmingly for Roosevelt.

But even while FDR campaigned, the state's economy continued to worsen. Overproduction of both agricultural and commercial commodities hastened the spread of unemployment. Once-prosperous industries, farms, and real estate developments were mired down by the national depression. Within a few months, banks—following runs on their holdings by nearly hysterical depositors—were threatened with collapse. To give the state legislature time to devise protective legislation, Governor James "Sunny Jim" Rolph, Jr., ordered a three-day "bank holiday" on March 2, 1933. Two days later, during President Roosevelt's inauguration, the governor of almost every state had imposed severe restrictions on the withdrawal of private bank funds. On the same day, Rolph extended the California bank holiday.

As the country neared economic paralysis, the scarcity of money reduced some businesses to using a barter system. Everyone hoped that Roosevelt's "New Deal" would spur recovery. The administration asked Congress to pass sweeping new legislation that virtually put government in partnership with business. Roosevelt proposed that thousands of unemployed workers be hired by civic work projects. Because the energetic new president demonstrated that he viewed the crisis as far from unsolvable, Californians looked to him for crucial leadership.

California's relief activities, now carried on through a State Relief Administration, were, initially, far from adequate to meet emergency conditions. Even at this time, thousands of new migrants descended upon the state, though they were warned not to come in search of jobs. Rumors of high wages "out West" nonetheless convinced many to make a cross-country trip they were to regret. Among the newcomers were 350,000 farmers from the parched Dust Bowl areas of the Middle West, disdainfully called "Okies" or "Arkies" by older-stock Californians. The overland trek of the Okies in their rickety "flivvers," old jalopies heaped with mattresses, children, and blankets, brooms and pails tied into the mess, and clanking all the while, also has been vividly described in John Steinbeck's poignant novel *The Grapes of Wrath*. *

Most of these migrants arrived during 1935 and in the four years thereafter. Because the labor situation was so gravely depressed, even responsible citizens supported legislation to close the border to indigents. (Later, in 1941, the U.S. Supreme Court declared such laws unconstitutional.) Farm owners became accustomed to paying starvation wages that desperate migrants were forced to accept. Faced with bankruptcy, employers claimed they could not possibly spend money they did not have to improve the working conditions of California's new refugees.

Both the AFL and Congress of Industrial Organizations (CIO), two rival labor groups, battled in the orchards of Marysville. In the packing sheds of Bakersfield and in the canneries of Fresno, both unions sought to

Migrant mother and baby wait for help with a broken-down truck that contains all of the family's worldly possessions. Dorothea Lange photo, courtesy of the Library of Congress, LC-USZ-16453.

organize migrant workers. Moving to combat these efforts, after a wave of field strikes, in 1934 a group of farm owners formed the Associated Farmers of California. This anti-union group came to number 40,000 members, providing more than a match for the United Cannery, Agricultural, Packing and Allied Workers of America, part of the CIO.

Governor Rolph had little idea of how to cope with the state's massive unemployment, especially among migrant workers. He opposed reform of California's tax structure and signed legislation that caused taxes to fall unfairly upon persons of the lowest income. A sales tax on retail items, including food, was blamed on Rolph. He also vetoed a progressive income tax bill and made the mistake of endorsing a brutal jailbreak lynching. When he died in 1934, "Sunny Jim" was succeeded by his dour lieutenant governor, Frank Merriam, who was more conservative in his rhetoric than in his actions.

The folksinger Woody Guthrie mocked Governor Merriam in one of his ballads about official indolence over just what to do about the Okies and Arkies. Public prejudice against these migrants was born of a combination of insecurity, shame, and racism: in short, it upset Caucasians to see their fellow whites working in the fields in deplorable conditions alongside persons of color. Guthrie's folksongs, like Steinbeck's novels, captured the spirit of the Great Depression. Born in Oklahoma, Guthrie had spent several years in Los Angeles, where he sang a ditty on a radio station that he dedicated to "the little man" and "drifting families," voicing both strength and bitterness in his "talking blues," a work that expressed his conviction that California was being misused by selfish, scared people. Guthrie, who composed over a thousand songs, is best remembered by his "folk national anthem" entitled *This Land Is Your Land.*

In addition to the influx of Arkies and Okies, a growing number of Mexicans slipped over the border in search of jobs, which were extremely hard to come by. Serious problems of education, housing, and assimilation subsequently developed around California's Mexican minority. Forced to accept the most unpleasant jobs at low wages or to remain unemployed, they clung to their Spanish language, clustered in their own organizations, and retained a largely separate culture. At Los Angeles, Mexican newcomers formed the largest Mexican community in the world outside Mexico. One Mexican immigrant, Ignazio Lozano, founded *La Opinión*, which became the nation's largest Spanish-language newspaper.

Members of another minority group, the Filipinos, also competed for jobs as houseboys, laundry workers, dishwashers, and fry cooks. Racist sentiment against Filipino farm laborers led to the Watsonville riot of 1930 and to another disturbance at Salinas in 1934, in which many Filipinos were manhandled. Repeating past patterns, by the mid-1930s proposals for the exclusion of Filipinos were voiced in the California legislature. The state eventually offered these immigrants free transportation back to the Philippines if they promised not to return to California.

Meanwhile, thousands of older folk, many of them no longer able to work, became dependent on curtailed incomes. They had believed that life in sunny California would rejuvenate them. During the Great Depression, elderly persons listened with great interest to schemes that promised to alleviate their hardships by redistributing America's uneven wealth. Among such plans in circulation at the time was a movement known as "Technocracy." Its chief advocate was Howard Scott, an engineer who wanted to create a utopian society by eliminating poverty. Equipped with elaborate blueprints, he explained his proposed new civilization in abandoned drug stores, garages, and unrented buildings. His ideas did not survive the period. Like Technocracy, other utopian plans hatched during the depression years were identified with a particular personality.

One of these characters was Upton Sinclair, the crusading journalist. Although eccentric, he was actually a highly disciplined writer of ninety books. In 1920, he unsuccessfully sought a congressional seat. After losing the election, he hosted séances in his home, even attracting such person-alities as Albert Einstein and Charlie Chaplin. He next ran unsuccess-fully for the Senate. In 1926, and again in 1930, he was the Socialist party candidate for governor. Sinclair's last attempt at public office was in 1934, when he sought the Democratic nomination for governor.

Sinclair's experimental EPIC ("End Poverty in California") plan was tailor-made for the downhearted. He advocated a monthly pension of $50 for widows, the aged, and the handicapped. Earlier, Henry George had championed a heavy tax on idle land. Sinclair too believed that home-owners should be exempt from taxation. His "production for use" scheme called for the state to buy up idle land and factories. This was to help the unemployed. Sinclair also wanted the legislature to issue a new substitute for money called "scrip currency." President Roosevelt considered Sinclair's extremist ideas impractical. In 1934, during a bitter gubernatorial election, the press, radio, and film industry (then in conservative control) united against Sinclair. His incumbent opponent, Governor Frank Merriam, por-trayed him as a fool and defeated him soundly.

Sinclair, however, was followed by even more radical messiahs. His was an age in which pundits of every description attracted huge audiences of discontented citizens. Among these was Dr. Francis E. Townsend, a retired physician who sold real estate at Long Beach. His campaign slogan was "Youth for work and age for leisure." In 1934, he proposed his Townsend Old Age Pension Plan. This scheme sought to provide a monthly pension of $200 for every person over the age of sixty. Recipients, however, would have to retire from work completely and spend each of these payments within the month it was received. A 2 percent federal tax upon all business transactions was to help finance the plan.

Townsend waged a personal "crusade" via his newspaper, *The Townsend Weekly*, and 5,000 clubs organized in his name. By 1937, national Townsend Club membership was estimated at from 3 million to 10 million persons. While even Upton Sinclair considered Dr. Townsend's plan economic madness, only slowly did Townsend's followers give up on his ideas.

In 1938, yet another visionary plan, the "Thirty Dollars Every Thurs-day," or "Ham and Eggs" proposal, emerged. Its proponents wanted to award a pension to every unemployed person over the age of fifty. Pay-ment of pensions and state taxes would be made in scrip or warrants fi-nanced by a compulsory stamp purchase system. In the state elections of 1938 and 1939, the measure actually came close to adoption, despite the fact that critics labeled it economically irresponsible.

This movement, like Sinclair's EPIC plan and Townsend's pension scheme, can best be understood in terms of the despair and confused thinking of the depression years. Yet President Roosevelt's unwilling-ness to include such locally improvised plans in his sweeping recovery-minded legislation undoubtedly contributed to their demise. Passage of the more realistic federal Social Security Act of 1935 was, however, influ-enced by and partly in response to California's experimental public welfare schemes.

A series of congressional measures, most of which survived Supreme Court tests of their constitutionality, enabled Roosevelt to deliver on his campaign promises of a "New Deal" featuring relief, recovery, and reform. Dozens of new federal agencies, with abbreviated alphabetic titles, were established to perform functions designed to bring back prosperity. Some of these organizations worked in partnership with state relief agencies.

With funding to construct Hoover Dam and the Central Valley Proj-ect, the federal government helped to finance other power, reclamation, flood-control, and navigation projects. These would affect markedly the very future of California. By the mid-1930s, the short-term relief benefits of massive government aid had become evident. Like their counterparts throughout the nation, destitute Californians depended upon weekly

Civilian Conservation Corps workers in California at Camp Rock Creek, 1933. Courtesy of the National Archives, NLR-PHOCO-A-48223762[27].

government checks to sustain them until they could find permanent employment. In addition to this direct relief, unemployed young men were given "make-work" jobs in the New Deal's Civilian Conservation Corps (CCC). Under the supervision of the CCC staff, young men in California constructed mountain trails and firebreaks on federal forest lands and in the six new state parks established in California during 1933. The CCC mailed the bulk of the workers' salaries home to their needy parents. Other young people in college were aided by funds dispensed by the National Youth Administration (NYA). Many of their fathers, meanwhile, worked on Works Progress Administration (WPA) or Public Work Administration (PWA) construction projects or as federally employed writers and artists.

Though resisted by conservatives, these New Deal initiatives helped to alleviate economic hardship. Their costs, moreover, seemed modest later when compared to federal expenditures made during and after World War II. No state benefited more from the federal relief programs than did California. There, the CCC built hundreds of new schools, parks, roads, and beach facilities during the Great Depression. In addition to the larger-scale projects previously mentioned, these new undertakings contributed materially to the development of the state.

Although the Democratic Franklin Roosevelt won California in four successive national elections, Californians had not seated a Democratic governor since 1894. In 1938, Culbert Olson, an advocate of President Roosevelt's reforms, broke the string of Republicans when he assumed the governorship near the end of the New Deal, just as public pressure for reform had abated. In supporting migrant laborers and confronting agricultural malaise, Olson butted heads with the Associated Farmers, the large growers fiercely opposing all forms of governmental intervention.

Nonetheless, following an upswing of business activity after 1937, labor became more popular. The CIO began to attract more unorganized laborers. That union renewed its interest in unskilled laborers, once represented by the IWW. For years, the Coast Seamen's Union had also agitated for better working conditions. Its Norwegian leader, Andrew Furuseth, a pioneer crusader for seamen's rights, had fought for the extermination of such evils as "the crimp." Sailors were then still forced to pay a fee to a "crimp," or labor broker, in order to join ship crews. Waterfront boardinghouses, providing seamen with beds, meals, and clothing, also charged exorbitant fees. Their operators regularly turned over to shipmasters those unemployed seamen who were deeply in their debt. Furuseth's struggle to obtain seamen's rights eventually was carried on to the Sailors' Union of the Pacific.

To obtain employment, waterfront workers joined the Longshoremen's Association, actually an open-shop company union through which shippers controlled hiring and wages. Worker discontent paved the way for the entrance of radicalism into the maritime labor movement, which now acquired new organizers. Among these was Harry Bridges, a spellbinding Australian-born longshoreman.

Maritime employers labeled the militant Bridges a dangerous alien radical, if not a Communist. But thousands of longshoremen up and down the Pacific Coast stood behind his leadership. By 1934, he staged a massive strike that affected all shipping from San Diego to Seattle. Bridges sought a minimum thirty-hour week for his dock workers at wages of $1 an hour. He also objected to the hiring of longshoremen by company foremen who selected their favorite workers.

During the great maritime strike of 1934, Bridges tied up ship traffic at San Francisco for ninety days. In sympathy with longshoremen, other transport workers went out on strike too. As hundreds of ships lay idle, entire cargoes rotted and rusted on piers and in warehouses. On July 5, known as "Bloody Thursday," a violent disturbance erupted. After the San Francisco police moved against picket lines with tear gas, two union pickets were shot to death and more than 100 men, including police, were wounded. Almost 150,000 workers then walked off the job, paralyzing the San Francisco Bay area. When the governor called out the National Guard, the move only intensified the resentment of strikers.

The 1934 "general strike" actually damaged the long-term interests of unionism. Eventually the longshoremen agreed to submit their demands to arbitration. Although they won some concessions from management, settlement of this strike by no means brought peace to the San Francisco waterfront. Other labor stoppages, though less intensive, occurred throughout the 1930s. These strikes only fueled the continuing public criticism of unions.

A jurisdictional altercation between Bridges and other labor leaders ultimately led Bridges to take his longshoremen into the CIO. Because of his power, from 1936 onward the Hearst press made demands for his deportation. Eventually, the House Un-American Activities Committee charged that various CIO unions were under Communist leadership and control. The courts upheld the legality of Bridges's radical unionization techniques, however, and he retained considerable power.

Demands for unionization also spread to Los Angeles, center of the open shop or "American Plan." By 1935, the port of San Pedro had been unionized. Similar pressures filtered back from the city's waterfront into Los Angeles proper. Its plasterers, hod carriers, plumbers, typographers, tire workers, steamfitters, and auto assemblers also made new demands upon management.

By the end of the 1930s, a revived era of negotiation had begun in the relations between California labor and management. Harry Bridges eventually came to call strikes an "obsolete weapon," while Roger Lapham, chairman of the board of the American-Hawaiian Steamship Company (and later mayor of San Francisco) agreed to participate in collective bargaining through the federal National Labor Relations Board.

Against the grave social dislocations of the depression years, the figure of William Randolph Hearst stands out in bold relief. Born into a wealthy family at San Francisco in 1863, his father, Senator George Hearst, had created a mining fortune. Young Will attended Harvard University and in 1887, at the age of twenty-four, was virtually handed the *San Francisco Examiner*. Through his willingness to invest vast amounts of his father's money, Hearst made the *Examiner* the most powerful paper on the West Coast. His reputation as a young and energetic publisher was first earned by the scathing attacks he made on the Southern Pacific Railroad. At first, Hearst was a reformist crusader, but by the 1930s he bore little resemblance to the liberal of earlier decades. Like many disgruntled businessmen, Hearst came to believe that reform had gone far enough and that conservatism must reverse the power of labor unions, of government, and, in particular, of flighty New Dealers.

Throughout his eighty-eight years, Hearst remained an enigma, even to close associates. Though outwardly shy, he made his power felt even at the international level through his chain of some thirty newspapers, thirteen magazines, and several radio stations. Hearst came to be associated with a remarkable number of issues and events. Prominent among these were the Spanish-American War, which he helped cause. Hearst hated the two Roosevelts and distrusted all minorities. He was an opponent of United States entry into both World Wars and of internationalism. Most thinking persons were offended by his prejudices and nearly always repelled by his personal tastes.

At the heart of Hearst's empire lay his newspaper chain. He bought up papers all over the country and made them successful. Their sensational reporting, as well as slanted editorials, appealed to a less-than-educated readership. His so-called "yellow journalism" became the despair of Hearst's critics. During California's depression decades, the "Chief" grew ever more eccentric, to the point that even his fellow conservatives shunned him. The Hearst press spewed hate at reformist Governor Olson and fulminated against attempts to "tinker" with the currency, "coddle" the unemployed, and "socialize" the country.

Aerial view of San Simeon, William Randolph Heart's Castle. Courtesy Hearst Castle® / California State Parks.

The headquarters of Hearst's domain was his San Simeon estate, located on the rocky coast north of San Luis Obispo. In the interwar years, he poured $35 million into the construction of an immense castle there. Stocking it with art treasures that he had acquired from all over the world, Hearst made San Simeon a rendezvous for guests drawn from the movie industry as well as the world of art, music, literature, and public affairs. Hearst, like his mother, Phoebe Apperson Hearst, also subsidized philanthropic and educational institutions.

By 1935, Hearst's personal empire was valued at $200 million. His holdings included: seven castles; warehouses full of antique furniture, paintings, and tapestries; ranches on which he raised 10,000 beef cattle; several zoos; hunting lodges; and beach homes.

Movie director Orson Welles's 1940 film *Citizen Kane* drew a stark picture of Hearst's life through its thinly veiled principal Hearst-like character, newspaper mogul Charles Kane. As times changed, the living anachronism that was "Citizen Hearst," as one of his biographers dubbed him, became ever more apparent. After World War II, the Hearst dynasty gradually crumbled. By the mid-1960s, his two major papers, the *San Francisco Examiner* and the *Los Angeles Examiner*, gave way to the *Chronicle* and the *Times*. Now the *Examiners*, both morning papers, had to be merged with the Hearst evening newspapers to meet the competition of suburban dailies as well as radio and television newscasts. Falling circulation led his heirs to enter other fields of endeavor.

The life of William Randolph Hearst continues to generate new biographies of the autocrat. He personified like no other public figure the enormous gap between wealthy and working-class Californians during the cruel depression that had enveloped their state.

SELECTED READINGS

Regarding this period see Leonard Leader, *Los Angeles and the Great Depression* (1991). See also William Mullens, *The Depression and the Urban West Coast, 1929–1933* (1991). On migration into the state, see James Gregory, *American Exodus: The Dust Bowl Migration and the Okie Culture in California* (1989) as well as Charles J. Shindo, *Dust Bowl Migrants in the American Imagination* (1997); Walter J. Stein, *California and the Dust Bowl Migration* (1973); Dorothea Lange and Paul S. Taylor, *An American Exodus: A Record of Human Erosion* (1939).

Other depression-era sources include Luther Whiteman and Samuel L. Lewis, *Glory Roads: The Psychological State of California* (1936); Jackson K. Putnam, *Old Age Politics in California* (1970); Abraham Holtzman, *The Townsend Movement: A Political Study* (1963); Gilman Ostrander, *The Prohibition Movement in California* (1957); Abe Hoffman, "A Look at Llano: Experiment in Economic Socialism," *California Historical Society Quarterly* 40 (September 1961), 215–36;

Regarding Upton Sinclair, see his *I, Candidate for Governor—and How I Got Licked* (1935). The latest biography is Anthony Arthur, *Radical Innocent* (2006). See also Greg Mitchell, *The Campaign of the Century: Upton Sinclair's Race for Governor of California and the Birth of Media Politics* (1992); Fay Blake and H. M. Newman, "Upton Sinclair's Epic Campaign," *California Historical Quarterly* 63 (Fall 1984), 305–19; Judson Grenier, "Upton Sinclair: A Remembrance," *California Historical Society Quarterly* 47 (June 1969), 165–69; and Grenier, "Upton Sinclair: The Road to California," *Southern California Quarterly* 56 (Winter 1974), 325–36.

On reform and labor, consult Tom Sitton, "Another Generation of Urban Reformers: Los Angeles in the 1930s," *Western Historical Quarterly* 18 (July 1987), 315–32; Woodrow C. Whitten, *Criminal Syndicalism and Law in California* (Philadelphia, 1969); Philip Taft, *Labor Politics American Style: The California State Federation of Labor* (1968); Robert W. Cherny, "The Making of a Labor Radical: Harry Bridges, 1901–34," *Pacific Historical Review* 64 (August 1995), 363–88; Hyman Weintraub,

Andrew Furuseth: Emancipator of the Seamen (1959); Robert Knight, *Industrial Relations in the San Francisco Bay Area, 1900–1918* (1960); Paul S. Taylor, *The Sailors' Union of the Pacific* (1923); Alexander Saxton, "San Francisco Labor and the Populist and Progressive Insurgencies," *Pacific Historical Review* 34 (November 1965), 421–38; Ira Cross, *History of the Labor Movement in California* (1935); Mike Quin, *The Big Strike* (1949); and Paul Eliel, *The Waterfront and General Strike . . .* (1934).

About California's governors, see H. Brett Melendy and Benjamin F. Gilbert's *The Governors of California* (1965). See also Robert E. Burke, *Olson's New Deal for California* (1952).

Hearst's biographers include Ben Procter, *William Randolph Hearst, The Later Years, 1911–1951* (2007) and *The Early Years, 1863–1910* (1998); Nancy Whitelaw, *William Randolph Hearst and the American Century* (2004); David Nashaw, *The Chief: The Life of William Randolph Hearst* (2000); W. A. Swanberg, *Citizen Hearst: A Biography of William Randolph Hearst* (1996); Oliver Carlson and Ernest S. Bates, *Hearst: Lord of San Simeon* (1937); John Tebbel, *The Life and Good Times of William Randolph Hearst* (1952); and John K. Winkler, *William Randolph Hearst: A New Appraisal* (1955).

Regarding competition between farm workers, see Gilbert Gonzalez, *Labor and Community: Citrus: Worker Villages . . .* (1994); Camille Guerin-Gonzalez, *Mexican Workers . . . and California Farm Labor* (1994); Wayne Cornelius, Leo Chavez, and Jorge Castro, *Mexican Immigrants and Southern California* (1982); Richard Griswold del Castillo, *The Los Angeles Barrio, 1850–1890* (1980); Vicki Ruiz, *Cannery Women, Cannery Lives . . . 1930–1950* (1987); Devra Weber, *Dark Sweat, White Gold: California Farm Workers* (1994); Cletus E. Daniel, *Bitter Harvest: A History of California Farm Workers . . .* (1981); and Harold A. De Witt, "The Watsonville Anti-Filipino Riot of 1930," *Southern California Quarterly* 61 (Fall 1979), 291–302. Regarding the field and citrus worker strikes of the 1930s see Gilbert G. Gonzalez, *Mexican Consuls and Labor Organizing* (1999) and Matt Garcia, *A World of Its Own: Race, Labor, and Citrus in the Making of Greater Los Angeles, 1900–1970* (2001).

CHAPTER THIRTY-TWO

TWENTIETH-CENTURY CULTURE

After 1900, California's mild climate and affordable housing attracted a wide variety of transient eccentrics. It became known as a land of spiritualist cults. Some of these engaged in bizarre social experiments. Organized religions flourished alongside fuzzy-minded Gurus, Yogi mystics, Swami palm readers, rainmakers, Hindu fakirs, and occultists. Theosophy, a sect that followed Buddhist and Brahman spiritual beliefs, also gained adherents.

Historians have too seldom featured the role of religious evangelism in California's story. After the turn of the century, Katherine Tingley, known as "The Purple Mother," established a theosophical community at Point Loma, outside San Diego. It lasted until 1929. Another theosophist, Annie Besant, settled in the peaceful Ojai Valley, inland from Santa Barbara. There she brought from India "The New Messiah," one Krishnamurti, to preside over her odd flock of converts.

Among fundamentalist preachers were two shouting evangelists. Both Robert "Fighting Bob" Shuler and Charles Fuller possessed a magnetic revivalist appeal. Fuller became a national radio presence whose popularity rivaled that of Hollywood celebrities. Before his death he founded today's Fuller Theological Seminary in Pasadena.

The best-known faith healer was Aimee Semple McPherson, a dynamic Canadian Pentecostal evangelist who founded the Four Square Gospel Church in Los Angeles. Her revivals, open to all races, had begun in open canvas tents. In the interwar years, "Sister Aimee" remained full of verve and high volume. On one occasion she scattered religious tracts from an airplane; at other times she held prayer meetings in a boxing arena. A talented show woman, she sometimes wore the white uniform and gold braid of an admiral. From the platform of her Angelus Temple, Sister Aimee, called a miracle woman, combatted the devil on behalf of the downhearted and lonely, for many of whom she had a potent appeal.

For twenty years, McPherson broadcast her emotionally charged services via her own radio station. In 1925, the station wandered off its assigned wave length. When Herbert Hoover, then secretary of commerce, ordered her broadcast license suspended, Sister Aimee cabled him: "PLEASE ORDER YOUR MINIONS OF SATAN TO LEAVE MY STATION ALONE . . . YOU CANNOT EXPECT THE ALMIGHTY TO ABIDE BY YOUR WAVE LENGTH NONSENSE." On another occasion Sister Aimee ceremoniously walked into the ocean and was presumed to have drowned. Thirty-five days later she reappeared in Mexico under suspicious circumstances, saying that she had been kidnapped. McPherson founded more than 200 branch churches, skillfully mixing entertainment with religion. She offered her followers healing by the "laying on of hands," or "speaking in tongues," as well as entertaining bell ringers and xylophone bands. During the national Great Depression of the 1930s, she also gave substantial aid to the sick and needy.

By the 1970s, the cinema treated "Sister Aimee" inaccurately in such films as *Chinatown* (1970). The exploitation of Los Angeles occultists by merchandisers of history also spread to television where her story was aired on several TV specials. Repeatedly, southern California was becoming damned as a magnet for eccentrics.

One sees a parallel phenomenon in the construction of its "funeral parks." These for-profit establishments advertised themselves as happy vales for the dearly departed. Unlike the staid and somber graveyards of the past, the new funeral parks promised mourners a glowing vision of the hereafter, glossing over death via slick advertisements. Swaddled in spongy euphemisms, burials were transformed into virtual celebrations.

Crude commercial campaigns opened southern California's funeral parks to lampooning by satiric authors, especially the popular English critics Evelyn Waugh and Aldous Huxley. Asked why he had settled in California, Huxley once quipped, "I stopped there on my way to India, and because of inertia and apathy remained." Los Angeles had a real influence on the way Huxley wrote. A critic of Victorian pomposities, Huxley grew ever more cynical; yet he sought solutions that might satisfy humankind's animal and spiritual needs. In *After Many a Summer Dies the Swan,* Huxley mocked ostentation and human hollowness. Impressed with eastern mystical thought, he began to attend meetings of the Vedanta cult, accompanied by yet another "southern California Englishman," Christopher Isherwood. Both hated the grotesquely palatial residences of the Hearsts and the movie magnates. Isherwood joined Waugh and Huxley in mocking advertisements for funeral parks ("the Beverly Pantheon, a Personality Cemetery").

Before World War I, writers from all over the nation continued to visit California. Some were more distinguished by their industry than by literary finesse. Zane Grey, a former baseball player and Ohio dentist, made a fortune publishing pulp westerns. Settling in Altadena, where he built a Zuni-style terraced house, Grey, like Jack London before him, sometimes wrote two novels in a given year. The most popular of Grey's works was *Riders of the Purple Sage* (1912). Another writer of pulp fiction, Harold Bell Wright, authored several dozen novels set in the Far West. His *The Winning of Barbara Worth* (1911), which focussed on the reclamation of the Imperial Valley from the desert, sold more than 1.5 million copies.

An aspiring poet was the eccentric George Sterling, who produced his romantic sonnets at Carmel. Sterling, in Jack London's words, "looked like a Greek coin run over by a Roman chariot." Nonetheless, Sterling's *Testimony of the Suns* (1903) was both imaginative and honest. In 1926 Sterling killed himself in San Francisco's Bohemian Club. A much greater poet was Robinson Jeffers who, after graduating from Occidental College, also setted in Carmel. There he built with his own hands a stone residence named Tor House. In his lonely work, Jeffers contrasted human depravity

Steinbeck's novel, *The Grapes of Wrath*, was made into a successful movie in 1940, directed by John Ford and starring Henry Fonda (center). Courtesy of the Museum of Modern Art, Film Stills Archive.

with the nobility of California's still pristine coastline, once writing "Cut humanity out of my being, that is the wound that festers." His respect for the primeval and for the wonders of the universe drew a loyal readership to his starkly beautiful poetry. Jeffers was at his best in such controversial narrative poems as *Roan Stallion* (1925) and *Be Angry at the Sun* (1925).

Upton Sinclair, the dedicated reformer and would-be officeholder, arrived in California after having written *The Jungle* (1906) and *The Money-Changers* (1908). He had an extraordinary career, at the same time exerting leadership in countless causes. Almost everything he stood for was detested by business interests. His platform, as divulged in his book, *The EPIC Plan for California* (1934), was inflammatory in its utopianism. Sinclair's writings, however, commanded worldwide attention. There is no question that his book *The Jungle* achieved specific reforms. Legislation such as the Pure Food and Drug Act remains in effect today. Sinclair, who died at the age of ninety, wrote almost fifty novels and more than twenty nonfiction books as well as plays.

Less blatant was the best-known of California novelists, John Steinbeck. Born near Salinas in 1902, Steinbeck poured the anger he felt over widespread social injustices into his California-based fiction. Whether describing exploited farm laborers, fishermen, or migrants seeking employment, he pleaded for tolerance and respect for the underdog. His *Pastures of Heaven* (1932), *Tortilla Flat* (1935), and *In Dubious Battle* (1936) reflected anger with all forms of social injustice. Steinbeck's most important novel, *The Grapes of Wrath* (1939), chronicled the plight of a family of Okie farmers forced to move westward and the cruel reception they received in California, which they had envisioned as a paradise. In 1962, he won the Nobel Prize for literature.

William Saroyan, of Armenian origin, discovered a rich literary lore in the San Joaquin Valley of his boyhood. His novels, *My Heart's in the Highlands* (1939), *My Name is Aram* (1940), and *The Beautiful People* (1942) are peopled by eccentrics who inhabit a dream world. Saroyan is best remembered for his short stories and occasional plays. The settings of these books do not venture far from the rural Fresno of his youth.

Because so many European refugees arrived there, southern California came to be called a boneyard for aging foreign intellectuals. Among them was the controversial English philosopher Bertrand Russell, who spent part of the World War II years teaching at UCLA. He ungratefully called Los Angeles "the ultimate segregation of the unfit." The German Nobel Prize–winning novelist Thomas Mann was another European refugee from Nazism. Between the wars, Sadakichi Hartmann, a Japanese-born historian of art and an aesthete, also wrote screenplays and exotic poetry in Hollywood and San Francisco.

Following World War II, much good writing began to come out of the state's colleges and universities. At Stanford, Wallace Stegner began earning acclaim for his books set in the American West, among them *Mormon Country* (1942) and *The Big Rock Candy Mountain* (1943). From Berkeley, Mark Schorer's *The State of Mind* (1947) and Henry Nash Smith's *Virgin Land* (1950) combined writing with teaching. Richard Armour, on the faculty of Scripps College, made a name for himself as the "playful poet," with light verse reminiscent of Gelett Burgess.

At Occidental College, historian Robert Glass Cleland produced engaging narratives on the fur trade, the California ranches, and the American West. At the University of California, George R. Stewart spanned both history and literature in his *Ordeal by Hunger* (1936) and *Storm* (1941). Walter Van Tilburg Clark, at San Francisco State College, wrote *The Ox-Bow Incident* (1940). This book split sharply with the tradition that glorified vigilantism in California.

The best-known novel of Niven Busch, *California Street* (1959), concerns a San Francisco newspaper dynasty, while James Edmiston's *Home Again* (1955) reflects a poignant criticism of the government's forced removal of Japanese Americans from the Pacific Coast during World War II. A related theme runs through Abraham Polansky's *A Season of Fear* (1956). The experience of San Francisco's Chinese form the backdrop of C. Y. Lee's *The Flower-Drum Song* (1956), which was adapted into both a musical play and a film.

Other postwar novelists include Jessamyn West, whose *The Friendly Persuasion* (1945) was transformed into a prize-winning film script. Her *South of the Angels* (1960) was set in southern California, as was James M. Cain's *The Postman Always Rings Twice* (1934) and *Mildred Pierce* (1941). Judy van der Veer evoked the San Diego backcountry in her *Brown Hills* (1938) and *November Grass* (1940). Both John Fante, in *Ask the Dust* (1940) and *Dago Red* (1940) and Joe Pagano in *Golden Wedding* (1943), portrayed Italian-American life in the Far West.

Among mystery authors who called California their home were Raymond Chandler, Dashiell Hammett, Ross McDonald, and Erle Stanley Gardner. Hammett is considered the father of the modern detective novel. Among his most popular creations was the hardboiled detective Sam Spade in the novel *The Maltese Falcon* (1929). Hollywood purchased the book and made a hit movie with it starring Humphrey Bogart as Spade, using a fog-shrouded San Francisco as the film's backdrop. Raymond

Chandler, a great admirer of Hammett, followed with his Phillip Marlowe, an incorruptible private detective who worked the streets and hills of 1930s and '40s Los Angeles. Chandler, too, would find success not only in his books but also with his screenplays. Among his key works are the novels, *The Big Sleep* (1939), *Farewell, My Lovely* (1940) and *The Long Goodbye* (1953). His films include *The Blue Dahlia* (1946) and *Double Indemnity* (1944), which he cowrote with Billy Wilder.

Erle Stanley Gardner was admitted to the California state bar in 1911, Gardner became best known as the creator of Perry Mason, a fictional attorney and super sleuth. Edgar Rice Burroughs, originator of the banal Tarzan stories, also kept up a voluminous production. Outpacing even these prolific writers was Louis L'Amour who, beginning with his book *Hondo* (1952), sold millions of copies of his western stories.

A totally different type of writer was Henry Miller, born in Manhattan in 1891. Most of his racy work was autobiographical. His best-known books are *Tropic of Cancer* (1934) and *Tropic of Capricorn* (1938), both of which he wrote during an expatriate period abroad. For some years, Miller lived on a mountaintop overlooking the Pacific Ocean. His book, *Big Sur and the Oranges of Hieronymus Bosch* (1956), described his dissolute life in California. Miller's *The Air Conditioned Nightmare* is a bitter book that claimed that Americans had lost the art of living. Yet, Miller ended up residing at Big Sur, south of Monterey.

In the 1950s, Miller influenced the "Beat Generation," among whom were writers Jack Kerouac and Allen Ginsberg. With San Francisco as their home base, the "Beatniks" expressed the frustrations of impatient young people disillusioned with post–World War II American society. At the City Lights Bookstore, Ginsberg joined Kerouac in publishing his writing in *Neurotica*, a journal that rebelled against the social "establishment," whom the Beatniks dubbed "squares." They averred that most Americans were conformists living safe but thoroughly dull lives. Defying society's conventions, the Beatniks clustered about the espresso cafés of San Francisco and farther south at Venice on the west side of Los Angeles.

These bearded Bohemians aroused the ire of critics who felt the Beatniks richly deserved the unpopularity they sought. As if to anticipate the Hippie rebellion of the 1960s, beat poetry readings, music sessions, and "kookie" artistic displays generated interest among the youth of the 1950s. The beatniks believed they were modern and avant-garde, which they may have been for a while, but most serious literary critics deemed their writings adolescent. Probably the most representative of the beat generation's works is Kerouac's novel *On the Road* and Ginsberg's long poem *Howl*

(1956), the latter called a tedious collection of raucous words by some but ground-breaking art by others. On occasion, the "beats" displayed a sense of humor. They encouraged the social commentary of the comedian Mort Sahl, a former University of California student who made a fortune in such nightclubs as San Francisco's "Hungry I" and Hollywood's Crescendo.

By the mid-twentieth century, the California press was also undergoing changes more suited to the new age of television. Syndicated news and editorial opinion, provided by eastern wire services, replaced home-grown journalism. Even local newspapers reflected a lack of variety and a high degree of monopolization. In large cities, one or two papers came to control the print medium.

As for book production, the University of California Press and Stanford University Press are first-rate scholarly publishers that serve a national as well as state market. In addition, a number of typographers and book dealers once established a tradition for fine printings in limited editions, supported by the Book Club of California and the Zamorano and Roxburghe clubs, all of which still honor fine printing.

The performing arts, however, have always flourished in California. At the turn of the century, the state's leading musical institution was the San Francisco Symphony, founded in 1911. For many years its most popular conductor was Pierre Monteux. San Francisco's Tivoli Opera House closed in 1913, but the San Francisco Opera Company appeared to fill the gap; after 1932 the company was given a permanent home in the War Memorial Opera House.

Ferdinand Rudolph (Ferde) Grofe, arranger and composer of the Grand Canyon Suite, began his career as an "extra" piano player at the Old Hippodrome Theater on San Francisco's Barbary Coast. On the eve of World War II, other foreign composers also sought refuge in California, among them Arnold Schoenberg and Igor Stravinsky.

By 1919, with the financial backing of William Andrews Clark, Jr., Los Angeles developed its own symphony, the Philharmonic. Although L.A. still had no central music hall, its new orchestra quickly gained acclaim because of its great open-air concerts. These have been held since 1921 at the Hollywood Bowl. Among the artists who appeared there were George Gershwin, who personally performed his "Rhapsody in Blue." In the 1960s, after the Los Angeles Music Center was finally built, the Philharmonic engaged world-renowned conductors, including Zubin Mehta and Carlo Maria Giulini. Los Angeles musicals also had long Broadway runs. Among their creators were Jerome Kern, Oscar Hammerstein, Sigmund Romberg, and George Gershwin. The city's Civic Light Opera Company staged these performances for more than fifty years.

Drama too has enjoyed a long history in southern California. In the 1920s, John Steven McGroarty's "The Mission Play" drew large crowds. Like Helen Hunt Jackson's *Ramona*, it embraced a Spanish fantasy heritage. As for the development of motion pictures, back in 1872 former governor Leland Stanford commissioned the English-born photographer Edweard Muybridge to take a series of action shots of Stanford's racehorse, named Occident. Stanford had bet a friend $25,000 that horses, while trotting, took all four hooves off the ground at one time during their stride. In order to prove this, Muybridge, with the aid of the engineering staff at Stanford's Southern Pacific Railway, lined up twenty-four cameras along a racetrack at Palo Alto. He then stretched fine wires across the track. As the horse broke these, a series of photographic prints were taken. The photos proved Stanford correct. However, when these exposures were projected onto a screen in rapid succession, the illusion formed pictures in motion. Muybridge had attracted attention to the possibility of designing a motion-picture camera. But credit for this invention is usually given to Thomas Alva Edison and his assistants.

For some years, film production remained confined to New York and New Jersey. By 1907, however, film producers moved to Hollywood for two compelling reasons. First, California's year-round good weather and variety of scenery made it an ideal location for motion-picture production. Second, the state was far from eastern debt collectors eager to hound delinquent movie producers. The first Hollywood filmmakers were, in addition, freed from the interference of New York State's motion-picture patent law, with its injunctions against producers who infringed upon the patents held by Edison and other developers of cinema equipment. The fugitive producers with their bootleg cameras had little capital with which to build a new industry. In southern California, however, labor costs were lower than elsewhere. Producers could operate on a shoestring budget if they could pool their resources, rent second-hand equipment, paint their own sets, and improvise lighting techniques.

In 1913, when Samuel Goldwyn, Jesse Lasky, and Cecil B. De Mille came west to produce *The Squaw Man* in a barn at the corner of Selma and Vine Streets, they had only few thousand dollars and the talents of an unknown actress, Clara Kimball Young, as assets. Such pictures enriched the producers as orders for prints of the films poured in from vaudeville houses and nickelodeons transformed into movie parlors.

In addition to independent producers from New York, film organizations began to spring up in California. One of these was the Selig Polyscope Company, which in 1907–08 filmed *The Count of Monte Cristo* near a Los Angeles suburb. In 1909 the Bison Studios of New York arrived in

Hollywood, followed by the Pathé organization and Biograph. The Vita-graph, Kalem, and Edison film companies followed thereafter. By 1914, when most of the eastern companies had sent workforces to California, seventy-three firms were producing pictures in California. In those early years of the film industry, one or another company ground out a "Western" every other day.

A sleepy little village founded by Kansas prohibitionists before the turn of the century, Hollywood had a town ordinance as late as 1903 that forbade driving more than 2,000 sheep down Hollywood Boulevard at any one time. Almost overnight, Hollywood became the film center of the world.

During the early years, the film industry passed through a "mega-phone-and custard-pie" comedy phase that drew to it both hacks and per-sons of talent. That era gave rise to the stereotype of the autocratic direc-tor, clad in riding breeches and a backwards cap, who shouted orders at droves of extras employed to fill the backgrounds of his pictures. Among the most imaginative men who came west to "shoot pictures" was David Wark Griffith, producer of *The Birth of a Nation*. Due to its high cost of production ($100,000), this was the first American picture to command a $2 admission fee. It opened at Clune's Auditorium in Los Angeles on February 8, 1915, and ultimately grossed $20 million. This was also the first film to be honored with a showing at the White House, where Presi-dent Wilson is said to have remarked, "It is like writing history with light-ning."

With the development of a "star system," the production of films be-came fantastically expensive. Outside the marquees of klieg-lighted pre-mieres, traffic stopped while fans ogled their favorite stars. Charlie Chap-lin, an English pantomime, became famous all over the world, soon joining Mary Pickford, known as "America's Sweetheart," at Mack Sennett's Key-stone Company. In two years Chaplin's salary skyrocketed from $150 to $10,000 a week. Both he and Pickford went on to command salaries in excess of $1 million a year.

Theda Bara, Dustin Farnum, Harold Lloyd, Lillian Gish, Rudolph Valentino, and Greta Garbo were other performers whom fans quickly grew to idolize. The retention of both beauty and youth was the goal of upcoming starlets like Marion Davies, the sexy mistress of publisher Wil-liam Randolph Hearst. "High cololonic irrigation" was one bizarre remedy against aging.

The cowboy stars William S. Hart, Tom Mix, and Ed "Hoot" Gibson became the heroes of countless small boys. A few of this group of actors actually had punched cattle on the range and were fine horsemen, as was the rustic comedian Will Rogers. In a category of her own, each week Pearl White left silent-film audiences breathlessly awaiting the next installment of *The Perils of Pauline*, a serial first produced in 1914.

The advent of World War I led to the collapse of moviemaking in Italy, Germany, and England. As a result, Hollywood producers gained control of the world movie market. Mergers and consolidations, brought on by postwar competition and price cutting, reduced the number of studios to a handful. By 1923, more than 20,000 actors were working before cameras, their weekly payroll amounting to more than $1 million.

The Hollywood of the 1920s is almost beyond recall today. In those lush years the flow of cash through the box offices staggered even the most avaricious of filmdom's pioneers. A baronial self-confidence led the movie moguls to festoon their studios with boastful pennants that read: "More Stars than There Are in Heaven" and "Hollywood, the Greatest Show on Earth." This was the era of matinee idols duly equipped with white silk shirts, bevies of aspiring starlets, sixteen-cylinder racing cars, and theatre-room white stucco palaces. Movie queens such as Pola Negri and Gloria Swanson spent thousands of dollars for perfume alone, helping to make

Scene depicting the assassination of Abraham Lincoln from D. W. Griffith's controversial *The Birth of a Nation*, 1915. Courtesy of the Museum of Modern Art, Film Stills Archive.

Hollywood one of the most talked-of towns in the world. Gossip concerning the industry and its stars was unquenchable. As early as 1923 the *New York World* wrote: "Hollywood has no art galleries, no institutions of learning, aside from primary schools and kindergartens—nothing that makes the slightest pretense to culture, civic or otherwise. . . . But Beauty, ye gods, the place is choked, blocked, heaped to the gunwales with female beauty. One has to elbow beauties out of the way to make a passage down Hollywood Boulevard."

Soon the private lives of the stars drew criticism. In 1921, the career of comic Roscoe "Fatty" Arbuckle was shattered by a scandal involving the death of a young actress in the course of a wild party in a hotel room in San Francisco. Arbuckle's comedies were thereafter banned in many communities. Will Hays, former postmaster general of the United States, was brought to Hollywood at a salary of $100,000 to impose discipline upon the industry. The Hays office restrained the industry from filming objectionable material. He encouraged the "moral ending," which transformed honestly controversial pictures into pious platitudes. Sentiment for censorship grew so strong that in 1922 the major producers banded together to form the Motion Picture Producers and Distributors Association.

Among filmdom's technological innovations was the addition of a sound track to film strips. *The Jazz Singer* was the first motion picture made with sound. This "talkie," starring song-and-dance man Al Jolson, revolutionized the film industry when it appeared in 1927. Suddenly, silent movie stars with squeaky, high-pitched voices vanished and were replaced by the likes of Clark Gable, Spencer Tracy, Claudette Colbert, and Joan Crawford. Sound pictures, attracting larger crowds than ever, led to the building of bigger theaters.

Brassy promoters encouraged a national craving for cheap entertainment combining the attractions of melodrama, vaudeville, and the circus. For 25¢, in a carpeted atmosphere of popcorn and Coca Cola, America's moviegoers—who numbered at least 50 million each week by the late 1920s—supported an industry built on opportunistic agents, stunt men, writers, scene painters, and thousands of hangers-on. Original and creative ideas often were squelched in the interest of moneymaking. Only half smiling could Hollywood's most famous lion (the MGM mascot) roar *"Ars gratia artis"* (Art for art's sake), the caption that accompanied his every appearance. Actually, commercial considerations almost always triumphed over artistic ones. In those profitable years director-producer Cecil B. DeMille indulged his audiences with pretentious "historical" productions such as *The King of Kings* (1927) and *Cleopatra* (1934), the purpose of which was spectacle, not significance. Such pictures were eminently vulnerable to the charge of tasteless vulgarity. De Mille himself one said, "Your poor person wants to see wealth, colorful, interesting, exotic." His films, with hundreds of paint-bedaubed extras, chariot races, and papier-maché replicas of the monuments of antiquity, set an unfortunate pattern. Hollywood came to worship the "colossal" and "stupendous" as elephantine epics became the norm and showmanship triumphed over art.

The rampart commercialism of the movie producers can be partially attributed to their early insecurity. William Fox was originally a cloth sponger on New York's Lower East Side. Marcus Loew had dealt in fur sales, later operating a penny arcade. Samuel Goldwyn was originally a glove salesman. Carl Laemmle, a German immigrant, had managed a Wisconsin clothing store. Louis B. Mayer, probably the most powerful of these pioneer "cellulords," had been a lowly scrap metal dealer. Though unprepared for making artistic judgments, these aspiring movie moguls produced some excellent films, often stressing middle class values.

Boy-meets-girl plots, big-laugh comedies, mawkish family dramas, and song-and-dance extravaganzas furnished an escape to viewers, especially during the years of the Great Depression, Hollywood soon set new fashions in dress, home furnishings, and married life, promoting the standardization of American "culture." Some films did glorify violence, corruption, and, to a limited degree, sex. In the 1920s civic groups claimed that sensational film titles promised unwholesome attractions for the young. A few such titles were: *Ladies Must Dress, Parlor, Bedroom and Bath, The Love Flower, Old Wives for New, Paid to Love, The Price She Paid,* and *Thedora Goes Wild.* Parents of teenagers resented the suggestive environment of comfy darkened theaters and came to feel that the movies undermined their children's morals. Churches too accused the moviemakers of marketing films that were spiritually debasing. One newspaper ad of the 1930s spoke of a movie featuring "beautiful jazz babies, champagne baths, midnight revels, petting parties in the purple dawn, all ending in one terrific smashing climax that makes you gasp."

Major novelists and playwrights were drawn to Hollywood as screen cotract writers. They included Sinclair Lewis, Theodore Dreiser, F. Scott Fitzgerald, Nathanael West, William Faulkner, and Clifford Odets. Ernest Hemingway sold enough of his fiction to make fifteen films. But, like Faulkner, he hated what Hollywood did to his books and short stories. Yet, the "studio system" was too lucrative for artistic talents to resist. The songwriters George and Ira Gershwin, David Rose, Vincent Newman, Dimitri Tiomkin, and Miklós Rózsa all ended up in Hollywood. Their music accompanied such films as *All Quiet on the Western Front* (1930), *The Informer* (1935), and *Citizen Kane* (1940).

In the late 1930s, the industry turned to foreign stars and themes to counter competition from such producers as England's Sir Alexander Korda. Among the new foreign talents were British actors Ronald Coleman, Leslie Howard, and Robert Donat, as well as the Irish actress Greer Garson. Their movies, such as *Mrs. Miniver* and *Goodbye, Mr. Chips*, earned international respect. On the eve of World War II, Hollywood attracted refugees from Nazism, including Jean Renoir, the director son of France's famous impressionist painter. Among other creative Europeans were Kurt Weill and Berthold Brecht.

One of the last big moneymakers of the pre-television age was *The Best Years of Our Lives* (1946), starring Fredrick March. After 1945, Hollywood flooded the country with B-grade pictures in larger numbers than ever before. A few postwar titles are illustrative: *Vice Raid, Drag Strip Girl,* and *High School Confidential.* Films of this type could hardly save the industry from sagging theater attendance caused by television, even as the cost of making movies rose steadily and actors demanded a larger share of the profits. Increasingly high taxes absorbed another large part of Hollywood's revenues.

In the postwar decades the movie industry was plagued by serious new problems. A federal investigation by the House of Representatives into alleged Communists in Hollywood tied the studios in knots. Then, after 1948, antitrust suits forced the major "Big Five" studios to divest themselves of lucrative theater chains. Gloom settled over a Hollywood beset by competition from paperback books, phonograph records, and new forms of recreation such as bowling, waterskiing, and boating. By the late 1940s, producers and directors found it financially advantageous to film pictures out of the country at studios in Rome, Paris, Montreal, and London.

The old studio-contract system was replaced by other modes of production. The film empires of Mayer and Goldwyn were no longer affordable. Heavy-handed administration was once shouldered by the likes of Darryl Zanuck. Adolph Zukor ruled the Paramount Studios for more than forty years; in 1975 at the age of 103, he was still on its board of trustees. A new generation of producer-directors replaced the pioneers. Billy Wilder, who had immigrated from Europe, produced highly successful films. The best of these, starring Marilyn Monroe, was *Some Like It Hot.* Other directors had directed successful plays on the New York stage. In the 1950s, Elia Kazan and actor Marlon Brando introduced a new raw approach in their films, *On the Waterfront* and *A Streetcar Named Desire.*

After World War II the cinema became a universal art form. The movies gave foreigners their first impression of the United States. Films reached into the lives of millions, not only as entertainment but also culturally. Film versions of classics such as *Anna Karenina, Wuthering Heights,* and *War and Peace* made these works familiar to many who would never have read them. The cinema has also featured Walt Disney's cartoons as well as newsreels, and documentaries. Hollywood now developed the independent production of films, home movies, educational films, drive-in theaters, wide-angle screens, and three-dimensional productions

The 1970s saw a long-awaited revival of interest in big-budget films. Francis Ford Coppola, Martin Scorsese, Dino de Laurentis, and Carlo Ponti (all of whom happened to be of Italian origin), produced films that resembled the earlier epics. The new titles included *The Godfather, Jaws,* and *King Kong.* Some big-budget productions, however, financially bombed. Among them were *Heaven's Gate, One From the Heart,* and a new genre of violent movies. By the 1980s, the use of video cassettes at home severely cut into film revenues. Yet a virtually new industry resulted from this adaptation. By the end of the twentieth century the digital video disk (DVD) replaced VHS cassettes and spawned new second-run revenues. In addition, films received wholly new competition from the Internet.

Television severely affected the movie industry. Few old-time directors, writers, or producers successfully shifted to TV production. Its marketing demands were totally different. Survival of the film industry in some cases came to depend upon the production of short "made-for-TV" movies. Like their East Coast counterpart, Hollywood and nearby Burbank became the West Coast center of television transmission. Soon, the upstart cable TV networks forged a virtually new industry, helping to push Hollywood light-years beyond the pioneer days of the silent screen.

The film industry and television industries aside, a variety of twentieth-century artists also helped shape modern California. Among notable painters were Phil Dike, Barse Miller, Rex Brandt, Millard Sheets, and sculptor Gutzon Borglum, who began his career in San Francisco. Ultimately, Borglum was commissioned to carve and drill out the features of four great U.S. presidents in the granite cliffs of Mount Rushmore in South Dakota. Another California sculptor and book illustrator, Joe Mora, also became well known outside the state, as did printmaker and painter Edward Borein.

Outstanding among California photographers was Carleton E. Watkins, for which Mount Watkins, a massive granite peak atop the Yosemite Valley is named. An equally distinguished photographer was the German-born Arnold Genthe. After the 1906 San Francisco earthquake and fire, Genthe wandered the streets of the city documenting the devastation in light and shadows.

Any list of the best-known modern photographers must include Ansel Adams and Edward Weston. Adams's Yosemite photos are especially sharp and vivid in tone, while Weston achieved an international reputation with his black-and-white depictions of nature and humans alike. Both men chose to live near Carmel, endlessly photographing its unique scenery.

As early as the 1920s, art colonies at Carmel, Santa Barbara, and Laguna Beach reflected a deepening interest in sculpture, painting, mosaicwork, and architectural design. Art institutes located in Los Angeles included the Otis, Chouinard, and Art-Center Schools. Museums too grew in the richness of their holdings. The Huntington Art Gallery in San Marino obtained increasing numbers of paintings in the English Renaissance style. The Crocker Art Gallery in Sacramento and the De Young Museum in San Francisco enlarged their collections. The Southwest Museum in Los Angeles likewise steadily improved its holdings of American Indian art and artifacts.

One of the most bizarre architectural phenomena in modern California was the artistry of an Italian immigrant, Simon Rodia, builder of the Watts Towers. Located near Los Angeles, these novel creations were fashioned out of bits of glass, tile, and artifacts garnered from junk heaps. Rodia built the first tower in 1921. By the 1960s, after thirty-three years, he had erected gigantic structures made out of concrete, steel, and rubble. His towers are enduring marvels of folk art.

After the turn of the century, the Mexican adobe ranch house inspired a "mission revival" architecture, a prime example of which is Riverside's Mission Inn. This style shared popularity with the mauve wooden California bungalows of Charles Sumner Greene and Henry Mather Greene, which derived from the arts and crafts movement. These dwellings combined the charm of European chalets with Asian-inspired ornamentation.

More modern architects, among them Frank Lloyd Wright, Rudolph M. Schindler, and Richard Neutra, built some of their first experimental structures in California. No one type, however, came to predominate the hodgepodge of styles still found throughout the state that include Queen Anne, Hawaiian, Oriental, Tudor, Jacobean, French chateau, Georgian, Mount Vernon colonial, Egyptian, Mayan, Cape Cod cottages, and even Hopi Indian dwellings replete with rope ladders.

In the interwar period, no architect was more popular than Wallace Neff. His designs were heavily influenced by Spanish and Italian buildings. Neff constructed residences throughout the wealthy enclaves of San Marino and Beverly Hills, also becoming a favorite designer of mansions for movie stars. Other architects also borrowed Neff's use of Spanish white-stucco walls, Tuscan red-tile roofs, and Romanesque arches; three of these who became popular from the 1920s to the 1940s were Reginald Johnson, Gordon Kaufmann, and Roland Coate.

In San Diego, Irving Gill became the best-known architect. Another prominent architect was Bertram Goodhue, who also used white stucco and red tile in his buildings. Except for his leaner, more angular, Los Angeles Public Library, Goodhue utilized architectural motifs found in California's Spanish and Mexican eras. In San Francisco, architects Willis Polk, Bernard Maybeck, and John Galen Howard also became popular. Polk had designed the Ferry Building, was one of the planners of the city's Civic Center, and also constructed the Hallidie Building, the world's first glass skyscraper.

By the mid-1930s, Richard Neutra, a Viennese architect, introduced functional houses in the Los Angeles area. His style evoked elements of Frank Lloyd Wright's modernism. Both Neutra and Wright stressed the practical in residential construction: their split-level houses offered increased living space, wide windows, and enclosed recreation areas.

Two outstanding women also made their mark in landscape architecture. Florence Yoch and Beatrix Farrand created dozens of designs for private residences, public courtyards, and educational institutions. Yoch also became known for designing sets for such films as *Gone With the Wind*. Farrand landscaped both the California Institute of Technology (Caltech) and Occidental College campuses and was a principal landscaper of the Santa Barbara Botanical Gardens. Both women skillfully adapted traditional eastern garden plans to suit the California environment.

By the 1980s, Frank Gehry became the darling of commercial building innovation. His Disney Hall, a part of the Los Angeles Music Center, is an example of extreme architectural modernism. But, like Wright, some of his ultramodern architecture did not hold up well against the weather. His garish Santa Monica Mall faced destruction because of changing public tastes. Whereas Wright's Hollyhock House in Los Angeles has been rebuilt, other Gehry structures, including a University of California at Irvine building, is being demolished. Still other architectural styles grace California's nearly 400 colleges and universities, including 110 two-year institutions.

The California Institute of Technology (Caltech) in Pasadena, founded as the Throop College of Technology, specializes in the hard sciences. In the 1950s its Jet Propulsion Laboratory (JPL) operated for the National Aeronautics and Space Administration (NASA), supervising the manufacture of the United States's first artificial Earth satellites. By the late 1960s, JPL landed a module on the surface of the moon.

The national press has repeatedly satirized California as a "land of pop and honey." Yet, its culture continues to take new eclectic forms. For example, today's Rand (Research and Development) Corporation at Santa Monica, a semipublic agency created to carry on strategic studies, brings together political scientists, physicists, and mathematicians. Other "think tanks"—from the Silicon Valley in the north to San Diego on the Mexican border—engage in cutting-edge research, the scope of which is universal.

Another research center is the Lawrence Radiation Laboratory of the University of California at Livermore. Cyclotrons (particle accelerators) exist at both the Berkeley and Los Angeles campuses of the university. California's law schools, medical facilities, observatories, and institutes all expanded rapidly. The Scripps Institute of Oceanography at La Jolla operates research vessels throughout the Pacific. Also at La Jolla is the Salk Institute for Biological Studies, named for the discoverer of the poliomyelitis vaccine. The Lick Observatory at Mount Hamilton near San Jose—technically a campus of the University of California—has been in operation since 1874. The Mount Wilson Observatory's 100-inch telescope operated from 1917 to 1985. It was astronomically superseded by the Mount Palomar Observatory's 200-inch telescope.

Paralleling California's educational and scientific institutions are the California Historical Society at San Francisco and the Historical Society of Southern California at Los Angeles. The Bancroft Library of the University of California at Berkeley and the Hoover Library of War, Revolution, and Peace at Stanford University are internationally known research centers.

Other tourist attractions in the Los Angeles area include UCLA's Hammer Museum, the Autry Museum of Western Heritage, the California African-American Museum, the Museum of Television and Radio, the Japanese American National Museum, and Pasadena's Pacific Asia Museum. The Museum of Tolerance and the Skirball Cultural Center are both devoted to the Jewish experience worldwide.

Two museums are administered by the J. Paul Getty trust. Although Getty lived his last years in England, he had made his first fortune in

J. Paul Getty Museum at its Los Angeles Getty Center. Photo: Tom Bonner.
© J. Paul Getty Trust.

the oil fields of southern California. He established his original museum along the seashore at Malibu. His will made possible the building of a cultural center inland from his facsimile Roman Villa. On a new hillside site near Brentwood, the ultramodernist architect Richard Meier supervised construction of a complex of buildings above a busy freeway. Opened in 1997, the new Getty Center, became yet another state cultural asset, as did the Getty Villa near Santa Monica.

The Getty's collections complement those of "the Huntington." The Huntington Gallery's renowned "Blue Boy," painted by Thomas Gainsborough, and "Pinkie," by Thomas Lawrence, are centerpieces of the finest group of British portraits that exist anywhere. In addition to its art galleries, the Huntington houses rare books and manuscripts. The thousands of visitors who come there stroll through English, Japanese, Chinese, Australian and world-renowned cactus gardens.

Other tourist attractions have evolved out of the film and TV industries. Daily tours are sponsored by the Universal Studios. Visitors are also attracted by Mann's Chinese Theater on Hollywood Boulevard, with its cement-cast footprints and signatures of movie folk, past and present.

Other amusement centers include the Knotts Berry Farm, the Autry National Center of the American West, and Disneyland. These and other theme parks continue to attract visitors from across the nation and the world.

SELECTED READINGS

Regarding novelists, see Brian St. Pierre, *John Steinbeck: The California Years* (1984); Harry T. Moore, *The Novels of John Steinbeck* (1939); Nelson Valjean, *John Steinbeck, The Errant Knight* (1975); and Martin Stoddard, *California Writers* (1984). William Saroyan's *My Name is Aram* (1940) and *The Human Comedy* (1943) are partly autobiographical. On Jeffers, consult Lawrence Clark Powell, *Robinson Jeffers: The Man and His Work* (1940); Frederick J. Carpenter, *Robinson Jeffers* (1952); Radcliffe Squires, *The Loyalties of Robinson Jeffers* (1956); and Melba Berry Bennett, *The Stone Mason of Tor House* (1966).

About architecture, see Diane Kanner, *Wallace Neff and the Grand Houses of the Golden State* (2005). Frank J. Taylor, *Land of Homes* (1929); Richard Neutra, *Mystery and Realities of the Site* (1951); Kurt Baer, *Architecture of the California Missions* (1958); Karen Weitze, *California's Mission Revival* (1984); Sarah Schaffer, "A Significant Sentence . . . Irving Gill, Progressive Architect," *Journal of San Diego History* 43 (Fall 1997), 219–37; also Bruce Kamerling, *Irving Gill, Architect* (1997). Harold Kirker, *California's Architectural Frontier* (1960); Geoffrey E. Bangs, *Portals West: A Folio of Late Nineteenth Century Architecture in California* (1960); Randell Makinson, *Greene & Greene: Architecture as a Fine Art* (1977); Reyner Banham, *Los Angeles: The Architecture of Four Ecologies* (1971); Esther McCoy, *Five California Architects* (1960) and McCoy, *Richard Neutra* (1960); Frank Harris, ed., *A Guide to Contemporary Architecture in Southern California* (1951); Joseph A. Baird, *Time's Wondrous Changes, San Francisco's Architecture, 1776–1915* (1962); David Gebhard and Robert Winter, *Los Angeles, An Architectural Guide* (1994) and their *Guide to Architecture in San Francisco and Northern California* (1995) as well as Winter's *Toward A Simpler Way of Life: The Arts and Crafts Architects of California* (1997); and Beth Dunlop, *Building a Dream: The Art of Disney Architecture* (1996).

Regarding printing, see James Hart's *Fine Printing in California* (1960) and Ward Ritchie, *A Bookman's View of Los Angeles* (1961). Photographic commentary is in Mary V. Jessup Hood and Robert Bartlett Haas, "Eadweard Muybridge's Yosemite Valley Photographs, 1867–1872," *California Historical Society Quarterly* 42 (March 1963), 5–26, and Haas,

Muybridge, Man in Motion (1976); Joyce R. Muench, ed., *West Coast Portrait* (1946); Edward Weston, *My Camera on Point Lobos* (1950); Charis Wilson Weston and Edward Weston, *California and the West* (1940); Ansel Adams with Nancy Newhall, *This Is the American Earth* (1959), and Adams, *Yosemite Valley* (1959); and Jonathan Spaulding, *Ansel Adams and the American Landscape* (1997).

About art, see Nancy Moure, *California Art: 450 Years of Painting* (1998); Paul Karlstrom, *On The Edge of America: California's Modernist Art, 1900–1950* (1996); Ruth Westphal and Janet Dominik, *American Scene Painting: California, 1930s and 1940s* (1991); Nancy Friedman, *Art of the State: California* (1998); and Edan Hughes, *Artists in California, 1786– 1940* (1989). Carl Oscar Borg and Millard Sheets, *Cross, Sword, and Gold Pan* (1936); Helen Laird, *Carl Oscar Borg and the Magic Region* (1984); Edith Hamlin, "Maynard Dixon, Artist of the West," *California Historical Quarterly* 53 (Fall 1974), 361–71; Patricia Trenton, *California Light* (1990); and Trenton, *Independent Spirits: Women Painters of the American West* (1997); Susan Landauer, *California Impressionists* (1996); Paul Karlstrom, ed., *On the Edge of America: California Modernist Art* (1996); Jeanne Van Nostrand, *The First Hundred Years of Painting in California* (1980); D. C. McCall, *California Artists, 1935 to 1956* (1981); and Harvey Jones, *Masterpieces of the California Decorative Style* (1980).

Hollywood is the subject of Steven Ross, *Working Class Hollywood* (1998); Giuliana Musico, *Hollywood's New Deal* (1997); Sumiko Higashi, *Cecil B. De Mille and American Culture: the Silent Era* (1994); Charles Clarke, *Early Film Making in Los Angeles* (1976); Tina Lent, "The Dark Side of the Dream: The Image of Los Angeles in Film Noir," *Southern California Quarterly* 69 (Winter 1987), 329–48; Richard Batman, "D. W. Griffith: The Lean Years," *California Historical Society Quarterly* 44 (September 1965), 195–204; Otto Friedrich, *City of Nets: A Portrait of Hollywood in the 1940s* (1986); Leo Rosten, *Hollywood: The Movie Colony, the Movie Makers* (1941); Raymond Moley, *The Hays Office* (1945); and novels by Harry Leon Wilson, *Merton of the Movies* (1922); Nathanael West, *The Day of the Locust* (1939); and Budd Schulberg's *What Makes Sammy Run* (1941).

Updating film history is David Thomson, *The Whole Equation: A History of Hollywood* (2004). The arrival in Hollywood of Arnold Schoenberg, Kurt Weill, and other European refugees is recounted in Reinhold Brinkmann and Christopher Wolff, eds., *Driven Into Paradise* (2000). On the movie moguls, see Scott Eyman, *Lion of Hollywood . . . Louis B. Mayer* (2005); Neil Gabler, *An Empire of Their Own: How the Jews Invented Hol-*

lywood (1989); Bosley Crowther, *Hollywood Rajah: The Life and Times of Louis B. Mayer* (1960).

Other sources include A. R. Fulton, *Motion Pictures . . . From Silent Films to the Age of Telev Balshofer* and Arthur C. Miller, *One Reel a Week* (1967); George N. Fenin and William K. Everson, *The Western, From Silents to Cinerama* (1962); Kenneth MacGowan, *Behind the Screen: The History and Techniques of the Motion Picture* (1965); Beth Day, *This Was Hollywood* (1960); Edward Wagenknecht, *The Movies in the Age of Innocence* (1962); Fred Powdermaker, *Hollywood: The Dream Factory* (1951); and Mervyn Le Roy, *It Takes More Than Talent* (1953).

The religious scene is described in Gregory Singleton, *Religion in the City of Angels: Protestant Culture and Urbanization, 1850–1930* (1997); see also Daniel Epstein, *Sister Aimee* (1993); Lately Thomas, *The Vanishing Evangelist* (1959); and Robert Bahr, *Least of All Saints: The Story of Aimee Semple McPherson* (1979). A whitewash of southern California's "cemetery culture" is Adela Rogers St. John, *First Step Up Toward Heaven* (1959), whereas Evelyn Waugh's *The Loved One* (1948) and Aldous Huxley's *After Many a Summer Dies the Swan* (1939) are both novels that debunk the phenomenon. Regarding utopian colonies see Robert V. Hine, *California's Utopian Colonies* (1953) and Hine, *California Utopianism: Contemplations of Eden* (1981) as well as Emmett A. Greenwalt, *The Point Loma Community in California, 1897–1942* (1955).

For literature see Pearsall and Ursula Erickson, eds., *The Californians: Writings of Their Past and Present* (1960); Richard Lehan, *Los Angeles in Fiction* (1981); Robert Kirsch and William Murphy, *West of the West* (1967); Lawrence Clark Powell, *Land of Fiction* (1952); Cynthia Lindsay, *The Natives Are Restless* (1960); and Jessamyn West, *South of the Angels* (1960).

Two histories of the state's major historical societies are Henry R. Wagner, "California Historical Society, 1852–1922," *California Historical Society Quarterly* 1 (July 1922), 9–22, and Jane Apostol, *The Historical Society of Southern California: A Centennial History* (1991).

On the "Beatniks," consult Gene Feldman and Max Gartenberg, eds., *The Beat Generation and the Angry Young Men* (1958); Thomas Parkinson, ed., *A Casebook on the Beat* (1961); and Lawrence Lipton, *The Holy Barbarians* (1959). More recent are John Maynard, *Venice West: The Beat Generation in Southern California* (1991) and Michael Davidson, *The San Francisco Renaissance* (1989).

Finally, L.A.'s musical development is described in Kenneth Marcus, *Musical Metropolis: Los Angeles and the Creation of a Music Culture, 1880–1940* (2004).

CHAPTER THIRTY-THREE

A CALIFORNIA WORLD OF SPORTS AND LEISURE

"Something for everyone" is the motto that makes California the ideal location for sports and leisure. Its outstanding climate fosters a wide range of sporting activities. The state is reputedly one of the few places in the world where one can go surfing in the morning and skiing in the afternoon. Encouraging a healthy lifestyle is a park system that allows Californians a wide range of year-round activities that include hiking, rock climbing, and bicycling. Along the state's coastline, visitors and citizens alike enjoy walking, surfing, or playing beach volleyball.

Early in the state's history, its free public education brought young people together and led to a wide range of sporting activities. With the goal of creating healthy minds and bodies, early public educators supported supervised competitions complete with coaches and referees. Today, regulated by the NCAA (National Collegiate Athletic Association), university students regularly compete for state and national titles. State schools have become dominant in baseball, golf, tennis, volleyball, swimming, and water polo.

On April 4, 1869, the first women's intercollegiate basketball game was played. It pitted Stanford against the University of California at Berkeley. Male spectators were actually barred from attendance. In the next century, President Richard Nixon signed Title IX, a 1979 federal law that barred gender discrimination in schools and colleges. This legislation forced universities and colleges to provide equal funding for women's and men's sports. Henceforth, women's collegiate athletic programs are thriving. In 1999, the U.S. Women's Soccer Team, playing to an audience of 92,000, won a 5-4 World Cup victory over China at Pasadena's Rose Bowl.

In figure skating, two southern Californians, Michele Kwan and Sasha Cohen, have repeatedly appeared on the world stage, including the Olympic Games. Also growing among women's sports are water polo, swimming, softball, volleyball, tennis, and basketball.

A legendary basketball coach at UCLA is John Wooden. He was the first to be inducted into the "Basketball Hall of Fame" as both a player and a coach. From 1964 to 1975 he led UCLA to ten national championships as the Bruins' coach. Wooden also instilled in his young players what he called his "Pyramid of Success," teaching them lifelong values useful on and off the court. Included in Wooden's "Pyramid" are integrity, reliability, and honesty—elements sorely lacking in today's hypercompetitive sporting world.

The most popular California college sport remains football. The state's "Big-time" football schools include the University of Southern California (USC), the University of California at Berkeley (Cal), UCLA, and Stanford. Programs at all four schools fell on hard times during the 1990s. But USC returned to national prominence in 2001 with the hiring of Pete Carroll, an upbeat coach who quickly led the Trojans to two national championships.

Professional baseball, however, remains the state's best attended sport. Five teams vie for spectators: the San Diego Padres, the California Angels, the Los Angeles Dodgers, the San Francisco Giants, and the Oakland Athletics. The state's ties with the national pastime began in the early twentieth century with the creation of the Pacific Coast League (PCL). Since there was no major league baseball team west of St. Louis until 1958, the PCL introduced minor league baseball via the San Francisco Seals, Oakland Oaks, Hollywood Stars, Los Angeles Angels and San Diego Padres. In their day, Joe DiMaggio, Jackie Robinson, and Ted Williams became well-known baseball stars. More recently, Barry Bonds of the San Francisco Giants, although controversial, surpassed Hank Aaron's home-run record.

By 1958, the Brooklyn Dodgers moved to Los Angeles while the New York Giants chose San Francisco as their new home. Each team achieved quick economic successes in California. In 1961, major league baseball came to include the Angels. And, in 1968 the former Kansas City Athletics became the Oakland A's. California's professional clubs have repeatedly won baseball's "Fall Classic."

The National Football League (NFL) came to California in 1946 when the Cleveland Rams moved to Los Angeles and the 49ers were established in San Francisco. By 1959, the American Football League (AFL) was organized. The next year this new league added two California-based teams, the Chargers and the Raiders, to its ranks. The timing was perfect. Their exciting play and colorful uniforms appeared at the very time when color television sets had become widely affordable. This encouraged the AFL to merge into the NFL. By the 1970s, the Oakland Raiders had

AT&T Park, opened in 2000, is served by more public transporation than any other ballpark in the country and is within walking distance of downtown San Francisco. © San Francisco Giants.

won three Super Bowl Championships. Their 'cross-the-bay rivals, the San Francisco Forty Niners, would win five titles by the year 2000. Meanwhile, Los Angeles has struggled to regain a franchise football team. In 1980, after 49 years (from 1946 to 1994), the Rams left for Saint Louis.

Professional basketball, like baseball and football, came of age in California during the 1960s boom decade. Recognizing the future of the state's sport markets, the National Basketball Association approved relocation of the Minneapolis Lakers to Los Angeles and the Philadelphia Warriors to the Bay Area (where they became known first as the San Francisco Warriors and later as the Golden State Warriors).

Basketball, with such gifted players as Wilt Chamberlin, Jerry West, and Elgin Baylor, rose to new heights with the arrival of Earvin "Magic"

Johnson to the Los Angeles Lakers. Johnson's impact proved immediate, leading the Lakers in 1980 to the first of five championship titles during that decade. His dazzling "no-look" passes to Kareem Abdul-Jabbar and James Worthy characterized the team's fast-breaking style. The term "Showtime" became their popular logo. Among the team's fans were Hollywood entertainment figures. After 2002, led by Coach Phil Jackson, with the talented Shaquille O'Neil and Kobe Bryant, the Lakers won three straight NBA Championships. Completing California's NBA roster are the Sacramento Kings and the Los Angeles Clippers.

Ice hockey has also gained a growing fan base, despite initial predictions that a sport played indoors on ice would not take hold in sun-drenched California. In 1988, helping to popularize this fast-action sport, came the recruitment of Canadian player Wayne Gretsky by the Los Angeles Kings. Called the greatest of all hockey players, Gretsky was a polite, indeed humble, athlete and a perfect ambassador for the sport.

Another figure who fascinated many fans came from East Los Angeles. Latino boxer Oscar de la Hoya was labeled by the press as its "Golden Boy." Handsome and likeable, the 1992 Olympic gold medalist became one of the best pound-for-pound boxers in history, defeating fourteen world champions.

Tennis, formerly tradition-bound, has entered the sports marketplace. Shaking up traditional tennis was Pasadena's May Sutton Bundy. She was the first American to win Wimbledon twice, in 1905 and 1907. Bundy shocked English spectators with her untraditional skirts which daringly allowed her ankles to show. She also rolled up her sleeves to bare her elbows when she competed. May and her sisters, Violet, Florence, and Ethel, were the sport's first tennis stars.

Many decades later, in 1994, the Williams sisters, Venus and Serena, from Lynwood, suddenly took the tennis world by storm with their hard-driving play. Given worldwide television coverage, today's advertisers signed them and other top athletes to endorse their products. With many World Tennis Association titles between them, the two sisters also set fashion trends and encouraged African Americans to take up the game. Other Californians had already become prominent in tennis history. These included Richard "Pancho" Gonzalez, Billie Jean King, Jack Kramer, Michael Chang, Tracy Austin, and Pete Sampras.

Few athletes have had more of an impact on a sport than has golfer Tiger Woods. Born in Cypress, California, Tiger took to the links at early age, appearing on television at age two. The very next year, at age three, he shot an incredible 48 for nine holes. By age nineteen, Woods had become the youngest golfer in history to win the U.S. Amateur Tournament. Be-

Golfer Tiger Woods, April 9, 2007. Photographer: M. Scott.

fore he turned thirty years of age, he had won ten major golf championships, ranking him third on the all-time list behind the golf legends Jack Nicklaus and Walter Hagen. Proud of his African American and Asiatic origins, Woods is an inspiration for young persons of mixed race.

Ocean surfing first made its appearance on the American mainland in 1885. That year three young Hawaiian princes demonstrated their skills off Santa Cruz. Although that region's frigid water temperature prevented the sport from gaining popularity there, two fellow Hawaiians, George Freeth and Duke Kahanamoku, later fostered surfing along the southern California shoreline. The adventure author Jack London, witnessing Freeth's surfing exploits off Waikiki wrote: "He is a Mercury—a brown Mercury. His heels are winged, and in them is the swiftness of the sea." Between 1907 and 1919, Freeth taught swimming, diving, water polo, and surfing to southern California's youngsters. He also formed lifesaving units responsible for saving hundreds of lives. Sadly, the young lifeguard met an early death. Known as the "man who could walk on water," and the recipient of a Congressional Gold Medal for ocean lifesaving, he succumbed at age thirty-five to the ravages of the flu pandemic of 1918–19. After Freeth's passing, his friend and Olympic gold medalist Duke Kahanamoku. traveled throughout California teaching both swimming and surfing.

The famed California lifestyle has evolved out of surfing, affecting popular music, the movies, and fashion. Swimsuit manufacturers in California annually register over $1 billion in sales. Linked to surfing is its impact on tourism. Driven to the state's beaches and neighboring cities were millions of visitors enticed by the music of the Beach Boys and the television show "Baywatch." Both projected an image of California as a place of "sun and fun."

Also popular is beach volleyball. In the early 1930s, the first two-on-two tournaments began on the beaches of southern California. Today this sport attracts millions of viewers and has been played as an Olympic competition. During the winter months, skiing and snow boarding thrive at Lake Tahoe, Mammoth, and Big Bear Lake. Water skiing too is popular on rivers, lakes, and sheltered bays.

Californians have invented some unique sports products. In 1963, a Santa Monica lifeguard, Larry Stevenson, fashioned today's skateboard. The word soon spread that surfers could enjoy the year-round thrill of riding on "concrete waves" via Stevenson's Makaha Skateboard. Its urethane wheels provided the grip needed to ride even rough surfaces.

Another recreation, developed early in the state's American era, was horse racing, which gained popularity even before California became a state. Its first adherents organized races on makeshift tracks inside pueblo plazas or in neighboring vacant fields. In 1899, Tanforan Race Track, then a state-of-the-art facility, was built on a Mexican land grant in San Bruno. Among its supporters and horse owners were a "who's who" of California history, including Leland Stanford, Adolph Spreckels, and Lucky Baldwin. The "Sport of Kings," however, gained its greatest popularity in California during the Great Depression. The Santa Anita track was dedicated in 1934 and was followed one year later by the opening of Northern California's Bay Meadows. Other tracks that opened up in the 1930s included Hollywood Park and Del Mar, best known as the track where "the surf meets the turf."

Auto racing, too, became a spectator favorite. In 1910, some 4,000 fans gathered to watch four cars race each other on a hastily constructed half-mile track at Playa Del Rey. There, legendary racer Barney Oldfield, riding his "Blitzen Benz" speedster, brought the packed crowd to its feet, breaking the then-unthinkable 100 km/h (60 miles per hour) barrier. By 1914, he was called the "Master of Speed" and was responsible for drawing crowds of over 50,000 to watch him race. By the end of the twentieth century, California possessed 200 racetracks. Among the sport's highest attended events in California are Nascar-sanctioned races, drag racing, and the annual Long Beach Formula One Grand Prix event.

AVP and Olympic Gold Medalists, Misty May-Treanor and Kerri Walsh at play, September 2006. The two are volleyball's most dominant doubles team, having won more than eighty professional beach volleyball tournaments. Photographer: Patrick Lee Mann.

The most prestigious of all athletic events are the Olympic Games. In 1932 the Tenth Summer Olympiad took place in Los Angeles. These games had the lowest participation by athletes from around the world, due to the Great Depression and the notion that Los Angeles was then a remote western outpost. Yet, Angeleños roared their approval of Mildred Didrikson as she won two gold medals and one silver medal in track-and-field events. Later known as "Babe" Zaharias, she became one of the best women golfers of all time, and arguably the best female athlete of the twentieth century.

California also held the 1960 winter Olympics at Squaw Valley. The Summer Games returned to Los Angeles in 1984. Despite dire predictions that these games would be plagued by terrorism, air pollution, traffic, and insufficient funding, they were one of the most successful on record. The organizers avoided the outlay of public funds by obtaining corporate sponsorships, selling advertising at high rates, and housing athletes at university dormitories. Some 50,000 volunteers helped to run the 1984 competitions.

The state's ties to such a variety of sports have made it a world leader in marketing. Sporting manufacturers, such as the Callaway Golf, Volcom, and Body Glove companies, sell their products around the globe. Other profitable companies include Nicket, based at the City of Industry, which manufactures clubs engineered for women golfers, and the Oakley Company of Beverly Hills, which specializes in sunglasses and ski goggles.

California's deep ties to sports and leisure make it an ideal location to hold competitive events. Its all-year climate allows a wide range of sports now televised to a global audience. The skills displayed and the clothing worn by the athletes have enabled the state to remain a worldwide leader in both sporting events and popular athletic fashions.

SELECTED READINGS

Regarding sports in California, consult Arthur Verge, "George Freeth: King of the Surfers and California's Forgotten Hero," *California History* 80 (Summer, 2001), 83–105; and Verge *Los Angeles County Lifeguards* (2005); Donald J. Mrozek, "The Image of the West in American Sport," *Journal of the American West* (July 1978), 3–15; Kevin Nelson, *The Story of California Baseball* (2004); Neil Sullivan, *The Dodgers Move West* (1987); Glenn Dickey, *San Francisco Giants* (1995); John Strege, *Tiger: A Biography of Tiger Woods* (1998); Matt Warshaw, *The Encyclopedia of Surfing* (2003); Michael Brooke, *The Concrete Wave: The History of Skateboarding* (1999); Pat Yeomans, *Southern California Tennis Champions, 1887–1987* (1988); B. J. King, *Billie Jean* (1975); Sinjin Smith and Neil Feineman, *Kings of the Beach: A History of Beach Volleyball* (1988); Laura Hillenbrand, *Seabiscuit: An American Legend* (2001); Richard B. Perelman and Mark Meyers, *Unforgettable!: The Hundred Greatest Moments in Los Angeles Sports History* (1995); Art Evans, *The Fabulous Fifties: Sports Car Races in Southern California* (2002); More general are Karl B. Raitz, *The Theatre of Sport* (1995); Kathryn Grove, *Hard at Play: Leisure in America* (1992); and Richard Krause, *Recreation and Leisure* (1997).

CHAPTER THIRTY-FOUR

WARTIME SETBACKS AND GAINS

During the years leading up to the United States' entry into World War II, the state also faced the threat posed by the European dictators and the Japanese military clique. The Japanese dive-bombing attack, on December 7, 1941, upon the U.S. Fleet in Pearl Harbor in Hawaii created widespread panic. Soon thereafter, Californians heard reports of the surrender of Sumatra, Borneo, and the Philippines. Could their state be next?

Wartime preparations would lead to great economic dislocations and social tensions. Labor shortages, rationing, and finding enough transportation, were only a few of the new challenges. The need to house defense workers became a high priority. Military training camps, shipyards, and aircraft factories had to be constructed quickly. Nothing could be allowed to impede the speeding of planes, tanks, and guns to the fighting front.

California's war industries drew workers from all parts of the United States. The state dismantled its depression-era "bum blockade" formerly erected against invading "Okies" and "Arkies." Border officials did an about-face, encouraging all workers to flock westward for employment in new war plants. Local chambers of commerce also encouraged related industries to move into the state.

Internal security became paramount. The state legislature passed the Dilworth Anti-Spy Bill, as well as the Slater Anti-Sabotage Act, and the Tenney Anti-Subversive Law. This legislation reflected a mounting antipathy toward the Japanese. By 1940, there were 120,000 Japanese and Japanese Americans in California. As fishermen, cannery workers, and farmers, those of Japanese heritage evoked growing public hostility. Their increasing affluence set them apart from the white majority. Jealous competitors resurrected nativist fears that Asians were not assimilable.

Fear of a Japanese attack spread from Hawaii to the mainland. In early 1942, a lone Japanese submarine surfaced near Santa Barbara and fired several shells at some oil storage tanks. Although the shelling did little

World War II evacuation sale at Okano Bros. five and dime store in San Francisco, 1942. Courtesy of the Franklin D. Roosevelt Library Digital Archives.

damage, jittery residents nearby put their houses up for sale and made plans to flee inland. On February 25, 1942, the *Los Angeles Times* boldly, and quite erroneously, reported that Japanese planes had bombed the city. Anti-aircraft fire had been shot into the sky, but against imaginary aircraft.

Many of California's Japanese-heritage residents were born and educated in the United States. There was no real evidence that they were disloyal. But there were hysterical demands that all those of Japanese heritage be interned, lest they manage to collaborate with the enemy. On February 18, 1942, President Roosevelt signed Executive Order 9066, placing Japanese Americans under military control. U.S. Army General John De Witt, head of the Western Defense Command, ordered 112,000 West Coast Japanese, two-thirds of them American citizens, subject to relocation. They were forced to quickly sell their homes, businesses, and land at a fraction of their value. Speculators greedily took advantage of their plight. In addition, radios, cameras, and all "suspicious" personal effects were confiscated by federal agents. Thousands of Japanese Americans were then herded onto buses that took them away to "relocation centers" at Manzanar and Tule Lake. At these camps, the evacuees lived in stark conditions behind barbed wire under military guard. The prisoners included *Issei* (persons born in Japan), *Nisei* (those born in the U.S.), and *Kibei* (American-born but educated in Japan).

Among the state's politicians supporting the move to detain these innocent persons was Earl Warren, then California's attorney general. Running for the governorship in 1942, he fell sway to arguments made by the American Legion, the Native Sons and Daughters of the Golden West, and the State Federation of Labor, all of whom supported evacuating those of Japanese heritage from the Pacific coast. Although Warren won against Culbert Olsen, he would later admit that supporting the internment of the Japanese and Japanese Americans was the greatest mistake of his life. Later, as Chief Justice of the U.S. Supreme Court, he would become a staunch defender of civil rights.

During the war, few citizens had the courage to speak out against the internment of "enemy" aliens, who also included Germans and Italians. In 1942, however, the German-born expatriate novelist Thomas Mann protested before the investigative Tolan Committee. From California, other famous artists, mostly foreign-born, including Lion Feuchtwanger, Bruno Frank, and Maestro Arturo Toscanini, sent telegrams to Washington on behalf of European internees. So did physicist Albert Einstein. In an atmosphere of suspicion, their efforts, however, were fruitless.

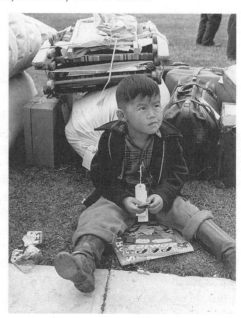

Japanese American boy waiting by his family's belongings to be transported to a War Relocation Authority Camp, Salinas, California, 1942. Library of Congress, LC-USZF34T01-72499D.

By 1944, the first Japanese American internees were allowed to leave relocation centers for coastal areas. Two years later the incarceration program ended. Some Japanese Americans never returned to California, settling elsewhere. Historians who studied the evacuation in calmer postwar years concluded that it represented a flagrant violation of constitutional rights. Only long after World War II did the federal government authorize payments of $20,000 to former internees. By then most of the Issei among them were already dead.

While the internment of Japanese Americans was not the finest hour in the history of the nation, a remarkable change has since occurred in the public attitude toward all minorities. The Japanese Americans who fought on behalf of the U.S. during World War II, even though their families were behind barbed wire, won the hearts and minds of Californians. Especially notable was the highly decorated all-Japanese American 442nd Regimental Combat Team.

Wartime racial tensions also spilled over into the state's Latino communities. Unforgettable were the infamous Zoot Suit Riots. Mexican Americans who were thought to be gang members, called *Pachucos*, aroused the ire of the Los Angeles police. Accused of carrying switchblade knives in their pockets and razor blades in their long hair, the Pachucos became the target of American servicemen on leave. In June of 1943, at Los Angeles, some white hoodlums joined sailors and Marines on leave in a two-week rampage against young Mexican Americans dressed in the "Zoot-Suit" style, which consisted of a long jacket, baggy pants, a pork pie hat, and an overlong watch chain. Although no one was killed in the riots, some persons were injured. The riots involved racist assaults on innocent persons. Yet, actual gang activity of some young Mexican Americans embarrassed their elders. Fortunately, such youths were in the distinct minority. Nearly 500,000 Mexican Americans served in the armed forces, winning thirty-nine Congressional Medals of Honor. Like the Japanese Americans, they had fought hard for acceptance.

As California's new governor in 1943, Earl Warren had played a big role in the Japanese internment program. Like the aging Hiram Johnson, whose picture he had proudly hung in his Sacramento office, Warren was a both a moderate and a progressive. Informal and easy-going, Warren projected a reassuring image during the stressful war years. Because of the war, he enjoyed a moratorium on political as well as labor discord. Most labor disputes were handled by arbitration. In some cases the governor himself acted as arbitrator. Warren easily won reelection in 1946 and 1950. He became the only California governor to serve three terms. In the 1946 election, Warren was also the only candidate ever to receive both the Republican and Democratic nominations. This was due to cross-filing, adopted by the legislature back in 1913.

Essential to winning World War II was the training of military troops and stepped up industrial production. Given California's strategic location, fronting the Pacific Ocean, the federal government pumped $35 billion into military bases and defense plants there. Hundreds of thousands of defense workers, soldiers, sailors, and airmen flooded into the state. Military posts became virtual cities with their own supply, transportation, and postal facilities. One of the largest, Camp Roberts, housed upwards of 50,000 men. Another big army depot was Fort Ord, located between Monterey and Salinas. At the Desert Training Center, over a million soldiers, including General George Patton's renowned Tank Corps, were trained. Camp Pendleton, near Oceanside, became a new west coast base for the Marine Corps. San Diego, Long Beach, and Mare Island were already major naval bases. There were also air training centers at March Field, the El Toro Marine Air Depot, and the Alameda Naval Air Station. California's ports too became huge troop embarkation centers for the Pacific war zone.

No segment of California's economy was so well poised to contribute to the war effort as its aircraft industry. As early as 1912, Glenn Martin had established an airplane production facility first at Los Angeles and later in Baltimore. In 1927, Charles Lindbergh, "The Lone Eagle," commissioned the San Diego–based Ryan Aeronautical Corporation to build his *Spirit of Saint Louis*. In this plane, "Lindy" became the first person to fly across the Atlantic Ocean.

Using the carrot of profit motivation, the federal government was able to get civilian aircraft and shipbuilders to convert their operations into massive wartime production centers. Once-small manufacturers evolved into major corporations. Donald Douglas, who had begun his aircraft company in 1920 in the back of a Santa Monica barbershop, oversaw six major aircraft plants that employed 160,000 workers by 1944. His Douglas Corporation would build almost 30,000 warplanes.

Henry Kaiser, who prior to the war had built roads and dams but never a ship, used prefabrication and assembly-line techniques to become the nation's leading shipbuilder. Kaiser put together cruisers, destroyers, and cargo carriers. The workforce at his Richmond Yard alone numbered more than 100,000. At the height of the war, Kaiser's "Calship" Corporation turned out one Liberty ship a day. He also constructed the largest steel mill in the American West at Fontana. Kaiser also formed today's Kaiser-Permanente health organization, originally to care for wartime workers. On the Richmond, Oakland, and San Pedro waterfronts, the Todd and

World War II assembly-line workers of boith sexes contribute to the pro-
duction of an A-20 attack bomber at the Douglas Aircraft plant in Long
Beach, California, 1943. Courtesy of the Franklin D. Roosevelt Library Digital
Archives.

Bethlehem shipyards hammered out hundreds of combat vessels. The
United States Maritime Commission also reopened shipyards at Sausalito
and Vallejo that had been idle since World War I.

In southern California, plane manufacturers took advantage of cheap
land and power to expand their plants. Once small in size and scope, the
region's aircraft industry prospered as never before. Favorable weather
even allowed planes to be built outdoors. Warplanes were tested over the
region's varied topography that included the ocean, mountains and deserts. California-based aircraft companies such as Douglas, North American, Northrup, Convair, Consolidated Vultee, and Hughes became known
throughout the world. Helping to turn the course of the war were the
mass production of the B-17 Flying Fortress, the B-25 Mitchell, the
Douglas-designed troop-and-cargo-carrying C-47 and North American's
P-51 Mustang fighters.

Among the giants of the aircraft industry was the Lockheed Company, founded by two Canadians, Malcolm and Allan Loughead. In 1932,
they sold their then moribund firm to investment banker Robert Gross
who restructured it. Later, two renowned pilots, Charles Lindbergh and

Amelia Earhart, set flying records in Lockheed aircraft. The twin engine Electra earned the company an international reputation. During the war Lockheed employed a 90,000-person workforce, producing Hudson bombers for Britain. The company also developed the P-38 fighter, the Ventura, and the 128-passenger Constitution.

California's production efforts relied heavily on recruiting defense workers. Over a million and half of them were drawn to the Golden State. As men went off to war, women joined the industrial work force. "We Can Do It," became their motto. Fondly recalled as "Rosie the Riveter," women war workers proved crucial in keeping production on schedule. In 1943, with over 40 percent of its workforce female, aircraft plants near Los Angeles turned out a new warplane every seven minutes.

The war also opened long-closed factory doors to minorities. President Franklin Roosevelt's Executive Order 8802 forbade discriminatory hiring practices by companies receiving federal defense contracts. Job opportunities served to improve worker's financial stability and self-esteem. Racial discrimination, however, did remain in segregated military units, labor unions, and local public housing.

As factory production increased, the environment suffered. *Smog*, a combination of the words *smoke* and *fog*, appeared rather suddenly. Overtaxed factory and municipal sewage lines also dumped waste water into bays, rivers, and the Pacific Ocean. Another problem was record population growth. For example, Vallejo, a war production center, soared from 20,000 residents in 1941 to over 100,000 by 1943. San Diego's population doubled during the war years. Housing and health issues also became paramount. G.I.s, when on leave, too often slept in movie theaters or public parks. In such cramped conditions, communicable disease rates soared. Law enforcement had to contend with record numbers of juvenile delinquents whose parents were away sometimes working at two war jobs. Californians dealt with gas and food rationing by utilizing public transportation and growing vegetables in backyards and vacant lots (called "Victory Gardens"). Those who complained about shortages, blackouts, or other related difficulties, were often rebuked with, "Don't you know there's a war going on?"

In April of 1945, as the war in Europe drew to a close, representatives of forty-six nations met at San Francisco. These delegates planned to transform their wartime alliances against the Axis powers into a permanent structure for world peace. They signed the United Nations Charter on October 24, 1945. Among the reporters covering this event was a young, recently demobilized, veteran named John F. Kennedy, future president of the United States.

World War II was one of the major turning points of California's history. The state rapidly emerged as the nation's "Arsenal of Democracy," a major staging area for the Pacific battlefronts. Its sped-up industrialization and urban growth encouraged 2 million defense workers to move into the state, many of them permanently. The natural beauty, good weather, and employment opportunities of the state, proved to be an irresistible beacon. Transformed as a portal to the Pacific world, the state once again became the land of golden opportunity.

SELECTED READINGS

Regarding World War II, see Arthur Verge, *Paradise Transformed: Los Angeles During the Second World War* (1993); Roger Lotchin, *The Way We Were: The Golden State in the Second World War* (2000); Marilynn Johnson, *The Second Gold Rush: Oakland and the East Bay in World War II* (1993) and Gerald Nash, *The American West Transformed: The Impact of the Second World War* (1985).

As to the internment of Japanese Americans, consult Lawson Inada, ed., *Only What We Could Carry: The Japanese Internment Experience* (2000); Peter Irons, *Justice at War* (1983); The United States Army version of Japanese relocation is *Japanese Evacuation from the West Coast* (1943). See also Stetson Conn, "The Decision to Evacuate the Japanese from the Pacific Coast, 1942," in Kent Roberts Greenfield, *Command Decisions* (1959); Miné Okubo, *Citizen 13660* (repr. 1983); Morton Grodzins, *Americans Betrayed: Politics and the Japanese Evacuation* (1949); Roger Daniels, *Concentration Camps USA: Japanese Americans and World War II* (1971) and his *The Decision to Relocate the Japanese Americans* (1975); Harry Kitano, *Japanese Americans, The Evolution of a Subculture* (1969); Bill Hosokawa, *Nisei, the Quiet Americans* (1969); Jeanne Wakatsuki and James Houston, *Farewell to Manzanar* (1973); Leonard Bloom and Ruth Riemar, *Removal and Return* (1949); Audrie Girdner and Anne Loftis, *The Evacuation of the Japanese-Americans During World War II* (1969); Michi Weglyn, *Years of Infamy* (1976); John Modell, *The Economics and Politics of Racial Accommodation: The Japanese of Los Angeles, 1900–1942* (1977); and Earl Warren, *Memoirs* (1977).

Regarding other wartime strife, Josh Sides, "Battle on the Homefront: African American Shipyard Workers in World War II Los Angeles," *California History* 3 (Fall, 1996), 222–97; Albert Broussard, *Black San Francisco...* (2001); Gloria Lothrop, "Unwelcome in Freedom's Land: The Impact of World War II on Italian Aliens in Southern California," *South-*

ern California Quarterly 81 (Winter, 1999), 507–44; Maurizio Mazón, *The Zoot Suit Riots* . . . (1984); Ralph Banay, "A Psychiatrist Looks at the Zoot Suit," *Probation* 12 (February 1944), 81–85; Harold De Witt, "The Watsonville Anti-Filipino Riot of 1930," *Southern California Quarterly* 61 (Fall 1979), 291–302; and Ricardo Romo, "Southern California and the Origins of Latino Civil-Rights Activism," *Western Legal History* 3 (Summer/Fall, 1990), 379–406.

Concerning wartime military production, see Wayne Biddle, *Barons of the Sky: From Early Flight to Strategic Warfare* (1991); William Schoneberger, *California Wings: A History of Aviation in the Golden State* (1984); Hugh Knowlton, *Air Transportation in the United States* (1941); Mark Foster, *Henry J. Kaiser: Builder in the Modern American West* (1989) and Roger W. Lotchin, *Fortress California, 1910–1961: From Warfare to Welfare* (1992).

In reference to women war workers, see Sherna Gluck, ed., *Rosie the Riveter* (1987); Susan Hartman, *The Homefront and Beyond: American Women in the 1940s* (1982) as well as Nancy and Christy Wise, *A Mouthful of Rivets* (1994).

CALIFORNIA
AFTER WORLD WAR II

As reconversion to a peacetime economy began, the fear of business mortality among war-born defense plants loomed over California. Domination of manufacturing by companies that had grown exponentially during the war posed another threat. A third source of anxiety concerned how to provide future employment for the huge number of wartime workers who had moved into the state. Thousands of returning service men and women swelled the tide of new residents. Fortunately most of these veterans obtained postwar employment. The "G. I. Bill of Rights" paid those who had served their country to enroll in a college of their choice. This bonus was also designed to help veteran employment prospects.

Wartime manufacturing had diversified the economy. Business was originally clustered around too few industries. Among them were citrus, film, aircraft, and oil. California suddenly enjoyed a larger share of national per capita income than it had ever known. Factories were going full blast. Everyone seemed to have a job, as airplanes and Jeeps, redesigned for peacetime, rolled off former wartime assembly lines. Among the new products that appeared in the postwar era were sportswear, jewelry, and footwear. Sorely needed were refrigeration equipment, technical instruments, chemicals, hardware, and cosmetics for national markets. Los Angeles continued as an automobile assembly depot second only to Detroit, as well as a tube and tire center. Before the war, only minor smelting and refining of ferrous metals had occurred. After 1943, Kaiser's Fontana mill began to process iron ore from Eagle Mountain and tungsten from the Rand Mountains.

More apartments, schools, business sites, and public facilities had to be built, and this required the services of engineers, architects, and all sorts of construction workers. There seemed to be no end to the migration of postwar newcomers who crowded into the Golden State. In 1940, California had a population of 6,907,387. It then ranked only fifth among the

California Freeway system. A large highway (I-405) near LAX. © Xavier Marchant/ Dreamstime.com.

states. By 1950, when the population reached 10,586,223, California had become the second most populous state in the nation. Schoolrooms were so crowded that teachers were forced to meet their classes in several shifts daily.

In those years of spreading housing tracts, thousands of war veterans formed new family units. Postwar California experienced one of the great construction booms of all time. For mile after mile, cities began to replicate themselves. Acres of raw lumber framework, stacks of bricks, and sacks of cement went into thousands of new dwellings. Large-scale tract development occurred at such "instant" cities as Westchester and West Covina in southern California and at Burlingame and Lafayette in the north.

During a single day in 1946, one real estate firm alone sold 107 homes at Lakewood Village within one hour! Its developers boasted that every fifteen minutes construction crews dug foundation trenches for a new tract home. Lakewood covered 3,300 acres of land with 133 miles of paved streets and driveways. Other unincorporated communities, such as Saratoga, Campbell, Monte Sereno, Los Altos, and Milpitas in Santa Clara County, as well as Pacifica and Woodside in San Mateo County, quickly incorporated themselves as new cities.

An incomplete freeway system became so jammed that California soon recorded the highest auto accident rate in the nation. In 1947, the legislature approved a ten-year highway construction program. The state proceeded to spend more than $1 million per working day on new freeways and highways. Transportation engineers planned a 12,500-mile statewide road system to link all cities with a population of 5,000 or more, as well as to tie into the federal highway network.

Automotive industries and services became a key element in all this planning. Organizations like the Automobile Club of Southern California grew politically powerful. By 1967, California had more drivers and cars registered—almost 10 million—than any other state in the union. The Los Angeles area had become the fastest-growing fuel market in the world.

Meanwhile, traffic congestion increased. Although the legislature in 1964 had approved a Southern California Rapid Transit District (RTD) to plan intracity transportation, new road construction could not keep up

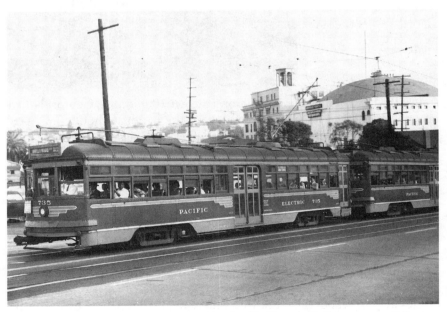

Once a popular form of mass transit, the Pacific Electric Railway system fell victim to Angelenos' love affair with the automobile. In the far right can be seen Sister Aimee Semple McPherson's Angelus Temple. Courtesy of Milton Slade.

with demand. At Los Angeles, sensible subway proposals were repeatedly killed. Legions of critics pointed out that the city had far too many urban centers. Some blamed politicians, auto dealers, tire manufacturers, and the threat of higher taxes for delays in developing viable systems of mass transportation. Others believed that there had been a conspiracy by the oil and bus industries to sabotage the city's Pacific Electric Railway System. Nevertheless, voters simply refused to abandon their freeway mentality and hostility to mass transit. Most commuters refused to abandon their autos for daily transportation.

In 1964, however, a San Francisco freeway revolt stopped construction of its Embarcadero Freeway. Voters had tired of endless freeway construction. Local conservation groups also struggled to keep the state's Panhandle Freeway out of Golden Gate Park. In place of these roadways, construction of the Bay Area Rapid Transit (BART) system began. This light rail and bus project, built with public approval, proved to be highly successful. It connected most cities of the East Bay. Tunnels dug under the bay then linked them to the peninsula via subway lines.

Other freeway revolts occurred at Laguna Beach and South Pasadena. In both cities, irate citizens prevented new freeways from bisecting residential areas as well as destroying parks and historic sites. In 1965, one plan involved destruction of the Santa Monica Pier. In its place, a freeway would traverse the coastline to Malibu. Governor Pat Brown vetoed such legislation. Freeways were also kept out of such beauty spots as Prairie Creek in Jedediah Smith Redwoods Park and Upper Crystal Springs Lake along the Junípero Serra Freeway.

For years the powerful Automobile Club of Southern California opposed mass transit beyond buses. Other pro-automobile concerns were the major oil companies and car dealers. They reminded the public that subway systems could not be built without some form of government-financed support. Subsidies were especially needed in areas of low population density. Because of steady postwar inflation, each year's delay led construction costs to grow astronomically.

Population growth, meanwhile, forced expansion and reconstruction of civic areas. San Francisco, confined to a peninsula, had to utilize its land space carefully. Thus, the process of building skyward accelerated. The city also built Candlestick Park as a home for the former New York Giants baseball club. In 1958, Los Angeles too attracted the Brooklyn Dodgers and constructed a new stadium in Chavez Ravine. L.A. also undertook reconstruction of its central city. Around a mall that covered 228 acres, new 20- to 40-story federal, state, county, and city government office buildings sprang up in formerly blighted areas.

Conservationists did not agree that all these changes represented progress. For example, Carmel's residents, in order to preserve their tiny community's decor, refused to install new sidewalks and house numbering, even though this meant they could not have home mail delivery. As the shift from single-family homes to apartments continued, California's urban skyline changed markedly, with more vertical construction ensuing. Rising land costs made it uneconomical to build single-family dwellings in downtown areas. Whether at Los Angeles, San Diego, or Oakland, a new style of supposedly efficient architecture featured multistoried apartments and office buildings, many of them built of high-rise lightweight metal and much window glass.

Continuing heavy defense expenditures underwrote a large share of California's postwar reconstruction. The state increasingly possessed what amounted to a nongovernmental civil service, with aircraft, missile, and instrument workers indirectly dependent upon the federal government for jobs. Obviously, this made a large sector of the state's economy vulnerable to national budget cuts. For decades, however, America's cold war and intensifying arms race with the Soviet Union provided California with juicy federal military contracts.

The establishment in 1954 of the U.S. Air Force's Space Technology Laboratory near Inglewood and Canoga Park, and the founding of the

B-1 bomber flies over Edwards Air Force Base. Official U.S. Air Force photo.

CHAPTER THIRTY-FIVE   331

IBM Research Laboratory at San Jose and Astronautics, Inc., at San Diego, further immersed California in missile, rocket, and satellite research and development. A significant event of the late 1950s was the activation of the nation's first privately financed nuclear power plant at Vallecitos. In that decade the new Pacific Missile Range also became a major launching site.

Meanwhile, the construction of Vandenberg Air Force Base changed nearby Lompoc from a rural town concerned with mining diatomaceous soil and flower raising to a city of 30,000 inhabitants. Several hundred technological companies, which employed more than 100,000 persons, settled within a mile of Los Angeles's new international airport. The 1950s also saw the dawn of the jet age. The first such experimental jet flight was by pilot Chuck Yeager at Edwards Air Force Base, a desolate moonscape on the Mojave Desert. This was followed by the supersonic flight of X-15, a combination of rocket and airplane.

By 1962, some 40 percent of the nation's $6.1 billion in contracts for military testing and research went to California. New university-industrial campuses housed sophisticated engineering and technology facilities. By 1968, one-third of California's industrial production was in the defense and space fields. The North American Company's El Segundo plant developed the XB-70 (Valkyrie) bomber and the X-15 airplane as well as the guidance and control systems of the Boeing Company's Minuteman missile. North American's Rocketdyne Division powered thirty-six of the first forty U.S. space probes. Rocketdyne also developed the H-1 Saturn Rocket. North American coordinated its efforts with those of NASA, Caltech's JPL, and the Space Technology Laboratories, operated for the Air Force by Thompson, Ramo, Wooldridge, Inc. North American was also the prime contractor of the Apollo moonship, while Rockwell International developed the B-1 bomber as well as NASA's first Space Shuttle.

In the nuclear age, the Lockheed Corporation of Burbank and Sunnyvale, like North American, remained active both in missile and aircraft production. Lockheed, in addition to producing the Polaris submarine missile for the U.S. Navy, was the main contractor for the Midas system of detecting ICBM (intercontinental ballistic missile) firings anywhere in the world. Lockheed played a key part as well in the development of the Samos spy-in-the-sky satellite.

By the 1970s, Lockheed's L-1011, a wide-bodied passenger jet, was featured in the fleets of major commercial airlines. Competing with that airplane was the McDonnell-Douglas DC-10, repeatedly modified after the war. This same firm had successfully converted from production of the Apache and Hornet warplanes, as well as Delta and Tomahawk missiles, to manufacturing commercial airplanes. The MD-11, the MD-80, and the MD-90 are now outdated. In 1997, McDonnell-Douglas merged with the Boeing Corporation. At San Diego, Convair, later General Dynamics, built the F-106 Delta Dart fighter and the 880 jet airliner. Its prize product was the Atlas ICBM Missile, with a range of nearly 10,000 miles.

In support of California's plane and missile industry, more than 200 high-tech electronic firms operated plants in the peninsula suburbs south of San Francisco alone. Among these were such national companies as IBM, ITT, Ampex, Hewlett-Packard, Western Electric, Raytheon, Remington Rand, Sylvania, Sperry-Rand, Zenith, Motorola, Philco, and General Electric. Today the phrase "Silicon Valley" connotes electronic specialization worldwide.

Increasing investment was centered in the state. As it moved beyond regional domination into national leadership, California has been described as "America only more so." In recent years its gross product has been exceeded only by that of the United States itself and six other countries!

Politically, too, California's power grew at the national level. In 1953, when President Dwight Eisenhower called Governor Earl Warren to Washington to become chief justice of the United States, California's "Warren era" of politics came to a close. Soon, another son of California, Richard Milhous Nixon, would rise to national prominence. A former Navy veteran, he first ran in 1946 for the seat held by liberal congressman Jerry Voorhis, a Democrat in Nixon's Yorba Linda home district. Nixon won and four years later ran for the U.S. Senate against Helen Gahagan Douglas, a liberal Democratic congresswoman and wife of film star Melvyn Douglas. In his campaign Nixon was quick to point his finger at alleged "Communists," suggesting that both Voorhis and Douglas were lacking in their anti-Communist convictions.

The nation's second Red Scare was spearheaded by Republican Senator Joseph McCarthy of Wisconsin. He and Richard Nixon accused various public officials, film personalities, and labor leaders of treasonable acts. As a fledgling congressman, Nixon also furthered his career by association with ultraconservatives who advocated severe restrictions on incoming foreigners. An almost hysterical fear of Communism led to passage of the highly restrictive Mundt-Nixon Immigration Act.

Also bolstering Nixon's image as a guardian of internal security was his seat on the powerful House Un-American Activities Committee. He helped bring to trial former State Department aide Alger Hiss for per-

After a remarkable political comeback that astonished friends and foes alike, Richard Nixon won the U.S. presidency in 1968. Courtesy of the Richard Nixon Library and Birthplace.

jury concerning espionage charges. In these politically tense years, state senator Jack B. Tenney headed a state committee that claimed to have detected Communists in California's government and educational circles. To uproot these alleged subversives in public life, Tenney recommended that teachers and government employees be required to sign a loyalty oath. Beginning in 1949, a test-oath controversy raged on the campuses of the University of California. Professors who bravely refused to sign an oath stating that they were not Communists and were loyal to the United States, lost their jobs. Ultimately the California Supreme Court ruled this oath invalid. But, in 1950, the legislature's Levering Act required an even more elaborate oath of all state employees. As a result, the University of California lost some of its most talented and independent-minded faculty members. In 1958, yet another California loyalty oath was struck down by the U.S. Supreme Court.

From 1952 until 1960, Nixon, who had become vice president under Eisenhower, occupied the most prestigious position of any California Republican. Nixon, like Earl Warren earlier, benefited from cross-filing. This unique political device was in force from 1913 to 1958, when it was abolished. Cross-filing permitted any candidate to file for the nomination of more than one party. In California, where Democratic registration has traditionally been heavier than Republican, cross-filing worked in favor of the Republicans. Successful candidates for public office, especially incumbents, could thereby capture both party nominations. By campaigning as a nonpartisan, any candidate who won the nomination of both parties could count on the support of the state's large proportion of independent voters.

In California, as well as nationally, candidates came to rely upon professional P.R. firms to publicize their campaigns. Since the 1930s, these organizations, by the use of mass-media techniques, learned how to manipulate public sentiment in favor of a particular candidate or ballot proposal. These public relations firms went on to devise many of the campaign posters, slogans, and clichés of America's recent political history.

A less excusable variety of political lobbying involved Artie Samish, the "Mr. Big" of California politics. Throughout the 1940s and into the early 1950s, the ruthless Samish ran the "Third House" of the California state legislature, receiving fat fees to lobby in the favor of truck and bus lines, liquor interests, race tracks, and other, confidential, clients. Samish romped through the legislature as though he had prerogatives superior to those of its members. His spree ended in 1953, when he was convicted of evading federal income taxes and sent to jail.

By 1958, the Republican hegemony in California had unraveled. A political squabble within the party helped cause its ouster. Republican Senator William Knowland, who wanted the governorship, forced the incumbent, Governor Goodwin Knight, out of the race. Into the breach stepped the Democratic state attorney general Edmund "Pat" Brown. Like Earl Warren, Brown knew how to conduct a nonpartisan political campaign. Brown too was swept into the state's executive office. He faced controversial and statewide problems, including traffic and smog control, water development, and a debate over capital punishment.

In Sacramento Brown was a new figure with novel ideas about building a state college system, improving water projects, streamlining government agencies, and creating modern transportation systems. Jesse Unruh, the powerful speaker of the state assembly, aided Brown in bringing the governor's hopes to realization. In 1959, he pushed through the legislature the far-reaching Unruh Civil Rights Act. This barred discrimination in business transactions and access to public facilities, including hotels, restaurants, and even clubs.

In 1960, Vice President Nixon became the nominee of the Republican Party for the presidency. Nominated at the Democratic National

Convention, in Los Angeles's new Sports Arena, was Massachusetts Senator John F. Kennedy. In the subsequent election, Nixon, the native son, won California by a narrow margin. But this proved insufficient to prevent Kennedy's election as president.

Two years later, in 1962, Nixon challenged Brown for the governorship. Failure to win this contest, political pundits predicted, might impair Nixon's chances of remaining a public figure. The campaign was a bitter one. Nixon accused Brown of being soft on Communists and of bungling administration of the state, but the governor won reelection by a wide majority. It seemed that Nixon's political career was indeed over. But, before the end of the decade, President Kennedy would be assassinated and Nixon would later go on to a presidential victory. But his presidency would be stained by deceitfulness uncovered during the congressional Watergate hearings.

In the early 1960s, the California Democratic Council, which had built up a productive statewide organization, began to disintegrate. The CDC was especially critical of Governor Pat Brown's timid leadership of the party, blaming him for having allowed factionalism to develop. This Democratic infighting resembled the bloodletting that had hurt California's Republican party back in 1958. The state's independent or "maverick" Democrats included Samuel William Yorty, elected mayor of Los Angeles in 1961, who had bolted from the party in 1960 to back Nixon against Kennedy. Assembly Speaker Jesse Unruh, who, like Yorty, had ambitions for higher office, became a lone wolf who guarded his powerful role in Sacramento, much as Artie Samish had done. The Democrats had become a fractured party.

Assembly Speaker Unruh was for a time a flamboyant national figure. After losing the speakership, Unruh became a critic of overlapping state, county, and city governments. He also voiced complaints against oil companies, housing-tract speculators, and moneyed interests interfering with the political process by what he called a "political ripoff" system. But Unruh also had to fight against his own image as a "Big Daddy" politico in an unsuccessful 1973 Los Angeles mayoral race against Tom Bradley, an African American Democrat.

Back in 1970, the *New York Times* had urged the election of Unruh against the incumbent Ronald Reagan in that year's gubernatorial race: "The Reagan-Unruh contest has significance far beyond California," said the *Times* in an editorial. "Ronald Reagan personifies non-issue politics. His approach is based on a contempt for serious discussion of real problems; it relies on glamorized images projected in carefully controlled public appearances and in intensive television advertising."

The special-interest groups that backed Reagan were to exert an enormous influence on the state legislature. The Reagan gubernatorial victory of 1967 signaled the dawn of a period that threatened to stop many Democratic reform hopes. Reagan subsequently opposed attempts to curb water pollution and to develop mass transportation, thereby encouraging the use of inefficient automobiles that befouled the air with carbon-monoxide emissions.

Although the Democrats controlled California politics from 1958 to 1966, the state had been in Republican hands during most of its history. By the late 1960s, a new voting pattern had emerged in California. It featured two political extremes—the far right and the far left. Hyperconservative rural southerners and retired elderly folk, yearning for a return to the simplicity of earlier days, disliked big government and looked distrustfully at the young and restless "human tumbleweeds" who, without money and responsibilities, flooded into the state. The ultraconservative John Birch Society maintained its headquarters in California.

Despite California's progressive past, nonpartisanship increasingly gave way to right-of-center sentiment. Reagan, like Nixon before him, projected the image of reasonableness, yet accused opponents of leftist extremism. By 1968, a new party, the Peace and Freedom advocates, arose to oppose U.S. involvement in the Vietnam War, but this group stood little chance of success. The championing of civil rights was also about to be drowned out by an ultraright tidal wave that washed over the state and nation.

SELECTED   READINGS

On postwar politics, see Kurt Schuparra, *Triumph of the Right: The Rise of the California Conservative Movement, 1945–1966* (1998) which maintains that Reagan has been severely underrated by historians. Also consult Montgomery Gayle, *One Step From the White House: The Rise and Fall of Senator William F. Knowland* (1998). Stephen Schwartz, *From West to East: California and the Making of the American Mind* (1998) deals with radicalism up to 1960. See also Edward Cray, *Chief Justice: A Biography of Earl Warren* (1997); Leo Katcher, *Earl Warren: A Political Biography* (1967); Richard M. Nixon, *Six Crises* (1962); Earl Mazo, *Richard Nixon: A Political and Personal Portrait* (1959); William Costello, *The Facts About Nixon* (1960); Horace Jeremiah (Jerry) Voorhis, *Confessions of a Congressman* (1947); and Ingrid Scobie, *Center Stage: Helen Gahagan Douglas, A Life* (1992).

Biographical accounts include Arthur H. Samish and Bob Thomas, *The Secret Boss of California* (1971); James Mills, *A Disorderly House: The Brown-*

Unruh Years in Sacramento (1987); Robert Dallek, *Ronald Reagan* (1984); John M. Allswang, "Tom Bradley of Los Angeles," *Southern California Quarterly* 74 (Spring 1992), 55–105; Lou Cannon, *Reagan* (1982) and his *Ronnie and Jesse: A Political Odyssey* (1969); as well as Roger Rapoport, *California Dreaming . . . Pat and Jerry Brown* (1982).

Electioneering practices are detailed in Robert Q. Wilson, *The Amateur Democrat: Club Politics in Three Cities* (1962); Francis M. Carney, "Auxiliary Party Organizations in California," *Western Political Quarterly* 11 (June 1958), 391–92; Currin V. Shields, "A Note on Party Organization," *Western Political Quarterly* 7 (December 1954), 683 ff.; and Robert J. Pitchell, "The Influence of Professional Campaign Management Firms in . . . California," *Western Political Quarterly* 11 (June 1958), 286 ff., and "The Electoral System and Voting Behavior: The Case of California's Crossfiling," *Western Political Quarterly* 12 (June 1959).

Regarding urbanization, see Merry Ovnick, *Los Angeles: The End of the Rainbow* (1994); more apocalyptic is Jared Orsi, *Hazardous Metropolis* (2004). See also Gray Brechin, *Imperial San Francisco: Urban Power, Earthly Ruin* (1999); Norman M. Klein and Martin J. Schiesl, eds., *Twentieth Century Los Angeles: Power Promotion and Social Conflict* (1990) and Schiesl, "Airplanes to Aerospace," in Roger Lotchin, ed., *The Martial Metropolis . . .* (1984), 135–49; Roger Lotchin, "The City and the Sword Through . . . the Cold War," in Raymond Mohl, ed., *Essays on Sunbelt Cities* (1990); Mel Scott, *The San Francisco Bay Area: A Metropolis in Perspective* (1965); Edward Eichler and Marshall Kaplan, *The Community Builders* (1967); Richard Street, "Rural California, A Bibliographic Essay," *Southern California Quarterly* 70 (Fall 1988), 299–328; and David Brodsly, *Los Angeles Freeway: An Appreciative Essay* (1981).

CHAPTER THIRTY-SIX

THE
BELEAGUERED
SIXTIES

The 1960s saw the explosion of severe social unrest throughout California and the nation. The state's material wealth had masked uneasiness beneath the surface. Students, dissatisfied with what they termed "The Establishment," joined older reformers in criticizing America's materialistic culture. Militants of the New Left openly criticized their parents as well as government, corporations, and even universities. Campus revolts, centered at the University of California's Berkeley campus, reflected a severe estrangement between the generations.

Disconcerting to conservative middle-aged taxpayers were a growing number of homeless street people who belonged to an angry underground culture. Youthful rebels, often drugged, let their hair grow long, wore sandals or no shoes, and crowded health food outlets wearing tie-dyed T-shirts. Dubbed "Hippies," this new generation of protesters resembled the Beatniks of the 1950s. Both had sought to change the world in hardly realistic ways.

In San Francisco, Oakland, or Venice Beach, alienated youths expressed their resentment against U.S. involvement in the Vietnam war. That conflict was absorbing millions of dollars for armaments and taking the lives of thousands of young Americans. Too many of those who served in the military came from disadvantaged families and minority groups. They could not, unlike privileged college students, evade the draft. Young people were also disgusted over what they saw as creeping automation, the suppression of individuality, and hypocritical middle-class morals. These factors combined to divide age, ethnic, and class groups. During the 1960s, a wave of transients descended upon Berkeley and San Francisco's Haight-Ashbury district.

Discontented Hippies, young and old, sought salvation in an alternative lifestyle. This included a relaxation of sexual mores and experimentation with psychedelic drugs. Disbelieving parents could not understand

Folk musicians and activists, Joan Baez and Bob Dylan perform at the Civil Rights March on Washington, D.C., August 8, 1963. Courtesy of the National Archives (ARC:542021, Loc: 306-SSM-4C93)24).

how children who had often enjoyed superior advantages could leave their middle-class homes and "turn on, tune in, and drop out." The coming-out of debutantes in California-designed Galanos dresses did not impress this new legion of young people.

Wide-eyed fans of a new wave of folksingers Bob Dylan and Joan Baez were mesmerized by the lyrics of discontent. Rebels of the 1960s also expressed themselves in an "underground press." In southern California the *Los Angeles Free Press* catered to reform-minded readers while in the Bay Area the *Berkeley Barb* and *San Francisco Oracle* featured anti-establishment views.

Scores of dissidents founded rural communes, some of which rejected traditional religions in favor of "New Age" spirituality. There was also a revived interest in Buddhism and Zen meditation. With social experimentation in the air, communal living emphasized "free love" and a brotherly sharing of both food and property. Ironically, these youthful critics, who paid no taxes, were creating their own conformity. Hippies did not diminish personal avarice. Some embodied the worst characteristics against which they rebelled. The new rebels were hardly freed from illegitimacy, murder, and suicide. The use of powerful LSD and other drugs resulted in "bad trips," even death.

In the fall of 1964, a boisterous "Free Speech Movement," broke out on the Berkeley campus of the University of California. Its agitators insisted upon a greater voice in college governance. During their sit-ins, Berkeley's police came on campus to restore order. Later, Governor Pat Brown ordered state police to break up a student demonstration that was disrupting university operations. This led to a confrontation by more than 700 youths, not all of whom were students. They were dragged out of Sproul Hall, the university's administrative center, and jailed. Pat Brown, jeered at by students and referred to by the *Los Angeles Times* as "a tower of jello," was actually a determined and consistent politician.

The actor Ronald Reagan, who succeeded Brown as governor, spoke even more forcefully of the need to clean up campus extremism and foul language. At San Francisco State College he found an ally in President S. I. Hayakawa , a respected semanticist who did not hesitate to confront rebellious students. Later the state's voters elected him to the U.S. Senate.

Undaunted, undergraduates in the 1960s questioned the wisdom of conservative, business-oriented university regents appointed by the governor for lengthy terms. Students at Berkeley and UCLA argued for decentralization of the university. Eventually the administration did take steps to reorganize its disparate campuses. At San Diego (UCSD) and Santa Cruz (UCSC) administrators approved the formation of small undergraduate colleges similar to those at Oxford. These seemed to promise the possibility of smaller classes and closer contact with favorite faculty members. The newer campuses also held out the prospect of greater curricular experimentation.

Under Governor Reagan's administration, public distrust of academia increased. In 1967, the regents of the University of California dismissed its president, Clark Kerr, whom conservative board members considered too wishy-washy toward student militants. Meanwhile, repeated confrontations by demonstrators on the campuses of public universities convinced most Californians that "left-wing" professors and administrators were spineless allies of student activists. For Reagan, government was not the solution but the problem. Yet, he had no hesitation in cracking down on campus demonstrators. In 1969 on the Berkeley campus and the next year at Santa Barbara, the governor repeatedly showed a stubborn adherence to his conservatism. Using National Guard troops, he authorized tear gas if necessary to break up student protests.

The 1960s have been described as "the ungluing of America." At a time when expanding educational budgets competed with accelerating welfare and health care costs, voters began to favor bond issues for public order and more police protection rather than more money for rebellious students and teachers. Confused taxpayers came to feel that state-operated campuses should teach students only those skills essential for employment and not become seats of public criticism, or sponsor distasteful dramatic and artistic productions. At Berkeley, a city in which the university dominates the community, the generation gap had opened wide.

The protestors of the 1960s should be credited with some positive changes. These include opposition to the unwinable Vietnam War and the raising of public awareness regarding civil rights. The era saw the dawning of "Gay Liberation." Young and old stridently called attention to environmental issues. In 1961, Walt Disney, and Roy, his nephew, founded the California Institute of the Arts at Valencia. This institution, like Pasadena's Art Center College, is a major arts center, which includes a cinematography program.

The '60s should be remembered as a new age for rock music. Adventurous California-based bands included The Doors, The Grateful Dead, and Creedence Clearwater Revival. These groups and The Mamas and the Papas changed the popular music industry. They were soon joined by other pop artists: David Crosby, Stephen Stills, Graham Nash, Neil Young, and Joni Mitchell. Adding to what became known as the "California Sound" were Jackson Browne, Linda Ronstadt, Fleetwood Mac, America, and the Beach Boys. All this musical outburst seemed to be captured in the 1976 album, "Hotel California," by the popular Los Angeles band, The Eagles.

As political protests wound down, a huge elderly population of indigent old folks became a heavy charge on the state's crowded welfare rolls. Most communities welcomed the elderly—as long as they had the means to support themselves. Some called Santa Barbara the home of America's rich unburied dead, while San Clemente was dubbed "the cemetery of the living."

California also continued to face the continuing problem of migratory laborers. These workers hoed and thinned sugar beets, cut spinach, fed livestock, and pruned vineyards. Uncertain market conditions and an oversupply of workers could quickly depress their wages or suddenly leave them unemployed. Traditionally nonunionized, blue-collar laborers also knew full well that any bad freeze or drought could drastically reduce their income. Too many workers still lived in substandard housing, consumed inadequate diets, and seldom saw their children complete even a grade-school education. In short, their working conditions were miserable.

During the 1960s migrant workers came into increasing competition with a human tide of illegal aliens from Mexico, brought to "El Norte" by employers desiring cheap labor. The debased condition of cherry pickers and almond harvesters had not improved markedly, in part due to the competition of thousands of *scabs* (strikebreakers) brought in temporarily from Mexico or Central America under the federal *braceros* (guestworker) program. Flooding the labor pool were *alambristas*, derisively called "wetbacks." These illegals were shepherded across the border by "coyotes," unscrupulous middlemen who marketed entire labor crews to American farmers and ranchers. If an attempted crossing into the U.S. went awry, the coyotes, simply pocketed the money they charged and fled, leaving behind the confused and hapless people to fend for themselves. Border guards arrested the most fortunate migrants, sending them back into Mexico. Others perished in the desert wastelands of the U.S. Southwest.

Some unemployed illegals wandered from farm to farm, following the harvests as birds follow the sun. Men, women, and children slept nightly in abandoned barns or warehouses. The hovels in which they lived had only dirt floors or tin roofs with no ceilings. Cheesecloth or flour sacks hung over window openings in a pathetic attempt to keep out insects. Flies swarmed amid these primitive sheds made out of scraps of lumber, flattened oil cans, discarded signboards, or tar paper. With no cooking or toilet facilities, migrants cooked their meals in the open over primitive fire pits. Too often they had no choice but to relieve themselves outside as well.

At first the IWW tried unsuccessfully to unionize the Central Valley's farmworkers. Later, in the 1930s, so did the AFL and CIO. By 1960, however, the Agricultural Workers Organizing Committee obtained wage increases of 12 to 17¢ for each box of peaches picked and from 15 to 17¢ per box for tomatoes. The next year, the Teamster's Union signed a union-shop contract at Salinas with various large ranches. But these were sporadic gains, without general significance. The Council of California Growers insisted that their unstable and unpredictable industry did not lend itself to traditional unionization. They claimed that once a crop was ready for harvest, strikes were out of the question, as they could not shut down their picking operations to negotiate.

Seasonal farm laborers, since before John Steinbeck wrote *The Grapes of Wrath*, wanted union recognition, better housing and working conditions, unemployment insurance, and the right to bargain collectively. Farm owners often refused to discuss these demands; some even dusted strikers with insecticides to drive them off. In 1965 at Delano, a Central Valley town, some laborers imported by the growers, however, met aggressive picketers who shouted *"Viva la Huelga!"* ("Long Live the Strike!") while firing marbles at the scabs with slingshots. Labor organizers of the farmworkers imposed a statewide boycott on Delano grapes and beverages. A few chain stores agreed not to stock these items. Leaflets explaining the boycott flooded into those stores that had not agreed to ban such merchandise.

Personally leading the farmworkers was Cesar Chavez, a magnetic idealist who had spent his youth in the labor camps of Imperial Valley. In 1966, his grape strikers marched 300 miles from Delano to the state capital in Sacramento to protest working conditions. Thereafter, Chavez began to reap the fruits of his patient organizing efforts. Grape pickers employed by the powerful Di Giorgio Fruit Corporation voted in favor of Chavez's United Farm Workers of America (UFW) against the Teamsters, who had also tried to organize the pickers. By the fall of 1967, Chavez had also struck against the Giumarra Vineyards, then the largest table grape growers in the world.

In February of 1968, Chavez completed a twenty-five-day hunger strike, which he brought to an end primarily because he feared violence. Senator Robert Kennedy joined him at the close of the fast, expressing sympathy. After the senator's assassination that year, Ethel Kennedy, his widow, continued the family's support for Chavez during his intensification of the grape boycott.

By the spring of 1970, the big grape strike approached its fifth year. Many believed that the growers would never give in. Then, in June, Chavez secured for the pickers a minimum wage of $1.70 per hour, a then unheard-of rate of pay for farmhands. Farmers, however, maintained that Chavez ran his union in a chaotic fashion. One of them remarked: "It isn't easy dealing with a man who thinks he's a saint, but who doesn't mind going back on his word."

Chavez, who continued to speak out against agribusinesses and exploitative labor contractors, next challenged lettuce growers in the Salinas Valley. On December 4, 1970, he was jailed without bail for refusing to obey a legal injunction restraining his strike activities. But this court action only drew further national attention to Chavez's lettuce boycott. Public pressure soon secured his release. Labor troubles in the fields, however, were far from over.

In the 1960s *Viva la Huelga, Viva la Causa,* and *Viva Chavez* became rallying cries for student activists, labor reformers, and clergy throughout California who joined Chavez's ranks. Some of the white-collar supporters were derisively labeled "limousine liberals." Nevertheless, Chavez, shy and even sad, in appearance, had become the mobilizer of a once-despised group. His typical manner of dress, a checkered shirt and blue jeans, had come to suggest a sincere wish to remain close to his people. He had come

Senator Robert F. Kennedy breaks bread with Cesar Chavez during a mass marking the end of Chavez's 25-day fast, March 10, 1968. Chavez fasted to bring attention to the peaceful disposition of the farm workers' strike against California grape growers. Archives of Labor and Union Affairs, Wayne State University.

from their ranks and knew what it was to do stoop work, picking grapes or harvesting lettuce all day long under a blazing sun. Yet, like India's Mohandas Gandhi, he refused to allow violence by his farmworkers.

Chavez, however, encountered opposition from the Teamsters Union, who repeatedly tried to organize his migrant workers. He was convinced that they were working with major growers to break up his organization. It took him years to patch up a working agreement with that rival union, allowing him to continue his personalized labor crusade. Day laborers remained loyal to Chavez. He had not only improved their wages, but had brought such amenities as ice water and portable toilets into the stifling fields.

By 1963, Chavez and his fellow Latinos were shocked by the assassination of President John Kennedy. A fellow Catholic, he had been nominated for the presidency at Los Angeles, hub of California's Mexican American population and home to the "Viva Kennedy" clubs that had sprung up during the 1960 presidential campaign. Less than five years after Kennedy's death, in June of 1968, Latinos mourned the loss of JFK's brother, Robert, assassinated in Los Angeles shortly after his stunning victory in the California presidential primary election in which Mexican Americans had strongly participated.

In the 1970s, discrimination directed against Latinos was not so blatant as that which African Americans encountered. Yet, a large percentage of Mexican Americans remained unskilled laborers with low incomes. They openly referred to themselves as *desgraciados*, those "born without grace." Years of employment as stoop laborers in the fields had cast braceros in an inferior role. Many Mexican American children were forced to drop out of school by the time they reached the eighth grade in order to help their families earn money in the fields.

Slowly, however, California's Mexican American community began to produce new leaders whose organizational aspirations exceeded even those of Cesar Chavez. Urbanized Latinos began to call themselves *Chicanos*, a politically charged term that proudly announced their Mexican heritage. Such upwardly mobile persons remained far removed from the marches of Chavez's farm workers. Instead, a new leadership founded such urban organizations as the Mexican-American Political Association and the Latino Legislative Council. After his early death, Chavez was awarded the Congressional Medal of Freedom.

During 1968, following demonstrations by Latino students and teachers in seven Los Angeles public high schools, the city's pressured school board promised to implement new racial reforms. Among these was the appointment of minority school principals, less restrictive policies regarding student hairstyles and clothing, more bilingual instruction, and a modernized industrial training program for minority-group students who would not go on to college.

Accused of sparking the school walkouts were the militant Brown Berets, whose goal stood in contrast to the Green Berets of the U.S. Army in Vietnam. Their leaders sought to unite *La Raza* (the race) in California's barrios. Wearing clothing that resembled the revolutionary garb of Fidel Castro and his Cuban followers, these critics carried signs that read *"Viva la Revolucion!"* An increasing number of young Chicanos were graduating from California's colleges and universities. This new generation was anxious to replace members of the old leadership whom they labeled *Tio Tacos* (Uncle Tacos) a slur parallel to "Uncle Tom."

By the 1960s, the inequities that faced California's African American population also caused them to cry out for reform. So said the oldest black newspaper in the state, *The California Eagle*. Black communities continued to grow in nascent ghettoes peopled by poorly paid custodians, waiters, railroad porters, handymen, and gardeners.

Increasing numbers of African Americans from the southern states moved into Oakland, Compton, and Inglewood. But California hardly proved a haven from prejudice. African Americans faced hurdles both as to residence and employment. Towns like Glendale and San Marino long remained lily-white. Blacks in California had always responded to such rejection by founding their own communities and organizations. As early as 1924, African Americans had founded their own resort community, Val Verde, near Santa Clarita in the Tehachapi foothills. They also started African American lodges, businesses, and churches. At Los Angeles, the black preacher William Seymour headed up the Pentecostal Holy Rollers, which influenced Aimee Semple McPherson and other evangelists.

Only slowly had African Americans entered the professions, sports, and politics. Dr. Ralph Bunche, a graduate of UCLA, went from a State Department career to become Undersecretary of the United Nations. Jackie Robinson began his baseball career at Pasadena Junior College. In 1947 he "broke the sports color line," becoming the first African American in the major leagues.

To help overcome discrimination against blacks, the Rumford Fair Housing Act was passed in 1963. It broadened prohibitions against discrimination in the sale or rental of private dwellings. But the next year the voters adopted Proposition 14, which nullified the state's open-housing provisions. This law, however, was invalidated in court.

Nevertheless, the sting of Proposition 14 had been felt on the eve of the bloody Watts riots in southeast Los Angeles. Although its streets were lined with palm trees, Watts was a crowded ghetto neighborhood. The August 1965 Watts uprisings epitomized the malaise of disenchanted blacks living in a segregated ghetto. Hundreds of frustrated rioters, shouting the antiwhite epithets "Burn, Baby, Burn" and "Get Whitey," looted stores, set buildings afire, and shot at firemen and police. Governor Pat Brown ordered National Guard troops out to help local police restore order. During the riots, which lasted for six days, 35 persons died and 600 others were injured. Some 4,000 persons were arrested within a square-mile burned-over area. In the chaos, looters invaded furniture stores, stealing television sets, freezers, and other electronic appliances.

The Watts riots underscored the deterioration of African American family life as well as a growing resentment over race-based inequities in society. Blacks were tired of seeing whites enjoy prerogatives denied them. Rootless youngsters were chafed by the harassment of the police. Although the riots resulted in great damage to the very place in which many African Americans lived, the outbursts did generate some moves toward reform, including a new cultural center, a hospital in Watts, and

First Lady "Lady Bird" Johnson, the conscientious wife of President Lyndon Johnson, visits a classroom for Project Head Start, Mar. 19, 1966. Courtesy of the National Archives (AR: 596401, Loc: C9080-17a).

the founding of California State University, Dominguez Hills. The Mc-Cone Commission, appointed by Governor Pat Brown to study causes of the riots, reported that Watts needed better transportation, recreational facilities, and job opportunities. Eventually, California did make progress in redressing racial inequalities. The state revamped run-down neighborhoods and poured money into welfare programs. But impatient Black Power advocates pushed for even greater antipoverty measures and for school programs such as Head Start and Upward Bound to help disadvantaged youths compete successfully.

By the end of the 1960s, California virtually functioned as an early warning system for the rest of the nation. The state had to cope with problems brought about by its seemingly endless growth, and in the new computer age, a segmented Balkanized society had become a definite possibility. No one really wished for such a future population distortion. But the future seemed very confusing.

SELECTED READINGS

Concerning educational ferment, see Clark Kerr, *The Gold and the Blue: A Personal Memoir of the University of California, 1949–1967* (2001); Rebecca Lowen, *Creating the Cold War University* (1997) concerns disruptions at

Stanford. See also Gerard J. DeGroot, "Ronald Reagan and Student Unrest in California, 1966–1970," *Pacific Historical Review* 65 (February 1996), 107–29; W. J. Rorabaugh, *Berkeley at War* (1989); also Arthur G. Coons, *Crises in California Education* (1968); Seymour M. Lipset and Sheldon S. Wolin, eds., *The Berkeley Student Revolt: Facts and Interpretations* (1965). An overview of education is in John Douglas, *The California Idea and American Higher Education* (2000).

For politics of the 1960s, see Ethan Rarick, *California Rising: The Life and times of Pat Brown* (2005), also Martin Schiesl, ed., *California Politics and Policy . . . The Pat Brown Years* (1997); Jackson K. Putnam, *Modern California Politics* (1996) and his "The Pattern of Modern California Politics," *Pacific Historical Review* 61 (February 1992), 23–52; Eugene C. Lee, ed., *The California Governmental Process: Problems and Issues* (1966); Thomas M. Storke, *I Write for Freedom* (1963); Charles M. Price, ed., *Consensus and Cleavage: Issues in California Politics* (1968).

Regarding African Americans in this period, see James de Abajian, compiler, *Blacks and Their Contributions to the American West: A Bibliography* (1974); Josh Sides, *L.A. City Limits: African American Los Angeles from the Great Depression to the Present* (2004); Kenneth Goode, *California's Black Pioneers* (1973); James A. Fisher, "Political Development of the Black Community in California," *California Historical Quarterly* 50 (September 1971), 256–66; Thurman A. Odell, "The Negro in California Before 1890," *Pacific Historian* 19 (Winter 1975), 321–45; Albert S. Broussard, *Black San Francisco: the Struggle for Racial Equality in the West, 1900–1954* (1993); Douglas Daniels, *Pioneer Urbanites: A Social and Cultural History of Black San Francisco* (1980); Lawrence B. De Graaf, "The City of Black Angels: The Emergence of the Los Angeles Ghetto, 1890–1930," *Pacific Historical Review* 39 (August 1970), 323–52; also De Graaf, "Recognition, Racism, and Reflections on the Writing of Black History," *Pacific Historical Review* 44 (February 1975), 22–51; and F. Ray Marshall, *The Negro and Organized Labor* (1965). Also see Albert S. Broussard, *Black San Francisco: The Struggle for Racial Equality in the West, 1900–1954* (1993).

On the Watts riots, see *Violence in the City: An End or a Beginning [The McCone Commission Report]* (1965), also Gerald Horne, *Fire This Time: The Watts Uprisings and the 1960s* (1995); Raphael Sonenshein, *Politics in Black and White: Race and Power in Los Angeles* (1993); Spencer Crump, *Black Riot in Los Angeles: The Story of the Watts Tragedy* (1966); Nathan Cohen, *The Los Angeles Riots: A Socio-Psychological Study* (1970); Paul Bullock, ed., *Watts: The Aftermath* (1970); Joseph Boskin and Victor Pilson, "The Los Angeles Riot of 1965: A Medical Profile of an Urban Crisis," *Pacific*

Historical Review 29 (August 1970), 353–65; and Mark Baldessare, ed., *The Los Angeles Riots: Lessons for the Urban Future* (1994).

On immigrants throughout this period, see George E. Frakes and Curtis Solberg, eds., *Minorities in California History* (1971); George J. Sánchez, *Becoming Mexican American* (1993); N. Ray and Gladys Gilmore, "The Bracero in California," *Pacific Historical Review* 32 (August 1963), 265–82; Mark Reisler, "Always the Laborer: Anglo Perceptions of the Mexican Immigrant," *Pacific Historical Review* 45 (May 1976), 231–54; Fernando Penalosa, "The Changing Mexican-American in Southern California," *Sociology and Social Research* 51 (July 1967), 405–17; Richard Griswold del Castillo and Richard D. Garcia, *Cesar Chavez: A Triumph of Spirit* (1995); John Hammerback and Richard Jensen, *The Rhetorical Career of Cesar Chavez* (1998); Susan Ferriss and Ricardo Sandoval, *The Fight in the Fields: Cesar Chavez and the Farm Workers Movement* (1997); Don Mitchell, *The Lie of the Land: Migrant Workers and the California Landscape* (1983); Gilbert G. Gonzalez, *Labor and Community: Mexican Worker Villages in a Southern California County* (1994); John Gregory Dunne, *Delano: The Anatomy of the Great California Grapeworkers Strike* (1967); Ernesto Galarza, *Merchants of Labor: The Mexican Bracero Story* (1964) and Galarza, *Barrio Boy* (1971); as well as Truman E. Moore, *The Slaves We Rent* (1965).

An overview of the "youth culture" is Kirse Granat May, *Golden State, Golden Youth: The California Image in Popular Culture, 1955–1966* (2002).

CHAPTER THIRTY-SEVEN

ENVIRONMENTAL
REALITIES

As hundreds of thousands of new residents continued to push into California, challenges to its infrastructure and environment grew urgent. These included overcrowded schools, hospitals, an outmoded freeway system, and severe water shortages. A beautiful land seemed headed for environmental decay. Californians had not yet learned how to balance their natural resources with population pressures.

The state's major cities were plagued by the baffling problem of smog—an acrid combination of smoke and fog. This haze not only irritates the eyes and lungs; it reduces visibility, affects crop yields, and discourages tourism. The Los Angeles Basin is especially afflicted by smog. In 1947, its Board of County Supervisors organized an Air Pollution Control District. As one of the first such regulatory agencies in the entire country, the APCD spent millions of dollars trying to reduce the noxious emissions of automobile and factory fumes. A full ten years later, the APCD finally convinced the city of Los Angeles to ban backyard incinerators. But, until tighter state regulations allowed the APCD to override local officials, its ordinances could not be applied to the sixty-three municipalities surrounding Los Angeles. Today the APCD strictly controls industries that produce sulphurous petrochemicals. It is also empowered to call a series of alerts when the smog danger becomes especially critical.

Los Angeles sits in a saucer-like basin and suffers from the lowest average wind velocity of any major city in the United States. The hot, sunny days for which L.A. is known cause a photochemical regrouping of exhaust-gas molecules. The emissions that billow out of industrial smokestacks then forms a dense layer of smog that hangs over the area for long periods. Particularly persistent smog areas are the Long Beach and Los Angeles ports where diesel pollutants spew forth from unloading ships, locomotives, and idling trucks.

"Mall Sprawl." Los Cerritos Shopping Mall in the Los Angeles area suburbs, August 5, 2006. © Xavier Marchant/Dreamstime.com.

Hydrocarbons, auto exhaust, and vapor leaks from gas tanks also contribute to smog. In 1956, when air pollution reached an unacceptable level, the APCD forced local industries to burn only natural gas. Alternative fuels for autos, buses, and trucks, such as ethanol, were also devised as a partial solution to the mounting air pollution. Eventually, auto companies began a lengthy attempt to market personal vehicles powered by natural gas or rechargeable batteries. Persistent air pollution contributes to higher-than-normal mortality rates from emphysema and other respiratory diseases. These include lung cancer, asthma, and allergies. In the last half century, however, the urgent need to scrub clean the filthiest air in the country has made L.A. an international leader in smog abatement.

Although smog seemed less of a problem in the north, San Francisco in 1955 organized its own Air Pollution Control District. This agency oversaw nine counties in the Bay area and began its mandate by banning rubbish fires. Municipal dumps, which released plumes of filthy air that hung over the bay on windless days, were forced to cover and fill over city refuse. Control of automobile emissions has been painfully slow. Commuting habits have changed only gradually. Carpooling has reduced auto exhaust somewhat.

No issue has become more important than ensuring a constant supply of fresh water. Whenever the annual rain and snowfalls dip below normal, an acute stress on the water resources of the Sacramento–San Joaquin

Delta occurs. This giant estuary serves California's farms as well as 16 million southern Californian households.

Developers wondered if southern California's sparse water supply could ever match the needs of its rapid urbanization. The state was no longer able to count on its annual water quota from the Colorado River (Boulder Canyon) beyond the 4.4 million acre-feet to which it is entitled, for that river is tapped by seven states and Mexico. One result of such anxiety over water has been the passage of legislation requiring future city planners to consider water availability before approving new housing tracts. Annual runoff from the Sierra and Cascade ranges remains undependable. Neither the Owens Valley Aqueduct nor the Boulder Canyon Project can permanently provide water to an ever-growing and thirsty southern California.

Yet, in 2003, the Los Angeles Water and Power Department finally, after decades of political bickering, agreed to restore water flowing into the long depleted Owens River. That river had been mostly dry since 1913. Water, now directed back into its riverbed, is the largest such restoration ever attempted in the American West.

Overpumping of underground aquifers has become serious. Near Long Beach, seawater has invaded freshwater basins, while in Suisun Bay and along the Sacramento–San Joaquin Delta, selenium and other toxic contaminants have polluted underground water reservoirs. Salt build-up has also resulted from excessive reuse of water, as has occurred in the Santa Ana River Basin.

Creeping salination has occurred in an improbable body of water called the Salton Sea. Located due east of San Diego, it straddles Imperial and Riverside Counties. Smelly and discolored, it has long been California's environmental invalid. The sea is not only cursed by rising salinity, but it also suffers from the flow of agricultural pesticides and sewage from neighboring Mexico. Since it was created by an accident nearly 100 years ago, alarmed conservationists have warned that the sea is steadily dying. Someday it will grow too salty even for carp and other bottom-feeding fish to survive. While still traversed by boat owners, Salton Sea water is of low-grade quality. Migratory birds and other wildlife are also endangered by toxic dust storms similar to those that blow off the shrinking Owens Lake farther north. There, acres of salt-laden former lake bottom are laced with chemicals that are a danger to campers.

Southern Californians live in a water-stressed area. Today's average family of four uses approximately one acre-foot of water (or 325,851 gallons) per year. But only a limited percentage of California's water is used by residential customers. Agriculture and industry consume most of it.

Makeshift flood control activity combined with conservation. Courtesy of the California Department of Water Resoures.

The Feather River Project harnesses the water resources of that important tributary of the Sacramento. Both rivers spill into 800 miles of canals and tunnels. The largest structure of this water network is the 730-foot-high Oroville Dam, part of a great "natural stairway" that provides fish and game protection as well as flood control.

Political sectionalism between northern and southern California slowed down the Feather River Project, only one part of an $11 billion statewide plan. Even after construction had begun on the centerpiece Oroville Dam, the legislature remained locked in discord over whether to complete the project. Controversy also brewed over building the accompanying San Luis Dam, in Merced County. Adamant southern legislators refused to appropriate money for water that could be recaptured by northern "counties of origin." This led to a ten-year stalemate. Meanwhile, the north required flood control as urgently as industrializing, but the parched south needed ever more water. The legislature also had to weigh protection of Yuba City, Butte, and Marysville from floods against the ravenous need for water in southern California.

As in past water-related controversies, critics of the Feather River Project feared the enrichment of huge corporation farmers whose thousands of productive acres would be nourished by water paid for by others. Another stumbling block to adoption of the Feather River Project remained its great cost. However, the main issue was the north's basic interests as opposed to the south's needs.

During his governorship, Pat Brown succeeded in breaking the north-south deadlock by persuading representatives of competing counties that it was in everyone's best interest to stop squabbling over water. This ensured the transfer of water from northern California as far south as San Diego. Protection of northern water rights in the counties of origin was also part of Brown's compromise. An intricate complex of dams and canals also conserves water, sending it to areas where shortages are endemic. Over a north-south artery, water from the southern San Joaquin Valley is lifted over the Tehachapi Mountains via tunnels and feeder lines into southern California.

A disappointing alternative to the state's costly water transport problem has been desalination. In 1967, the federal government provided funds to help build the largest desalination plant in the country near San Diego. But so far it has not proved economical to convert seawater into freshwater.

Chronic water shortages are not only due to weak rainfall. The state has not built enough facilities to store water that flows into the ocean. By the 1970s Californians, however, did authorize a forty-three-mile peripheral canal to divert water around the Sacramento–San Joaquin Delta. Ecologists maintain that diversion of too much water out of the Delta's marshes could destroy waterfowl and fish life. Urban sprawl has also resulted in the loss of scarce wetlands.

Onshore and offshore water pollution has posed yet another mounting problem. Paved areas not only cause more toxic runoff, but they increase the velocity of hazardous waste water as it races to the seashore. Dangerous bacteria and viruses are present in the water that spills out of storm drains, forming layers of muck in the Pacific Ocean. In some places polluted sediment is as thick as fifteen feet. There are still not enough sewage treatment plants to render pesticides and hazardous chemicals inert. In addition, the sludge disgorged by ships has amounted to millions of tons of slimy pollutants, a black mayonnaise that befouls both underwater systems and beaches.

In addition to coastal blight, pesticide-laden water runs onto agricultural fields and enters the maritime food chain. Recreationists increasingly encounter mutant frogs as well as deformed pelicans, sea lions, and

Tunnel under construction through the Tehachapi Range bringing water into southern California. Courtesy of the California Department of Water Resoures.

dolphins in and around California's once pristine waterways. Municipal sewage-treatment systems cannot handle peak loads, leading to contamination of the water table. Worse yet, cities have released raw sewage directly into the ocean. Surfers become mysteriously ill, probably because of toxicity. Persons who eat ocean mollusks and other seafood risk ingesting harmful bacterial contaminants.

Overfishing has, furthermore, depleted the state's fish population. High-tech fishing vessels, using sophisticated technology, harvest too many fish. In recent years the offshore fish population has fallen by an estimated 90 percent. Even such staples as red snappers and crabs, once abundant, have become scarce. In 2001, the last cannery on San Pedro's Terminal Island closed. For forty-five years that cannery had processed one hundred tons of tuna and salmon per day. Because of decreased tuna supplies, strict environmental regulations, and world competition, it was no longer feasible to operate that plant. Terminal Island was once a world fishery center. All of its sixteen canneries are now defunct.

After 1972, the California Coastal Commission joined the Sierra Club in seeking to preserve 1,000 miles of prime seaside properties. In recent years, however, the pressure to open up the state's offshore petroleum resources, and to develop oceanside tourist facilities, have led to accusations that the commission has engaged in bureaucratic overkill.

Counties of California

Del Norte
Siskiyou
Modoc
Humboldt
Trinity
Shasta
Lassen
Tehama
Plumas
Mendocino
Glenn
Butte
Sierra
Colusa
Yuba
Nevada
Lake
Sutter
Placer
Sonoma
Yolo
El Dorado
Napa
Sacramento
Amador
Alpine
Solano
Marin
Contra Costa
San Joaquin
Calaveras
Tuolumne
Mono
San Francisco
Alameda
Stanislaus
Mariposa
San Mateo
Santa Clara
Merced
Santa Cruz
Madera
San Benito
Fresno
Inyo
Monterey
Tulare
Kings
NORTHERN COUNTIES
SOUTHERN COUNTIES
San Luis Obispo
Kern
Santa Barbara
San Bernardino
Ventura
Los Angeles
Orange
Riverside
San Diego
Imperial

0   50   100   150
Miles

Ironically, as sports and recreation boosters call for loosening environmental restrictions, the state's tourist industry annually loses considerable income because of pollution fears. Beachgoers are increasingly warned away from unsafe swimming or fishing zones located near storm drains. Popular beaches are occasionally closed to swimmers due to high bacteria levels in the water. Conservationists also issue warnings concerning chemicals that do not break down in the soil and are eventually drained into wildlife refuges and the water table.

Some pure-water remedies have made possible California's agricultural success. Among these is massive water recycling, even from sewage. As 95 percent of its crops are grown on irrigated land, the state remains first nationally in the production of almost forty different crops. An estimated 25 percent of America's table food comes from the great Central Valley alone. No other region comes near the quantity of its production of fruits and vegetables. California continues to produce more than 275 crops—from cut flowers to kelp.

More than one hundred years after California's hide-and-tallow trading days, large corporate ranchers have extended their operations into shipping and processing. Today's cattle ranchers breed, feed, ship, and sell their own livestock; some grow the alfalfa and sorghum used in cattle-fattening pens. Rancher-farmers operate motor pools and buy costly harvesters, tractors, and automatic potato pickers.

Modern corporate farming has largely replaced small family farms incapable of successfully competing. Among the state's mechanized agribusinesses is the Kern County Land Company. Its holdings were once gargantuan. Such firms are frequently absorbed by even larger companies. One of these, the Irvine Ranch Company, once controlled much of Orange County. It became a major subdivider, managing properties as far away as Imperial County. The huge Newhall Land and Farming Company also converted large blocs of farmland into real estate subdivisions. Valencia is a model community created by that company.

In the San Joaquin Valley, the Di Giorgio and Sawyer fruit and vegetable farms still generate millions of dollars of income annually. The Maggio Company in the Imperial Valley is the largest grower of carrots in the United States. The Brock Ranches near El Centro, and the Antle Ranches, growers of lettuce and carrots in the Imperial Valley and Arizona, are perhaps the leading producers of vegetables in the nation.

But California's agricultural land remains threatened. Each year 20,000 acres of prime farmland are gobbled up by industrial plants, space-consuming highways, and housing tracts. From Bakersfield to Reading, suburbs are sprouting on land that once produced milk, tomatoes, cantaloupes, peaches, apricots, figs, and almonds. After 1999, in just two years, Santa Clara and Alameda Counties alone lost more than 7,000 acres of farmland.

California, however, remains the nation's leading dairy state, producing more than 130 varieties of cheese. In the year 2000 almost 170 million pounds of mild and white Monterey Jack, first marketed in 1882 by David Jacks, were sold. Yet, less than 10 percent of the state is still farmland, even in the prized Central Valley. Fueled by a huge population growth rate, the state continues to squander its prime farm land, as acres of open space succumb to urban developers.

In addition to paving over a farming paradise, California has been losing agricultural and manufacturing markets to foreign competitors who pay lower wages. The state, once second only to Texas in oil production, has become a net importer of petroleum products. As California's oil wells produced less and less high-grade petroleum, a battle arose with the federal government over vast oil deposits that extend outward from its shoreline. Long Beach, after World War II, leased its offshore reserves to independent oil operators in defiance of both state and federal claims. Only after a lengthy dispute was a three-way agreement reached between the federal government, the state, and California coastal municipalities.

Federal versus state tension over offshore oil drilling has become almost violent because of repeated oil spills that destroy wildlife and putrify beaches. Santa Barbara residents bitterly recall one particular offshore platform blowout. In 1969, a leak developed and for the next twelve days oil poured onto nearby beaches. This oil slick eventually covered 660 square miles, killing thousands of birds, mammals, and fish. The devastation ruined marine life for years. Only some 2,100 California sea otters remain in the wild. Once hunted to extinction, today they are menaced by industrial pollution, human waste, and parasites.

Oil companies are now prevented from developing coastal leases obtained before a 1990 moratorium on new drilling rigs. As many as a billion barrels of oil lie locked beneath the sea as far north as Morro Bay. Despite pressure for exploitation of this treasure, environmentalists vigorously oppose further exploration of tideland oil. Unfortunately remaining on-shore oil reserves are of thick viscosity and, therefore, of low quality.

California is menaced by yet another natural phenomenon. Earthquakes continue to be of great concern to federal, state, and local authorities. Along the San Andreas Geological Fault, which crosses the San Francisco area, serious tremors occurred in 1906, 1933, and 1971. The later Sylmer quake killed seventy-eight people. In 1989, the Loma Prieta quake caused the collapse of an entire freeway in Oakland and crumpled stretches of the double-decker bay bridges. In addition to the loss of fifty-seven lives and millions of dollars worth of damage to property, the 1989 quake interrupted the cross-bay World Series between the San Francisco Giants and Oakland A's. As a broadcast of the game was disrupted and television screens across the nation temporarily went blank, thousands of frightened fans in Candlestick Park were evacuated from the stadium, which had sustained some physical damage.

Mount Shasta, a towering volcanic peak of the Cascade Range, viewed from the north. © Sydney Deem/Dreamstime.com.

Other serious tremors jolted the Los Angeles Basin. A 1994 North-ridge quake killed sixty-one people, snarled rail and air transportation, and caused severe power and water outages. Another natural phenomenon, albeit one aggravated by manmade erosion, is landslides. Some hillside zones resemble a slithering deck of playing cards. At poorly chosen building sites, the power of nature can easily sweep away plaster-and-wood constructions.

As the population has grown, a widening stain of confusion marred California's shift from an agricultural to a postindustrial way of life. The missions and ranchos of the Spanish period had long ago made way for film and television studios, oil derricks, aircraft factories, airports, steel mills, and countless subdivisions. In too many areas rising land costs have made it uneconomical to build single-family dwellings. Urban dwellers increasingly orient their lives around high-rise housing, strip malls, and industrial parks.

Dynamite and bulldozers have gouged deep scars in the landscape. The National Park Service estimates that there were once more than 2 million acres of redwoods between Monterey Bay and southern Oregon. Only a fraction of that virgin forest remains. As buzzing chain saws continue to log whole groves of ancient trees, new cities ooze out over the countryside. Suburbia is cluttered with billboards that mar the landscape.

In a single generation smog has altered, perhaps permanently, the Mediterranean environment of southern California.

The English architectural historian, Reyner Banham, actually admired the state's "knockdown, throwaway, and constantly reinvented car culture." A populist, he felt that not all urbanization has led to spoliation. In 1965, the legislature created a Conservation and Development Commission to stop communities alongside San Francisco Bay from filling in seaside lagoons and inlets in order to create more land for development. Also, the U.S. National Resources Conservation Service began to pay out millions of dollars to ranchers and farmers who promised to convert thousands of acres of their wetlands into refuges for migratory birds and other wildlife. The Sierra Club and Calpers, the nation's largest pension fund, have also strongly opposed the cutting down of old-growth redwoods.

Population has spilled over into the wine-growing Napa and Livermore valleys. Yet, a few agricultural reserves have been created and some seashore areas have also been preserved. Another unusual development has been the orderly opening up of the former Irvine Ranch in Orange County. This area, six times the size of Manhattan, once extended twenty-two miles inland from the coast. After 1960, a future master plan for the area was drawn up, including a new campus of the University of California.

Instances of protecting California's manmade landmarks include restoration of San Francisco's Palace of Fine Arts, the last remnant of the 1915 Panama Pacific International Exhibition. Its 160-foot-high rotunda was the tour de force of architect Bernard Maybeck. Nearby, the Ghirardelli Chocolate Factory also has been restored as a place to wine, dine, and shop. Conversion of an adjacent antique cannery near Fisherman's Wharf and of the city's cable-car barn combines preservation of historic sites with today's functional needs. Although threats to such green belts as San Francisco's Golden Gate Park and Los Angeles's Elysian Park have been unceasing, the U.S. Army has surrendered the San Francisco Presidio to National Park Service supervision.

Greedy developers in the state continue to sell cheaply constructed tract homes, which too quickly fall into disrepair, sometimes even lapsing into the hands of homeless migrants. Some of these slum nests become magnets for gang activity; all of them undermine community pride. California's failure to provide enough public parks and playgrounds has hardly been made up for by the construction of privately held commercial theme parks. Now found across the nation, these synthetic recreation centers such as Knotts Berry Farm and Six Flags Magic Mountain, were started in California. Disneylands have become worldwide amusement parks.

Such for-profit centers form part of an artificial landscape that is a poor substitute for the lost greenery of a countryside increasingly paved over by freeways. Each freeway consumes twenty-eight acres of land per mile of construction. An interchange eats up as many as eighty acres. At Los Angeles, two-thirds of the center is occupied by streets, freeways, parking facilities, and garages. Not only do freeways take valuable property off the public tax rolls, but they fragment once stable neighborhoods. Only a few communities, among them San Francisco and South Pasadena, have stopped new freeway construction. The extension of Freeway 710 from Long Beach to Pasadena has been held up for years by legal squabbles. A proposed tunnel under South Pasadena remains under consideration.

Indignant environmentalists, including animal rights groups and the Sierra Club, continue to press for the regulation of development. These no-growth advocates have been frustrated by the construction industry, which claims to protect the rights of home buyers. Indeed, a number of developers as well as manufacturers have left the state because of its perceived proenvironment, antibusiness climate.

As the whine of rubber tires on concrete grows more intense, such suburbs as Daly City, Pacifica, and an unwieldy conglomerate called City of Commerce have come to resemble industrial moonscapes. California's supercities now stretch inland and northward from San Diego, beyond Los Angeles, toward Santa Barbara and San Luis Obispo. In northern California a second sprawling complex has created a contiguous metropolis around San Francisco Bay. Californians have begun to question whether such unabated growth is really "progress."

SELECTED READINGS

On water development, see David Carle, *Drowning the Dream: California's Water Choices* (2000); Norris Hundley, *The Great Thirst* (1991); William L. Kahrl, *Water and Power* (1982); John Walton, *Western Times and Water Wars . . . Rebellion in California* (1992); Mary Montgomery and Marion Clawson, *History of Legislation and Policy Formation of the Central Valley Project* (1946); Vincent Ostrom, *Water and Politics* (1953); Erwin Cooper, *Aqueduct Empire* (1968). John Hart, *Storm Over Mono* (1997) concerns a seemingly endless environmental struggle. For the 1938 and 1970 floods, see Betty Lou Young and Thomas R. Young, *Santa Monica Canyon . . .* (2005).

See also Carolyn Merchant, ed., *Green Versus Gold: Sources in California Environmental History* (1998); Arthur McEvoy, *The Fisherman's Prob-*

lem: Ecology and Law in California Fisheries (1986); Michael Black, "Tragic Remedies: A Century of Failed Fishery Policy on California's Sacramento River," *Pacific Historical Review* 64 (February 1995), 37–70; Andrew Rolle, "Turbulent Waters: Navigation and California's Southern Central Valley," *California History* 75 (Summer 1996), 129–37; and *The California Water Atlas* (Sacramento, 1979).

Regarding the Los Angeles environs, see Norman Klein, *The History of Forgetting: Los Angeles and the Erasure of Memory* (1997) and his *Los Angeles and the Memory of Many Hopes* (1990) as well as Blake Gumprecht "51 Miles of Concrete: The Exploitation and Transformation of the Los Angeles River," *Southern California Quarterly* 79 (Winter 1997), 431–86; John Chavez, *Eastside Landmark* (1998); David Rieff, *Los Angeles: Capital of the Third World* (1991); David Clark, *Los Angeles, A City Apart* (1981); Stephen Longstreet, *All Star Cast: An Anecdotal History of Los Angeles* (1977); Christopher Rand, *Los Angeles, The Ultimate City* (1967); Alison Lurie, *The Nowhere City* (1966); Robert M. Fogelson, *The Fragmented Metropolis* (1967); John L. Chapman, *Incredible Los Angeles* (1967).

Other environmental sources include Rob Kling, Spencer Olin, and Mark Poster, eds., *Postsuburban California: The Transformation of Orange County since World War II* (1991); Clark Davis, "From Oasis to Metropolis, Southern California and the Changing Context of American Leisure," *Pacific Historical Review* 61 (August 1992), 357–86; Raymond F. Dasmann, *The Destruction of California* (1965) and his *California's Changing Environment* (1981); William Bronson, *How to Kill a Golden State* (1968); Richard Lillard, *Eden in Jeopardy, Man's Prodigal Meddling With His Environment: The Southern California Experience* (1966); Ronald F. Lockman, *Guarding the Forests of Southern California* (1981); Robert Kelley, *Battling the Inland Sea . . . Public Policy and the Sacramento Valley* (1989); and Harold Gilliam, *Between the Devil and the Deep Blue Bay: The Struggle to Save San Francisco Bay* (1969).

Regarding offshore oil, see Ernest R. Bartley, *The Tidelands Oil Controversy* (1953); Robert B. Krueger, "State Tidelands Leasing in California," *U.C.L.A. Law Review* 5 (May 1958), 427–89; and Robert Easton, *Black Tide: The Santa Barbara Oil Spill and its Consequences* (1972).

CHAPTER THIRTY-EIGHT

FROM REAGAN CONSERVATISM TO "GOVERNOR MOONBEAM"

Political conservatism remained strong in California. The elections of the 1960s reflected a serious alarm over an increased crime rate, high property taxes, and widespread civil disturbances. Urban unrest, riots, and large-scale student protests at Berkeley deeply disturbed voters. Racial tensions also lurked in the background as Governor Edmund "Pat" Brown sought a third term against a new challenger, the film actor Ronald Reagan.

During the 1967–68 campaign, Reagan, formerly President of Hollywood's Screen Actors Guild, stressed that his political inexperience was an asset. He also made effective use of campaign funds provided by conservative business backers. A veteran of more than fifty motion pictures, Reagan projected a relaxed self-possession before television cameras. Convincing the electorate that he was a moderate weary of massive social welfare programs, Reagan defeated Governor Pat Brown by nearly a million votes.

Reagan promised tax relief, which voters had come to expect. In order not to raise taxes, the governor hoped to make government more frugal. But, after he proposed slashing the state budget by 10 percent, Reagan faced a movement to recall him. He had barely assumed the governorship when his proposed university budget cuts placed him at odds with the state's professoriat. Yet, his "anti-intellectualism" was applauded by some. He also hoped to impose higher tuition fees upon California's public universities and sought to control radicals on their campuses. When Reagan next sought to trim public assistance agencies and to close some mental health clinics, he faced another uproar. One of his chief goals was cutting bogus medical care for the elderly, the indigent, and chronic welfare recipients. Reagan unapologetically sought "to squeeze fraud and abuse out of California's welfare system." His opponents labeled these measures as heartless.

Some of the governor's proposals did seem petty. Toll collectors on bridges were forced to surrender their state-issued revolvers. Reagan ordered these to be sold. Travel by state employees was to be curtailed as was the use of teletype and telephone services. Equipment and supply budgets were also slashed. The governor's office suspended the publication of road maps, brochures, and even a state parks recreation magazine. Reagan announced that he saved $50,000 in typewriter ribbons alone and $2 million in the governor's phone bill during his first few months in office. He also sold a state-owned airplane.

Nevertheless, Reagan ran up against ingrained governmental programs. He found it difficult to cut budget items enacted by the state legislature. Yet, early in 1968, the state's medical program, known as "MediCal," was running an annual deficit of $210 million. Fortunately, a flourishing economy covered that expenditure, especially after Reagan severely cut expenses for mental health services.

The governor, however, had his own costly agenda. He proposed stronger penalties for rape, armed robbery, and theft. Reagan, an ardent opponent of gun control, nevertheless faced a fearful public that forced the legislature to pass a stronger gun control law. Passage of that measure was ensured after an armed group of Black Panthers scared legislators witless by bursting into their chambers as the law was being debated. Reagan met fierce opposition over his repeal of an open-housing law, passage of obscenity laws, and the establishment of welfare fraud units.

Reagan filled his administration with business persons who served on task forces and commissions without pay while urging the loosening of state controls over business. Conversely, labor unions hated Reagan. When farm labor grew short during the 1968 harvest season, the governor sent convicts to help pick crops. He also ordered the employment, during harvest seasons, of able welfare recipients as pickers. Labor leaders called such moves a subsidy to growers. Despite Reagan's tough talk, in the eight years he served as governor, his attempts to stem the growth of government were repeatedly defeated by a Democratic legislature hostile to him. Governmental inertia made it difficult to overhaul a lumbering bureaucracy in Sacramento. Welfare rolls actually increased under Reagan.

The governor's attempts to coax state employees into voluntarily working on holidays showed how distant his views were from those of entrenched civil servants. In addition, by 1974, Reagan's last year as governor, his annual budget reached over $10 billion. This was more than double the amount spent by his supposedly spendthrift predecessor, Pat Brown. Although Reagan's promises to reduce the size of state government fell flat,

Ronald Reagan (right) campaigning for Barry Goldwater in 1964. That year Goldwater won the Republican presidential nomination. The Goldwater campaign was the starting point of Reagan's own national political career. Courtesy of the Ronald Reagan Library.

his opponents underestimated both his tenacity and popularity, since he went on to become president of the United States.

California's next governor was Pat Brown's son, Edmund G. "Jerry" Brown, Jr. (1975–83). The senior Brown had unquestionably overseen an era of explosive growth. His son, however, exhibited a self-imposed retrenchment when faced with the proliferation of state projects. Indeed, Jerry Brown repeatedly reminded audiences that there was a limit to what government could undertake, even criticizing the spending philosophy of old New Dealers like his father. Although an advocate of civil rights, racial integration, and ecology, Jerry Brown turned out to be both an ascetic and a rather quirky fiscal conservative.

Only thirty-seven years old when he became governor, the young Brown stated that he had no national political aspirations. In 1975, he refused to attend the National Governors Conference, claiming to be more concerned with California's problems: unemployment; crime; the rising cost of medical insurance; the plight of farmworkers; and fighting the highway and auto lobbies. Only one year later, young Brown entered the presidential primaries as a "favorite son" candidate. He did not gain the Democratic nomination, which went to Jimmy Carter.

Brown came to be called "Governor Moonbeam," for he promised his generation a respite from post–Vietnam War disillusionment with big government, big business, and big unions. His refusal to live in a new governor's mansion or to use an executive airplane or official limousine struck a positive chord with his own baby-boom generation.

Even in Orange County, the largely Protestant and conservative home of Richard Nixon and "the world's first drive-in church," Brown, an unmarried ex-seminarian who had dabbled in Zen meditation, remained quite popular. But, as with Governor Reagan, the public expected almost magical solutions to difficult problems. During 1975, a malpractice crisis inundated the medical community. This concerned the soaring rates that physicians had to pay for malpractice insurance. Hundreds of physicians throughout the state temporarily ceased practicing medicine.

The governor's boyish charm made him appear to be an old-fashioned Populist as well as a pseudo-monk committed to sacrifice. "We're going to have to work harder," he stated in a 1976 speech to the California Democratic Council. One assemblyman chided the young governor's inaction: "I've heard that goddamned sanctimonious speech too many times. He lectures people who know a lot more about public policy than he does."

Brown, however, did act upon some of his convictions. A new state Office of Appropriate Technology advocated environmentally designed buildings and supported wind power, solar heating, home organic farming, and bioconversion (the use of human waste to produce energy). He also appointed numerous women, persons of color, and consumer advocates

Edmund G. "Jerry" Brown, Jr., the youthful Democratic Governor of California, 1975–83.

to commissions and court offices. The governor's admonition that "we are entering an era of limits" hardly impressed his fellow politicos. The press too grew tired of his sermonizing.

Brown did find a politically valuable soul mate in Cesar Chavez, the union farm organizer. In 1975, Brown sponsored the pathbreaking Agricultural Labor Relations Act, which strengthened the bargaining power of Chavez's United Farm Workers. Chicanos, however, looked in vain to Chavez as an organizer of urban barrios. Although Chavez was not an efficient administrator or a strong orator, the legislature in 2000 enacted a state holiday in his honor.

In 1976, Los Angeles County reached a population of 7 million persons. It had become the most populous county in the United States. San Diego was now the state's second largest city, whereas San Francisco dropped to third place. An American love affair with the Sun Belt cities of the Southwest accounted for some of modern California's growth. But it was also due to a tremendous increase of foreign-born immigrants, both legal and illegal.

Jerry Brown's governorship showed continuing tolerance for homosexuals, in an era when many gay people found the courage to come out of the closet. San Francisco became a tolerant center for homosexuals. In 1978, a tragedy occurred there involving Mayor George Moscone and a member of the Board of Supervisors, Harvey Milk, an avowed homosexual. Both men were shot to death in San Francisco's city hall by a disgruntled former official; in the shadows lurked an unexplained love affair.

A marked change in population demographics occurred in the Brown years. Upwardly mobile aspirants to power and material affluence called Yuppies, a term used to describe Young Urban Professionals, took the place of the Hippies of the 1960s. Some Yuppies were, ironically, former Hippies who had graduated and entered the workplace. This generation of baby boomers increasingly influenced journalism and law in particular.

Californians professed to an interest in urban renewal and mass transit. Yet, potential commuters remained uninformed about fixed light-rail systems already operating throughout the world. Jerry Brown realized that the state's freeway program had to be curtailed due to inflation, skyrocketing construction costs, and wavering tax collection. To combat air pollution, Californians erected tough new emission standards that succeeded in reducing exhaust emissions from a typical new car by a startling 90 percent. The state henceforth cracked down on those who owned and operated pollution-spewing old jalopies.

But such measures depended upon adequate funding. An energy crisis hit the United States in the mid-1970s. This was followed by severe federal budget cuts. Dependent upon a massive public-sector workforce, California was seriously hurt by the reduction of federal defense spending after the U.S. withdrawal from Vietnam. The number of aerospace jobs declined from a high of 616,000 to fewer than 400,000. The state treasury went from a surplus of $2.9 billion in 1979 to a deficit of $541 million by 1983.

The attitude of the idealistic young governor reflected voter dissatisfaction with the state's uneven system of taxation. This touched off a taxpayer revolt. In 1978, Howard Jarvis, a harsh critic of government taxation, came up with a property-tax reduction initiative (Proposition 13) that the voters passed by a landslide. It stabilized assessments on real estate for years to come. That measure also encouraged tax rebellions in other states throughout the nation. Education was the largest single item in the state budget. Expansion of the state college and university systems alone placed heavy fiscal burdens on taxpayers. The community colleges, comprising 109 institutions, would become the largest system of higher education in the world.

Between 1987 and 1991, public spending soared. As we shall see, yet another wave of new immigrants would further complicate the state's fiscal liabilities.

SELECTED READINGS

Recent California politics and society are analyzed in Jackson K. Putnam, *Modern California Politics* (1990) and his *Old Age Politics in California, From Richardson to Reagan* (1970) as well as Putnam's *The Political Career of Jesse Marvin Unruh* (2005); Michael P. Rogin and John L. Shover, *Political Change in California* (1970); Royce D. Delmatier, Clarence F. McIntosh, and Earl G. Waters, eds., *The Rumble of California Politics, 1848–1970* (1970); and Raymond A. Mohl, ed., *Searching for the Sunbelt* (1990), 124–48.

Regarding the two Governor Browns and Reagan, see John C. Bollens and G. Robert Williams, *Jerry Brown in a Plain Brown Wrapper* (1978); J. D. Lorenz, *Jerry Brown: The Man on the White Horse* (1978); Robert Peck, *Jerry Brown: The Philosopher Prince* (1978); Roger Rapoport, *California Dreaming: The Political Odyssey of Pat and Jerry Brown* (1982); Orville Schell, *Brown* (1978); Gladwin Hill, *Dancing Bear: The Inside Look at California Politics* (1968); Bill Boyarsky, *The Rise of Ronald Reagan* (1968); and Joseph Lewis, *What Makes Reagan Run? A Political Profile* (1968). Edmund G. Brown, Sr., wrote two books: *Reagan and Reality: The Two Californias* (1970) and (with Bill Brown) *Ronald Reagan, The Political Cha-*

meleon (1976); see also Lou Cannon, *Ronnie and Jesse: A Political Odyssey* (1972); Gary Hamilton and Nicole Biggart, *Governor Reagan, Governor Brown* (1984); Gerard J. DeGroot, "Ronald Reagan and Student Unrest in California" *Pacific Historical Review* 65 (February 1996), 107–29.

Regarding labor and racial strife, see Francisco Balderrama, *In Defense of La Raza* (1982); Roger Daniels and Spencer C. Olin, eds., *Racism in California: A Reader in the History of Oppression* (1972); George D. Horowitz, *La Causa: The California Grape Strike* (1970); Ralph de Toledano, *Little Cesar* (1962); Ernesto Galarza, *Barrio Boy* (1971), as well as Galarza, *Spiders in the House and Workers in the Field* (1970); Leo Gobler, Joan W. Moore, and Ralph Guzman, *The Mexican-American People* (1970); Joan London and Henry Anderson, *So Shall Ye Reap* (1970).

Books about Cesar Chavez include: Richard Griswold del Castillo and Richard Garcia, *Cesar Chavez: A Triumph of Spirit* (1995); Ronald B. Taylor, *Chavez and the Farm Workers* (1975); Jacques Levy, *Cesar Chavez: Autobiography of La Causa* (1976); Peter Matthiessen, *Sal Si Puedes* (1969); James Terzian and Kathryn Cramer, *Mighty Hard Road: The Story of Cesar Chavez* (1970); Mark Day, *Forty Acres* (1970); Linda and Theo Majka, *Farm Workers, Agribusiness, and the State* (1982); and Cletus E. Daniel, *Bitter Harvest: A History of California Farmworkers* (1981).

For modern agriculture, see Lawrence J. Jelinek, *Harvest Empire: A History of California Agriculture* (1979); Donald J. Pisani, *From the Family Farm to Agribusiness* (1984); Ellen Liebman, *California Farmland* (1983) rebuts Paul Gates's assertion that land monopolists exploited former ranchers. Instead, she asserts that most land holdings came from the public domain.

For more on Chicanos, in agriculture especially, see David Gutiérrez, *Walls and Mirrors: Mexican Americans and the Politics of Ethnicity* (1995); Carey McWilliams, *Brothers under the Skin* (1951) and his *North from Mexico* (1949); Matt S. Meier and Feliciano Rivers, *The Chicanos* (1972); Raul Morin, *Among the Valiant* (1963); Julian Samora, ed., *La Raza: Forgotten Americans* (1969); Charles Wollenberg, ed., *Ethnic Conflict in California History* (1970); Gilbert Cruz and Jane Talbot, *Chicano Bibliography, 1960–1972* (1974); Gilberto Lopez y Rivas, *The Chicanos* (1974); Albert Camarillo, *Chicanos in California* (1985); Ricardo Romo, *East Los Angeles: History of a Barrio* (1984); Rodolfo Gonzalez, *I Am Joaquin* (1973); Edmund Villaseñor, *Macho* (1973); Herschel T. Manuel, *Spanish-Speaking Children of the Southwest* (1958) and Wayne Moquin, ed., *A Documentary History of the Mexican Americans* (1971).

CHAPTER THIRTY-NINE

AN ETHNIC TAPESTRY

In the early American era, a raw and sparsely settled new state needed every immigrant it could entice. California's population then numbered only some 7,500 persons, most of whom spoke Spanish. Today's burgeoning California is home to a rich variety of ethnicities, languages, and cultures. Yet, recent conflicts related to overpopulation and ethnicity have marred the state's social fabric.

By 2005, the population of California surpassed the 36 million mark. It also marked the first time in the state's history that no one racial or ethnic group constituted a majority. Simply put, everyone in California was in the minority. Leading the change was the dramatic growth of ethnics. In 1980, they constituted less than one-third of the state's population. Today, former minorities have come to make up 64 percent of the state's population. Almost 40 percent of these speak a language other than English at home.

California's population growth raises difficult questions as to the state's future. Concerns continue to mount on how its infrastructure, especially in the fields of education and health care, can meet the needs of its diverse peoples. With 21 percent of the nation's minorities living in California, the debate over bilingual education, for example, has raised issues of fairness. If it is offered to those speaking Mandarin Chinese or Spanish then some ask, why is it not offered for immigrants from Eastern Europe?

Tied to these difficult issues is the contentious debate over illegal immigration. Although opinion polls show that Americans are overwhelmingly opposed to illegal immigration, many businesses and farmers as well seek an inexpensive labor force. Ironically, those who argue for the need to secure the state's border against Mexico (the number one source of illegal immigrants) include the same residents who want ethnic laborers to wash their cars, pick their lettuce, and watch their children at bargain prices.

State lawmakers tout the importance of making sure "no one is above the law," yet they enact legislation favoring the rights of "undocumented workers." In California, criminal suspects cannot be asked questions about their immigration status. Its banks offer illegals personal accounts without identity documents while some Health Management firms accept undocumented aliens as members.

Meanwhile, illegal immigration has placed huge strains on the state's ability to provide adequate social services for its citizens. Its hospitals, schools, and criminal justice system are stretched beyond capacity. Critics of illegal immigration further point out that an "underground economy" exists in which forged documents are rampant. Also, unscrupulous employers pay illegals "under the table," depriving society of vitally needed tax dollars.

Illegals searching for work flock toward the San Diego–Tijuana border, long a sieve for the undocumented. Los Angeles and the San Francisco Bay area have provided sanctuaries for illegals. The L.A. Catholic hierarchy openly defends the harboring of undocumented aliens. Other groups which protest federal immigration restrictions include *La Raza* as well as the strident Aztlán Movement.

Today, L.A. contains the largest concentration of Latinos of Mexican origin outside of Mexico City. Those illegals who cross the border into "El Norte" face significant physical dangers. Once filthy rivers are forged and deserts crossed, undocumented immigrants live a life of fear. If discovered, they can be sent back homeward. Also, smugglers, referred to as "coyotes," are not above stealing and abusing the very people who have hired them.

The jobs that these workers take include low-paying car washing, lawn mowing, trash-hauling, construction work, and road building. Given the huge demand for such workers, it is understandable why illegal immigration has soared. To stem the tide of illegal immigrants from around the world, the Immigration and Naturalization Service (INS) has sporadically tightened controls at airports, seaports, and along the state's porous border with Mexico. Occasional violence continues between border patrol officers and illegals.

Traveling northward along the coast from San Diego, motorists pass through INS toll booth checkpoints. While most drivers are waved onward by uniformed agents, those cars suspected of carrying illegal immigrants are hailed to the roadside for examination. All illegals are sent back below the Mexican border.

Illegal immigration has fostered strong political debate throughout California and the nation. In 1986, federal legislation granted amnesty to large numbers of undocumented aliens. This legislation encouraged the arrival of even greater numbers of illegals. By 1996, the seemingly unstoppable tide of illegal immigration led to a public backlash. That year, mired in a recession, the voters, by a landslide, enacted Proposition 209. This law limited schooling and medical care for undocumented immigrants. Repeated legal challenges to Proposition 209 were mounted.

Such restrictive legislation hardly ended the debate over race, gender, and class tensions. Corporations and farmers alike, seeking cheap labor, continued to fight against ethnic restrictions. Yet, in 1998, another restrictive Proposition 227 was approved by 61 percent of state voters. That measure abolished most bilingual education programs. At the time, some 1.4 million California children spoke little if any English. Again, critics of bilingual education maintained that it actually hurt minority students who desperately needed to speak, read, and write English if they hoped to succeed.

During the 1990s, Ward Connerly, an African American Regent of the University of California, led a national fight against affirmative action. He asserted that such laws actually hurt minority students by letting unqualified applicants gain admission into colleges and universities in which they could not successfully compete. With little support once they had gained admission, such students dropped out of school altogether. Connerly's point was that the administrators were simply filling quotas, not really helping the minority students they had accepted.

Racial and ethnic strife continued to rise, associated with disparities in schooling and income. According to one study, Asians were three times more likely to finish high school than were Latinos, who form the backbone of the low-paid service economy. Asians were also twice as likely to earn incomes above $60,000. Marginalized Latinos, whose families clustered in ethnic enclaves, found themselves locked into low-paying jobs with few benefits or opportunities for advancement. Today, fewer than half of foreign-born Latinos complete high school.

Illegal immigration has also had profound effects for California's African Americans. Realization of their civil rights remains a protracted struggle. Latino demographics have steadily eroded the electoral power of black voters. Yet, black Californians continue to assume leadership positions. Los Angeles and San Francisco have both elected black mayors. Willie Brown, who served as the first African American mayor of San Francisco, was also the state's first African American speaker of the state assembly. Despite such high profile political gains, many blacks remain disenchanted by the growth of crime and long-term joblessness among inner-city youths.

Taken in Los Angeles on April 30, 1992 near the intersection of Kenmore Avenue & Beverly Boulevard. Later that day, a dusk-to-dawn curfew was imposed in portions of the city. Polaroid photo by Dana Graves.

Racial discord has also increased between African Americans and Latinos, tightening the job market in the formerly black-dominated communities of Compton and Inglewood. In south-central Los Angeles, black residents came to resent Asian merchants who operated stores in their neighborhoods but who refused to hire blacks. Asian merchants were perceived as giving little back to the black community, spending their profits elsewhere. As they bought up more corner groceries and coffee shops, polarization mounted. L.A. convenience stores owned by Korean merchants were firebombed after a highly publicized case in which a young African-American girl accused of shoplifting, was shot dead by an angry storeowner.

The tensions between blacks, Koreans, and Chicanos have remained unresolved. Black breadwinners regularly complain of losing jobs to undocumented workers. Feelings of victimization have sometimes gotten out of control as black gang members clashed with Latino rivals.

In April of 1992, full-scale violence broke out near Watts for the second time in twenty-seven years. This followed the acquittal of two Los

Angeles police officers accused of beating Rodney King, a black motorist who resisted arrest after he had been stopped by the police. Although a third party provided the prosecution with a videotape that clearly showed the officers hitting and kicking King, the first jury trial failed to convict the involved officers.

When that verdict was announced, enraged blacks took to the streets. Live television coverage captured the resulting riots. Violators of all races used the King verdict as an excuse to steal merchandise and to attack innocent motorists trapped in their vehicles. Some fifty-three persons subsequently lost their lives. Arsonists set fire to business establishments, some of which were Asian owned. Proprietors, with their buildings looted and burned to the ground, refused to reopen their doors, leaving predominantly African American neighborhoods with even fewer services.

In May of 2007, another Los Angeles ethnic disturbance occurred. An "immigration rights" demonstration was marred by rocks and bottles thrown at Los Angeles Police Department officers who began moving troublemakers into a local park. Overreaction by the police, in which over 140 rubber bullets were fired into the terrified flag-waving crowd, created a political firestorm. Astute handling of a potential maelstrom by the city's Latino mayor and police chief did calm the situation. But anger against the Los Angeles Police Department again increased.

Such public demonstrations remind one that ethnics have forever changed California society. Los Angeles saw its Latino population soar from 260,389 in 1960 to nearly 1.8 million by the year 2000. Neighboring Santa Ana, once a predominantly white suburb, has become only 12 percent Caucasian. In 2001, the U.S. Census Bureau reported that 76 percent of Santa Ana's residents speak Spanish, the highest community figure in the nation. Anaheim, Riverside, and Los Angeles are also nationally among the top ten cities in the percentage of Spanish-speaking persons. Overall, California has the greatest number (39 percent) of persons who speak languages other than English.

It has been argued that Latinos from Mexico, as compared to other immigrant groups, have had more difficulty assimilating into the mainstream of American society because their homeland is so close by. One study, however, indicates that most immigrants climb the upwardly mobile economic ladder within a relatively short time after their arrival.

Some simply bypass the traditional melting pot concept. Increasing numbers of Latinos appear on television shows. Among such entertainers are Eva Longoria, George Lopez, and Carlos Mencia. And a dysfunctional model scarcely applies to Latinos elected to public office. In 1996, the legislature selected its first Latino speaker, Cruz Bustamante, the

"Victory Smile." Antonio Villaraigosa gives his victory speech after defeating incumbent James Hahn, May 17, 2005. Villaraigosa's became the first Latino mayor of Los Angeles since 1872 when the city was still a frontier town. Photo by Julio Cortez/www.JulyThePhotoGuy.com.

son of a Dinuba barber. In 2005, Antonio Villaraigosa, a product of East L.A., was voted the first Latino mayor of Los Angeles since 1872.

Critics do, however, warn that California could become a new Bangladesh, an overpopulated country that has not controlled the entry of illegal immigrants. The increased use of fraudulent documents allow newcomers to qualify for employment and relief benefits. This increases the drain upon the state's welfare, educational, and health systems.

After the fall of Saigon in 1975, some 50,000 Vietnamese refugees suddenly became legal California residents. Today's Westminster, known as "Little Saigon," contains the largest concentration of Vietnamese in North America. Thousands of Laotians and Cambodians, also displaced by the Vietnam War, subsequently took up residence in Los Angeles and Orange Counties.

By the 1950s, numerous second-generation Japanese Americans, or *Nisei*, had moved out of Boyle Heights into nearby Monterey Park. By 1990, that community was 58 percent Asian American and 30 percent Latino, becoming known as the "Asian Beverly Hills." Meanwhile, in the real Beverly Hills, foreign-born storeowners along its posh Rodeo Drive have transformed that suburb of L.A. into one of the wealthiest Jewish American and Iranian communities in the nation. Each lives side by side.

Similarly, the number of Glendale's Armenian residents has risen to over 30 percent of its population. More than a third of L.A. County's 153,000 persons of Armenian descent now live in Glendale. That city has the second largest population of Armenians in the nation. In this once predominantly white community, however, tensions between Armenian and Latino youth have resulted in several violent high school gang clashes. Also, when the city's American flags were lowered to half-staff on Armenian Genocide Day, some Glendale citizens were appalled. Elsewhere too, immigrants have changed the face of various communities. Today's South Gate boasts an Asian majority. Further northward, numerous Filipinos reside in Daly City near San Francisco. Asians and Latinos alike have begun to replace black majorities in Watts and South-Central Los Angeles. This was due to the recent movement of African Americans out of south L.A. into adjacent suburban areas, including the San Fernando and Antelope valleys. East Los Angeles's population is close to 100 percent Latino.

During these huge population shifts, Caucasians virtually disappeared from such suburbs as Baldwin Park, Rosemead, and El Monte. Enhanced real estate values, rather than "white flight" alone, led the formerly white majority to cash out their equity in older homes. Whites moved into less expensive retirement havens at La Verne, Claremont, San Dimas, Walnut, and Diamond Bar. Across southern California, restaurant menus, traffic signs, and even graffiti, feature Latino and Asian phrasing.

Religious diversity has also accompanied the state's multicultural pattern. Some 40 percent of both Asians and Caucasian Buddhists in the United States live in southern California. Its new architectural structures include mosques, churches, and temples constructed by followers of Muslim, Christian, Jewish, and Hindu faiths.

The myth that foreigners would inevitably be integrated into one pattern of life has given way to the phrase "ethnic pluralism." Clinging to native folkways, each subculture does risk becoming antagonistic toward other competing groups. Latinos hail from several dozen nations. Spanish-speaking persons prefer to be called Mexicans, Cubans, or Salvadorans. The Vietnamese, Laotians, and Thais accuse affluent Chinese from Hong Kong and Taiwan of "moving in at the top," when they possess better homes and automobiles than other foreign groups.

Among these are California's Sihks, members of the world's fifth largest religion. The state possesses fifteen Sikh temples. In April of 2007, more than 10,000 turbaned Sikhs, anxious to affirm their presence, paraded in downtown Los Angeles. As with other minorities, class origins, linguistic skill, and educational status play a large part in whether immi-

Los Angeles & Vicinity

0 — 5 — 10 Mi
0 — 10 Km

grants are employable in white collar positions or head toward poverty in a new land.

Asians are stereotypically viewed as industrious and respectful of "family values." Statistics show that Asian teenagers drop out of high school at lower rates than whites. As a result, these immigrants tend to arrive in California with English-language and technical skills. These high-status newcomers need not begin at the bottom of the job ladder. They frequently enter medical, computer, and engineering specialties or are employed as property managers. Asian names also have begun to be cited for political achievement as well as economic success. In 1974, March Fong Eu, a Chinese American and former member of the legislature from Oakland, was elected California's Secretary of State.

California's cities reflect their continuing foreign population growth. A "Koreatown" has emerged along Olympic and Vermont Boulevards in Los Angeles. It has become the largest Korean settlement outside Seoul. San Marino, once an upper-class white enclave surrounding the Huntington Library, is now a Chinese-dominated community. Further north, Fremont now has a 40 percent Asian school enrollment.

The longer most immigrants stay, the better off they become. Over time, they usually achieve home ownership and better financial security. Among Asians employment is high and claims for public aid marginal. One result of their recent migration has been to help make California a center of trans-Pacific commerce. Foodstuffs, scrap iron, paper, oranges, cotton, and beef flow out of San Pedro and San Francisco harbors, to be exchanged for computer microchips and television sets from Asia. Automobiles by the thousands continue to be unloaded off Asian container vessels.

One group that has been ignored historically are those of Middle Eastern ancestry. As recent as the 2000 census, people of Middle Eastern descent were not included in the nation's population figures. The tragic events of September 11, 2001, however, renewed fears, as with Japanese experience along the Pacific coast during the Second World War, that innocent ethnics would again be punished by a vengeful public. Middle Easterners saw a drop in their businesses immediately after the 9/11 terrorist attacks in New York City and elsewhere.

One further minority which until recently has not received widespread attention are the state's Indians. Some of its tribes now profit handsomely from legalized gambling. Approved by California voters, they operate numerous gambling casinos, exempt from federal and state taxation. Not all reservations have gambling. Some are located on small, remote, and bleak reservations. Other tribal groups, including the Morongos, operate casinos and luxurious recreation facilities situated near urban areas. Among their investments is San Diego's venerable U.S. Grant Hotel.

California's Indian gaming facilities now take in 7 billion dollars annually. This revenue surpasses the collective intake of all Las Vegas casinos. The state possesses more than fifty Nevada-style gambling resorts with over 60,000 slot machines and hundreds of blackjack and poker tables. Gamblers, who once flocked to Las Vegas, now head for glitzy Indian lounges outside Palm Springs and Indian Wells. The impoverished and disease-plagued forebears of Indian casino owners could not have imagined the growing affluence of their descendants.

Finally, California continues to offer hope for those seeking a better life. But, will the state's attractiveness last forever? It has become a kaleidoscope in which its many nationalities and races face myriad social, economic, and political challenges.

SELECTED READINGS

Recent ethnic scholarship includes Mark Wild, *Street Meeting: Multiethnic Neighborhoods in . . . Los Angeles* (2006). See also Victor Hanson, *Mexifornia: A State of Becoming* (2003); McKanna, Clare, *Race and Homicide in Nineteenth Century California* (2002); Lawrence Bobo et al., *Prismatic Metropolis: Inequality in Los Angeles* (2001); Davis Wyatt, *The Fire This Time . . . Race, Catastrophe and the Shaping of California* (1997); Kevin McCarthy and George Vernez, *Immigration in a Changing Economy: California's Experience* (1997); James Allen and Eugene Turner, *The Ethnic Quilt: Population Diversity in Southern California* (1997) and their *Changing Faces, Changing Places . . .* (2002); Roger Waldinger and Mehdi Bozorgmehr, eds. *Ethnic Los Angeles* (1996); Diane Hart, *Undocumented in L.A., An Immigrant's Story* (1997) and Robert Self, *American Babylon: Race and the Struggle For Postwar Oakland* (2003).

Chicano references include: David Hayes-Bautista, *La Nueva California: Latinos in the Golden State* (2004) and Mary Pardo, *Mexican American Women Activists . . . In Los Angeles Communities* (1998) as well as Anibal Yanez-Chavez, *Latino Politics in California* (1996); Lydia Chavez, *The Color Bind: California's Battle to End Affirmative Action* (1998); Francisco E. Balderrama and Raymond Rodríguez, *Decade of Betrayal: Mexican Repatriation in the 1930s* (1995); Juan Gómez-Quiñones, *Mexican American Labor, 1790–1900* (1995) and his *Chicano Politics: Reality and Promise, 1940–1990* (1992); David G. Gutiérrez, *Walls and Mirrors: Mexican Immigrants and the Politics of Ethnicity* (1995); Ricardo Romo, *East Los Angeles: History of a Barrio* (1983); Marguerite Marin, *Social Protest in an Urban Barrio* (1991); Rodolfo Acuña, *Community Under Siege: A Chronicle of Chicanos East of the Los Angeles River* (1984); Edward J. Escobar, "The Dialectics of Repression: The Los Angeles Police Department and the Chicano Movement," *Journal of American History* 79 (March 1993), 1483–1514; Mario Barrera, *Race and Class in the Southwest* (1979); Alfredo Mirande, *The Chicano Experience* (1985); Zena Pearlstone, *Ethnic L.A.* (1990); Antonio Ríos-Bustamente and Pedro Castillo, *An Illustrated History of Mexican Los Angeles, 1781–1985* (1986); Gilbert G. Gonzalez, *Labor and*

Community, Mexican Citrus Worker Villages . . . (1994); George J. Sanchez, *Becoming Mexican American . . .* (1993) and Douglas Monroy, *Mexican Los Angeles From the Great Migration to the Great Depression* (1999). Blacks are the subject of Josh Sides, *L. A. City Limits: African American Los Angeles* (2003) and Douglas Flamming, *Bound For Freedom: Black Los Angeles. . .* (2004) as well as Lawrence de Graaf, Kevin Mulroy, and Quintard Taylor, eds., *Seeking El Dorado: African Americans in California* (2001); Delores McBroome, *Parallel Communities: African Americans in California's East Bay, 1850–63* (1993); Gordon Wheeler, *Black California* (1993); E. Frederick Anderson, *The Development of the Black Community of Los Angeles* (1980); Mark Baldessare, *The Los Angeles Riots* (1994); Rudolph Lapp, *Afro-Americans in California* (1980); W. Sherman Savage, *Blacks in the West* (1976); Byron Skinner, *Black Origins in the Inland Empire* (1983); Douglas Daniels, *Pioneer Urbanites: A Social and Cultural History of Black San Francisco* (1980); Nathan Cohen, ed., *The Los Angeles Riots: A Socio-Psychological Study* (1971); Fred Viehe "Black Gold Suburbs . . . of Los Angeles, 1890–1930," *Journal of Urban History* 8 (November 1981), 3-26; and Michael Goldstein, "The Political Careers of Fred Roberts and Tom Bradley," *Western Journal of Black Studies* 5 (Summer 1981), 139–46.

American Indians appear in Robert F. Heizer and Alan F. Almquist, *The Other Californians: Prejudice and Discrimination Under Spain, Mexico, and the United States* (1971); Joan Weibel-Orlando, *Indian Country: L.A.* (1991) and Diana Bahr, *From Mission to Metropolis: Cupeño Indian Women in Los Angeles* (1993).

Regarding Asians, see Nancy Abelman and John Lie, *Blue Dreams: Korean Americans and the Los Angeles Riots* (1995) and Lon Kurashige, *Japanese American Celebration and Conflict . . . in Los Angeles* (2002) as well as Leland Saito, *Race and Politics: Asian Americans, Latinos, and Whites in a Los Angeles Suburb* (1998), centered on Monterey Park.

Also consult Sucheng Chan, *Asian Californians* (1991) and her *This Bittersweet Soil: The Chinese in California Agriculture* (1996); Paul Ong, Edna Bonacich, and Lucie Cheng, eds., *Down By the Station: Los Angeles Chinatown, 1880–1933* (1997); Yong Chen, *Chinese San Francisco* (2000). See also Ronald Takaki, *Strangers From a Different Shore* (1989); David Yoo, "Enlightened Identities: Buddhism and Japanese Americans of California, 1924–41," *Western Historical Quarterly* 27 (Autumn 1996), 281–302; Thomas Chinn, *Bridging the Pacific: San Francisco Chinatown* (1989); Benson Tong, *Unsubmissive Women: Chinese Prostitutes in Nineteenth Century California* (1994); Judy Yung, *Unbound Feet: A Social History of Chinese Women in San Francisco* (1995); Julia Costello, *Rice Bowls in the Delta*

(1988); Timothy Fong, *The First Urban Chinatown, Monterey Park* (1994); Karl Yoneda, *Ganbatte: Sixty-Year Struggle of a Kibei Worker* (1983); Pyong Gap Min, *Caught in the Middle: Korean Communities in New York and Los Angeles* (1996); Ivan Light and Edna Bonacich, *Immigrant Entrepreneurs: Koreans in Los Angeles, 1965-1982* (1988); E. Y. Yu, and E. H. Phillips, *Koreans in Los Angeles* (1982); Gary Peters, "Migration . . . Among the Vietnamese in Southern California," *Sociology and Social Research* 72 (October, 1987), 33–38; Craig Scharlin and Lillia Villanueva, *Philip Vera Cruz: A Personal History of Filipino Immigrants and the Farmworkers Movement* (1992); Michael Showalter, "The Watsonville Anti-Filipino Riot of 1930," *Southern California Quarterly* 71 (Winter 1989), 341-48.

Italians are the subject of Gloria Lothrop, "Unwelcome in Freedom's Land: Italian Americans in Southern California . . . During World War II," *Southern California Quarterly* (Winter 1999). See also Sidney Lawrence, "The Ghirardelli Story" in *California History* 81 (Winter 2002), 90–115. The Jewish experience is described in Ava Kahn and Mark Dollinger, eds., *California Jews* (2003). Arabs are the subject of Janice Marschner, *California's Arab Americans* (2003).

A TRANSFORMATIVE SOCIETY

"The Golden State" was an apt motto for early Californians to adopt. The land's beauty and climate drew widespread praise long before modern chambers of commerce began their incessant boosterism. The accounts of explorers, hide-and-tallow traders, visiting sailors, and gold hunters all suggested a new utopia in that far-off province. Today millions of newcomers continue to savor California's allure. Even its overcrowding, high rates of crime, smog, earthquakes, floods, landslides, and annual fires have not quite marred the state's appeal.

Though radical challenges of modernity are constant, San Francisco, with its small population, has managed to preserve its cable cars and palatial hotels. Called the center of America's "left coast," the city's image as a gracious metropolis has been stained by a rising crime rate, high housing costs, and environmental decay.

Los Angeles too is no longer a nirvana of waving palm trees and fragrant citrus groves. Today its county comprises eighty-eight cities whose population totals over 10 million inhabitants. Urban sprawl has created a fragmented new global crossroads. Less affluent residents are moving eastward to an "Inland Empire" that provides less costly housing and lower taxes. Other counties and states also offer cheaper housing and better jobs.

In Oakland, San Diego, and San Jose, crime, deteriorating neighborhoods, and the homeless have also changed these cities' image. By the 1960s, California's crime rate reached well above the national average. Among its lurid events were the 1969 mass murders by the deranged female groupies of cult leader Charles Manson. Five years later came the sensational kidnapping of Patricia Hearst, heiress of the Hearst newspaper dynasty. During that episode, Hearst had strangely sided with her captors, even helping them to stage a bank holdup. Los Angeles police swat teams finally cornered Hearst and the bizarre group called the Symbionese Liberation Army, with a bloody shootout following.

Instant critics, seizing upon such bizarre events, have repeated tired stereotypes about California as "a land of fruit and nuts." Back in the 1940s, Hollywood's unsolved Black Dahlia murder almost seemed to forecast a later series of lurid assassinations. In 1975, Lynette (Squeaky) Fromme attempted to kill President Gerald Ford in Sacramento. Other psychopaths included the Zodiac Killer, the Zebra Murderer, the Night Stalker, and the Hillside Strangler. The most brutal offenses to mar the state's image featured the "Reverend" Jim Jones. His 1978 flight from San Francisco to Guyana in South America resulted in mass murder-suicide. Jones led some 900 of his religious followers to their deaths by drinking a poisonous substance. Extensive media coverage was given to trials involving such Los Angeles and Hollywood figures as former athlete O.J. Simpson, actor Robert Blake, and singer Michael Jackson. Each was acquitted of a variety of alleged serious crimes.

Alarmed by so many outrageous crimes, Governor George Deukmejian, as state attorney general, authored the "Use a Gun, Go to Prison" law. But he never really managed to make real inroads into the crime problem. California's media repeated tired negative stereotypes, claiming that urbanites stood a greater chance of dying by knife or gun than in an auto accident. Some freakish urban murders were gang-related. Replete with nicknames, hand signals, and an array of weapons, young gang members formed a veritable counterculture. Competing gangs engage in fatal drive-by shootings. In Los Angeles, Latinos and African American gang members continue to kill each other over turf wars and drug deals. During their street warfare, innocent bystanders are also slain.

High rates of unemployment and family breakdowns are linked to such inner-city crime. Disoriented youngsters turn to gang membership for the support they fail to get at home or school. They pollute the learning atmosphere of their classrooms. Rapes, aggravated assaults, robberies, and burglaries at one point reached epidemic proportions. In an attempt to make California a zero-tolerance zone for criminals, in 1994 the legislature instituted a draconian measure. This "Three Strikes Law" mandates 25-year-to-life sentences for anyone convicted of three felony crimes, including even minor possession of drugs.

By 1991 a new conservative governor inherited a budget swollen by escalating prison costs and welfare entitlements. This was Pete Wilson, a harsh foe of illegal border crossers. By 1994, he led a ballot measure to exclude them from most public services. This legislation passed but was then declared unconstitutional by a federal court. The governor also advocated steep cuts in welfare grants to children, the elderly, the blind, and education. The new governor also opposed affirmative action for minority university applicants.

Education became a steadily larger item in the state's inflated budget. Although 40 percent of state funding went to public schools and colleges, California became one of the lowest-ranked states in expenditure on education. The need to improve public education and to address social problems heightened tension between liberal legislators and each conservative governor.

When Wilson favored raising state taxes, this set off an ultraconservative antitax movement. That year, the voters adopted Proposition 218, which supplanted the 1978 "Jarvis-Gann Taxpayer's Revolt." Both measures limited property taxation. Proposition 218 also required a popular vote before local governments could raise new taxes. As a result, some city and county services, even garbage collection, faced curtailment. After eight years in office, Wilson was forced out of the governorship by a term limit law. He had maneuvered the state through a financial crisis and had run a scandal-free administration. But, Wilson's confrontations with the legislature and union officials alienated even his supporters.

In 1999, Gray Davis, the Democratic lieutenant governor, was swept into office. The Republicans had scared off minority voters by holding firm to immigration restriction. As a result, there arose a stereotype of illegal hordes overwhelming the state. Indeed, it almost seemed as though southern California might become America's new Ellis Island.

By 2001, Davis encountered a statewide energy shortage. Back in 1996, the legislature had deregulated energy production, hoping to increase competition and to lower rates for consumers. This move backfired, leading to high bills for electricity and for natural gas. The governor's anger did not solve the problem of outrageous pricing by utility companies. Davis maintained that, because of deregulation, control over power generation had been handed over to companies operating outside California. These utilities had set prices as high as they pleased, which led the state into a panic of wholesale buying of energy, sending prices even higher.

The governor also charged that such private firms were deliberately manipulating a fragmented energy market at the very time when national gasoline prices had also trebled. No major generating plant had been built within California in more than a dozen years. The result was a chaotic situation. Davis termed the Federal Regulatory Commission a do-nothing "culprit agency," thereby shifting part of the blame for the current crisis to the federal government.

The utility companies, meanwhile, charged the California Public Utilities Commission with preventing them from collecting proper rates for power. The utility firms, in turn, had to purchase electricity and gas at ridiculously high wholesale rates. Furthermore, the commission had frozen the amount that utility companies could charge their customers. Davis did not admit that the crisis was partly caused by environmental regulations which had contributed to a stagnant power supply. Nor did he mention how millions of illegal aliens had overburdened the state's infrastructure. Davis came up with the idea that the state government would buy power from generating firms outside California, then resell it to consumers. This, however, created a steady drain on the state's treasury.

Governor Davis, never a charismatic leader, blamed others for his own inaction. Critics charged that California's energy crisis had been partly due to a foolish spending spree. This had led to weaker credit ratings on state bonds. Also the state had not encouraged incentives to invest in new generating plants. The utility companies asked that revenue bonds be issued to bail them out of almost certain insolvency. In February of 2001, Davis signed a bill to sell $10 billion worth of bonds to finance the purchase of electricity under long-term contracts. The state's reeling utility firms had paid inflated prices for power. The Pacific Gas and Electric Company, barred from increasing rates, declared bankruptcy. The energy crisis dwarfed all other problems. In May of 2002, the state's attorney general filed suit against four big energy firms, charging them with wild profiteering.

Due to expensive power costs and threatened blackouts, some industries simply shut down. Citrus growers, dependent upon gas heating and electric wind fans to protect their crops from frigid temperatures, feared potential brownouts. Dairies, flower growers, and poultry farmers also grew nervous about their future. Skyrocketing power prices especially affected high-tech companies in the Silicon Valley south of San Francisco. The Santa Clara Valley had evolved from a dried-fruit packing center to large glass-walled factories populated by engineers and internet tycoons. Venture capitalists had irrationally backed the high-tech boom. When the E-commerce bubble burst, only the strongest digital companies, among them Intel and Cisco, survived. Suffering from slumping revenues, one electronics firm after another either crumbled or resorted to mass layoffs.

Alarmed, Governor Davis raised the budgets of virtually every department of state government. The state's shortfall quickly ran into the tens of billions of dollars. With his administration in deep trouble, the voters sought his recall. Back in 1911, this procedure had been installed by civic-minded populists and progressives. By October of 2003, a rising tide of public anger would topple Davis from the governorship just eleven months after he had been reelected.

Arnold Schwarzenegger, popular film actor and body-builder turned politician, campaigned vigorously for Davis's recall. His engaging Austrian accent and charm created a new political atmosphere for star-struck voters. For pure melodrama nothing matched Schwarzenegger's outsized persona. He came across as a combination of superhero and comforting leader. Determined to unseat Davis, he rode his celebrity into the governorship.

In the new "age of Arnold," Republicans found an outsider whose charisma reminded voters of Governor Reagan. Yet, his moderate stands on abortion, gay rights, and gun control made him palatable even to most conservatives. Straddling both left and right positions, he cast himself as a centrist who favored government reform of state spending and taxation.

Schwarzenegger resembled a street smart salesman with little book learning. He quickly vetoed $116 million from $105 billion in the 2004–05 budget. This still left a huge shortfall. Although Schwarzenegger promised to transform California's economy, he was criticized for divert-

Speaker of the House of Representatives Italian American Nancy Pelosi, alongside California's Austrian-born Republican Governor Arnold Schwarzenegger on February 27, 2007, Washington, D.C. Used by permission, Photographer: Oscar H. Metaquin.

ing funds from transportation and welfare programs in order to shore up the state's financial mess. His agenda soon lost traction after he teased Democratic Party legislators calling them "girlie men."

In California's prosperous decades, its citizens had repeatedly voted for more government programs than they were willing to fund. Each required endless borrowing. Too many ballot initiatives had spiraled out of control. This led to some awkward contortions in responsible budgeting. Tax-cutting measures had originally been passed in order to reign in spending. But reductions in property taxes placed three-fourths of the budget out of the control of both the governor and legislature.

A strong antitax mood was backed by powerful special interests. Yet, the state's mounting deficits made its economy almost ungovernable. A two-thirds majority in the legislature was required to curtail addictive spending. Throughout the 1990s, Sacramento's debits had regularly exceeded revenues by 18 percent. To cover this gap, voters continued recklessly to pass new bond issues. This produced a rock-bottom national credit rating.

Schwarzenegger also railed against overlapping jurisdictions between state, county, and city layers of government. But reinventing government lay beyond the power of one rookie governor. The legislature repeatedly resisted his proposed spending cuts. Desperate to move the state's economy back into a pattern of growth, he urged voters to show the legislature who was their real boss. By appealing directly to the people, the governor sought to circumvent entrenched politicos.

Although the Democrats held on to both houses of the legislature, the governor's call for urgent retrenchments enraged legislators. So did his support for reform of gerrymandering that made reelections a foregone conclusions. Instead, he proposed nonpartisan retired judges to head up committees that would redraw congressional district mapping.

In short, the new governor aimed to strip legislators of much of their power. As the state faced a structured deficit of $1 billion per month, California remained in a deep financial hole. The governor warned: "No single budget can fix a broken system that puts our state into a deficit year after year." He accused legislators of borrowing from one fund to transfer money to another, giving the appearance of a balanced budget while continuing to run up debt. They, he countered, had turned the state into an economic basket case.

With the budget teetering on a tower of borrowed money, Schwarzenegger challenged powerful employee unions. Firemen, nurses, teachers, and even the widows and orphans of police officers, objected to reductions in salary and pension payments. His school reform plan called for merit pay for teachers, also eliminating easy tenure. Schwarzenegger also angered Latinos by praising Arizona volunteers who patrolled the Mexican border against illegal entrants. Next the new governor vetoed legislation to legalize same-sex marriages. The "Terminator's" opponents portrayed him as a hard-hearted despot who labeled them losers.

Eventually Schwarzenegger had to alter his reform program. Despite a continuing budget crunch, the voters did authorize a controversial $3 billion stem-cell research program. This was meant to place California at the center of biomedical research. At Sunnyvale, the shares of one company, Stem Cells Incorporated, suddenly rose exponentially.

The governor, meanwhile, also reached a deal with the state's Indian casinos to recoup billions of dollars from their tax-free gambling profits. In return, the Cahuilla and Cupeno tribes asked for permission to open Las Vegas–style casinos 600 miles way from their ancestral lands. California now ranks second to Nevada for revenue raised from gambling. Its Indians even have the right to keep competitors out of the state. Each Indian-owned casino is each allowed 2,250 slot machines!

With his political honeymoon fading, Schwarzenegger provoked a backlash that paralyzed the legislature. Both the Republican governor and the Democratic majority saw their agendas shredded by acrimony. A drumbeat of criticism against Schwarzenegger was unceasing in the *Los Angeles Times* and via union-bought TV ads. Both sides raised large sums of campaign money.

The drop in the governor's popularity coincided with his push for a special election in the fall of 2005. He sought to curb the power of the Democratic legislature and public employee unions. The governor encountered a barrage of public criticism. A union-led campaign defeated every one of his reform proposals. The public was especially upset by his bickering with the Democratic legislature.

Walloped in the 2005 election, he apologized to the voters by stating "message received." He then assumed a centrist position, outlining a blueprint of infrastructure renovation. This included a proposed megabond issue to strengthen leaky levees along the Sacramento and San Joaquin rivers. Central to the governor's plans was improving the state's battered roads, reducing air pollution, constructing new schools, and adding prisoner facilities. Critics called his future borrowing grandiose, resembling his movie career. But cooperation with the Democratic legislature rescued several more of his controversial proposals.

In November of 2006, the dominating force of his personality easily propelled Schwarzenegger into reelection. He soon also became a

Gross Domestic Product in Selected Countries and California, 2002*

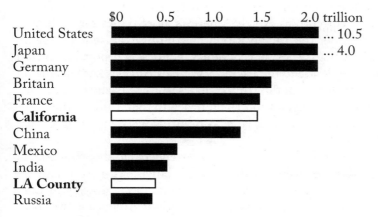

	$0	0.5	1.0	1.5	2.0 trillion
United States					... 10.5
Japan					... 4.0
Germany					
Britain					
France					
California					
China					
Mexico					
India					
LA County					
Russia					

* Adapted from Los Angeles Economic Development Corporation.

national figure by boldly proposing a variety of legislation on pressing social issues. These included the extension of health care to all residents, including illegals. He also took strong stands on improving the environment as well as support for funding stem-cell research. Indeed Schwarzenegger's leadership skills propelled the state forward on complicated social issues.

The labyrinth of state and federal regulations which California's governors encounter raises the question of whether the state has become ungovernable. Once it was the progressive model for the entire nation. Its citizens possessed excellent schools, a renowned university system, modern highway and street rail systems, and an enviable water conservation program. Such achievements occurred under two conciliatory governors—Earl Warren and Pat Brown. Today that centrist tradition has broken down. Politicians have become fiercely partisan, with regular feuding between northern and southern legislators. Coastal city councils battle for funds against a conservative heartland. Berkeley, Santa Monica, and San Francisco seem hyperliberal as compared to Orange County and San Joaquin Valley voters.

Throughout the 1990s, California's economy had grown at some 10 percent annually, twice the national average. By the year 2005, accompanying an inflow of talented specialists, its output of goods and services reached almost $1.50 trillion per year. Indeed, its economy almost challenges that of France and Italy in world ranking. The state now possesses the sixth largest economy in the world and produces one-eighth of the U.S. gross domestic product, or GDP.

Economically, California has emerged as a virtual nation, indeed a global center. It currently is North America's chief outlet for trade with countries that border the Pacific Rim. One-third of the state's economy is tied to trade with Asia. Also, economics, politics, and population have shifted from the Atlantic to the Pacific coast. Los Angeles has become the largest cargo entry-point in the United States. A new "Alameda Corridor" links the ports of Los Angeles and Long Beach to train yards in the center of L.A. The city's economy is as large as South Korea's and is larger than that of Switzerland and Taiwan.

Once sprawling alfalfa fields have now surrendered to shopping centers. Gnarled orchards have given way to housing subdivisions. L.A. is now the most populous county in the nation. California has been growing by more than half a million persons each year. One in eight Americans live there. It faces the biggest population growth of any American state. By 2006, the figure had reached some 37.4 million persons. California, as the nation's most populous state, has almost the same number of people as Texas and New York combined. Orange County alone has more residents than the entire state of Montana. By the year 2040, as many as 65 million people may be living in the state. In excess of 10 percent of the nation already lives in California. This is more than the entire population of Canada.

Such unparalleled growth has placed enormous pressures on the state's infrastructure. Indeed, growth is California's Number One problem. In 2005, Westwood (a suburb in west Lost Angeles) residents protested that their area had reached near saturation. Its clogged roads could hardly tolerate further intense development. Motorists complain about the state's crowded and crumbling highway system. Money to fix the deteriorated roads has repeatedly been diverted to social programs.

Suburban decentralization, as mentioned, has created a car-centered culture. Endless standing traffic on California's freeways reminds one that all this growth has been uneven. The three counties of the San Francisco Bay area have seen their population stagnate while Riverside County experienced the state's highest rate of increase. Escalating costs have driven 30 percent of the state's population inland. Bakersfield, Modesto, Ontario, Palmdale, and Santa Clara have had their populations increase exponentially. Sutter and Yuba counties in the Sierra foothills have seen an even faster growth as has tiny San Benito County, south of the Silicon Valley.

Long before that area became a computer center, Californians achieved exceptional progress in science and technology. The cyclotron was invented by Ernest Lawrence who founded the center that bears his name at

Livermore. Astronomer Edwin Hubble's discovery that The Milky Way was only one of many galaxies made Pasadena a scientific center. Back in 1889, at nearby Mount Wilson, Harvard University had installed a 13-inch photo telescope. By the 1930s, Hubble was working with a 100-inch telescope, then the largest in the world. He developed the theory of an expanding universe. A later scientific generation would place astronauts on the moon, tracked by Caltech's Jet Propulsion Laboratory.

Federal defense spending encouraged national fiber optics, electronics, and plastics firms to relocate to California. The state's tax and environmental laws and high labor costs have led some technology companies overseas. In 2006, the Japanese auto maker, Nissan, moved its North American headquarters from crowded Los Angeles to rural Tennessee. The year before, the Boeing Aircraft Company shuttered its Long Beach assembly line. During World War II this plant had produced an airplane every two hours as part of the Douglas Aircraft Company. By 2007, it had become the last facility to assemble Boeing's 717 commercial airliner. Its valuable property was to be turned into a real estate development. In Burbank too, Lockheed Aircraft's secret Skunk Works facility has moved to Marietta, Georgia. Its land had become too valuable to maintain as a plant there. An out-migration of some high-tech industries has also occurred. The Internet Bubble which burst in 2001, dumped many specialists onto the job market.

Yet, the buying power of Los Angeles continues to exceed the combined total of Houston, Baltimore, Cleveland, Miami, and Denver. The city anchors a hinterland of more than 15 million persons. L.A. has emerged as the first metropolis of the American West, also a center of the nation's entertainment, aerospace, and defense companies. Further north, the Napa and Sonoma valley vineyards generate more jobs than does the entire state of Rhode Island. Near San Diego, some 800 technology companies have created a digital coastline of research complexes and laboratories. These biotech, software, and telecommunications facilities cater to national as well as international markets. Located there are branches of Sweden's Ericsson, Finland's Nokia, and Japan's Kyocera, as well as Qualcomm and Motorola. Genentech, a manufacturer of cancer drugs, operates in south San Francisco.

Via television, film, and the print media, foreign manufacturers follow the state's cutting-edge trends. Nearly a quarter of a million workers still remain employed in software development and high-tech jobs. This provides a gigantic market for computers and their peripherals. Rising international demand has made San Jose the top national metropolitan area in export sales of these products.

California fueled the postwar national defense program, aerospace design, and the computer revolution. Caltech graduates spawned a new technology center along Orange County's Tech Coast. This zone encompasses parts of San Bernardino, Riverside, Los Angeles, and San Diego Counties. That region currently hosts 20 percent more high-tech (especially biomedical) firms than the Silicon Valley. For a time some production was lost to other states and countries with more favorable labor costs and tax incentives. But, by 2006, Cisco Systems, the Intel Corporation, and Sun Microsystems began to rehire workers. At Redwood Shores, Oracle too began to expand into a software giant. Of the nation's 500 fastest-growing companies, eighty-two of them are located within the state.

Today's California can truly be called a transformative society. Frontier rurality has given way to a suburban lifestyle. In the state's cities the old is becoming new. Long-neglected districts are being revived to create affordable housing. This has led to gentrification, slum clearance, and rejuvenation of old commercial buildings in depressed areas. Despite L.A.'s race riots, Latino, Asian, and African American investors are moving back into Watts and other low-income suburbs.

As one looks back at California's story, some key turning points seem obvious. Its Gold Rush era was a defining moment, even in the nation's history. A deluge of people coming from all over the world gave birth to a new state. Rather quickly California became the leading agricultural state in the nation. Its year-round sunshine and once-affordable labor supply encouraged ranching, farming, and the stunning film industry. When the automobile age dawned, the state still had ample supplies of oil locked away in its subsoil. Offshore too were huge pools of untapped oil.

No longer can California claim to be a Garden of the World in which magical things happen. Its unstoppable population avalanche causes serious problems. But, neither is the state a Paradise Lost. It has moved beyond the postwar images of the Beach Boys, the ultraconservative John Birch Society, and its monochromatic Pleasantvilles filled with aerospace workers. Even California's harshest critics acknowledge the recent appearance of a bicoastal society linked to the wider world of art, music, theater, and gastronomy.

A magnet to so many races and creeds, the state continues to struggle with the social problems such as homelessness and drug addiction. There is also a great gap between the gated communities of Beverly Hills and Rancho Santa Fe as compared to virtual slum conditions in the agricultural ghettoes of the Coachella Valley. The human wave which keeps breaking over California has flooded its infrastructure. Disputes continue over water and power shortages, education, and how to solve endless traffic jams on deteriorating highways. The extreme environmentalism of the 1970s led to cancelling of freeway construction as well as that of sorely needed electrical plants and sewage-disposal facilities. Overzealous conservationists retarded the repair of worn-out public facilities as runaway urban development triumphed.

It is, however, beside the point to wallow in what went wrong in the state's past. Californians have long known about their failures to preserve the environment. Historians too continue to stress California's sorry legacy of discrimination. But successful gender, race, and class fusion has also occurred. History is not only the study of human strife. The state's novelty and bigness alone cannot assure a healthy future. Its past optimism has been sidelined by political and economic blundering. Yet, other societies too suffer from poor planning, stretching vital resources to the limit, and widening the gap between rich and poor. Smog, traffic jams, and skyrocketing home prices are making the Golden State a markedly different place in which to live, not in crisis but with its future in doubt.

Californians are faced with some serious population projections. By the year 2050, almost 60 million people are expected to live in the state. The questions arise whether it can successfully absorb another 24 million persons in the intevening forty-three years from 2008 onward.

California once symbolized exceptionalism. Newcomers who wanted to start a different life within their own country came from all over America, lured by its promised riches. Visitors saw golden beaches fading into rolling green hills. Endless vistas of blue water lay offshore. Vast stretches of farm acreage grew a rich variety of products, even in midwinter. But is the sun really setting over California? It may be wise to consider the words of Florence's Niccolò Machiavelli, who in the 1500s wrote: "Make no small plans, for they have no power to stir the soul."

SELECTED READINGS

Regarding recent trends in California, see Robert Gottlieb, Mark Vallientos, Regina Freer, and Peter Drier, *The Next Los Angeles: Struggle For a Livable City* (2005). A bicoastal comparison is in Halle, David, ed., *New York and Los Angeles* (2003). Dydia DeLyser, *Ramona Memories: Tourism and the Shaping of Southern California* (2005).

About culture, consult Lawrence Clark Powell, *The Creative Literature of the Golden State* (1971); William Storrs Lee, ed., *California, A Literary Chronicle* (1968); Leslie Freudenheim, *Building With Nature: Roots of the San Francisco Bay Tradition* (1974); Mellier Scott, *Partnership in the Arts: Public and Private Support of Cultural Activities in the San Francisco Bay*

Area (1963); Arthur Bloomfield, *The San Francisco Opera* (1961); and William Wilson, *The Los Angeles Times Book of California Museums* (1984).

For town and city developments, see Edward Lyman, *San Bernardino: The Rise and Fall of a California Community* (1996); Judy Wright, *Claremont, A Pictorial History* (1999); Richard De Leon, *Left Coast City: Progressive Politics in San Francisco, 1975–91* (1992); George A. Pettit, *Berkeley: The Town and Gown of It* (1973); Gloria Lothrop, *Pomona: A Centennial History* (1988); Augusta Fink, *Palos Verde Peninsula: Time and the Terraced Land* (1987); Andrew Rolle, *Los Angeles: From Pueblo to City of the Future* (2d ed., 1995); and Lauren Cordley, *Napa: The Transformation of An American Town* (2004).

Architectural studies include Reyner Banham, *Los Angeles, The Architecture of Four Ecologies* (1971); Leonard and Dale Pitt, eds., *Los Angeles A to Z* (1997); Michael Dear, ed., *Atlas of Southern California* (1996); also Michael Dear with H. Eric Schockman and Greg Hise, *Rethinking Los Angeles* (1996). William Fulton describes his book, *The Reluctant Metropolis . . . Los Angeles* (1987) as "an amalgamation of political science, history, sociology, and urban planning, but ultimately . . . journalism." Other works that feature architecture and society include: Richard Longstreet, *The Automobile and Retailing in Los Angeles* (1997); Allen J. Scott and Edward W. Soja, *The City: Los Angeles and Urban Theory* (1996); William McClung, *Landscapes of Desire: Anglo Mythologies of Los Angeles* (2000); Dana Cuff, *The Provisional City* (2000); also Fred Siegel, *The Future Once Happened Here: New York, D.C., L.A.: The Fate of America's Big Cities* (1997).

For recent politics see Larry Gerston and Terry Christensen, *Recall: California's Political Earthquake* (2005); John Allswang, *The Initiative and Referendum in California* (2000); Jackson Putnam, "The Pattern of Modern California Politics," *Pacific Historical Review* 61 (February 1992), 23–52; Charles G. Bell and Charles M. Price, *California Government Today* (1988); Richard B. Harvey, *Dynamics of California Government and Politics* (1995); and Dan Walters, *The New California: Facing the 21st Century* (1992). Social and cultural matters appear in Norman M. Klein and Martin J. Schiesl, eds., *20th Century Los Angeles* (1990); see also Schiesl and Mark Dodge, eds., *City of Promise: Race and Historical Change in Los Angeles* (2006); Robert Kling, Spencer Olin, and Mark Poster, eds., *Postsuburban California* (1991); Peter Theroux, *Translating L.A.* (1994); Pamela Hallan-Gibson, *The Golden Promise: An Illustrated History of Orange County* (1986).

For journalism, see Marshall Berges, *The Life and Times of the Los Angeles Times* (1984); Robert Gottlieb and Irene Wolt, *Thinking Big: The Story of the Los Angeles Times (1977); and Dennis McDougal, Privileged Son: Otis Chandler and the Rise and Fall of the L.A. Times Dynasty (2001).

Regarding the future see Janet Abu-Lughod, New York, Chicago, Los Angeles: America's Global Cities (1999); Christophe Lecuyer, Making Silicon Valley and the Growth of High Tech (2006). Also Mark Baldassare, California in the New Millenium (2000) and his A California State of Mind (2002). City planning is discussed in Greg Hise, Magnetic Los Angeles: Planning The Twentieth Century Metropolis (1997). Highly speculative is Peter Schrag, Paradise Lost: California's Experience, America's Future (1998).

APPENDIX

SPANISH REGIME, 1767–1821

(Dates of service for each governor are from assumption to surrender of office.)

Gaspar de Portolá

November 30, 1767, to July 9, 1770
From May 21, 1769, Portolá was *comandante-militar* for Alta California. From July 9, 1770, to May 25, 1774, the position of comandante was filled by Pedro Fages; and from May 25, 1774, to February 1777, by Fernando Rivera y Moncada.

Matías de Armona

June 12, 1769, to November 9, 1770

Felipe de Barri

March ?, 1770, to March 4, 1775
Governor of *Las Californias,* residing at Loreto.

Felipe de Neve

March 4, 1775, to July 12, 1782
In February 1777, Neve took up residence at Monterey. Rivera y Moncada went south to assume the lieutenant governorship at Loreto. The acting lieutenant-governor, pending Rivera's arrival, was Joaquin Cañete.

Pedro Fages

July 12, 1782, to April 16, 1791
On July 18, 1781, Rivera y Moncada was killed on the Colorado River, and Joaquín Cañete served as lieutenant-governor until November 1783, when he was succeeded by José Joaquín de Arrillaga.

José Antonio Roméu

April 16, 1791, to April 9,1792

José Joaquín de Arrillaga

April 9, 1792, to May 14, 1794
During this period, Arrillaga was lieutenant-governor and comandante of Lower California, and governor of *Las Californias ad interim.*

Diego de Borica

May 14, 1794, to March 8, 1800

José Joaquín de Arrillaga

March 8, 1800, to July 24, 1814
Until March 11, 1802, when he died, Pedro de Alberni was *comandante-militar* for Alta California. The decree making Alta California a separate province bore the date August 29, 1804, and it reached Arrillaga November 16.

José Darío Argüello

July 24, 1814, to August 30, 1815
Governor *ad interim.*

Pablo Vicente de Solá

August 30, 1815, to November 10, 1822
Held over from Spanish regime to November 1822.

MEXICAN REGIME, 1821–1847

Luis Antonio Argüello

November 10, 1822, to November ?, 1825
Until April 2, 1823, Argüello's authority derived from the Spanish Regency. After that date it derived from Iturbide as Agustin I. After November 17 it derived from the *Congreso Constituyente* (National Congress). In March 1823, Iturbide named Naval Captain Bonifacio de Tosta governor of Alta California. In 1824 José Miñón was appointed governor of Alta California but declined the office.

José María de Echeandía

November ?, 1825, to January 31, 1831
Antonia García was appointed as Echeandía's successor, but the appointment was revoked.

Manuel Victoria

January 31, 1831, to December 6, 1831

José María de Echeandía

December 6, 1831, to January 14, 1833
De facto *jefe politico* and *jefe militar* in the district south of, but not including, Santa Barbara.

Pío Pico

January 27 to February 16, 1832
Jefe politico by appointment of the Diputacíon for only twenty days.

Agustín Vicente Zamorano

February 1, 1832, to January 14, 1833
De facto *jefe militar* only in the district north of and including Santa Barbara.

José Figueroa

January 14, 1833, to September 29, 1835
Early in 1833 Figueroa asked to be relieved of office. On July 16, 1833, José María Hijar was appointed *jefe politico*, but the appointment was revoked by Mexico's President Santa Anna on July 25. On July 18, 1834, Figueroa withdrew his request to be relieved.

José Castro

September 29, 1835, to January 2, 1836
From October 8, 1835, to January 1, 1836, the position of *jefe militar* was held by Nicolás Gutiérrez.

Nicolás Gutiérrez

January 2 to May 3, 1836

Mariano Chico

May 3 to August 1, 1836

Nicolás Gutiérrez

August 1 to November 5, 1836

José Castro

November 5 to December 7, 1836
Castro was *jefe militar* until November 29, when he was succeeded by Mariano Guadalupe Vallejo. He then became acting governor.

Juan Bautista Alvarado

December 7, 1836, to December 31, 1842
Until August 7, 1839, Alvarado was governor *ad interim*. On June 6, 1837, Carlos Carillo was appointed governor, and on December 6 he assumed office at Los Angeles, but was arrested and deposed by Alvarado on May 20, 1838.

Manuel Micheltorena

December 31, 1842, to February 22, 1845

Pío Pico

February 22, 1845, to August 10, 1846

By the departmental junta Pío Pico was declared governor *ad interim* on February 15, 1845. José Castro served as *jefe militar* for the same period.

José María Flores
October 31, 1846, to January 11, 1847

Andrés Pico
January 11 to January 13, 1847

AMERICAN GOVERNORS UNDER MILITARY RULE
(Dates given are beginning of term.)

Commodore John D. Sloat
July 7, 1846

Commodore Robert F. Stockton
July 29, 1846

Captain John C. Frémont
January 19, 1847

General Stephen W. Kearny
March 1, 1847

GOVERNORS OF THE STATE OF CALIFORNIA
(Dates given are of inauguration.)

Colonel Richard B. Mason
May 31, 1847

General Persifor F. Smith
February 28, 1849

General Bennett Riley
April 12, 1849

Peter H. Burnett
Ind. Dem. Dec. 20, 1849

John McDougal
Ind. Dem. Jan. 9, 1851

John Bigler
Dem. Jan. 8, 1852

John Neely Johnson
Amer. Jan. 9, 1856

John B. Weller
Dem. Jan. 8, 1858

Milton S. Latham
Lecomp. Dem. Jan. 9, 1860

John G. Downey
Lecomp. Dem. Jan. 14, 1860

Leland Stanford
Rep. Jan. 10, 1862

Frederick F. Low
Union Dec. 10, 1863

Henry H. Haight
Dem. Dec. 5, 1867

Newton Booth
Rep. Dec. 8, 1871

Romualdo Pacheco
Rep. Feb. 27, 1875

William Irwin
Dem. Dec. 9, 1875

George C. Perkins
Rep. Jan. 8, 1880

George Stoneman
Dem. Jan. 10, 1883

Washington Bartlett
Dem. Jan. 8, 1887

Robert W. Waterman
Rep. Sept. 13, 1887

Henry H. Markham
Rep. Jan. 8, 1891

James H. Budd
Dem. Jan. 11, 1895

Henry T. Gage
Rep. Jan. 4, 1899

James N. Gillett
Rep. Jan. 9, 1907

George C. Pardee
Rep. Jan. 7, 1903

Hiram W. Johnson
Prog. Rep. Jan. 3, 1911

William D. Stephens
Rep. Mar. 15, 1917

Clement C. Young
Rep. Jan. 4, 1927

James Rolph, Jr.
Rep. Jan. 6, 1931

Frank F. Merriam
Rep. Jan. 7, 1935

Culbert L. Olson
Dem. Jan. 2, 1939

Earl F. Warren
Rep. Jan. 4, 1943

Goodwin F. Knight
Rep. Oct. 5, 1953

Edmund G. Brown
Dem. Jan. 5, 1959

Ronald Reagan
Rep. Jan. 5, 1967

Edmund G. Brown, Jr.
Dem. Jan. 5, 1975

George Deukmejian
Rep. Jan. 5, 1983

Pete Wilson
Rep. Jan. 5, 1991

Gray Davis
Dem. Jan. 5, 1999

Arnold Schwarzenegger
Rep. Nov. 17, 2003

INDEX OF AUTHORS CITED

SUBJECT INDEX

California: A History, Seventh Edition
Developmental editor: Andrew J. Davidson
Copy editor and Production editor: Lucy Herz
Proofreader: Claudia Siler
Cartographer: Jason Casanova, Pegleg Graphics
Indexer: Pat Rimmer
Printer: Versa Press, Inc.